National
Popular Politics in
Early Independent Mexico

NATIONAL POPULAR POLITICS

in
Early
Independent
Mexico,
1820 – 1847

Torcuato S. Di Tella

University of New Mexico Press

ALBUQUERQUE

Library of Congress Cataloging-in-Publication Data
Di Tella, Torcuato S., 1929–
National popular politics in early independent Mexico, 1820–1847
Torcuato S. Di Tella.—1st ed.
     p. cm.
Includes bibliographical references and index.
ISBN 0-8263-1673-5
1. Social classes—Mexico—History—19th century.
2. Political participation—Mexico—History—19th century.
3. Mexico—Politics and government—1821-1861.
I. Title.
HN120.Z9S624 1996
306.2'0972'09034—dc20   95-41729
CIP

Contents

Tables

Preface

I have been driven to the study of the early nineteenth-century Mexican labyrinth as a result of my search for clues to an understanding of Latin American politics, from the perspective of a sociologist with historical and comparative inclinations. But then, why concentrate on a single case? In the field of comparative sociology, it is necessary to try out new approaches, as the methodology is in the making and continually evolving. I could have taken four or five historical processes, using mostly secondary literature, and tried to establish similarities and contrasts among them. This is a valid approach, known to have given excellent results. But comparatists must also try their hand at the study in depth of a single case, so as to have a better look at the trees in the forest, getting involved with the vagaries and contradictions of the local scene. Of course given time, patience, and resources, it is possible to bestow this treatment not only on one but on several instances. Indeed this is necessary, but it need not be done in the same book, nor even by the same person.

In my analysis of the Mexican situation during the early decades of the republic, I have always kept in mind contrasting experiences both from the area and period considered and from outside of them. In a previous work, I tried to develop a general framework for the study of Latin American politics. I do not intend to inflict a summary of it on the unsuspecting reader, but of course I will use it and explain that use when necessary, tucking into footnotes the more complex references. I believe that the comparative method, nay more, theory building in general, must be capable of expressing its results in a plain language. But on the other hand, tentatively at least, some classificatory frameworks or schemata should be developed, in which to nest empirical materials and lower-level generalizations, so that results might be additive and open to easier contrast.

I have been working on Mexican history for quite a long time, moving back and forth between it and other research and theoretical endeavors. I have published in part the results of these efforts, and in this book I refer to them only tangentially. I have tried to see Mexican events as a sample, so to speak, of what was happening in other parts of Latin America. Not that the situation was similar everywhere; rather the contrary. Mexico was at one extreme of variation, due to its sheer size, the severity of its decay, and the violence of its attempts at independence. In spite of the differences, however, in analyzing a given Mexican political phenomenon I often had the impression of observing, with a magnifying glass and in changed circumstances, the behavior of familiar actors.

The period comes to an abrupt end with the American war: afterward, things could never be the same. One is tempted to invert a well-known phrase, and say that what had earlier been a comedy, became after the war a tragedy. Actually it had always been a tragedy, beginning with the massacres of the Insurgencia and including the frustrating changes of government, legal and otherwise, during the intervening decades.

My focus of interest is the connection between the class structure and the political system, particularly the factions, parties, and corporative and ideological groups vying for power and entering into the most complex and bewildering alliances. The pattern of these alliances (too often attributed to personality traits or sheer opportunism) is a central theme of study and so is the degree and form of popular participation in what appeared to be the war of all against all. I was particularly attracted by the prevalence of political coalitions that included as an essential part of their formula an element of popular participation. These combinations could be liberal or conservative, clerical or anticlerical, or (to use only partially anachronistic terms) of the Right or Left. The prevalence of military interventions, together with the less emphasized incapacity of the system to generate a solid dictatorship (in contrast with other Latin American cases) contributed to my fascination with it.

During the period studied, mainly the years between 1820 and 1834, with occasional glances to the 1840s, a definite cyclical pattern emerges, its causes being traceable to three main characteristics: the contraposition between protectionist and free-trading interests; the high level of popular menace hanging over the heads of the upper classes; and the overarching economic and ideological role of the church.

These three characteristics were present in Mexico, in the first part of the nineteenth century, to a much higher degree than in practically any other part of Latin America. One can think of countries and periods when one or the other of the above-named traits existed, but not to such a high degree, and particularly not all of them together. The presence of these three factors produced a wide assortment of social actors and a seemingly endless series of coalition making and unmaking. Outcomes depended on combinations of events, personalities, and international conjunctures. But given the basic data, political changes were bound to follow certain patterns, independently of the individuals involved. It was difficult to have a political vocation or a political responsibility thrown on one's shoulders in those days, and posterity has not been kind to most contemporary practitioners. Maybe it is time for some compassion, if not rehabilitation, as the basis for a better understanding.

In the following pages, it will be easy to discern the influence of the social scientists Richard Adams, David Apter, Oscar Cornblit, Karl Deutsch, Gino Germani, Helio Jaguaribe, Seymour Martin Lipset, José Nun, Guillermo O'Donnell, Bryan Roberts, Stein Rokkan, Alfred Stepan, and Charles Tilly. Among historians I owe many insights to Nettie Lee Benson, David Brading, Germán Carrera Damas, Enrique Florescano, Moisés González Navarro, Luis González y González, Tulio Halperín Donghi, Herbert Klein, Enrique Semo, and Eric Van Young, not to mention the whole dedicated cohort of Mexicanists, too long to enumerate here. My assistants, Patricia Chomnalez and Adriana Novoa, provided much-needed conversation and fresh ideas. My two stays in Texas, at the Institute of Latin American Studies in Austin, in 1988 and 1990, were essential for the completion of this work, begun too long ago to remember, during a prolonged residence in London and Oxford, whose large repositories of tract literature often disturbed my sleep and made me dream of passions and hopes astonishingly similar to those of our own times.

National
Popular Politics in
Early Independent Mexico

Introduction

In order to unravel the tangled yarn of early independent Mexican politics, it is necessary to begin with a consideration of the chasm that separated the upper from the lower classes. Nobody denies the existence of this chasm; but what is open to discussion is its magnitude, the relevance of the intermediate sectors, and the degree to which the popular strata could channel their antagonisms into political action. The very violent nature of the Insurgencia makes it impossible to overlook the fact of popular participation, and recent scholarship has pointed to the prevalence of mass violence in the early stages of political development, both in Mexico and elsewhere, adopting a perspective "from below" to compensate for the more classical study of the elites. This approach must be complemented, though, with an analysis of what happened at the level of the middle strata: how numerous they were, how estranged from the dominant order, and how determined to get involved in unorthodox alliances. An excessive concern with violence and revolution leaves out of consideration a significant aspect of the political scene. The conflicts between Escoceses and Yorkinos and their numerous offshoots and transmutations did not contrapose actors across a simple class line, but they did have an important anchorage in the class structure, if the latter is properly interpreted and subdivided. This was obvious to contemporary observers and has also been pointed out by an early generation of sociologically inclined historians. Thus Luis Chávez Orozco referred to the Yorkinos as "the party of the people, of the . . . impoverished middle class, of the miserable rabble," contraposed to the "interests of the feudal and militarist sector, supported by the deceived rural masses."[1] Much earlier the British minister, Henry Ward, saw the Yorkinos as very dangerous, attributing to the faction twelve thousand "affiliés," conjuring up, by giving them that name, scenes from the French revolution.[2] Though a bipolar characterization oversimplifies the issue, the conflicts involved are central to an understanding of the Mexican predicament and often were not much less violent than those emerging from the many local peasant uprisings of the time. It is true that some of the major upheavals, like the Insurgencia, spread mostly among the rural population, but one should not underrate the role of the urban masses as bases of populist, if not revolutionary, politics.[3]

Marxist analyses of this type of situation were for many years marred by their excessive concern with class consciousness, which it is difficult to assign to peasants and urban laborers in preindustrial times. More recent studies in this theoretical field, under the influence of the pioneering work of Eric Hobsbawm and E. P. Thompson, have revised that rigid orthodoxy. Popular participation has thus been revalued, regardless of ideology, especially when it involves violence. What is necessary now is to complement this new vision with an equally open one for the less violent forms of such popular participation. These range from voting, joining political clubs, and assiduous reading of (or listening to) newspapers and pamphlets, to serving in the militia or getting involved in street demonstrations, strikes, and rioting: in other words, the usual arsenal of nineteenth-century Latin American politics, with the addition of military interventions and influence peddling or corruption of officials. In this obscure and unsung experience, political parties were formed and constitutional traditions forged, while a widening of participation took place.

The violent substratum of politics, always present (though usually at quite a few removes) in any society, was very near the surface in Latin America, and especially so in Mexico at the time of independence. This was the result of the peculiar nature of the Conquest and the ensuing superposition of races and cultures. In spite of this, and of the initial confrontations with the *encomenderos*, during most of the colonial era the crown did not need much of a regular army to keep order in its colonies. Admittedly the church had created a high degree of consensus across classes, and many colonials were armed in defense of the established order, but it is surprising that the various factions of the dominant classes were not at each other's throats more often. Probably it was the magnitude of the potential threat under which they lived that brought them to their senses and instilled in them a feeling of solidarity and a loyalty to the royal government, a feeling also shared by the intermediate strata. However, when the crown (or international economic and military forces) introduced serious alterations that affected business or bureaucratic interests, widespread revolts erupted. This happened during the Gálvez reforms of the 1760s and, on a colossal scale, in Peru and Upper Peru during the 1780s. As a result of these internal tensions, in addition to international conflicts, the regular army experienced a notable expansion in New Spain after the latter part of the eighteenth century.

The mechanism of civil society's violent resistance to changes often occurred in two stages. First, sectors of the elites, feeling their interests severely threatened by government action, reacted strongly in defense of their interests, come what may. Once the united front of dominant-class social control was thus broken, the usually subdued tensions from the underworld could more easily erupt. This happened on a limited scale in New Spain at the time of Gálvez, but became a major catastrophe in Peru, where disaffection among the white and mestizo populations helped trigger the Túpac Amaru rebellion. In a not too different situation, the disruption caused by the French Revolution between white and mulatto settlers in Saint Domingue (Haiti) opened the gates to slave insurrection. In Brazil things were different, because there the Portuguese authorities, not necessarily out of foresight, had since at least the Methuen treaty of 1703 opened their kingdom to British interests, thus allowing more time for a gradual adaptation to the new international economy. In New Spain the opposite was the case, and this, added to the Consolidación and other ill-advised measures, created such havoc among the elites that many of them became decidedly disloyal to the status quo. Still in Mexico the upper classes, centered on the capital, expressed their opposition only mildly, during the Iturrigaray episode of 1808. Lower sectors of the dominant classes, however, especially provincials and the middle classes, were more ready to resort to extreme measures, which ignited the powder keg.

Forms of Popular Participation

Since the Insurgencia, one could ignore the possibility of violence in everyday life and in politics only at one's grievous risk. Politics became, more than ever before, the continuation of civil war by other means, which included scarcely veiled appeals to violence or ritual invocations or exercises of it — in militia training, in elections, and in a strongly worded press. To what extent was there mass participation in all of this? Contemporary observers, often participants, of various shades of opinion, from Alamán to Zavala, Mora to Bustamante, Tornel or Zerecero, consistently emphasized the strategic role of the masses in the political process. One of the objects of the present inquiry is to see how and why those masses had to be taken into account, because it cannot be said that in all preindustrial or premodern societies popular participation in politics was as high as it was in Mexico. Though the level of participation, or the necessity to take into account wide sectors of the population, has probably been higher in most historical instances than is usually realized, in some cases it was markedly important. In New Spain the nature of the Conquest bequeathed a potential for popular violence to the dominant order, which made the control of these tensions an affair of the first priority. The concentration of the population in rather large cities, in mines, and in other centers of production, and the nature of rural-urban migrations, all helped generate an available mass ready for incorporation into episodes of violence. At the same time, economic and international upheavals beginning in the late eighteenth century had created the conditions for intense factional behavior among the dominant classes, making them blind to the dangers of agitating the masses. Involved, against better counsels, in this risky business, the elites eventually acquired some expertise in the art of channelling and controlling a crowd.

In other words: violence being always around the corner, it was necessary for any political group, even in peaceful and constitutional times, to flex its muscles and be in readiness for direct action at any moment. "Direct action" was basically of two types: one involved appealing to the military, the other to the people. The latter was particularly strategic in an era when one man could rather easily provide himself with a gun and eventually a horse and become a good match for a trained soldier. But how to appeal to the people convincingly enough to make them risk their tranquility and eventually their lives? Some special inducements had to be provided, from the grossest to the noblest kind. Maybe it was enough to distribute a few *reales*, or to provide opportunities for plunder. But as for the latter, not everyone could risk encouraging it, particularly those who had something to lose, or with wealthy friends and backers.

On the other hand, looking at things from the popular side, we must explore a wider gamut of motivations for violent or semiviolent action than those involving immediate economic gain. Some sectors of the population were more readily accessible than others and would respond to different stimuli. Politicians had to cultivate an audience, through charismatic or other forms of personal appeal, and feed their followers with ideas or at least some motives for enthusiasm. It was also necessary for them to exercise their troops occasionally; hence the party press, the gatherings and street agitations, the enrollment in the militia, the show of strength and counting of numbers (at least of the brave) on election day, and so forth. All these things were meaningful, not necessarily in terms of the constitution (that is, for the purpose of forming a majority in Congress or getting a president elected), but rather as preparation for civil strife if the situation arose. That is to say, it was not always enough, if one wished to topple or to defend a government, to have recourse to the military; it might be sufficient in some circumstances, but not in others. And in all cases, the availability of potentially armed people in the streets could go a long way toward making up the minds of the military or of other influential sectors of society. The people were not kingmakers, but they did play a role in the kingmaking process. They could, consciously or not, set some rules and requirements for those who would attempt to use them. It was only a participation of sorts, but still participation after all.

The Dangerous Classes: Which Ones?

Mexico had a large component of "dangerous classes" in its population, some quite visible, especially the *léperos* in the large cities, the miners, and the socially mobilized Indians, uprooted from their communities. There is no doubt that these groups were menacing; my hypothesis, though, is that the really dangerous ones were the middle classes. It would be out of place here to go into a discussion as to what constitutes a class, or how to define a middle position within the stratification pyramid. But within the social hierarchy there are lines of discontinuity at different levels. A very important, though often fuzzy, line of separation generally runs between manual workers (urban or rural) without property or control of a means of production, and others, who are situated above them. As there are many doubtful cases, to which one must add incongruent locations (high in one dimension and low in another), it may be convenient here to refer to some special problems.

First, in the urban sector, below the line, factory workers, artisans without a shop of their own, service personnel of various kinds, and the host of street vendors and marginals formed the bulk of the lower classes. Above the line, foremen, shop-keeping artisans or small traders, and white-collar employees formed what may be called a middle class. Needless to say, there are always straddlers, such as the classical well-paid artisan without a shop of his own, or the equally familiar scribbler unable to pay his bills. Self-employed people were below the line when they came near to being street vendors or marginals, while in other cases they had a position similar to that of a small shopkeeper, above the line.

Second, in the rural sector, the salaried *peones* were below the line, as were many subsistence agriculturists, even if they rented or owned (individually or collectively) a patch of land. Small property holders, renters or even squatters, and some members of Indian *pueblos* who managed to occupy a position of privilege within their communities were above the line.

The existence of a middle class, and the internal stratification within each group, became more evident the closer one looked at them. Local statisticians, like Ciríaco Iturribarría in a study of San Luis Potosí, included among the middle class the *dependientes de comercio* and the *maestros* of the main trades, such as silversmiths, carpenters, blacksmiths, and shoemakers. By contrast Mariano Otero, a well-to-do liberal writer and politician, in an analysis of social stratification in Mexico, argued that a class that could properly be called upper did not exist or was too weak, and he designated as proletarian all those who did not have other resources than "mercenary work." He reserved the use of "middle class" for those who "represent the greatest sum of wealth, including all the professions which cultivate the intellect." Obviously Otero had a very peculiar definition of the middle class, including only what we would call today the bourgeoisie, or upper middle class. In fact he was pointing to another line of relative discontinuity within the social pyramid, namely, that which divided the middle classes into a lower and an upper layer, the latter enjoying better and more secure positions, through property, business, the professions, or important jobs in private or public administration, the church, or the armed forces. In a similar vein to that of Otero, Baron von Humboldt and Bishop Abad y Queipo tended to see only extremes of wealth and misery, which probably was a commonplace observation in well-educated circles at the time.[4]

This dichotomous view reflected the weakness of an upper middle class, that is, of people who might be the interlocutors of those highly placed observers. The lower middle classes, both urban and rural, suffered from penury and frightful insecurity, so that in a sense they could be seen as living in misery. But they and those below them were very conscious of the differences. Guillermo Prieto, who had known hard times in his youth, saw that the populace "had its hierarchies, its nobility, its aristocracy." Artisans, and the politicians who sought their support, were quite conscious of the differences between a maestro and a worker in a factory, who was assimilated to an *oficial*, that is, a non-shop-owning artisan who worked in a dependent position. During a discussion in 1829 in the Puebla congress, a deputy expressed the fear that the conversion from

maestros into salaried workers in large factories would bring disaster to
the country, "as the expansion of the glebe serfs had done to Poland."
Another visualized the despondency of the "artisans, seeing that by becoming oficiales and dependents on the privileged, their industry would
be reduced, limits would be set to their ingenuity, and they would be
condemned to indigence."[5] This forecast became true in many places, as
artisan work was affected either by foreign imports or by the competition
of local large-scale factories, as in Querétaro. In Rafael Durán's *Memoria
sobre el Censo de la República Mexicana*, written in 1863, it was stated
that "modern and scientific industry had forced the disappearance of an
infinite number of cotton and wool looms, which, though they produced
less, occupied many people," who were compelled to migrate. The cigar
industry was also subject to the menace of mechanization. In 1846 a
group of *maestras* and *oficialas* petitioned the government to stop the
proposed purchase of a machine, which would have left without work
"thirty thousand needy and unhappy families," a not too exaggerated
estimate of the total number employed in the industry, though of course
not all would be left jobless by the contemplated machine. The women
(or their politically inspired counselor) exhorted the government "not to
follow blindly the economic principles which have extolled the use of
machines," and to take notice of what happened in "the more industrial-
ized countries of Europe, where every day one can see the diminution of
salaries . . . and multitude of workers remaining without occupation."
The only alternative left for those women would be domestic service, but
this was too "repugnant, because of its humiliation.[6]

In the countryside there was also a social pyramid with something in
the middle between the extremes of wealth and squalor. The majority of
the rural population, particularly in the central and southern parts of the
country, was made up of Indians. Colonial policy had tried to entice them
away from their communal landholding pueblos into the wage-working
world of the Spanish economy. But the villages retained a considerable
amount of land and autonomy, and most had a *república*, with *alcaldes*,
regidores, a governor, and often a *cacique*. The Indian república was a
world in itself, with its own social scale and its pyramid climbers, and in
many cases the old distinction between *principales* and others was retained. Observers to this day complain about the Indians' tendency to
spend their savings in feasts and celebrations connected with their positions in the república or the religious *cofradías*. But the fact that they did
so testifies to the importance they attached to enjoying a position of pre-

eminence in their immediate surroundings. There were also some solid advantages for those who were at the top of that microcosm. Some of them had in many cases obtained tracts of land in private property or special access to the use of the fields held in common. In addition the principales by inheritance and others having offices in the república, as well as those working for them, were exempt from the *repartimiento*.

Could one call the principales and other privileged sectors of the Indian communities a middle class? The top people in the village were conscious of their superiority, they spent money to back it up with prestige and legitimacy, and surely they were envied by the others. Calling them a middle class, in the theoretical perspective here adopted, does not imply a full host of consequences as to their behavior. Some do follow, though, because the fact of occupying a position of relative privilege in social space leads people to act in forms different from those they would adopt if positioned lower down in the pyramid. How different is a matter that should be studied in each case, refraining from lumping all apparently "poor" groups in a single, undifferentiated mass of peasants or Indians. Common sense might indicate that the upper crust of villagers would act conservatively. This was so in some instances, but in other cases they were the leaders of rebellion, because they harbored more resentments than the others, as a result of comparing themselves with the dominant Spanish or mestizo society. They also had more resources to use in the defense of their positions. One of those resources was the loyalty of their fellow villagers, which could be gained and consolidated in a number of ways, including setting off a few fireworks on special days. When sectors of the Indian elite got some education, or when they ventured out of the enclosed world of the village, they suffered severe strain and status incongruence, a fact not lost on the more conservative *criollo* observers of the scene, who took it to be a source of radicalization.[7]

Outside of the Indian communities, most land was taken up by *haciendas*, but there was some left for middle-class *rancheros*, as well as for squatters and renters of subdivided *ranchos*, which had become rancherías, or *cuadrillas*, as they were called. Though the percentage of land occupied in this manner was small, the number of people making a living on it was not negligible, and their social status was rather heterogeneous, so that they also formed a social-stratification pyramid. In the large haciendas, on the other hand, the permanent and resident labor force, the *peones de raya*, enjoyed some "secure dependence" (in the best of cases), to use John Tutino's concept, but were quite low on the social scale. Below their level one could find most temporary workers, drawn from the poorer or younger sectors of nearby pueblos or rancherías. In many haciendas there were also tenants, occasionally very numerous, and probably very heterogeneous, so that they included a wide gamut of status levels.[8]

The Politics of Status Incongruence

If there was a social pyramid, one could hopefully rise in it, or (more probably, given hard times) fall, or lose status relative to others. If the middle positions within the pyramid were quite numerous, then the number of people potentially affected was large. Their attitudinal and political reactions would be a function not only of their class position at any given moment, but also of changes in it, or of particular configurations of the various dimensions of their position in the world. This could arise mainly from downward mobility (or the threat of it) and from status incongruence. When the economic dimension of status was high, it was easier for the individual to withstand some low marks in education or prestige, unless serious social ostracism was involved, which was mainly focused on ethnicity. The latter was the case of the rich or the educated Indian, two situations that were not equivalent. The rich Indian (an infrequent but real character) could to some extent buy his way into the upper strata or at least marry his daughters into them. Agustín Paz, who started as an *albañil* and finished as an Escocés deputy and then senator for the state of Mexico (he died in 1829) was probably an example of this type. His critics maintained that he could scarcely speak Spanish, though he had filled himself with ill-digested readings. Actually the word albañil was used to designate both a mason and a builder, and in his case probably encompassed a process of upward mobility. The prospect was more difficult for the well-educated Indian, who was very likely to turn radical, as exemplified by Benito Juárez and Juan Rodríguez Puebla. The latter, son of an *aguador*, got a scholarship to San Gregorio and rose to become rector of that college in 1829. He was active in the Gómez Farías reforms of 1833–34, but opposed the disentailment of Indian communities, a pet project of other liberals. More common as a case of status incongruence was the middle-class person with more education than economic resources or occupational possibilities. Relatively high education involved contact with radical ideological sources, but it also generated (if in a less conscious way) aspirations to a better life, that is, what has been called the revolution of rising expectations. The resulting frustration was an added cause of anti-status-quo ideas, of any sort, a fertile ground for new combinations and political strategies, of which José Joaquín Fernández de Lizardi and Pablo Villavicencio were prime examples. Higher up in the social pyramid, one could also find instances of status incongruence, above all the old aristocracy in reduced circumstances, with which Iturbide's entourage was so well endowed, and (increasingly, with the accumulation of economic crises) merchants, miners, and industrialists facing bankruptcy.

Apart from status incongruence, direct and simple downward mobility was also present. Of course to a certain extent downward mobility always implies some elements of incongruence, not only for those who suffer it but also for those who are seriously threatened by it. The downwardly mobile always keep some elements from their previous station in life; but particularly for some lower-middle-class sectors, such as artisans or small rancheros, the capacity to counter downward mobility was not very great, unless they resorted to some form of political action. Even then the struggle was an uphill one.

Obscuring such mobility problems were the more brutal ones of unemployment or eviction from tenancies, a subject well covered by the literature and easier to document. In a sense losing a job and becoming destitute is a form of downward mobility. But if the image one has of the social pyramid is that of a small elite confronted by a basically homogeneous miserable mass, the issue of downward mobility does not arise or is irrelevant for most members of the popular strata. My hypothesis is that in many of these cases what was involved was a fall from purgatory into hell, a distinction that has its significance. I do not intend here to overemphasize the reality of the dividing line, though for the sake of exposition it is handy to use the metaphor. What is importance is to perceive the existence of a social pyramid, its form, and the internal distance between positions, as well as movements between them.

A clearly different perspective from the one adopted here can be seen in a work by J. Iturriaga on social stratification in Mexico, based on the census of 1895. A "rural popular class" is there defined as including peones, small agriculturists (including members of *comunidades)*, and some country artisans and small traders, forming 77 percent of the total national population and 97 percent of the rural one. Above it a "rural middle class," made up of middle-size landowners, traders, and white-collar workers, encompasses 1.7 percent of the national total, while above it a "rural upper class," made up of hacienda owners, includes an additional 1 percent. Frank Tannenbaum, in his influential book on the Mexican revolution, also adopted this view, accepting the fact that "in 1910 the large majority of the Mexican population were classed as peons" (in the census). He recognized that in some cases, notably in Oaxaca and in the mountainous areas of Veracruz and Puebla, comunidades had retained more land and that therefore their members enjoyed a better position than hacienda workers. But he was not interested in determining internal differences, which, by the way, are very difficult to measure and can only be gleaned from indirect or fragmentary evidence. The contrast to the approach adopted in this volume is obvious, and certainly does not depend on the different time periods covered. It is certainly not that Tannenbaum or the other authors lacked the capacity to perceive distinctions inside the popular classes, but rather that they believed them to be unimportant. It could even have seemed frivolous, when considering the prospects of a major social revolution, to be concerned with such minor differentiations.[9]

The dichotomous view of social stratification is also shared by more recent scholars. Thus according to Nathan Whetten, "till recently, Mexico has lacked almost completely a middle class." In a similar vein, Stanley Green argues that from an overview of contemporary statistical materials (mostly contained in state governors' *memorias*) the picture that emerges is that of a "feudal society . . .with a few hundred storekeepers, a handful of doctors and lawyers, several dozen churchmen, a few score tradesmen or possibly miners, and thousands upon thousands of laborers (*jornaleros* or *labradores*)." He is more discriminating for the urban sector, where he estimates that 20 percent of the total population formed a middle or upper class, on the basis of Frederick Shaw's study of an 1849 census for the city of Mexico.[10]

Other authors recognize the presence of a middle class, especially in the urban sector, though without estimating its numbers. Thus John Chance and William Taylor locate a middle class made up mostly of mixed bloods in Oaxaca, and John Kicza, in his study of merchants in Mexico City, considers that there was "a very large and highly differentiated middle sector" and that "there is no way in which the many retail merchants, functionaries, artisans, managers, and processors can be relegated to the lower class." Similarly Guy Thomson sees in Puebla a four-layer stratification pyramid, with a small elite on top and then a middle class, followed by "la plebe" and the underclass. In his concept of middle class, Thomson includes a smaller group than the one I would think justified, as he only takes a few of the more solid artisans and shopkeepers. In his category of "la plebe" there is a mixture of what I would consider lower-middle-class and working-class elements; however, it is important to differentiate, as he does, a plebeian mass from the underclass of léperos. Richard Salvucci, in his work on textiles, recognizes loom operators in the non-*obraje* sector as part of a "class" that included rancheros, *pegu-jaleros* (small producers of tobacco and other crops), and artisans, among whose upper reaches there were some petty capitalists, blending downward into the working poor.[11]

There is thus, in this debatable area, an important current of opinion recognizing the existence of quite sizable intermediate occupational groups, emerging above common wage-workers and the marginally self-employed, constituting the equivalent of what we call today a middle class, though of course their role was peculiar to the times. The fact that they did not look nor necessarily act like today's middle classes should not detract us from using the term to describe them. They lived often in what can appear as poverty, and especially in awesome insecurity, but they had an abyss beside them, from which they were happy to be spared, and into which they might slip at the least oversight. The subject has theoretical relevance, because the search for a better position in social space, the comparison with others, and the fear of falling lower down the scale, can all play a very central role in determining the attitudes found among wide sectors of the population.

Cleavage Lines

Apart from class conflict, which separates those above and below the various horizontal lines dividing the social pyramid, it is necessary to take into account the conflict between groups seeking a modern form of organizing production, education, or government, and those bent on maintaining the old system. The latter included the corporatist organization of many business and educational and artisan guilds. It froze a large amount of property in civil and ecclesiastic entails, including the Indian comunidades. In practice it involved a considerable amount of economic protectionism, unwittingly facilitated by the cumbrous regulations and the trade monopoly with Spain. There was then a confrontation between what might be called corporatism and the oncoming economic liberalism. At each side of this rather vertical line, very heterogenous groups could be found, located at different levels of the social pyramid. The fact of being on the same side in the corporatism-liberalism tussle created bonds of interclass solidarity, which compensated for the effects of class differences within each sector.

The corporatist and ecclesiastic aggregate was the dominant one in colonial society, and therefore it could be expected to have conservative attitudes. But it faced a potentially very strong liberal force, which, though somewhat fragile in national society (even after independence), was hegemonic on the international scene. Therefore the corporatist and ecclesiastic resistance was to some extent an opposition of "the weak" against new menacing powers, and as such it tended toward populist forms of expression. Quite a few members of the popular or lower middle classes could thus find themselves better interpreted, or defended, by the upper sectors of the old corporatist regime than by the enthusiasts of the new modernizing ideas. The bases were created for the rise of a popular-conservative and a liberal-bourgeois coalition. However, there was a group of ideologues and politicians who supported the disestablishment of the old order, because they believed that liberalization of productive forces would in the long run benefit the popular classes. A sector was thus created within liberalism that resisted the directives coming from the more doctrinaire of capitalist-minded components of that political hemisphere, complicating the panorama of possible alliances, because it was tempting for it to come to tactical agreements with sectors of the old establishment. To all this one should add the incidence of regional interests, as well as of other more specific economic and ideological variables. The resulting criss-cross was responsible for a great proliferation of social actors and for the formation of apparently contradictory coalitions. These coalitions were highly unstable, due to the tensions between their mutually antagonistic members, and to the oscillations of economic circumstances. Political leaders and caudillos operating in this chaotic environment acted with a high degree of apparent independence from class or other structural determinations. What was involved in fact was a more indirect relationship, mediated by the formation of elites in various particularly stressed locations of the social pyramid.

The shaky character of coalitions led to what at the time was often called "anarchy," associated with continuous changes of cabinet or military interventions. In the latter case, more often than not a "military anarchy" followed the civilian one, and it was as difficult to establish a presentable dictatorship as a solid civilian regime. Though to some extent these conditions also existed in other Latin American countries, the type and intensity of the unsettling forces was different in each case. As a result strong civilian governments could be organized in places such as Chile and Brazil, or more enduring dictatorships could take their place, as in Argentina.

On the other hand, it is also necessary to consider the distribution among social and cultural groups of the capacity to generate political loyalties. Political action, even of the more economically oriented type, needs a certain amount of expertise in the art of organization. When this is scarce, it can be substituted by traditional loyalties and habits of collective cohesion and solidarity. This is true at all stratification levels, and it is particularly dramatic at the lower ones. Among these lower strata, autonomous associationist practices must often be replaced by a mobilizational mode of participation, with external leadership. For this leadership to succeed, it must propose actions congruent with the interests of those to be mobilized; but something more is needed: a cultural or social-psychological component that establishes a common language, a shared symbology. In this field the corporatist and ecclesiastical sector enjoyed a great resource — religion. An appeal to the other world usually took paternalist and conservative forms, but it might also adopt a newer, more mobilizational aspect. The poorer or more rural parish priests, as well as the friars, were experts in these matters. Though they were part of the traditional system of domination, they could easily become agitators of the masses, due to the closeness of their positions in social space.

Within the liberal hemisphere, there were less ideological resources of this traditional type, but other new ones could be created. The army, both the regular one and the militia, was in many cases a vehicle for the generation of new loyalties, which very well might take a liberal hue. The same happened with the charismatic caudillos, who represented a mutation of classical paternalistic figures. Often their leadership was not traditional and conservative, but rather mobilizational (occasionally revolutionary), pitted against the upper classes. Politicians seeking mass support also used elements of nationalist or *indigenista* ideology. Of course all of this produced divisions, because mobilizational strategies were frowned upon by the better-off sectors of each political hemisphere, and as a result further lines of cleavage were generated. If there ever was an ungovernable country, Mexico was it.

1

Social Stratification

Artisans and Fabricantes

In what could broadly be called the urban plebs, the artisans enjoyed a relatively privileged position, though they were also internally stratified. They had considerable organizational experience, expressed since early colonial times in *gremios*, recognized and controlled by municipal *ordenanzas* that gave them the right to elect a governing body each year, composed of an alcalde or *mayoral* and two or three *veedores*, mostly in charge of conducting examinations and granting licenses to set up a shop. One of the aims of the regulations was to maintain the privileged status of the artisans as independent producers selling directly to the public. One can also discern a trend toward increasing differentiation within the guilds, as a result of population and economic expansion and division of labor. Some *ordenanzas* expressly forbade the formation of cofradías by the oficiales. This prohibition was common in the contemporary literature on artisans. Thus Campomanes warned against oficiales who had not yet risen to the status of maestro forming "a guild, and much less a cofradía, nor an association separated from that of the maestros, as was the case in some guilds, trades and arts of Madrid," because in that case lack of subordination and no end of quarrels would follow.[1] The skill categories and the names given to them in each trade were not uniform, but the tendency was toward establishing a top level, that of shop-owning maestro, followed by another one of oficiales, occasionally called *laborantes* or *menestrales*, and by yet a lower one of unskilled helpers or *obreros* and the young apprentices.[2]

After independence market forces could operate more freely, though it took considerable time before they had their full effect. Artisans demanded the prohibition of imports, mostly textiles, while a large portion of the consuming public wanted cheap foreign goods. On the other hand, many financiers were looking for new investments, and a protected industry seemed a promising new field. Industrialists and independent artisans, though jointly interested in tariff protection and capable, therefore, of occasional common political action, had many other opposed interests. Their alliance was always unstable, artisans having as much, if not more, to fear from a thriving local industry than from foreign imports; against the latter it was always possible to mobilize nationalist feelings. On the other hand, local industry would predictably produce at high cost, thus providing some sort of shield, and it would create new jobs, but many of them for women and children. Even for men the earnings and status of a factory worker would be predictably lower than those of an independent artisan.[3]

In a statistical study of 1838 for the city of Orizaba (Veracruz), artisans were classified according to the old categories of maestros, oficiales, and apprentices, though by this time the divisions did not correspond as before to a clear process of gremio regulation, which had been disposed of as part of the old colonial regime. The author pointed out that by maestros he meant those who had a shop of their own, and for each trade he gave the percentage formed by the maestros over the total work force. In most trades between a fourth and a third of their practitioners were classed as maestros. Leaving out the albañiles, the very special musicians, and another peculiar occupation, that of *cargadores*, the adjusted figures for the total of Orizaba give 29 percent as the proportion of the artisan work force that could be classed as maestros. This can be taken as a first approximation to the proportion of the total artisan work force that could be considered middle class. The figure is useful for the interpretation of other statistical materials where only the total number of artisans is given.[4]

In a study of Guadalajara, Rodney Anderson gives data for 1821–22, taken from the census and from registers of exams and voters in artisan guilds, in which the proportions appear as very different from those in the Orizaba report. This is because Anderson's information comes from two different sources, which are not totally comparable. The lists of maestros taking the required exams, as well as those of voters, refer to a very reduced and probably elitist sector of the trade. Thus for example among *zapateros* just one maestro was listed as voting or being examined for every twenty-three oficiales in the census. This is unlikely to have been the proportion between shop-owning artisans and their employees, because it would have implied an excessively large number of oficiales per shop. According to a study by Jorge González Angulo in the city of Mexico in 1801, most *zapatería* shops had between one and four oficiales, though there was a minority (about 10 percent) with as many as a dozen, these data being in line with the Orizaba figures. It should be taken into account that in the larger cities, especially Mexico, greater productive units were bound to exist, thus reducing the percentage of the shop-owners over the total working force in the trade. On the other hand, in a small town the relative social status of an independent producer, even if self-employed, would generally be higher than in a big urban concentration.[5]

The textile trade was very extensive in New Spain and very heterogeneous, the nonorganized sector being very numerous. Traditional activities such as spinning and home weaving with small looms were usually not included in the artisan sector by census takers. Of course workers in the rather large-scale obrajes were also not considered artisans, of any level, except for the very few maestros, who in this case were managers or owners, clearly differentiated from the rest. Workers, many of them forced, convicts, or even slaves, would have been called fabricantes.[6]

At the time of the above 1838 census, Orizaba was beginning its industrial revolution, with the establishment in the city itself of a large-scale textile factory, Cocolapan, owned by Lucas Alamán and partly financed by the Banco de Avío. This factory was then being built and already producing cotton yarn (*hilaza*), which it sold to the eighty existing manual looms operated by the artisan sector. After completing the installation of its projected one hundred power looms, the factory would consume its own yarn, thus leaving the manual looms without raw materials and forcing them to close, according to the local *jefe político*. Be that as it may, the following decades would see a radical transformation of Orizaba, which was destined to become, by the end of the century, the "Mexican Manchester." By then (1898) it included, apart from Cocolapan, which employed five hundred people, the nearby Río Blanco, with seventeen hundred workers, and Los Cerritos and San Lorenzo, with three hundred each, all located at about 4 kilometers from the city and dedicated to cotton spinning and weaving, using hydraulic power. A jute factory, employing eight hundred people, the railway repair shop with four hundred workers, and a number of other establishments for marble cutting, wheat milling, sugar and beer production, and cigar manufacture, as well as tanneries, contributed to the formation of a new working class, which soon would have a major confrontation with management and government in the violently repressed Río Blanco strike of 1907.[7]

The "industrial revolution" had brought prosperity to some sectors of the town population and misery to others. The blacksmiths, who with their noise had kept the Calles de Guadalupe alive, ceased their activity, unable to compete with foreign imports. Something similar, but due to the pressure of cheaper local factory production, had happened to the mostly female cotton spinners. It is not possible to tell whether all the women thus displaced got jobs in the new factories, but probably there were fewer new occupational positions in this field than there had been. The impact was felt with particular intensity when no new jobs appeared in the same community. For these women, in any event, their previous position was already quite low. But for the blacksmiths who were displaced by foreign products, the likely prospect was one of downward mobility, in case they got a factory job, unless it was as a foreman. By the 1830s these industrial changes were only beginning to take place and were fiercely resisted by very thorough protectionist legislation.[8]

Manufacturing workers who were not artisans were generally called fabricantes in the early censuses, though in some cases they were classified as *operarios*. They included the non-guild-organized spinners and weavers (mostly Indian) and people employed at tanneries, obrajes, factories, and tobacco enterprises. Wool, in distinction to cotton, was also worked mostly by fabricantes, in medium- to large-size obrajes. Tobacco elaboration gave work to some of the larger concentrations of the working population in the country and also included a sizable proportion of supervisory personnel. In the city of Mexico, there were between five and nine thousand people engaged in this activity, partly in a large factory and partly working at home. They did not have a guild, but from colonial times they had had a mutual-benefit association, La Concordia, which also performed some representative functions. Like many other census or occupational categories of the time, that of fabricantes was heterogeneous, as it included some owners of small units of production as well as the mass of their wage workers, in addition to self-employed people doing piecework. Querétaro and other towns in the Bajío, in the neighboring state of Guanajuato, such as San Miguel and Acámbaro, were centers of the wool trade. Before independence, Querétaro, with its 35,000 inhabitants, was the third or fourth largest town in New Spain, closely vying for that honor with Guadalajara and Guanajuato. It had some twenty obrajes, all concentrated in one section of the town, and many spinners and small loom operators spread not only throughout the city but also in the surrounding countryside. At the time of Humboldt's visit, toward the turn of the century, there were in the obrajes some 1,500 operatives, mostly weavers, another 1,500 in smaller textile mills, and 300 spinners in surrounding villages. Of this textile labor force of 3,300, some 800 were estimated to be women. An additional 3,000 people could be found in tobacco elaboration, most of them in one large factory, including 1,200 women;

and an estimated 2,300 *menestrales* worked as artisan helpers, journey-men, or at such less skilled jobs as albañiles and *arrieros*. If we take 10 percent of the tobacco workers as performing supervisory functions, the low-status categories added up to 8,300, in an employed population of slightly over 11,400 people; that is, they made up 73 percent of the total, leaving the rest for the middle and upper classes of artisans, shop keepers, administrators, and owners. Social tensions were potentially high, due to the large concentration of obraje and tobacco workers and to the vulner-ability of textile production to international economic conditions and regulations. Obrajeros were considered to be militia officers (their facto-ries doubled as prisons, since some of the workers were convicts); the high incidence of women in the labor force probably weakened the fam-ily structure and with it some of the conservative controls against vio-lence and the lack of discipline.[9]

Textile interests all over New Spain were very much affected by the opening of the port of Veracruz to neutral (that is, mostly American) ships, between 1805 and 1808, and by the continued introduction of British products even after that date.[10] When the Consolidación de Vales Reales was sanctioned for New Spain, in 1805, the whole credit structure received a mortal blow, generating a series of petitions for reconsidera-tion, including one by Corregidor Miguel Domínguez.[11] In 1808, when criollo elites made an attempt at autonomy using Iturrigaray's ambitions as a prop, Domínguez was in the forefront of those who demanded the formation of a congress and was later known to have had associations with the Insurgencia.[12]

The main center of the cotton-textile industry was Puebla. With its 70,000 inhabitants at independence, it was second only to Mexico City in size; it was larger than all other towns in the Spanish or Portuguese empires. In early colonial times, obrajes had been numerous, but they had decayed by the end of the eighteenth century, when textiles were organized in small-scale, independent artisan shops. Due to the stimulus provided by the Banco de Avío and by capitalists in search of secure in-vestments, Puebla soon became a hub of what for the time was large-scale industry. By 1841 it included ten factories employing between 45 and 300 people, for a total of 1185, mostly dedicated to power spinning, with some mechanical looms, while outside, in small, independent units, another 1,500 people worked in weaving (independent spinners had been all but eliminated).[13]

Puebla was considered to be a very conservative and religious commu-nity; this probably had something to do with its threatened artisan population, which tended toward populist political attitudes, tinged with a certain nostalgia for the good old days of corporatist organization. The ease with which the Puebla popular classes could be aroused under religious banners was a commonplace of early independent Mexico. Already in 1820 the Troncoso brothers, moderate liberal printers and publishers of *La Abeja Poblana*, though enthusiastic about the Spanish constitution and the new elections for representatives to the Cortes, lamented that the clericals had won at the polls as a result of abusive practices, which included distributing leaflets with lists of candidates and such other actions as forming juntas and associations. The Troncosos used the Rousseaunian differentiation, according to which the sum of particular wills can err, particularly if channelled through cabals and juntas, while the "general will" is a purer concept, based on public opinion without "sects and partisans." Three years later, during the last days of the empire, the Iturbidista José Manuel Posada, provisor (bishop's substitute) of Puebla, had created a "popular commotion under pretext of religion," agitating in favor of the tottering regime.[14]

Before the *Abeja*, another serial appeared, called *El tejedor y su compadre*, whose intended public is clear enough from the name. It was clerical, though constitutional, and warned against new, poorly understood principles, which according to some maintained that "we are all equal now." In one of the issues (no. 3), the *Tejedor* reprehends the Oficial for slackness in work, only to receive what by then must have been the standard response that "these are no longer the old days, when I had to bear with whatever you fancied . . . now, thank God, we are all equal and free to do whatever we wish." It was necessary for a third character, the Compadre, to cool down tempers by pointing out that the constitution only meant "civil equality."[15]

One of the main representatives of Puebla industrialists was Esteban de Antuñano, owner of La Constancia Mexicana, a large cotton factory outside Puebla. He was of Veracruz origin, but had concentrated his investments in Puebla and later branched out into other areas, such as Guadalajara. His Constancia factory was somewhat cruelly satirized by Manuel Payno, a liberal writer and politician, friend of Guillermo Prieto and editor with him of *El Museo Mexicano*, the literary journal where he published some travel notes. The rather crude allegories painted in the entrance hall of the factory were an easy target, though they might not have been out of place in any Quaker-owned mill in the more advanced part of the globe. Those were the days (1841–44) when the Santa Anna regime was supporting protectionist policies for cotton manufacture, which included the prohibition of several types of textile products. Payno repeated the usual argument, that only capitalists profited from this, and that three million pesos per year were lost in import duties, thus rendering the Treasury impotent with respect to financiers, some of whom were also cotton-factory owners. However, he noticed that the factory was surrounded by a barrio of very neat small houses for workers and acknowledged that if there was any part of the republic where protectionism was beneficial, it was Puebla, whose common people were "lively, intelligent and of mercurial passions; it is necessary to give them bread to eat, and work so as not to be idle. Since the establishment of factories in Puebla there have been very few revolutions and never so bloody and terrible as when they were hungry." Realizing that this might sound contradictory when compared with his earlier tirade against protectionism, he concluded that what may be good for some regions may not be so for others, a general maxim of difficult application under the circumstances.[16]

Urban Stratification Profiles

Frederick Shaw, in his study of urban poverty in the city of Mexico, based on the occupational data of the 1849 census, has established a three-tiered stratification profile. He defines a higher group formed by professionals, civil servants, industrialists, prosperous merchants, and other people engaged in business, paying over seven pesos monthly rent, which he calls "middle-upper." These formed 20 percent of the total male occupied population, a very important figure, considering that practically no artisans were included in it. Below this first tier, a second one appears, mostly made up of small shopkeepers (paying between three and seven pesos monthly rent), tradesmen, and artisans, not differentiated according to maestro or *oficial* status (which generally cannot be deduced from census information). This second tier comes to 42 percent of the total, forming the "skilled," better-off part of the *plebe*, or laboring poor, practically coinciding with the artisanate, with the exception of a few very solid master craftsmen, who were counted among the businessmen. In a third level we find the "*plebe ínfima*," 29 percent of the total, made up of unskilled workers, peddlers, and artisans in low-prestige trades. This stratification analysis is an important contribution to our knowledge of the social structure of Mexico by midcentury. The second tier, however, should be further analyzed, as it is excessively heterogeneous, including many maestros who, though not making it into the "middle-upper" level, were, however, differentiated from the rest of the artisanate, composed mostly of oficiales or journeymen. Medium-size merchants should also be differentiated from that common mass.[17]

Rodney Anderson, in a study based on the censuses of Guadalajara taken in 1821 and 1822, detects two upper strata (the elite and the auxiliary elite) forming 21 percent of the total male occupied population. Below there is a very broad artisan group, subdivided into two groups according to status criteria such as the designation of *don*. The upper-status artisan group forms 17 percent of the population, which if considered middle class and added to the two elite groups, would yield a total of 38 percent for the middle and upper classes.[18]

Other published local censuses, combined with the estimates derived from Orizaba for the relative proportion of maestros or shop-owning artisans, help to develop a picture of the social pyramid. For Guadalupe, the religious center near the capital, we have the occupations of its economically active population for 1856, including some rural categories besides the typically urban ones. Within the urban categories the following can be discerned:

1. Clearly middle (or upper) class: *comerciantes, corredores de arrieros, funcionarios, empleados, dependientes de comercio, estanquilleros, fondistas, clero, preceptores, maestros*; 198 persons, all males.

2. Artisan categories, male: *sastres, zapateros, talabarteros, herreros, carroceros, carpinteros, hojalateros, pintores, pasteros, cereros, carniceros, canteros, ladrilleros, barberos, fruteros, jaboneros, veleros*; 125 persons.

3. Artisan categories, female: *costureras, torcedoras de cigarros*; 31 persons.

4. Micro salespeople, half of them estimated to be males: *placeros* and *billeteros*; 32 persons.

5. Micro salespeople, females; 32 persons.

6. Transportation, construction, and service workers: *arrieros, cocheros, carretoneros, albañiles, aguadores, empleados de policía, cocineros, "jornaleros en la población"* (in contrast to *"jornaleros del campo"*), musicians, and an estimated half of the domestic servants; 288 persons, all males.

7. Female service workers: *tortilleras, atoleras, lavanderas*, and half the domestic servants; 54 persons.[19]

These figures can be further elaborated, classifying, according to the Orizaba figures, 30 percent of the artisans (of either sex) as middle class and including all the micro salespeople in the lower strata. The lower strata, comprising some 60 to 70 percent of the population of a town like Guadalupe, could in turn be subdivided into a settled working-class sector and an unstable or marginal one. The lines of division were not clear, nor can they be deduced easily from the census materials. One approximation would include among the settled working-class sectors the non-shop-owning artisans (that is, the oficiales or menestrales), plus the people working in factories and in tobacco elaboration, and maybe half those involved in transportation (arrieros, carretoneros, cocheros), construction (albañiles), and such services as musicians. This group in Guadalupe would consist of 147 people, that is, 23 percent of the urban males, leaving for the lowermost, shifting proletariat a good 40 percent of the total, made up of domestic servants, street peddlers, quite a few albañiles and transportation workers, and jornaleros. This lower 40 percent would be somewhat larger if self-supporting women and rural people residing in the town were included. According to this estimate, then, almost half the population, could be considered as forming a shifting proletariat, not exactly léperos, but close to them, and of course including them. A high percentage, and a very visible one, but still not more than half the population. The rest included the more solid components of the manual working class and the insecure but relatively privileged middle class. It was easy to fall from this middle class to the lower abysses; but one could also fight back through family solidarity and eventually some corporatist or political action, as well as with help from private patrons and religious welfare organizations.

For Mazatlán, a port town with a military garrison in Sinaloa, there are also occupational data for 1858. Excluding the military and women, but retaining the few agricultural professions (because jornaleros are not subdivided between rural and urban), the breakdown is as follows:

1. Clearly middle class; 549.

2. Artisan maestros (30 percent of artisans); 152.

3. Menestrales (the remaining 70 percent of artisans); 355.

4. Other stable working class (half of all albañiles, musicians, arrieros, carretoneros); 55.

5. Unstable working class (half of the above, plus an estimated male half of sirvientes domésticos, plus jornaleros, sailors, *vendedores ambulantes*, *revendedores*, and other low-status manual jobs); 1009.[20]

Adding up the corresponding categories, the resulting profile yields 33 percent for the middle (and upper) classes, 19 percent for the stable working class, and 48 percent for the unstable working class.

For the municipality of Durango, there are occupational data for 1849. At that time the population of the city and its environs of ten or twelve leagues was 29,198, of which the total with some declared occupation was 9,777. There was a tobacco factory employing 487 people and a textile mill (located ten kilometers from the town) with 280 workers, practically all women in both cases, and 27 wool obrajes. In order to get an idea of the stratification profile in the nonagricultural sector of the municipality, that is, mostly the town and its satellite industrial village, we must substract the 2,324 *agricultores*, leaving a total of 7,453 gain-fully employed people in the nonagricultural, or "occupationally urban," part of the municipality. Applying criteria similar to those used above, 2,456 people enter into the urban middle-class category, making up 33 percent of the total.[21]

The port of Carmen, center of wood export in Tabasco (which was then a part of Yucatán), also has occupational data for its *partido*, for the year 1869. As usual there is a large category of agricultores, with 1,872 members, of whom it is stated that 1,510 were indebted, which reflects the fact that most must have been peones. The remaining "occupation-ally urban" population has a total of 287 people in the middle class, that is, 32 percent of the urban, or nonagricultural, total.[22]

For Querétaro there are also significant data on social stratification. We have already seen the situation in Humboldt's time. Toward the 1840s it had undergone its "industrial revolution," the traditional obrajes being superseded by a large cotton-spinning and weaving establishment, the Hércules, owned by Cayetano Rubio, a less prominent version of Puebla's Antuñano. The Hércules, around 1844, employed 876 operarios, includ-ing 584 women, and as it was building an extension, 400 albañiles also found work there. By 1855 his factory had grown, using 9,200 spindles, 450 power looms, and 270 manual ones, and giving employment to a total of 2,500 people, a figure that may include some independent pro-ducers linked through the homework system. The governor of Querétaro in 1844, Sabás Antonio Domínguez, also owned a cotton factory, smaller than the Hércules; and the author of the statistical study we are using here, Antonio del Raso, also said he had had textile experience beginning in 1801. The city was crossed by two rivers, which powered the factory and obraje machines and several wheat mills, serviced the tanneries, and then irrigated haciendas and ranchos. The city and its relatively nearby San Juan del Río were the "gate to Tierra adentro," that is, to the north, and thus centers of intense commerce and *arriería*, particularly San Juan, where a cavalry squadron of permanent troops was also stationed. The town itself was subdivided into two *parroquias*, the newer one established on the "otra banda del río." A league and a half to the south, another pueblo, San Francisco Galileo, called Pueblito, was inhabited by some nine thousand Otomí Indians, while to the east La Cañada, also heavily Indian, was another satellite population center. So population estimates of the city of Querétaro varied according to the enthusiasm of the visitor. Zelaa thought it had fifty thousand inhabitants, while Father Morfi reduced the figure to forty-three thousand in about 1777–78, and even earlier the careful census taker Villaseñor y Sánchez put the figure at over forty-six thousand. Quite an explosive place, all things considered, as was to be attested by its early role in the Hidalgo revolt.[23]

Antonio del Raso made estimates of the occupational distribution of the total population of the state of Querétaro for the year 1844, giving also what he considered to be the income generated by each group. This allows us to have a glimpse of how a statistician of the time saw the social-stratification pyramid.[24] The occupational categories he considered may be divided into basically "urban," that is, linked to secondary, tertiary, or mining production; and "rural," or primary, except for mining. Many secondary or tertiary occupations were practiced in small pueblos or hamlets or haciendas, so strictly speaking they were not urban. We may consider them occupationally urban, though, as a first approximation to the situation in the towns. Let us now examine the occupationally "urban" categories, collapsed into five strata.

In the "urban" sector, we find a first level of *censualistas* (rentiers), professionals, merchants, and clergy, with an estimated annual income of more than 900 pesos. Some of these categories are quite heterogeneous, such as the clergy, most of whose members would really belong in some of the groups below. The merchants, by their numbers and income, do not include the mass of semiambulant vendors, occasionally opening a *tendajón* or selling under a *tianguis*.

A second level, with incomes between 300 and 900 pesos per year, included government officials, *escribientes*, and fabricantes. The latter, given their estimated income, obviously do not include most of the workers traditionally called fabricantes, or low-status, nonguild manual workers. They would include the owners of small- and medium-scale industries, some of them almost of artisan level, though their income was much higher than that of shop-owning artisans. Wageworkers in factories were explicitly excluded from this group; as operarios they belong to a category two steps lower in the ladder.

The third level was made up of *dependientes de comercio* and shop-

owning artisans, explicitly defined as operating *talleres* of their own. This
group had incomes varying between 150 and 200 pesos per annum.

Below this point the proletariat began, and it is not easy to differentiate it according to income data. Probably security of employment was
much more important there. We might tentatively form a first group,
located at the fourth level, of those who had what appear to be more
permanent jobs (except domestic service, which is demoted to the lowest
level, whatever its security). We have here the *menestrales* (oficiales and
apprentices) working for the shop-owning artisans, the operarios in large
or small-scale industries and tobacco manufacture, and the miners.

A second group of the proletariat, occupying the fifth and lowest stratification level, would be formed by the menestrales not working in the
artisan sector, that is, the albañiles, arrieros, aguadores, hortelanos, and
vendimieros, plus the ambulant or semiambulant vendors and the domestic servants. It should be noted that the number of "male domestics"
is too high to justify thinking of them simply as domestic servants. Many
must have been doing service jobs of the peddler or street-vendor variety,
connected with fulfilling household needs; hence their name. The category of jornaleros, so often used in other census materials, does not
appear in this study (nor in the rural sector). This is because their members have been assigned to other groups, notably the nonartisan
menestrales and the male domestics.

Here what may be called the middle classes make up 21 percent of the
"urban" total, somewhat less than in the small-town studies of Orizaba,
Guadalupe, and Mazatlán. In interpreting the difference, we must take
into account that these data correspond to a whole state, including mi-
nuscule hamlets, and that this was the center of the traditional wool industry; apart from the new large-scale cotton factories, it still accounted
for some obrajes and many *trapiches*, giving work to the poorer strata.
We also have to take into account the proletariat-creating capacity of the
tobacco factory and the tanneries, plus several mescal and *chinguirito*
installations. By the 1850s another local statistician commented that "industry . . . was reduced to nullity since after independence the ports were
opened . . . Neither trapiches, nor obrajes, nor other talleres can work, so
the multitude are reduced to the sorry condition of proletarians."[25] Admittedly these were the days of the last Santa Anna dictatorship, inspired
by Alamán, so the argument about the bad effects of opening up to the
international market may have had some political aims. This perception
of its effects at the time, however, was very widespread. Lucas Alamán,
who ought to know, recognized that "modern machinery, which has been

so useful in multiplying and cheapening production for the benefit of consumers and a few businessmen, [has been] detrimental to the producing class, whose misery it has caused."[26]

Haciendas, Ranchos, and Pueblos

In the rural areas, in the early part of the nineteenth century, a majority of the population was Indian and lived for the most part in pueblos, with their own relatively autonomous institutions. Most of the land, however, was not in the hands of the pueblos but in those of Spanish, criollo, or mestizo owners and squatters. Large properties were called haciendas and smaller ones ranchos, though the latter name was used with different meanings, as we shall see presently. In haciendas and ranchos, a certain part of the population was established as resident peons or tenants, while others came to work from the neighboring pueblos, as temporary wageworkers and also as nonresident tenants.

The proportions of these categories varied from place to place. In southern Oaxaca the traditional structure of pueblos and caciques had been least touched by Spanish influence. Indian communities had managed to retain considerable amounts of land, and caciques and their relatives in many cases had obtained large fields as private property. The production of *grana* from the cochineal insects in the *nopal* cactuses was undertaken by Indian and other casta families, and though commercialization was in the hands of Spanish traders, a certain modest well-being (by comparison with what happened in other areas) existed among the rural popular classes. Thiéry de Menonville, a French traveler of the eighteenth century who was entrusted by the king of France with the task of getting some *cochinilla nopales* (the export of which was of course prohibited), so as to transplant them to Saint Domingue, left a description of Oaxaca, which he found very similar to Europe, due to its fertile lands and wheat fields. In San Juan del Rey, he visited a black who was the local alcalde and who owned one and a half *arpentes* (about half a hectare) of *nopaleras*. In the city itself, he met a watchmaker who turned out to be a "corregidor" (surely a mistake for regidor), and after bargaining unsuccessfully with a small tradesman (*apothicaire*), by posing as a botanist he was able to buy the precious plant from another "corregidor," who employed five or six Indians. A strong impression emerges of a society of small cultivators, petty bourgeois entrepreneurs, and upwardly mobile Indians or castas engaging in the trade.[27]

In the pueblos there was a social stratification with an upper stratum of caciques, principales, members of cabildos, and leaders of cofradías, along with some other enterprising commoners who emerged from the community as small traders, arrieros, or renters of particular tracts of land in nearby haciendas or in the pueblos themselves.[28] The poorer members of the pueblos went to work temporarily or permanently in the haciendas, as peons or as tenants, the latter being a very heterogeneous category. In some cases tenancy involved managing a productive unit of some economic significance, while in others it merely implied having a very small plot for building a hut and doing some subsistence agriculture, waiting until the owner required some extra help for the harvest or other seasonal labor-intensive activity.

In colonial times those Indians who left their pueblos and went to live in the haciendas or ranchos were called *gañanes*, *laboríos*, or *naboríos*. These Indians were not subject to control by their repúblicas, particularly if their residence in the haciendas had been long or extended to a succeeding generation. In this way the class of hacienda or rancho peones was created, and to it other mixed bloods were added with the passage of time. Toward the end of the eighteenth century, Guanajuato had the greatest concentration of laboríos in the viceroyalty, some two-thirds of the total. This was partly due to the fact that most of that intendencia was established in a frontier land with little settled Indian population; mining prosperity, too, attracted migrants.[29] The economic and demographic expansion of the Bajío area did not mean that prosperity spread down the social ladder. Rather the contrary was the case, the increased population implying an unfavorable relation between the supply and demand of labor, as has been remarked recently by John Tutino in his study of the conditions leading to agrarian rebellions in Mexico. The vast proportion of Indians uprooted from their ancestral pueblos and a large increase in population, due in part to internal migration, must be taken as factors explaining the development of the Insurgencia in the Guanajuato area. In contrast to Oaxaca (and to much of the rest of New Spain) the Bajío had a large socially mobilized population, which had broken its links to traditional forms of community control.

Side by side with the pueblos and occupying a position generally above most of its residents, the rancheros formed a very strategic social group, which has been the subject of an increasing number of studies that focus on their capacity to subsist (though occasionally at the cost of becoming *minifundia* operators) and their political explosions when harassed by the state.[30] A rancho, in the common usage of the time, meant a small- to medium-size property, or a similar-size unit rented from an hacienda, larger than what most arrendatarios or medieros would have had. It could also refer to a portion of an hacienda, worked centrally but separated because it was somehow differentiated from the rest in terms of production; it might be oriented more toward stock, or more irrigated, or dedicated to a special crop, or be separated from the rest by some geographical accident. For administrative and census purposes, though, a rancho was a center of delegated order-maintenance and recording functions. This is the sense in which the term was used in most censuses, in which the whole territory of an intendencia or a state was subdivided into haciendas, ranchos, and pueblos. Thus in a *reglamento de policía* for the state of Guanajuato in the 1830s, the role of ayuntamientos in order maintenance was classified as "internal" and "external." Internal security applied to the built-up part of towns, where each regidor, helped by a resident neighbor termed *vigilante*, was in charge of a *cuartel*, while further subdivisions by block and street were allotted to subordinate vigilantes. As for external security, ayuntamientos were instructed to see that in haciendas and ranchos houses should be built close to each other and that in each congregation thus formed, a *custodio* should be appointed, with the name of "encargado de rancho o hacienda." These people had the responsibility of making lists of all residents with their occupations and reporting on *vagos* and animals without known owners, and they were empowered to make detentions.

　　In the hacienda the administrative unit generally coincided with an individually owned or nonsubdivided family property, and in the pueblos the municipal authority was usually present. The land that was neither hacienda nor pueblo-owned was in a sense residual, but many people made a living there. In what probably was the oldest or most important settlement in each one of these residual areas, an official "rancho" was erected, which in its origin may have coincided with a unit of property or production, later subdivided by inheritance, sale, or new settlement. Pedro García Conde, in a statistical essay on Chihuahua made in the 1850s, gave a list of the "subdivisiones políticas" of the state, classified as follows: *ciudad con ayuntamiento, villa con ayuntamiento, pueblo con ayuntamiento, pueblo con junta municipal, pueblo con juez de paz, pueblo sin autoridad, mineral* (classified like the pueblos), *hacienda con juez de paz, hacienda sin autoridad, rancho con juez de paz, rancho* or *ranchería sin autoridad.* The latter class, though in fact "sin autoridad" in Chihuahua, was taken by García Conde as a census unit, and obviously coincided with those congregations of ranchos that in the Guanajuato regulation of the 1830s were supposed to have a delegated municipal authority.[31]

In another statistical study, for Salvatierra in Guanajuato in 1865, there are references to a Rancho del Sabino, "subdivided among more than fifty owners who cultivate their small lands." The Hacienda de la Zanja was still called by that name, even though it had now been sold to twenty different people; the Hacienda de la Magdalena had been subdivided into thirteen fractions; and that of Esperanza, in the suburbs of the town, now had four new owners and a textile factory. The census criterium was maintained up to the twentieth century. Thus in a book published by the Dirección General de Estadística in 1952, a *localidad* was defined as any place formed by a group of houses, huts, or constructions of any type, which was permanently inhabited, known in the area by a name, and possessed a political category based on law or custom. The book further went on to give a list of all municipalities, subdivided into localidades, with the corresponding "political category," which could be: ciudades, villas, pueblos, congregaciones, haciendas, fincas, estaciones de ferrocarril, "pequeñas localidades sin categoría política," ranchos, rancherías, and ejidos.[32]

There are many cases of the ambiguous use of the term *rancho*. When in the second half of the eighteenth century Father Morfi made his trip to the far north, he saw in the latifundium of the Marqués de Aguayo a locality called Puerto de los Ojuelos, "known as such because of an estancia or rancho of the same name that [was] nearby . . . It is a hapless hut with a small stream . . . and many lands, which the marquis, so as not to abandon totally, has given to some poor fellows [who] in arrendamientos pay a tenth of their crops." But other ranchos he visited belonged just to one owner or one occupier. By the 1820s, in a similar voyage, Berlandier and Chovel described a number of localities, each of which they designated as "ranchos," in the plural, such as the "ranchos del Encinal, which are ten or twelve," while in other cases the rancho de las Norias, located in a saline area, was described as basing its income on selling water, which was the main income of "its rancheros." When economic rather than population data were recorded, often for tax purposes, for example in a study of the pulque trade coming into the city of Mexico from the central plateau, the units of production were classified into haciendas and ranchos; in those cases the latter were individually owned and rather sizable in value. In more recent studies, ranchos occasionally appear as singly owned units of production, but this is often due to the source used. Thus Isabel González Sánchez, in a study of Tlaxcala, uses a list of donations to Philip

V from landowners, who were classified into hacendados and rancheros. These were, of course, the more substantial rancheros, as the others would not even dream of appearing in such a list.[33]

A detailed description of haciendas was made in a statistical study of two partidos in Zacatecas in 1830. One of them, Encarnación, was said to "have" eleven ranchos, one of which was called an hacienda, another two estancias, and the remaining eight were inhabited "by a few arrendatarios and sirvientes, whose livelihood depends on employment in the hacienda." This was most probably a case, like that of the Hacienda de Bocas, where the arrendatarios or medieros lived in sites inside the property, called ranchos, and were so registered statistically. In another area a large hacienda, Plateado, was located in a plain where there were "quite a few ranchos belonging to small owners,"and in San Andrés "there is a good number of ranchos, some annexed, some independent, and most of them subdivided among a multitude of arrendatarios or owners who get in each other's way due to the small amount of land they cultivate." There were also some landowning pueblos and several haciendas that belonged to religious cofradías controlled by their Indian parishioners in association with the priest. The author, deferring to the spirit of the times, proposed that all those collectively-held lands be subdivided, so as to stimulate the animal spirits of property.[34]

Existing legislation, during the early decades of the republic, facilitated the formation of new pueblos. This was the result of statutes enacted by the Spanish Cortes during the liberal periods, which remained in force after independence. That legislation allowed people to "denounce" unoccupied fiscal lands up to a certain extension and get them in private property; Indian communities could also ask collectively for such lands, and even petition for parts of private haciendas which were not used by their owners. Of course a lot of litigation could ensue as to what it meant to have a certain part of a large hacienda in operation. Rancherías, even if not made up of Indians, could also petition for the right to become a pueblo, which gave them some legal protection and the possibility of establishing an ayuntamiento. Once an ayuntamiento was organized, it had to be manned, and this was the golden opportunity for the "*leguleyos* and *rábulas.*" At any rate this was the opinion of the *prefecto* of Cuernavaca, who in a report for 1850 expressed relief at the fact that there were not many of such types in his jurisdiction, because "when one of them gets appointed secretary of the ayuntamiento he causes more iniquities due to his control of affairs" than if he had continued in private practice. The prefect went on to recommend a sweeping reduction of the ayuntamientos, which were a good score or so, to just five, one in each dependent partido.[35]

Rural Stratification Profiles

Several hacienda studies undertaken by Jan Bazant in San Luis Potosí allow us to gain an idea of the rural occupational structure, even if they refer to a somewhat later period than the one covered in this volume. The Hacienda de Bledos in 1840 had a population of 2,124 inhabitants (some 400 families) and worked about half its land directly (one is tempted to call that sector a "demesne"), while the other half was worked by tenants, called alternately arrendatarios or *aparceros*. Bazant calculates that the directly operated half used 100 peones, who lived near the *casco*, and the other half was given to 300 tenants, who lived in rancherías distributed throughout the hacienda. Peones, apart from their wages, got a good amount of maize to feed their family and a small plot of land for cultivation. Tenants received free of charge their hut, firewood, seeds, and some pasturage, and had to give half the crop to the owner in exchange for the land they used. Occasionally tenants worked for hire, receiving a money payment. It is not clear from this study whether there was a difference in status between the two groups. The peones had a certain security, especially because they had food regardless of the weather. The tenants depended on the rain, and some of them, if they had a sizable plot of land and a pair of oxen, might make some money in a good year. Others were forced to rely on occasional employment and had no secure food supply. Thus some tenants were above the peones and others below them. David Brading considers the resident peones a relatively privileged, less unstable group, a fact reflected in their lower level of debt as shown in the Bazant study; Brian Hamnett is of the same opinion. On the other hand, Eric Van Young, in his study of Guadalajara haciendas, refers to the heterogeneity of the tenants, claiming that some of them deserved the name of *kulaks* and got the more important one of *don*.[36]

John Tutino does not differentiate so much between peones and tenants, but rather contraposes the whole hacienda work force, which generally enjoyed a "secure dependence," with the pueblo Indians, who though more autonomous, were highly insecure, due to the vagaries of the weather. Tenants would be, from this perspective, in a position nearer to that of the pueblos, though in a crisis they would have had somewhat better access to hacienda grains and credit than people from the comunidades. On the other hand, James Taylor, in a study of Guanajuato at the time of the insurgency, considers the arrendatarios in general clearly to have been above the peones and much more ethnically mixed, including many of criollo status, than the resident peones or the pueblo inhabitants.[37] Guillermo Prieto, in a study of Mexican public finances for 1850, referred to the medieros, one of the names given to arrendatarios or aparceros. He was trying to differentiate for the Indian population those who were "more independent, because they [were] as though more emancipated from the tyranny of the owners . . . , [including] . . . the *medieros*, that is, the tillers of other people's lands, in contracts which give all the advantages to the landlord." His proposal was to give them lands in ownership taken from uncultivated latifundia and from the Indian comunidades (the latter, preferentially, for their own residents), thus forming what he thought might become the equivalent of the farmers of more prosperous countries.[38]

Actually such broad categories as arrendatarios or even resident peones are too heterogeneous to serve as basic units of social stratification. Bazant's data for the Hacienda de Bocas, also a very large one in San Luis Potosí, help to provide a closer look at the internal stratification of the rural population. In 1852 the hacienda, like Bledos, subdivided its work force into sirvientes (permanent or occasional) and arrendatarios or aparceros. But the so-called sirvientes included an elite group of five people, who were very far from the *peón* category: they were the administrator, the *capellán*, the *mayordomo*, the shop assistant, and the "accountant," who earned between 300 and 1000 pesos per year. Below them there was a group of 55 "*peones acomodados*" who were not really peones: they included the escribiente, the *sacristán*, and much supervisory personnel. They all got their ration of maize and between 4 and 10 pesos per month. Below them, still in the category of "sirvientes," another 360 "*peones corrientes*" could be found, who were paid some 1.5 reales per day, without maize, but they could buy it at half the market price. Finally, 95 muchachos, surely kin to the rest of the work force, were also employed at lower wages. All permanent sirvientes (420 without counting the muchachos) had some small lots given to them for sowing and could obtain the seed at reduced prices. Still in the category of "sirvientes," there was a widely oscillating number of temporary peones, or *alquilados*, who at peak harvest moments could number as many as 500 and in winter almost nil. Among them some were *capitanes*, making 3 reales per day, but most earned from 1 to 1.5 reales, without maize and without credit. Many of these temporary peones were arrendatarios, and others may have come from nearby pueblos or ranchos.[39]

The arrendatarios, in this case, in contrast to their situation at Bledos, had to pay 5 pesos per year for their right to have a hut and corral (*pisaje*) and an extra amount according to the extension they used or the number of heads of cattle they had. In 1852 there were 794 arrendatarios, some 200 of whom were called aparceros. They lived scattered among twelve rancherías; estimating five persons per family, they made a population of 4,000 people. To this number Bazant adds 1,500 residents, corresponding to the 420 adult permanent servants; supposing that among them there were many who belonged to the same family, the hacienda would have a total of 5,500 inhabitants, corresponding to an economically active population of 1,309 people. Among the arrendatarios many paid only pisaje; that is, they just had a place to live in the hacienda and were available for temporary work. Probably the 200 who were called aparceros were those cultivating larger portions of land, who did not need to employ themselves as transitory wageworkers in the hacienda. So the 794 arrendatarios can be broken down into the 200 better-off aparceros and the rest who had scarcely a plot of land at their disposal and who reappeared statistically as the 500 temporary peones "alquilados" at peak moments. Actually there would still be an extra 94 to account for, but probably those who took temporary work were not always the same ones, so the total of these workers would be larger than the 500 working in December.

Considering, then, the 200 people distinguished in this document by the name of aparceros as forming a relatively privileged group, a first classification of the 1852 data for Bocas gives the following social stratification profile:

1. A middle class, including the 5 elite, the 55 "acomodado" supervisors, and the 200 aparceros, making 260 in all, or 20 percent of the total employed.[40]

2. A lower class, including the 360 peones corrientes, the 95 muchachos, and the 594 arrendatarios not classed as aparceros, for a total of 954 people; to avoid double counting, the temporary workers are not included, as they were recruited from the poorer arrendatarios.

Obviously percentages must have oscillated widely from hacienda to hacienda and from time to time, according to the state of the market and management's choice between directly working the "demesne" or giving out tenancies. The holders of the latter, however, did enjoy some traditional moral rights of security, even if no legal ones. When these rights were infringed upon, rebellions might follow.

It is difficult to generalize these figures to other locations, conditions being exceedingly heterogeneous on haciendas, ranchos, and pueblos. I would estimate, however, that at least 10 percent of those classed as peones and 30 percent of those appearing as labradores, *terrazgueros*, or arrendatarios should be considered as being "above the line," whether one calls them a class, stratum, caste, or whatever. These estimates can be useful in the interpretation, however tentative, of some of the numerous census materials of the time, which do include some occupational data.

There was a continuum between the rancheros and the aparceros or arrendatarios, including squatters in frontier lands, especially in the less controlled *tierra caliente* areas. The worse-off arrendatarios or aparceros could fall into the category of peones, while those better situated merged with the rancheros.[41] An eighteenth-century report for the zone between the Mescalapa and Coatzacoalcos rivers, in what then was Oaxaca, describes the cabecera of San Francisco Ocuapan as being composed of 26 Spanish families, 80 Indian, and another 233 of mulattoes living "spread out among the woods at distances of 12, 14 or 16 leagues . . . cultivating cacao and maize."[42] In such situations it was difficult for census takers to distinguish something called a rancho, and it was common to enumerate simply pueblos and "rancherías." This was typical of frontier areas where haciendas had not yet been established, as can be seen in a study of the district of Tuxpan, on the gulf coast south of Tampico.[43] In it the traditional division between villas, haciendas, ranchos, and pueblos gives place to another one, where the villa is reported, plus the pueblos and a large number of rancherías. Surprisingly no haciendas appear in this report, which may be due to the lack of development of solid estates worthy of that name, in an unhealthy area of sparse settlement.[44] From the people living in such environments, ranging from squatters to rancho owners and the lower levels of hacienda foremen, derived such figures as the "*jarocho*," the traditional rural dweller of the Veracruz plains. Among them there were more prospects for bettering their condition than among the more traditional estate peons, however secure these may have been, and their life chances were completely different from those of the mass of pueblo dwellers. For them participation in civil wars was just another occupational possibility, implying a way of life not too different and not much riskier than the one they were accustomed to.

If the rancheros are a rather mysterious class, the nature of the labradores is obscured by a still greater darkness. Rhetorically, the word could be used for anyone engaged in agriculture, even of the loftier status. In the censuses the term was often used in contrast to *jornalero*. Referring to the Bazant studies we have analyzed, it may be stated that the labradores more or less coincided with the arrendatarios and the jornaleros with the peones, taking into account that those categories were quite heterogeneous. In some statistical studies, however, the all-encompassing term of *labrador*, or alternately *jornalero*, was used to refer to the whole of the working rural population, as in a census for Aguascalientes. Yet another report, published in 1862, this time for Chiapas, gives the occupational categories in some detail for the urban sector, but the rural population falls either into the "labrador" or the "ganadero" class. Equally rough is a study of Durango, where apart from the rather detailed urban categories, all others are reduced to the condition of "agricultores."[45]

More information can be gathered from a census for the state of Guanajuato, taken in 1825, which gives data by districts; these were mostly rural ones, since the capital was not included in the returns. The occupational categories, not very rich, are different from those used in the more detailed urban censuses seen in the previous chapter or in the Querétaro study (table 1).[46]

The first four categories are predominantly "urban" (in the occupational if not the residential sense of the term). The labradores were of course rural, but the jornaleros could be either urban or rural, most probably moving from one branch of activity to the other, as is usual in this type of situation. Their numbers were very large, though not so overwhelming as some impressionistic descriptions would have us believe; they formed 57 percent of the total. If they were all classified as rural, then the remaining "urban" stratification profile would be weighted too much toward the upper layers of the pyramid. It is not possible to allot the jornaleros proportionally to the urban and rural spheres, so we must be content with having a look at the total ("urban" plus rural) social pyramid in each locality. However, in such a state as Guanajuato, especially with the capital left out of consideration, most jornaleros must have been rural. So we can take as an indicator of the rural character of a district the percentage formed by the sum of labradores and jornaleros over the total.[47]

Before proceeding, the categories of fabricantes and labradores must be analyzed. As stated earlier, "fabricantes" was a heterogeneous and shifting census category, most members of which were very low level manual workers who did not make it into the artisan group, even at its lower sector of *menestrales* (that is, "oficiales" plus apprentices and operarios). In the census we are considering, about half the "fabricantes" were concentrated in San Miguel el Grande, one of the cradles of the Insurgencia, with many wool obrajes and tanneries, employing a basically unskilled and impoverished labor force. As for the labradores, they were distinguished from the mere jornaleros, as we saw earlier. On the basis of estimates made earlier in this chapter, we may include 30 percent of labradores, that is, the more self-sufficient aparceros, and 10 percent of the peones or jornaleros (bearing in mind that they were overseers), in the rural middle class. When the two categories of labradores and jornaleros were mentioned in a census, the mass of the pueblo-community Indians were likely to be taken as jornaleros, except, of course, those of them who were renting lands on the haciendas. At any rate, this is evidently the situation in the Guanajuato census, because there are some districts called "pueblos" where only or almost only jornaleros were listed (Rincón de Tamayo and San Miguel Octopán), and none where all or a vast majority were defined as labradores.[48] In most census districts classed as pueblos, though, there were both labradores and jornaleros.

So we will include in the relatively higher status group, for each district, both the urban and the rural middle classes, comparing them with the total economically active population (urban plus rural) for the district. The urban middle class will be formed by the professionals, the clergy, the merchants, and 30 percent of the artisans. The rural middle strata will incorporate 30 percent of the labradores and 10 percent of the jornaleros. Let us now look at the comparative results for some census units (there were twenty-nine of them in the state)(table 2).

There is a striking contrast between the obraje center, San Miguel, and the cotton-producing townships of Celaya and Salamanca. Cotton-textile elaboration tended to accompany a more complex division of labor and

Table 1. Occupational Categories, Guanajuato, 1825

Occupation	Statewide total
Professionals, clergy,and administrators:	340
Merchants (comerciantes)	1,794
Artisans (with no further specification)	11,764
Fabricantes	1,745
Labradores	17,136
Jornaleros	43,508
Total	76,287

the emergence of artisan middle sectors. It also happened that in San Miguel not only was the "urban" sector quite destitute of middle strata, but so was the rural area. Already in the 1740s, when it was head of a prosperous *alcaldía mayor* that included the "Pueblo Nuevo de Dolores," it had according to Villaseñor a "large number" of Indians, some on the outskirts of town, but most living in the haciendas as *operativos* or *gañanes*, or as *arrendatarios de las tierras*. Prosperity for some was accompanied by proletarianization for others, given its particular productive structure. The town had an unstable economy, perhaps as a result of overspecialization in wool production. When Father Morfi visited it in 1777, he was somewhat inconsistent in his evaluation. On the one hand, he said that it had "a better society than Querétaro," but he found the obrajes in decadence and the streets full of unemployed vagrants, that is, léperos. The forces of social control were weaker there than in cotton-producing regions.[49]

In commercial Salvatierra, placed in a highly rural district, the weight of the urban middle strata within the total was slight; but if we include the countryside, a large group of labradores raises the figures for the middle classes.[50] The same happens with small and highly rural Dolores. As for the state as a whole (excluding the capital), the percentage of middle classes, due to the weight of artesanos and labradores, was also relatively high, leaving San Miguel by itself as a strongly off-average district. On the other hand, the city of Guanajuato and its environs (not included in this census), with its heavy concentration of mining population, was another powder keg, which exploded as the Insurgente armies approached.

The study of Querétaro state's occupational and productive structure undertaken by José Antonio del Raso in 1845, which was examined earlier in this chapter for its urban data, can be used also for the rural scene.[51]

There was a first level of hacienda owners and large-scale renters (who rented a whole hacienda), who had nothing to do with the "arrendatario" category seen earlier in the Bazant studies. Immediately below, a second level of rancho owners and hacienda administrators can be distinguished. These two groups made up a very small percentage of the rural total (4 percent). At a third level, there were two occupational categories, making up the typical components of the rural middle class and merging upward into the ranchero sector. They were the "arrendatarios de ranchos," also called "*colonos*," and the extractors of wood, charcoal, and tuna ("*vivanderos*"), who payed a rent to the haciendas. This group of vivanderos is similar to that of the arrendatarios, "medieros," and "aparceros" in the Bazant studies, or the "labradores" in other census

Table 2. Stratification Profiles for Some Communities in Guanajuato,
1825 (percent of economically active population)

	Percent rural	Urban middle strata (%)	Total middle strata (%)
San Miguel el Grande (wool obrajes)	68.7	9.4	11.1
Celaya, with dependent Sta Cruz (cotton)	52.0	19.0	26.6
Salamanca (commercial and mixed textile center)	60.1	14.8	23.9
Salvatierra (commercial center)	80.2	9.8	17.9
Dolores Hidalgo (diversified agriculture, wine)	89.1	3.9	19.0
State total, except capital city	79.5	7.4	19.9

Source: Memoria que presenta el gobernador de Guanajuato 1824 y 1825 (1826).
The "rural" sector is considered to be formed by labradores and jornaleros.

materials. It probably had less stability, and its conditions of work were hard and insecure, but Raso estimates the income of both groups to have been similar, and double or treble that of the peones and vaqueros. They formed 23 percent of the total rural population. As stated earlier in this chapter, they were a heterogeneous group, as they included some extremely small operators. There is no way of deciding whether Raso has included all of them in this category. The figure of 23 percent, however, ties in well with the estimates for the Hacienda de Bocas, considering average values.

The permanent salaried work force is included in a fourth level, divided into a somewhat higher paid group of vaqueros and a larger one of peones de raya. The peones de raya, for reasons not explained by the author, appear as receiving wages for only nine months of the year, though they were residents in the haciendas. Maybe this allows for the fact that some of them held other lands in the pueblos or doubled up as arrendatarios.

Finally a fifth and last level refers to peones (adults and youths, or muchachos) who lived in pueblos and worked in haciendas only for three months yearly, the rest of the time being employed on their own or other pueblo residents' lands. Raso was referring only in an indirect way to the pueblo population, supposing that the whole of it had some connection with the hacienda or rancho system. This might have been quite a realistic assumption in the Bajío, where most pueblos had been reduced to small extensions of land and could not maintain themselves without resorting to the haciendas or ranchos. In fact the population resident in pueblos was implicitly classed into basically three categories in this study. One of them, probably the better off, rented lands in the haciendas, adding to what they already had in the villages. A second group could manage most of the year with their pueblo lands, but had to complement their income with a brief stint of salaried work. The third group might be made up of those who had very little access to pueblo lands and who therefore had to go to the haciendas as peones acasillados; some of these might yet retain links to the village, especially of a family type, going there occasionally, while others might have cut their connections totally, at least concerning productive activities. There is no place in this scheme for prosperous members of the pueblos who might have enough land to employ themselves and their families fully the whole year, possibly using the labor of other villagers. That group must have existed, but its numbers in Querétaro at the time were probably too small to merit attention.

Mining Reales

Mines provided the greatest source of concentrated wealth in New Spain, covering the territory with a very large number of small reales, in addition to a dozen or so really large conglomerations. Some of the more significant ones, such as Guanajuato, Vetagrande-Zacatecas, and Real del Monte–Pachuca, were in the vicinity of medium-to-large cities.[52]

Guanajuato was a large town in late colonial times, especially if one included in its population the nearby mining reales, situated at less than two leagues from the urban center. According to an enumeration of 1803, it had just over 55,000 inhabitants, including the mines in nearby Marfil, Santa Anna, and Santa Rosa, thus approaching Puebla and outstripping Querétaro and Guadalajara.[53] Guanajuato, together with Querétaro and the smaller San Miguel el Grande, were typical productive rather than service centers, with a rigid social stratification and a concentrated and menacing working-class sector. In this sense the three towns contrasted with Puebla, also productive but based on artisans (until by midcentury it witnessed the establishment of large power-driven factories), and with

Guadalajara, more service and government oriented. The Valenciana silver mine, one of the largest in the world, employed almost 3,300 people in 1803 (including 732 women) distributed among the underground shafts and surface and refining work, while nearby Rayas had a labor force of 572 people.[54]

Vetagrande, a few leagues from the city of Zacatecas, had a population of 4,000 in 1833, which meant a working force of some 1,500 or more, given the likely employment of several members of the same family. According to a later report, Vetagrande, with just 5,000 population, employed 2,550 workers in the mining enterprise.[55] In Fresnillo, also in the state of Zacatecas, a private company mostly formed by Mexicans was established in 1835 to take over the working of the mines from the provincial state (recently subdued by the centralist government of Santa Anna), and soon it had 3,700 workers distributed in various mines and haciendas de beneficio in the locality. Three years later 1,287 employees had been laid off, and in 1845 the total was reported to be 2,950.[56] In Tlalpujahua, in the state of Mexico, after much destruction brought about by the wars, an English mining company was trying to revive operations in 1826, employing some 1,600 workers plus another 600 or 700 charcoal burners.[57]

There was constant movement between agriculture and mining, and when farms prospered due to good weather or other economic factors, it was hard for the mineowners to get labor, especially in northern areas such as Zacatecas, where population was sparse. Wages necessary to attract workers were quite high by international standards, and "abuses" had to be tolerated, especially the apportionment of a part of the produce for the workers themselves to use and sell to intermediaries.[58]

In the mining towns, there was a shifting social scale above the operatives, made up of overseers, traders, moneylenders, intermediaries who bought the mineral in order to process it on a small scale (rescatadores, maquileros), and the mineowners, resident or not. Some of them could be counted among the wealthiest people in the country, but not all were big men. It was not too difficult to "denounce" a mine that had not been worked by its owner for some time, and this gave a right to exploit it as long as a minimum level of activity, involving four operatives, was maintained. In the Diputación de Minería of Guanajuato during the year 1860, 122 denuncias of mines were made, almost all by different people. In old or flooded mines, the buscones, always working at partido, kept reworking parts of the old wealth, making a scant living most of the time, but quite likely to round up a fair sum with a bit of luck.[59]

Mining areas had always been centers of violence, due to problems with labor recruitment. Anastasio Zerecero, in his memoirs, recalls that in Guanajuato the antagonism between the rich and the poor was very high in comparison to other parts of the country. The minerales located in the midst of old established Indian lands could rely during colonial times on the repartimiento, but by the end of the eighteenth century this system was falling into disuse. In the northernmost districts, it had been necessary from the beginning to rely either on free labor attracted to the reales or on slaves. Guanajuato, which was just outside the frontier of the old settled Indian lands, had a unique position. It had benefited while it could from the repartimiento, though for this it was necessary to scour the pueblos from a considerable distance — more than double the legal ten miles. As time passed it was necessary to force the *vagos y malentretenidos* of the real itself to work, which they did not want to do when there were no prospects of a bonanza. As labor requirements expanded during the second half of the eighteenth century, the definition of *vago* became more elastic, provoking anxiety among artisans and their dependants.[60]

2
Conservatives and Liberals at Independence

When Iturbide made his move for independence, he was far from imagining the kind of social forces he would unleash or the contradictory alliances his subsequent attempt to hold on to power would stimulate. Classical historiography has pointed to the conservative nature of those who supported him as a means to oppose the liberalizing measures coming from Spain. On the other hand, the popular pressure and street agitation accompanying his military coup of May 18 and 19, 1822, are also well known, though there may be doubts about their real nature. Less often mentioned is the strategic support he got from those who might be called the Left of their times, people such as Fernández de Lizardi, Gómez Farías, or Zavala. The problem is how to give relative weights to each one of these components and how to combine them in a coherent interpretation.[1]

The distinction between liberals and conservatives is quite well known, with liberals favoring anticlericalism, extension of the operation of a free market, and disentailment. Less clear is their attitude toward government intervention and stimulus, what might be called (taking a word from modern usage) *desarrollismo*. Of course everybody wished the country to develop and prosper, and some thought it would be enough to let loose the forces of private competition and a free market to accomplish it. But others, without being traditionalists, believed an important element of state intervention was necessary, whether in the form of tariff protection, bank support, infrastructure building, or stimuli to immigration, colonization, and education. In this sense Alamán, rather than (or apart from) being a conservative, was a typical *desarrollista*, and so were quite a few of the ill-famed *agiotistas*.[2]

On the cultural side of politics, nationalism must also be considered, though it is often seen as a passion only later developed. In fact it was

43

already present, but it certainly took forms different from those it acquired in the twentieth century. For some it implied a reference to the
particularly mixed ethnic traditions of the country, with a high respect
for its Indian past, at least rhetorically, as was the case for Carlos María
de Bustamante and fray Servando Teresa de Mier, while for others Spanish European roots were all-important.

In the more strictly political sphere, the attitude toward checks and
balances was an important dividing line, not always neatly separating
conservatives from liberals. It contraposed those who emphasized the need
for a strong executive, eventually dictatorial, against believers in the role
of congresses, political parties, and various forms of association and the
expression of citizens' concerns. The opponents of authoritarianism, along
this dimension, might be called pluralists, but to avoid confusion with
religious tolerance, it would be better to call them representationists. Carlos
María de Bustamante, while not anticlerical and only a very mild believer
(if one at all) in the virtues of the free market or of opening up to the
world, did favor representative institutions as against one-man rule; in
that sense he would be on the liberal side. He preferred a representational
system, inspired by medieval Spanish traditions, and was averse to absolutism; but as he rejected religious tolerance and the diversification of
culture through English, French, or American influences, the word *plu-
ralism* cannot really be applied to the position he symbolized.

The other specifically political dimension was that of popular participation, which in principle liberalism wished to broaden in contrast with
conservatism. But within the liberal fold, there were those who, like Mora
and the Escoceses, wanted to proceed very slowly along this path, while
others, like Zavala and the Yorkinos, based their political action on the
mobilization of ample sectors of the population.

Liberalism and Corporatism

However paradoxical it may seem, corporatism could have become the
basis of liberalism. Liberalism seeks, among other things, an equilibrium
of forces, the distribution of power among sectors of society outside the
state; from the perspective of a Montesquieu or a Burke, this could per-
fectly well have been achieved as a result of the interplay of corporate
interests. The Ancien Régime in many countries did allow a considerable
distribution of power between its corporatively organized interests, but
these were subject to excessive intervention by the state. If that intervention were controlled by an adequate constitution, and if more groups

were brought in, so as to have wider citizen participation, a liberal polity, even if not a fully democratic one, would most probably ensue. This is very close to what happened in Great Britain and in some of the northern countries of Europe. In Spain the last struggle to maintain medieval corporative rights and to base on them a free polity was defeated by Charles V at Villalar, but the tradition remained.

One of the representatives of that tradition was Carlos María de Bustamante. From colonial times he had been engaged in journalism, in association with progressive intellectuals, such as Jacobo de Villaurrutia and Juan Wenceslao Barquera. Together they founded in 1805 the *Diario de México*, which was connected with such influential figures as Francisco Verdad y Ramos, a lawyer who pleaded cases in the Audiencia and who was a member of the Ayuntamiento. They all represented the criollo autonomist faction that, led by Villaurrutia, would find expression in the aborted Iturrigaray attempt in 1808 and would cost Verdad's life. The newspaper often managed to get around censorship and express implicitly favorable opinions about the Insurgencia. When freedom of the press was established in 1812, Bustamante tried journalism on his own, starting *El juguetillo*, competing with Lizardi's *El Pensador Mexicano*, but both battling for greater freedom within the colonial system or eventually outside of it. When censorship was reinstituted again that same year, Lizardi went to jail and Bustamante fled to Insurgente territory, where he continued to publish journals and tracts. He acted mostly in the area controlled by Morelos, for whom he became a constant panegyrist in later years. He also performed judicial functions in the tottering independent regime. In 1817 he asked for an indult, was confined to house arrest, and having attempted escape, was imprisoned in San Juan de Ulúa for over a year. In 1819 the liberal local governor set Bustamante free, though confining his movements to the port city. He became a prolific writer of chronicles of his times, purportedly continuations of the *Diario*, which he had edited as a younger man. Immediately after independence he published *La Abispa de Chilpancingo*, as a self-appointed guardian of the principles of the Republic of Anáhuac, whose authorities had been based in Chilpancingo under Morelos's leadership.[3]

Bustamante took a staunchly anti-Iturbidista position and was thus close to the Escoceses, though he shunned freemason involvements. He was in favor of an important role for representative institutions, and despite being a fervent Catholic, he hated the friars and supported an active role for government in exercising the *patronato*. He opposed the collective political action of the clergy and thought that some limits had to be set to the proliferation of canons and other sinecures in the cathedral chapters. When in 1831 Vicente Rocafuerte was imprisoned for writing a tract on religious toleration, the matter was taken up in Congress, of which Bustamante was a member. Rocafuerte was supported by the federalist liberal Juan de Dios Cañedo and set free by a jury. Bustamante commented that it was insane to support toleration in a country where everybody was a Catholic. As he was writing his chronicle some years after the event, he could comment on Rocafuerte's later experience, when he returned to his native Ecuador and had to exercise the presidency, where he found "the difference between governing a people according to the theories of the philosopher of Geneva and doing it following the laws, uses and customs of their forebears." Bustamante was certainly no admirer of the "philosopher of Geneva," nor of the rest of the antireligious French enlightenment thinkers. However, his constant criticisms of the friars led him to defend himself against accusations of Jansenism, saying that Mexico should join the ranks of nations that were "Catholic, *but* enlightened." He explained that he realized the friars had done a fine job during the Conquest, because if it had not been for them, "not a single Indian would have been left alive." The regular orders should be reformed by the bishops, with help from the secular arm.[4]

Bustamante did not have much of a liking for the military in politics, especially when it came to Santa Anna, but he cooperated with the Jalapa revolt of 1829, led by General Anastasio Bustamante, and approved of his repressive measures, which he deemed necessary. He disliked military abuses and the practice of dueling to intimidate critics, but he thought in times of crisis it was better to have a firm hand from the beginning; otherwise conflict would continue forever. Thus he lamented that ill-advised mercy toward a Yorkino rebel in San Luis Potosí, who should have been shot when caught with arms in hand, had allowed him to be a strategic support for the new rebellion led by Santa Anna in 1832. He also thought that it was correct to have condemned to death a man who had stolen a golden cup with consecrated wafers from a church. His defense of national and Hispanic traditions led him to oppose "all" the articles of the treaty of commerce and recognition with the United States; he even wished that none of the treaties with foreign nations had been signed. He was particularly incensed at the news that Gómez Pedraza had published in the United States a manifesto outlining the recent political turmoils of Mexico. He thought that it was particularly scandalous to do this from the United States, "our enemies." His animadversion against foreigners was much abated with regard to Spaniards, and though he had fought against them during the war of independence, he tried to avoid their expulsion.[5]

His determined opposition to what he thought was Yorkino dema-
goguery or military agitation of the rabble made him adopt conservative
attitudes. When Santa Anna started an insurrection against the Jalapa
regime in early 1832, Bustamante observed that he was financed by foreign merchants resentful of the protectionist and industrializing policies
of the Alamán ministry. Joseph Wells, the British vice-consul, was particularly active, joining a crowd of "cobblers, tailors, boys and vile and
drunken people." Santa Anna, coming from his nearby hacienda in Manga
de Clavo, collected a large number of "horsemen, called *jarrochada*,
negroes . . . who don't even know how to ride," plus foreign adventurers
and recruits from "both castas," according to our chronicler.[6]

Bustamante became more conservative with age, and he was a stalwart of the centralist regime inaugurated in 1837, again with Anastasio
Bustamante as president. Carlos María became a member of the new
"fourth power," or Poder Conservador, entrusted with the responsibility
of intervening in the public realm during particularly acute crises that
could not be resolved by the normal constitutional process. It purported
to be the representative of the "conscience of the nation," performing a
role similar to the Poder Moderador wielded by the emperor in Brazil.

On economic matters Bustamante never inveighed against the artisans'
defensive institutions, their guilds, nor against the collective property of
the Indian pueblos. The main onslaught against Indian property came
only during the Reforma of the 1850s, but it was already being proposed
in the 1820s. Bustamante did not join this more modernist liberal project,
nor did he oppose protectionism. He happened to be close to government
circles during the two presidencies of his namesake Anastasio, who with
the cooperation of Alamán, adopted a decidedly protectionist policy, from
which not only traditional artisans but also the newly established large-
scale industrialists benefited. In general Carlos María had only words of
encomium for Alamán's policies, including his promotion of economic
development. At some point Carlos María said that Alamán's memory
should be perpetually extolled, if for no other reason than that he had
introduced the merino sheep into Mexico.[7]

Bustamante's interest in Mexican history is well known, as is his respect for the Indian past, about which he was continually trying to get
information. Brading has commented on this, and sees him as well as
Fray Servando as forerunners of Mexican nationalism, which indeed they
were, especially in the cultural field. Apart from this, Carlos María de
Bustamante's prolific writings and chronicles full of side comments and
digressions give enough material to locate him in a special niche within
Mexican liberalism, though his antipopulist fervor more usually brands

him as a conservative, a similar fate to that which befell Edmund Burke. But Bustamante had an Insurgente past, and his Morelista fervor never abandoned him. Admittedly in Morelos he saw the man who could lead Anáhuac to independence, using the popular forces unleashed by Hidalgo but controlling them under appropiate institutions, developed with regard to local traditions and Spanish precedent. He probably did not know much about Burke, since he did not favor books coming from heretical countries. Without knowing it, however, he was a Burkean or, more appropriately, a Hispanic traditionalist liberal steeped in the long history of medieval corporations, fueros, and cortes of the peninsula.[8]

Not too far from these positions were the brothers José María and Juan Nepomuceno Troncoso, who called the printing press they owned "Imprenta Liberal de Troncoso Hermanos."[9] In the *Abeja Poblana*, the newspaper they started publishing soon after freedom of the press was reestablished in 1820, they quoted freely from Montesquieu, D'Alambert, and Filangieri, stopping short, of course, at Voltaire or Rousseau. They also opposed the more radical and "vulgar" tracts of Fernández de Lizardi, *El Pensador Mexicano*, from whose excesses they wanted to be distinguished.[10] They believed economic reform would allow a modernization of industry, but they were not prepared to see a dismantling of the existing productive structure. One of them, Juan Nepomuceno, was among the members of the Puebla local congress in 1829 who supported the retention of import prohibitions.[11]

Despite the Troncoso brothers' affinity with Bustamante and Mier, they supported Iturbide's bid for the crown, though they would have liked it to take place legally and in a moderate way, not through "cuatro gritos." Despite these warnings, José María accepted the important symbolic post of capellán of the emperor. He later became a conservative member of the legislatures of Puebla and Veracruz and senator for Puebla. His brother, Juan Nepomuceno, the main editor of the *Abeja*, was independent enough to merit a good word from the furiously anti-Iturbidista author of a humorous *Testamento de Iturbide*. Under the cloak of Iturbidismo, as we shall later see, many different political families converged, as widely opposed as the conservative clericals, the radical populists, and quite a few progressive liberals.[12]

The Clerical Conservative Faction

The church, especially its higher levels, was the main center of ideological elaboration of the Ancien Régime. Not the only one, of course, because there was also a strong current of regalist thinking, expressed in the Spanish version of the Enlightenment, which gave pride of place to civil power. But due to the weakness of peninsular authorities after the Napoleonic invasion and the oscillations of the Spanish regime between autocracy and liberalism, the church remained in Mexico the most solid refuge of traditional thinking. It was flanked by some old viceregal officials and members of the Audiencia, though among these there were also some who had been won over by the new ideas.

At the time of Iguala, the head of the Mexican church was Archbishop Pedro José Fonte, a man with no ability to fulfill that role in times of troubles. When independence was proclaimed he had no alternative but to accept it, hoping that the fiction of the Treaty of Córdoba would materialize, bringing some compromise with the mother country and the crowning of a Bourbon. When he realized that Ferdinand VII would have no part in this, he abandoned his seat, and with the excuse of a pastoral visit, he avoided being compromised in the crowning of Iturbide and went to Spain, where he survived obscurely for many years.

The other bishops were not so soft in character, and the more active ones were clearly Iturbidista. Juan Ruiz de Cabañas, of Guadalajara, lent 25,000 pesos to Iturbide when he marched to the south in November 1820, supposedly to clean up the remnants of the Insurgencia. The money, of course, was used to fight the Spanish government, not Guerrero. It was not a case of bad financial judgment or naiveté, but collusion. In early republican days, Ruiz de Cabañas would foment, from Guadalajara, various types of political movements favorable to the exiled monarch, under the cover of federalism.[13]

The bishop of Puebla, Antonio Joaquín Pérez, was also a bellicose man very favorable to Iturbide, whom he had the honor of crowning. He had been a deputy to the Spanish Cortes, where he distinguished himself leading the group of "Persas" who in 1814 gave the welcome to Ferdinand as absolute ruler. Back in his native Puebla, where he was given the episcopate in recognition for his services, he had to face the revenge of the liberals in 1820, who wanted to make him pay for his past servility. His flock (equally if not more "servile" than himself) was preparing to defend him, when independence made this unnecessary. Iturbide put him in first place in the five-men regencia he established immediately after liberating the capital. The other members were two unobjectionable figures, Manuel de la Bárcena, éminence grise of the vacant Bishopric of Michoacán, and Manuel Velázquez de León, secretary of the viceroyalty, plus the less reliable *oidor* Isidro Yáñez, whose nomination was aimed at keeping the liberals quiet. Iturbide was the fifth man in this supreme executive body, destined to rule the country until a decision was made regarding who would accede to the crown. According to the Treaty of Córdoba, the government would be monarchical, and the crown would be offered to Ferdinand himself, if he wanted to come to Mexico, or to some other Bourbon; in case none of them accepted, the decision as to which other person would be called to that responsibility would be in the hands of a soon-to-be-elected national Congress. Bishop Pérez suffered, together with Bárcena and Velázquez de León, the affront of being relieved by Congress from his position in the regency in April 1822, when the conflict between Iturbide and the constituent legislature was raging. Iturbide had been unable to form a majority in that body, which was elected between December 1821 and January 1822, and where a combination of moderate liberals and republicans of Insurgente sympathies held sway.

The Bishopric of Michoacán was vacant, but Manuel de la Bárcena ruled it efficiently. In a report for the Quai d'Orsay, he was called "bishop," and he was marked as a strong Iturbidista, the most cultured member of the Consejo de Estado, another institution created at the time to advise the government. He published, right after the Plan of Iguala (January 1821), a manifiesto arguing the rights of the *nation* of Indians and the *colony* of whites and castas to become independent, due to their maturity, bringing in some citations from Montesquieu. He added that opinion in Spain was more "advanced" than in Mexico, where the "violent extinction of so many monasteries and the deprivation of the clergy from its legal privileges [fueros]" caused alarm. In passing he remarked that despite the theoretically liberal measures taken by the viceregal government, "imported products cost three times as much what they should be worth . . . just to please the monopolists." This was a clear blow against the commercial sector, which under the guise of moderate liberalism wanted to preserve ties with Spain through a sort of commonwealth, under laws sanctioned by a cortes with American representation. After the fall of the empire, Bárcena was one of those who returned to the provinces to agitate in favor of a restoration. According to Carlos María de Bustamante, the plan then would be to bring back Iturbide from exile to one of the cities of the Bajío and confront from there the authorities in Mexico City.[14]

The Bishop of Durango, Juan Francisco Castañiza, who had inherited a title of marqués, belonged to one of the more important plutocratic clans of Mexico at independence, which had its conservative side, the Castañiza-Bassocos, and its liberal wing, the Fagoaga-Villaurrutias. The

Fagoagas were in the forefront of the moderate-liberal project of establishing a sort of commonwealth with Spain, under a Bourbon monarch, and were open to the new ideas coming from Europe. The Castañiza-Bassocos were immune to this contagion, particularly the bishop and his brother, a Jesuit who had returned to Mexico to reorganize the company when Ferdinand reestablished it in his domains. As for Bassoco, his principal interest had been to accumulate capital, which he had done very successfully. He died without children in 1814, bequeathing to his widow one of the largest fortunes in the country. When she in turn died in 1816, she left most of the money to the Jesuits, and the title fell to the grandson of Bassoco's brother, a young man in holy orders who was thought to be of "no consequence" in 1825 when the British legation provided information about him. Bishop Castañiza was an important supporter of Iturbide. In the ironic *Testamento de Iturbide,* published by an opponent of the emperor, Castañiza was recognized for having been president of the *"juntilla"* established after the dissolution of Congress in October 1822.

The bishop of Oaxaca, Manuel Isidro López, also sided with the emperor, though he was a less important man. He did merit mention in the *Testamento,* however. Farther away from action were the bishops of Yucatán and of Sonora, though the latter, the Carmelite friar Bernardo del Espíritu Santo, also an Iturbidista, would distinguish himself a few years later for reminding the nation, after the sanction of the constitution of 1824, that sovereignty did not reside in the people but in God. This earned him a strong rebuke from the Pensador Mexicano, who advised him to wipe his lips before pronouncing the names of Voltaire, Rousseau, Montesquieu, Hobbes, and other philosophers. As for the Chiapas seat, Salvador Sanmartín, its latest occupier, had died recently, but as a Deputy to the Cortes he had joined the "Persas."[15]

In the city of Mexico, the weakness of the archbishop had created a place for the consolidation of other figures. One of the main ones was the vicar and provisor, Félix Flores Alatorre, who was in charge since Fonte's abandonment of his responsibilities. Iturbide made him teniente de limosnero mayor, an honorific post in the "Imperial Family." Only a few months after independence, he had to exercise his apostolic zeal by excommunicating Fernández de Lizardi, who had published a *Defensa de los Francmasones,* a tract in which the Pensador was trying to see how far he could go in treating irritating religious subjects, and by the way selling a few more pamphlets, his sole source of income. Félix Flores Alatorre was well connected. He had a brother, Juan José, a permanent member of the Audiencia of Guadalajara and ad interim member of the Audiencia of Mexico (he would later belong to the Supremo Tribunal de Justicia, which would replace it). Another relative, Ignacio Flores Alatorre, was procurador general of the Indian parcialidades of the city of Mexico.[16]

Another bastion of the archbishopric was José Guridi y Alcocer, priest and lawyer, curate of the Sagrario, active in the Puebla curia and then in that of the capital, of which he became in time vicar and provisor, succeeding Alatorre. He had been to the Cortes, was very legalistic, and was staunchly opposed to the idea of a republic. During the final crisis of the empire, he played a very central role, trying to avoid its downfall, and afterward continued to favor the policies of those who sought the return of the exile. He had a brother who for years was secretary of the ayuntamiento, an influential bureaucratic post that allowed him to have rooms in the Cabildo. Guridi's legalism had led him to oppose the crowning of Iturbide after the coup of May 1822, despite being his strong supporter; he argued that electors had to be consulted. He was also a member of the Junta de Censura Eclesiástica, which excommunicated the Pensador. Toward the end of the empire, when Andrés Quintana Roo, a liberal who had supported it throughout, jumped onto the victorious republican bandwagon by declaring himself in favor of freedom of worship, Guridi was preparing to have him accused for excommunication.[17]

José Manuel Sartorio was another member of the capital's clergy who enjoyed a wide reputation for his literary gifts, as revealed in his sermons. He had had his inklings of sympathy for the Insurgentes, against whom he had refused to preach, thus achieving popularity. The Insurgente chief Ignacio López Rayón had proposed him in 1813 for a high ecclesiastic position in charge of relations with Rome. At the outset of independence, he made an effort to have the Jesuits once again readmitted to Mexico but did not get the necessary majority in the Ecclesiastic Affairs Committee of the Junta Gubernativa. His solid support for the empire earned him persecution after its demise, when he narrowly avoided being expelled from the country.[18]

Among the strong supporters of Iturbide was Canon Juan Bautista Arechederreta, rector of San Juan de Letrán College, half-brother of Alamán. Though one cannot deduce Alamán's opinions through those of his brother, it is quite possible that had he been in the country at the time of the crowning, he would have been in favor of it, even if with qualms as to the means used, as were so many other conservative clericals. However, when he returned to Mexico, it was already too late for that, and he soon took up the main ministry, that of Relaciones. From there he had to oppose the remnants of Iturbidismo, who by then had become allied to federalists and populist republicans in what was going to become the Yorkino party. We will return to this transmutation; for the moment, going back to Arechederreta, it must be said that he attempted to dissuade Iturbide from accepting the crown in the *golpista*, popular manner he obtained it. But when in August 1822 Iturbide had several opposition deputies jailed, the canon, as rector of Letrán, was somewhat fainthearted, expelling from his college two of the jailed deputies who were its members, and he even tried to break open the door of their rooms to get rid of their belongings, if we are to believe the author of the *Testamento*.[19]

Yet another ideological and political pillar of the church and of Iturbidismo was Dr. Matías Monteagudo, rector of the university. He was also director of a small but select congregation, the Oratorio de San Felipe Neri, installed in an old Jesuit house known as La Profesa, where spiritual exercises attracted a veritable think tank of the Right. He was the one who stimulated Iturbide to procure independence, taking advantage of the armed expedition against Guerrero, thereby isolating New Spain from the secularizing measures emanating from the Old. Though surely the hero of Iguala was not a simple tool of this "complot de la Profesa" (as classic historiography has considered him), it is highly probable that the project existed. Admittedly, since its authors were not omnipotent and needed allies to obtain their ends, the results did not coincide exactly with expectations. Monteagudo, an active and bellicose man, had already taken a dominant role in 1808 as head of the Spanish clique loyal to the mother country who opposed Iturrigaray's autonomist bid. Not that he had changed from legitimist to autonomist; his position remained the same, that of loyalty to the traditional social order anchored in the church and opposed to liberal reforms. On both occasions he was accompanied by Oidor Miguel Bataller, and in the Profesa affair by other clerics, among whom was Bárcena, Iturbide's friend in charge of the Michoacán mitre. Monetary support was obtained from the Spaniard Gregorio Mier y Terán, who in time would be referred to as the "Mexican Rothschild."[20]

Others in the clerical camp who supported Iturbide were the inquisitor José Tirado, who took part in the Profesa; Juan José García Torres, of the sanctuary of Guadalupe; José Manuel Posada, provisor of the Puebla bishopric in Pérez's absence; the Veracruz curate José María Becerra, who would become one of the leaders of the "party of retrogression," according to José M. L. Mora; and the Jesuit Basilio Manuel Arrillaga, tutor to the emperor's children. Also favorable were the Troncoso brothers of

Puebla, Juan Nepomuceno and José María, the second of whom was made capellán of the emperor. They had published a moderately liberal paper under the Spanish government, *La Abeja Poblana*, and had been early supporters of the Plan of Iguala, but toward the end of Iturbide's rule, they became independent enough for Juan Nepomuceno to receive a compliment from the author of one of the several Testamentos published by enemies of the deposed monarch. Another cleric, Miguel Valentín, of Tlaxcala, was outside the main trend, as he was a solid opponent of Iturbide but conservative enough to be included also by Mora as a member of the "party of retrogression."[21]

Among the regular clergy, both in the upper and lower layers, Iturbide also had many friends. Among the Dominicans a solid partisan was Provincial Luis Carrasco, who according to the author of the *Testamento* "gave him the money of the order" for his political purposes. In his convent the deputies accused of sedition in August 1822 were imprisoned. In the Franciscan convent of nearby Toluca there was an Iturbidista clique that planned special operations for rescuing the regime during its last days. N. Ortigosa was its moving spirit, and he used other friars, La Santa and Juan Luzuriaga, as contacts with the emperor.[22]

The role of the *mercedario* Aguilar, of Mexico City, as popular agitator, has already been mentioned before, and in Puebla there were others also prepared to react against a liberal government that was seen as destroying, wittingly or not, the delicate equilibrium of interests and inter-class solidarities of the Ancien Régime. The provisor of the Puebla bishopric, José Manuel Posada, had promoted a popular mutiny in 1823, at the end of the empire, to resist the Veracruz liberal rebels, and would have produced a massacre had it not been for the prudence of Gral Vivanco, head of the incoming troops, according to the author of one of the testamentos. The meddling of friars in politics was so obnoxious that Bustamante, despite his Catholic faith, was led to exclaim that "republic and friars are as incompatible as freedom and slavery, grace and sin." He also made an incursion in the comparative method, rhetorically asking his readers: "Who would not see the similarity between the rule of Robespierre in France and that of Iturbide in Mexico?" Maybe in making this comparison he did not have in mind the similarity in the social support of both regimes, but rather in their allegedly sanguinary nature. However, there were other examples he might have taken from his knowledge of world history as paradigms of tyranny. The connotation of Iturbide's rule being a popular dictatorship was certainly present in the diatribe and also emerges from all his other remarks about that regime.[23]

Mining Plutocrats

The largest mine in the country, the Valenciana, had been discovered by Antonio Obregón y Alcocer, who became in 1780 the first conde de Valenciana, with a complicated group of descendants who formed one of the several clans into which the elite (and to some extent the politics) of New Spain were divided. His namesake, the second count, was a weak personality who according to the British legation had "gambled away [his fortune] and was left in penury in his old age." This was an excessively pessimistic interpretation of his temporary financial straits, due to the destruction wrought by the Insurgencia, however, because when he died in 1833, he was still worth over a million pesos. The first count had a natural son, Ignacio Obregón, who inherited more of his animal spirits and made another fortune in the real de Catorce, in San Luis Potosí, while commanding in his spare time a militia of dragones. He had been a friend and business partner (somewhat illegally) of Viceroy José Iturrigaray, who in 1808 attempted, with the help of some criollos of Mexico City and the provinces, to render New Spain autonomous. When Iturrigaray was challenged by the Spaniards, Ignacio Obregón headed south with his dragones, but he was too late to prevent the coup that deposed the innovating bureaucrat-turned-political-precursor malgré lui. The first count also had two daughters. One of them married Diego Rul, a Spanish military man who was made Conde de Rul in 1804 and "conde consorte de la Valenciana" for a time, while Antonio was a minor. He died fighting the insurgents in 1812, but his son continued the grand strategy of alliances, marrying the daughter of Juan Francisco Azcárate, enterprising mining lawyer, stalwart of the Iturrigaray faction in 1808, and later associated with Iturbide. Rul's grandson, Miguel, became in time the main administrator of the Valenciana interests.[24]

The second daughter of the old conde de Valenciana married another Spanish soldier, Antonio Pérez Gálvez, who became conde de Pérez Gálvez in 1805, and also temporarily, after the death of his brother-in-law, "segundo conde consorte de la Valenciana." During the war of the Insurgencia, it was rumored that he had republican sympathies and that he was in touch with General Félix María Calleja, who despite being the main repressor, was approached by rebel delegates to tempt him into doing what Iturbide would later do, becoming ruler of a new nation.[25] Pérez Gálvez's son, Juan de Dios, who married a Rul cousin and died without offspring in 1848, was the head of another mining, landed, and commercial Mexican fortune of the early independence era. His interests were inherited by a sister, Francisca, known as the condesa de Pérez Gálvez (though true republicans shunned these titles). It fell upon her to preside over a turning of the wheel of history: in 1838, after the British company that had leased the mine in 1825 ran into difficulties, the Pérez Gálvez family took back the administration of the concern (they had been the nominal owners throughout). As she also died without descendants, everything went to Miguel Rul, who found himself inheriting the Valenciana, Pérez Gálvez, and Rul titles. The family had a good political connection, via Azcárate, with the latter's son-in-law, Manuel Gómez Pedraza, a Queretano military man who was a solid supporter of Iturbide until the very end, and who afterwards reemerged as a very influential political figure, under liberal colors, but clearly opposed to radical or populist excesses.[26]

The other great mine on the outskirts of Guanajuato, Rayas, was developed in the early eighteenth century by José Sardaneta y Legaspi; his son Vicente was made marqués de San Juan de Rayas in 1774 and was active in the local ayuntamiento and diputación de minería. The third marqués, José Mariano Sardaneta y Llorente, who died in 1835, was also prominent locally and nationally, residing much of the time in Guanajuato, though he was a member of the Tribunal de Minería. He became a close friend of Iturrigaray, to put it mildly, and when the viceroy was deposed, the marquis was made his attorney. This turned out to be a difficult job, because there were many things to be explained in the juicio de residencia involving a few hundred thousand pesos of dubious origin. He was suspected of being a partisan of independence, and when he was elected to the Cortes in 1812, he was not allowed to attend, but rather was jailed in 1814 on the basis of some evidence found in the captured Morelos's papers. He was absolved in 1820 but condemned to exile in Spain, which through influence he was able to avoid. A supporter of Iturbide and member of the Junta Gubernativa established in 1821, he remained associated with the Iturbidistas and was implicated in 1823 in a plot to bring back the emperor. The Insurgencia seriously affected his interests, so much so that in the British legation they believed, by 1825, that he was "poor, but the propietor of the richest mine in the country," adding that he was "a man of moderate talents." Rayas was a cousin of Lucas Alamán, a member of a well-to-do mining family of Guanajuato, who was also related somewhat more distantly to the Valenciana family.[27] Alamán, too young to participate in politics during the Iturrigaray events of 1808, was given a good technical education in Mexico and Europe and in 1820 became a deputy to the Spanish Cortes, where he was the foremost expert on mining matters. The declaration of independence by Iturbide caught him in Europe, and before returning he took the opportunity of establishing contacts with British companies eager to invest in Mexican mining ventures. He was thus made a representative of the United Mexican Co., which had as one of its main contracts the association with the marqués de Rayas in Guanajuato. Alamán managed this company with an excessively "Mexican" viewpoint, protecting local employees and the like, thus incurring the displeasure of the British chargé d'affaires, Henry Ward. Alamán arrived in Mexico when Iturbide had just been deposed, so he did not have to take a position vis-à-vis the emperor during his reign. In his works he was moderately critical of Iturbide's agitational methods and military coup as methods for achieving power. However, most of Alamán's friends and relatives had been Iturbidistas, including his half-brother Juan Bautista Arechederreta, a canon and counselor of convents, rector of the San Juan de Letrán college in the 1820s, and a solid bastion of the church (as was Alamán). He had also been very favorable toward what he considered Iturrigaray's attempt to obtain a "provisional independence" for the duration of the Napoleonic threat.[28]

A closely knit group, these criollo mining entrepreneurs of Guanajuato were nucleated in the Valenciana-Pérez Gálvez-Rul and Rayas families and their related political specialists Azcárate, Alamán, and Gómez Pedraza. They were connected with the church, ideologically conservative (with the exception of Pedraza), with an element of nationalism, strong Iturbidista connections, and early experience of favoring a moderate form of independence using Iturrigaray, and later even Calleja, as figureheads.

About a hundred miles northeast of Mexico City lay the Pachuca-Real del Monte mining area, where the fortune of the "Croesus of New Spain," the Spanish immigrant Pedro Romero de Terreros, was made, earning him the title of conde de Regla. The third count, Pedro José, who attained the title in 1809, actively managed his business, which had been neglected by his father, and in 1824 entered into a contract with a British company to finance operations and take over the management.[29] Pedro José also engaged in some behind-the-scenes political activities as an early supporter of Iturbide, whose access to power he helped finance. He married the daughter of the "Güera" Rodríguez, a "very superior, but profligate woman," who had placed her three daughters very well.[30] So the young count found himself a brother-in-law of the marqués de Aguayo and the marqués de Guadalupe Gallardo, two very important men.

The marqués de Aguayo owned latifundia in Coahuila and Durango, in the fertile area of La Laguna; nobody had measured them, but it was said they were as big as the Kingdom of Castile. In spite of this, the marquesado was very much indebted, and by 1816 it was in the hands of its creditors. He became the mayordomo of the imperial family, the top post in that courtly institution, just above that of the conde de Regla. Aguayo's brother, the conde de San Pedro del Alamo, also a strong Iturbide supporter, was a middle-ranking military man who stayed with the emperor to the bitter end. The Alamo family, very much linked to the Aguayos, had owned a banco de plata in colonial times, as well as mines.[31]

Regla's other brother-in-law, the marqués de Guadalupe Gallardo, was the owner of lands in the Bajío and San Luis Potosí. The San Luis Potosí area, where the rich mines of Catorce (developed by Ignacio Obregón) were located, also had an influential mining nobility, whose investments had been converted largely to land by the time of independence. The conde del Peñasco, large landowner and erstwhile miner in Catorce, performed important military functions in Iturbide's project. A similar position was that of Juan Nepomuceno Moncada, marqués del Jaral, who preferred to use the older title of conde de San Mateo Valparaíso, with mining roots during colonial times, and great meat *abastecededor* of San Luis, Guanajuato, and Mexico City. This "potente condazo" had spent much money fighting the Insurgencia, and it was said that in 1817 Mina had taken 300,000 pesos from him in a single day. His house in Mexico was large enough to house first Calleja and then Iturbide.[32]

The San Luis Potosí nucleus also included Félix María Calleja, a Spanish military man married to the heiress of the Hacienda de Bledos. Calleja, who was in the process of becoming a local caudillo, reacted quickly to the Hidalgo revolt, summoning the loyal local militia. He became the most prominent repressor of the Insurgencia, though he was also well connected with criollo circles. His friends in due time tried to cajole him into using his newly acquired military power to take over from the viceroy and declare independence. As the story goes, he was about to connive in this plot, in early 1813, when he got his designation as the new viceroy; thus he changed sides, or rather refrained from a change of sides. It was necessary to wait until Iturbide for a similar operation to succeed, though in a different political context. An important member of Calleja's entourage was Anastasio Bustamante, a military man from Michoacán who had started a medical career and was residing in San Luis Potosí by 1810, a member of the local Batallón de Comercio militia. He immediately joined the force recruited by Calleja, working under him for the duration of the emergency. In 1821 he became an early supporter of Iturbide and was faithful to him almost until the end. Though his military career took him to many parts of the country, his connections were mainly in San Luis Potosí and secondarily in the Bajío, where he held military positions in Guadalajara, especially during Iturbide's rule.[33]

Zacatecas, one of the richest mining states, which did not suffer much destruction during the wars, boasted a mining *real*, Vetagrande, near the capital, and two other large ones farther north, Fresnillo and Sombrerete. Much of this wealth was or had been owned by the Fagoaga family, who had the title of marqueses del Apartado, very prominent members of the Mexican establishment and provided with a large and complex clan, to which we will return. The Fagoagas themselves, more financiers of mines than miners, were leaders of the moderate liberal faction, the Escoceses, thus opposing Iturbide's quest for the crown; but other noted members of their family, notably the bishop of Durango, Juan Francisco Castañiza, marqués de Castañiza, were Iturbidistas.

Finally, completing the list of important reales, Bolaños, in the hilly north of Jalisco, was the great discovery of the late eighteenth century; it had been owned by the marqueses de Vivanco. The heiress, by the time of independence, was married to José Morán, a distinguished military man known by his wife's title, who remained loyal to the Spaniards and later, as a moderate liberal, was an opponent of Iturbide and friend of the Fagoagas.

Economic Transformations and Liberal Ideas

The main business community was divided between the mining sector, organized in the Tribunal de Minería, and the merchants, nucleated in three consulados: the traditional one of Mexico and the two newer ones of Veracruz and Guadalajara. The mining group was very heterogeneous, because it included both producers and financiers of mining activities, roles not always clearly differentiated. On the other hand, the more powerful groups had diversified their investments, particularly by buying land, which gave them more security. All of them, however, were passing through a period of crisis, due to the destruction and paralysis brought about by the Insurgencia. One of the wealthiest groups, a leading creditor of the colonial state, was that of the Fagoagas. Its most distinguished member at the time of independence was José María, born in Spain but with a long career in Mexico, who had been a deputy to the Cortes. He was virtual chief of the moderate liberal sector, an opponent of Iturbide since the beginning. He had been very much involved in the liberal reforms promoted from the peninsula in 1820 and associated with others of his same ideas in the Escocés masonic lodges.

The Fagoagas were a very special family, quite influenced by their relative Jacobo de Villaurrutia, who had been a member of the Audiencia, a man filled with the spirit of the Enlightenment, which he tried to transmit to others through the pages of the *Diario de México*, founded in 1805. He was a great believer in congresses and meetings of representatives and had been prominent in the Iturrigaray attempt at autonomy in 1808. He had traveled widely, as would his two nephews, the marqués, Juan Francisco, and his brother Francisco. However, the group had its more conservative and clerical wing in the Bassocos and Castañizas, merchants and mine financiers, closely related among themselves and with the Fagoagas. Francisco de Castañiza was bishop of Durango, but his social position was marked by that of his father, who had been prior of the Consulate of Mexico. Antonio Bassoco, a Spaniard who married the daughter of his employer, the first marqués de Castañiza, and who would later receive the title of count, was one of the greater money lenders in the realm. As was true for many others, he played astride the roles of both merchant-banker and miner, but in him the former roles predominated.[34] During the liberal interlude of 1820, the Fagoagas had financed a weekly, *Semanario Político y Literario de México*, which carried long articles about freedom of trade and the need to reduce the taxes that were preventing the recovery of the mining industry. After Independence the Escocés lodges got an important accretion from the civilian and military personnel who came with O'Donojú, one of whom, the military medical doctor Manuel Codorniú, was the editor of the newspaper *El Sol*, launched two months after the liberation of the capital and also supported by the Fagoagas. It promoted new educational experiences, such as the Lancaster schools, and in economic matters its orthodoxy was reflected in an editorial that stated that Mexico had to be "first agricultural, then mining, and by no means industrial or commercial." The "by no means" was a bit strong and probably not intended for all eternity, but the phrase was addressed to very concrete issues and people. To begin with, it denied the utility of making an effort to protect local artisans or textile obrajes, due to their low international competitiveness. As for commerce, the target were those merchants who enjoyed a position of privilege and monopoly supported by the institutions of the Ancien Régime, notably the Mexican Consulado. The hoped-for opening to the international market could not help hurting that "commerce" to which Mexico was admonished not to dedicate itself. As for mining, the phrase reflects the disenchantment with an activity in crisis that would be very difficult to revive, as it would require enormous (foreign) capital and official support better concentrated on other activities. Which other activities? Preferably agricultural ones, in the expansive frontier and lowlands, in the form of tobacco, sugar, cotton, coffee, and other export staples. It would have implied following the Brazilian or Río de la Plata roads to economic growth.[35]

Veracruz, due to its climate and geographic position, could hope to become the leader in such an economic overhaul. In its more temperate slopes lay Orizaba and Córdoba, where tobacco growing was allowed during colonial times; the *estanco* was then one of the main sources of revenue, producing some four million pesos net, remitted to Spain. The government bought all the produce, fabricated cigars and cigarettes in its own factories, and sold them in so-called *estanquillos*, making a very large profit.

Tobacco growers were rather medium-to-small producers. They were organized into a gremio that, as did many other corporative institutions of the time, included in the same organization the producers and their creditors. Small producers, large ones, and *aviadores* (financiers) were all members of the gremio, and they elected a *diputación de cosecheros* in each zone, whose directors (a president, a secretary, and a treasurer, all paid by the gremio's funds) negotiated conditions with the administrador de la renta. In Orizaba the Tornel family was closely connected with the tobacco economy. José María Tornel, the noted politician who started his career as a Yorkino and remained one of the few solid friends of Santa Anna, had his hometown and family connections in Orizaba. His brother José Manuel was administrador principal of the renta in Orizaba in 1844. His other brother, José Julián, was an attorney for the diputación and secretary of the Ayuntamiento in the 1830s and early 1840s.[36] Tobacco cultivation provided some avenues of social mobility for middle-size producers, owners, or renters of land. It was rather easy to start with a small plot of land, though one had to depend on financing, either from aviadores or from the Renta de Tabaco itself. The potentially "democratic" or consensus-building nature of tobacco growing was such that in 1816 the Spanish authorities devised a plan to allow a temporary extension of the permitted area, so as to cajole back into obedience some sectors of the population that had shown insurgent sympathies.[37]

Not only tobacco, but also other tropical crops such as coffee, indigo, sugar, rice, and cotton were waiting to be "liberated" or allowed the freedom to expand in an international market opened up by the elimination of trade barriers. Some of these crops, such as sugar and cotton, had been produced for a long time; others had been tried beginning in the early years of the nineteenth century, either in medium-altitude localities, such as Orizaba, Córdoba, and Jalapa, or in the fertile but unhealthy lowlands. The interests around this possible frontier zone were basically bent on changing the economic rules of the game and had a lot to do with the Santa Anna faction in Mexican politics. Some, though, while interested in the long run in opening up to world trade, might fear an inflow of cheap and well-ginned American cotton, or even tobacco, and thus could accept protectionist policies at least for some items. A frontier, indeed, but a difficult one, as there were powerful economic interests in the country capable of resisting the changes.

When rapid economic development took place under the Porfiriato, there was more expansion in the north than in such tropical zones as Veracruz, though the latter also grew. The Veracruz model, however, is important for an understanding of the political strategy of Santa Anna and some liberals from this state who were often allied with him. It was a developmentalist and economic liberalism, which rather than confronting the conservative and corporatist structures of the Meseta preferred to ignore them or seek occasional allies among them. Some of the liberals of the Meseta, especially the more radical ones, as well as some provincial groups, were set, by contrast, on a more adversarial path against the corporatist Ancien Régime.

The aforementioned editorial from *El Sol* was a somewhat extreme expression of the moderate liberal group. The same journal also dedicated its pages to a more concrete defense of mining interests, a program that had ample consensus among influential circles. The Junta Gubernativa, after some vacillations due to lack of funds, decided to reduce drastically the main tax on miners (levied on production) from 10 percent to 3 percent, and also diminished other taxes that hit silver at the moment of minting. This reduction, in fact, was an example of what the intransigent editorial had warned its readers about, because after all, someone had to pay for the cost of government. What was expected, of course, by those who enacted the new legislation, was that the revolutionary opening up to the world market would increase customs receipts and convert all others into a bad memory from the past.

Optimism about the possibilities of the Mexican economy was unbounded. A spate of proposals vied with each other as to how many taxes to eliminate, including the alcabala and the mining dues, which were considered to be another form of alcabala. There was a belief that a new direct contribution charged on property or incomes would be the fairer way to collect revenues. An anymous author, signing J.M.G., who declared himself a follower of Francisco Severo Maldonado, the progressive liberal writer from Guadalajara, published a *Proyecto de ley sobre contribuciones*, with a study of the capacity of the rural sector of the country to pay the very high direct tax he was proposing, especially for large producers. He also suggested a 100 percent import tariff, because it was unwise to allow foreign products to be cheap; there should be international commerce, but based on the exchange of products, not pure importation paid for with silver coin.[38] Later on, in June 1822, José María Gutiérrez de Rozas, a lawyer associated with the Mexican Audiencia and erstwhile member of the Ayuntamiento, published another *ensayo*, dedicated to José Antonio Andrade, military commandant of the capital, with ideas similar to those of J.M.G.[39] In any case, whether they were the same person or not, both works represented the tradition of progressive *haciendistas* who cooperated with Iturbide. In the case of Maldonado, this economic projecting was coupled with a very strong dose of Enlightenment liberalism.

The Moderate Liberal Nucleus

Liberalism was baptized with that name toward 1810, and by the early 1820s the concept had wide circulation in Mexico. The liberal stem, never too clearly defined, divided itself into several branches, of which it is possible to distinguish a moderate (or conservative) one and a more radical (or populist) offshoot. As for the radical branch, it is necessary in turn to distinguish between its more extreme sectors, which can be termed liberal populist (or simply populist) and those in an intermediate position, for whom the designation of *progressives* can be reserved; most of the latter were convinced federalists. The three strands were not distinctly separated, but will serve as a first approximation to an understanding of the ideological spectrum, though of course additional variables must be considered for an explanation of concrete political involvements.[40]

Let us begin by examining the moderate liberal group, closely linked to the upper reaches of the bourgeoisie in the process of adaptation to capitalism. The Fagoagas' central role in this group has already been referred to. They had good connections with the Audiencia, which included their relative Jacobo de Villaurrutia, plus Hipólito Odoardo, Isidro Yáñez, and Juan Bautista Raz y Guzmán, fiscal agent, who had had sympathies and contacts with the insurgentes but had managed to keep his official

64   CHAPTER TWO

position.[41] In the old bureaucracy, permeated by Enlightenment, liberal ideas also influenced Ignacio García Illueca, a lawyer registered in the Audiencia, legal advisor to the Spanish army during the time of Calleja. According to Bustamante, he was a minion of José María Fagoaga, "though an honorable man," a landowner in Toluca of distinguished family, and somewhat aggrandized when, after the fall of Iturbide, he was made universal minister for a short transition period.[42]

Contacts in the army were not very numerous, because the majority was with Iturbide, but some did exist and were quite strategic. They included José Morán, from Querétaro, who had married the marquesa de Vivanco, whose title he adopted and whose mining investments he helped manage. He had an important role in the Liberating Army gathered against Iturbide in 1823, and after the emperor's overthrow, he was named commandant general of Mexico and chief of staff, posts he lost in 1827 due to Yorkino pressure.[43]

Two other important military contacts of the Escoceses were Nicolás Bravo and Manuel Mier y Terán, old insurgentes who had held important positions during Morelos's times. The imperial government did not give them central roles in the new military structure, but their prestige was very high, and they increased in stature, especially after Iturbide's fall. As potential allies one might count Generals José Antonio Echávarri and Pedro Celestino Negrete, Spaniards who had supported the Plan de Iguala, so much so that Negrete became the "second personality in the empire."[44] Both defected toward the end and became linked to the Escoceses. Two other Spanish military men of the same persuasion, though of lesser stature, were Juan de Orbegoso, who later made a career in the Mexican army, and Nicolás Campero.

In the intellectual field, two important members of the group were Francisco José Sánchez de Tagle and José María Luis Mora, whose paths later diverged widely. Sánchez de Tagle, who occasionally wrote poems and was the secretary of the Academy of San Carlos (of Beaux Arts) was also a lawyer, member of a family who had owned a banco de plata, regidor of the Mexican Ayuntamiento, and well connected to the church. So much so that he later became a member of the "party of retrogression" and the artificer of most simulated sales of church properties to preserve them from the voracious fisc. Mora, despite having been trained as a priest, underwent an intensive radicalization. He was a good friend of the Fagoagas, but he left them behind when he joined the radical reformers in 1833, and he thereafter became a pundit of anticlerical liberalism in Mexico. As the clergy never forgave him for what he had done to them during the few months of the Gómez Farías ascendancy (1833–34), he had to go into exile. His trajectory indicates the possible transmigrations from one liberal branch to the others, but by the early twenties those developments were still in the future, and Mora was quite moderate.

Other liberals near the moderate nucleus were Mariano Michelena, precursor of independence in Michoacán, where he plotted in 1809 and was then exiled to Spain; Vicente Rocafuerte, an Ecuadorian who would later become president of his country, an enterprising innovator in business ventures, involved with Michelena in the financial negotiations that led to the first loans in London; Joaquín Infante, a Cuban, collaborator on *El Federalista* with Francisco Ortega, a moderate federalist; José María Cabrera, a close friend of Mora who was a prominent Escocés; and Miguel Santamaría, a Veracruzan who had participated in Mina's expedition and resided in Colombia, where he became an admirer of Bolívar's centralist constitutional ideas (and later a representative of that country in Mexico).[45]

Two other intellectuals close to the Escocés faction, but who retained their independence due to their very strong and idiosyncratic personalities, were Fray Servando Teresa de Mier and Carlos María de Bustamante. Both had been determined partisans of independence almost from the start and came close to the centralist (or very moderate federalist) version of Escocés liberalism. Fray Servando, since his expulsion from New Spain in 1794 for an unorthodox sermon on the apparition of the Virgin of Guadalupe, had never known quiet. In exile in England, he began writing a history of New Spain, financed by Iturrigaray, who hoped his own efforts during the 1808 crisis would receive a favorable light, but the money was cut short when it became clear that the cleric was extolling the insurgentes. His labors in favor of independence and his agitated life had made him very popular in educated circles, but he was considered naive and exaggerated in his opinions.[46]

In the commercial sector, the Fagoagas had good connections with Manuel de Heras Soto, whose father had obtained the condado de Casa Heras for his strong financial contributions to the Spanish fisc, and with Tomás Murphy, a Spaniard of Irish ancestry resident in Veracruz, of whose consulate he had been prior, owner of mines and linked with other members of his family resident in Britain and Spain in an international trading partnership. He had become a real economic power at the turn of the century, due to his friendship with Godoy. Since 1823 he represented Mexico in Paris and London, a post that he said required great expense and that had reduced him to straitened circumstances. Other important

merchants did not sympathize very much with the new liberal ideas, perhaps because of their close connection with the trade monopoly symbolized by the Consulate of Mexico. This was the case of the conde de Agreda,
one of the richest men in Mexico, and the conde de la Cortina, also pos-
sessor of a handsome fortune, both Spaniards who had been priors of the
consulate and supporters of the viceregal government up to its final moments. They did not have a tendency to get involved in politics, though,
and Cortina emigrated soon after independence (his son returned later
on, to become a respected man of culture of conservative and pro-inter-
ventionist preferences). Gregorio Mier y Terán, a powerful financier who
was known as the "Mexican Rothschild," had supported Iturbide's bid
for independence and was associated with his political fortunes. In sum
the commercial sector, as revealed by some of its more conspicuous members, was very much divided, as it was difficult to see clearly advantages
and disadvantages in the economic changes that were in the offing, though
it had a predominant moderate-liberal nucleus among its politically active members.

Many established merchants had much to lose as a result of international events. Their semimonopolistic position, linked to Spain, was going to pieces, and independence was not a solution but rather the
permanent confirmation of their losses. They would prefer to retain some
link with Spain, in a commonwealth type of arrangement. Their fears
about further liberalization of trade had been expressed since 1810 by
several Cassandras, among them Juan López Cancelada, a journalist on
the colonial government's *Gaceta*, who in search of allies and a better
image argued that it would mainly be the artisans who would suffer from
foreign competition.[47]

Iturbide's Entourage

Iturbide, a "Basque from all four sides," as he liked to characterize himself, was the son of an immigrant with pretensions of nobility who owned
an hacienda in Michoacán. The future Liberator took to the career of a
soldier, without neglecting the haciendas, and particularly during the wars
of the insurgencia, he mixed in an unpleasant fashion his military prow-
ess with quick commercial operations, profiting from the confusion that
followed each battle. He also suffered, however, from the destruction the
insurgentes effected on some of his properties. The viceregal government
finally rewarded him with the lease of the large ex-Jesuit hacienda of
Chalco, in the vicinity of Mexico City. Iturbide's condition was typical of

what can be considered the provincial hidalgos, some of them relatively well-to-do, others in penury, owners of lands never too well worked nor linked to an international market. Many were indebted, among them Iturbide, though at moderate rates of interest and very long terms, with that solid and very understanding bank that was the church. When they fell in the hands of private financiers, the situation became more difficult. In contrast with what happened in other parts of the Americas, large landowners were not the more powerful economic class, but were the solid base of the social order. Of course some of them, who owned the largest latifundia, did get into the higher echelons of society, but this was more the exception than the rule. The more solid fortunes were those that combined various types of investments, particularly if they had passed through mining and knew how to get out in time.

These provincial hidalgos, in the process of becoming mere landowners in a capitalist society, included some of the members of the more traditional nobility, descendants of the conquistadores and the early officials of the crown, who had earned their titles with their blood, not their money. They were no friends of innovations, accustomed as they were to the exercise of authority over a working population whose needs they knew quite well and whom they could rule paternalistically, the opposite of the conditions of mining entrepreneurs. Among them a prominent position was held by the family that held the condado of Santiago Calimaya and the marquesados of Salinas and Salvatierra. At the time of independence, three closely related people were members of this clan: Miguel Cervantes y Velasco, the most distinguished one, who proceeded to a mediocre military career under the republic; his brother José María; and his uncle Juan María Cervantes y Padilla. Both of the latter had had short-lived military experience and had already retired from arms. The three members of the clan were used by Iturbide to pack the Junta Gubernativa, and he did the same with another man of similar origins though lesser ancestry, José Manuel Velázquez de la Cadena, whom he made marqués de la Cadena.[48]

Significantly, Iturbide did not include many military men in active duty in the junta, either because of civilianist prejudices or out of jealousy. He did include two important ones, however, Manuel de la Sotarriva, whom soon after the coup in May 1822 he made minister of war, and his friend and close collaborator Anastasio Bustamante, who would have a long and brilliant career under the republic as a representative of right-wing Iturbidismo, and who on more than one opportunity tried to capitalize on his past associations with the mythical figure of the executed Liberator.[49] Two other military men of lower rank whom Iturbide included in the junta were Nicolás Campero, retired, and Juan Orbegoso, who joined the opposition. Many of the military chiefs were people of similar social extraction to that of the provincial hidalgos. In the close blending between landowning and military roles, the upper middle class of the provinces was being consolidated, becoming the main social prop of the republican order. This order, of course, recognized its summits in the financier, merchant, and mining grandees, as well as in the really large latifundistas.

The greatest of these was the marqués de Aguayo, already referred to, who despite his great possessions was heavily indebted. He also had a clan, as his wife was one of the daughters of the Güera Rodríguez, but apparently she was too pretty to limit herself to a conventional marital life. It was rumored that Iturbide, after courting the mother, gave her the grief of fixing his attentions on the daughter. The opposition, of course, could not refrain from relishing this *boccato di cardinale* in their gossip mongering; the deputies and others jailed in August 1822 were accused, among other things, of trying to make political capital out of this affair.[50] Aguayo was made a member of the junta, and later on mayordomo mayor de su majestad, the highest position in the so-called Imperial Family. His brother, the conde de San Pedro del Alamo, also of the Iturbidista faction, was a middle-level military man who remained loyal until the end. Bustamante in his chronicles accuses him of having been part of an unrealized last-resort attempt to consolidate the tottering regime by terroristic repression in the capital, an allegation also reported in an anonymous pamphlet immediately after the end of the regime. In October 1823 he was jailed for taking part in a plot destined to bring back Iturbide from exile.[51] One of Aguayo's two brothers-in-law, the mining potentate conde de Regla, was also put in the junta by Iturbide and given a high honorific position in the Imperial Family.

The San Luis Potosí clique of the conde del Peñasco and the conde de San Mateo Valparaíso (who was also marqués del Jaral), landed and erstwhile mining families, were also staunch Iturbidistas, and so was the Marqués de Rayas, the strong miner of Guanajuato, who became a member of the junta and after the demise of the empire plotted for its return.

Mining, as can be seen, was quite well represented in the junta. The sector also counted among its members the mine-owner José María Bustamante (no kin to the chronicler Carlos María nor to the military Anastasio), who had taken part in the campaigns against the Insurgencia. He was an intimate friend of Alamán and very much associated with the liberal faction.[52] The Valenciana group was not directly involved in the junta, perhaps due to the prudence it displayed in these matters; but indirectly it was represented by Azcárate, who retained the post allotted to him in the provisional draft. As for Lucas Alamán, he was in Europe at the time.

In contrast with the great number of provincial hidalgos, military men, and miners, merchants were not sufficiently represented in the junta. The two strong leaders of the Mexican Consulado, Ignacio Aguirrevengoa and the conde de la Cortina, were absent, though Juan Bautista Lobo, from the Veracruz Consulate, was present. That province's interests were taken into account by also including Manuel Montes Argüelles, a landowner of Orizaba who was lawyer to the tobacco cosecheros. The moderate liberal group did not get the dominant position it could have expected either, given its weight in society, though it was not ignored; Sánchez de Tagle and José María Fagoaga were there, and so was the oidor Yáñez; and another closely associated oidor, Raz y Guzmán, as well as the military judge Ignacio García Illueca, the merchant conde de Heras Soto, and Colonel Orbegoso all received posts.

Among officials, the oidor Bataller was dropped, despite his role in the Profesa plan, and he soon emigrated. Juez de Letras Suárez Pereda was included, as were several oidores — the above-mentioned liberals Isidro Yáñez and Raz y Guzmán, the Spaniard Manuel Martínez Mansilla, and the creole José Domingo Ruz, of the Audiencia of Guadalajara (where Iturbide had many friends). Two other respected figures were also included: Manuel Velázquez de León, former Secretary of the viceroyalty, and Mariano de Almanza, founder of the Consulado of Veracruz and designated member of the Spanish Regencia during Fernando's imprisonment, though he had never left New Spain.

The clergy had an important position: apart from the inevitable Monteagudo and Guridi y Alcocer, other heavyweights also found places. These were Bishop Pérez of Puebla; Provisor Bárcena of Michoacán; Sartorio, of the Archbishopric; Isidro Ignacio Icaza, of the Colegio de San Ildefonso (a former Jesuit house); and Miguel Sánchez Enciso, of the Colegio del Seminario. Thus the three main university-level institutions maintained by the church were included, because the university itself was headed by Monteagudo.

The junta was completed with four other lawyers, who merit some detailed consideration. Espinosa de los Monteros, later to become a determined liberal anticlerical, was then visualized as a leading legal expert, who "knew all the property titles of Mexico," according to Mora. He was closely connected to Iturbide, who made him an important member of the ministerial staff during his government. Another advocate, an intellectual and writer interested in social reform projects, was Francisco Severo Maldonado. Of early Insurgente sympathies, he had been editor of *El Despertador Americano*, but was soon taken prisoner by the royalists and forced to continue publishing another, pro-Spanish periodical. This lack of nerve, perhaps necessary to save his life, was compensated by his great activity during the liberal spring of 1820, when he published an influential *Pacto Social propuesto a España*, to which he added other works with very progressive orientations, including the distribution of land to the Indians and protected industrialization. He was a determined partisan of Iturbide, for whom he published the periodical *El Fanal del Imperio*, which he continued from his native Guadalajara after the downfall of the regime. A third lawyer of this somewhat heterodox group was José María Jáuregui, who had secretely supported the insurgentes from Mexico and who would later evolve toward radical liberal positions in the Yorkino party. Less well known was Antonio Gama, of the Colegio de Santa María de Todos los Santos.[53]

In the Junta Gubernativa, which had been nominated directly by Iturbide, but also taking into account the state of public opinion, the Liberator did not have a majority. His position was more solid in the executive body he created, the Regencia, charged with running the administration provisionally until an answer came from Spain to the offer made to Fernando or another Bourbon to accept the crown. In the Regencia, of five members, he reserved for himself the role of president, compatible with the command of military forces, which also gave him the title of generalísimo. He reserved a post, in case Spain accepted the proposal, to O'Donojú, after whose premature death he appointed Bishop Pérez of Puebla. Flanking him were the faithful Bárcena of Michoacán, the malleable Velázquez de León, and the less trusted oidor Yáñez. In sum three or four votes out of five, because Pérez and Bárcena were unshakeable.

In the Cabinet he made a decision that surprised many. In Relaciones, a combination of Interior and Foreign Affairs, and which was thus the main post, he designated José Manuel Herrera, an erstwhile priest very active under Morelos, who had sent him on a mission to the United States to buy arms. Herrera, whose critics said he was thought cultivated because he did not speak, had interpreted the sad story of the Republic of Anáhuac, torn to pieces by the internecine fights of its diminutive congress, in the sense that what was needed was a strong executive. So much so that Carlos María de Bustamante (a member of that congress) gossiped that Herrera had once advised Morelos to proclaim himself king.

What is certain is that throughout his collaboration with Iturbide, he supported in every instance the consolidation of strong personal power, even if it was not totally legal. No wonder the *Testamento* referred to him as "hijo primogénito."[54]

Iturbide put Rafael Pérez Maldonado in Hacienda; he was an old haciendista from colonial times. He appointed Antonio Medina to War, a man with experience in the Spanish navy, whom he had to replace with the more energetic General Sotarriva when the confrontation with Congress took a violent turn. Justice, the fourth and last ministry, was offered to José Domínguez Manso, a personal friend from Michoacán, the son of a modest employee of the tobacco organization, who was quite respected even by his political antagonists.

To these collaborators others have to be added, forming his intimate circle. One was Juan Gómez Navarrete, a lawyer from Michoacán, who had been elected to the Cortes in 1820, a personal friend who became Iturbide's legal attorney after the exile. Even before Iturbide's departure, Navarrete started publishing a journal, *El Aguila*, as a means to defend the political interests of the deposed emperor, determined to engage in a complex policy of alliances and ideological transmutations. The newspaper became one of the more important ones in the country, together with the moderate-liberal *El Sol*. The French journalist Germán Prissette, persecuted in his home country by the Restoration, was a member of its staff. The following year Lorenzo de Zavala took over, for a few months, to be replaced by Antonio Valdés, a Cuban federalist who had an official job during the empire. In August 1826 *El Aguila* was entrusted to Juan Wenceslao Barquera, an intellectual of high prestige, who had had sympathies for the Insurgencia and later cooperated with Iturbide, of liberal but accommodating orientation.[55]

Among the military, almost the only support Iturbide retained until the very end was that of Manuel Gómez Pedraza, son-in-law of Azcárate, who also stayed in the emperor's entourage. Pedraza was the chief of the loyal forces besieged in the City of Mexico by the rebel Liberating Army from Veracruz. In spite of that, he survived the collapse and had a prominent role in the first few years of the republic, as minister of war under Victoria and a candidate to succeed him in 1828, supported by *El Aguila*.

On a more personal level, the Italian adventurer and military man Miguel Cavaleri could always be relied upon for a game of cards, and was selected by Iturbide at the time of his exile to accompany him on the long trip; but he was not allowed by the republican authorities to go aboard.

3

Mobilizational Leadership

After the whirlwind of the Insurgencia, politics could never be the same as before. The experience of massive participation in armed struggle left a residue, both in the countryside and in the towns. In the countryside small-scale rebellions, as well as grander ones such as those in the Sierra Gorda and in Yucatán in 1847–48, continued to erupt, with the prospect, both for alarmed contemporaries and for some present-day observers, of reenacting the Insurgencia.[1]

The possibility of agrarian rebellion leading to a more widespread movement affecting the whole country depended, however, on the participation of other, nonrural political actors. Though the contraposition between the upper classes and the agrarian masses may have been the most profound one, there were other conflicts, among the elites and the middle classes, which had more saliency because of the greater weight (if not numbers) of their protagonists. Given the criss-cross of cleavages, all sorts of alliances could ensue, including those between popular groups and sectors of the upper classes. In the larger towns, in particular, conditions existed for the incorporation of large sectors of the population into the political struggle. As mentioned in the Introduction, the fact that at the time one man meant one gun, made rebellion or the threat of it easier; technological advantage was not so much on the side of government and the regular army as it is today. Admittedly, though, the popular strata did not possess organizational and leadership skills in sufficient quantity, despite experiences with the Indian repúblicas, the artisan guilds, or even the religious cofradías. Leadership, then, had to be provided by middle- and upper-class sectors, which was only possible if enough social tensions were operating at their level so as to generate anti–status-quo elites. These elites' capacity to incorporate the masses, and the latter's availability to enter into a political movement, then become major variables in the explanation of successful revolutionary upheavals. Availability is greater as the masses become socially mobilized, that is, as they abandon their traditional deference patterns. But their lack of organizational experience leads them to seek a new father figure, charismatic rather than traditional—a caudillo or a Bonapartist leader.[2]

Once it is realized that mass political movements are to a large extent the result of a coalition or convergence between sectors of the elites and the masses, it becomes more necessary to analyze the social pressures leading some members of the middle or upper classes to set themselves against the existing order of domination and seek a popular alliance or coalition. The concept of coalition does not necessarily refer to a process of explicit transactions between group representatives, which would be a special instance of coalition formation. In most cases the term refers to what might be called a latent structure, determining a marked tendency on the part of individuals and politicians to act in a certain way.

To gain a better grasp of the concept of social mobilization, let us consider how it applies to various situations. The Indian pueblo population, in general, could not be considered to have a high degree of social mobilization, especially if they were far away from urban centers and not excessively irked by neighboring haciendas. A greater connection with the market, especially labor mobility, usually implies a beginning of social mobilization. Long stints of forced labor in far-away places, such as in the Peruvian mita (even if people afterwards returned to their villages), also contributed to breaking traditional vertical bonds, which were replaced, eventually, by charismatic ones centered on substitute father figures. In New Spain forced labor was much less widespread and involved only short displacements, both in time and space, so it did not alter the traditional pueblo social structure as much. However, if the pressure from the haciendas excessively eroded the lands available to the communities and forced too many of their members to hire themselves out permanently, even if at short distances, then a process of breakup of vertical links within the pueblos and eventually intense social mobilization could set in. In the Cuernavaca area, for example, the pueblos had been losing out against the sugar estates from colonial times; most of the estates were worked by slaves or liberated blacks, who in time mixed with the Indians. In this case the coexistence of social mobilization with elements of the autonomous organization of the old pueblo repúblicas helped increase the potential for revolt.

In the haciendas the resident labor force, made up of peones and some arrendatarios (other arrendatarios came from the pueblos) had been uprooted from its ancestral homes, and to that extent it could be considered to be socially mobilized. Of course in time new family and social links developed, but they were not propped up by the república structure, and the links with the patrón were weakened by the very large number of residents present on many haciendas. Ethnic differences also worked against the integrative effects of classical rural life.[3]

On the other hand, social mobilization and its associated charismatic, caudillista, or mobilizational mode of popular involvement must not be seen as the only formula for mass violent conflict. If for a number of reasons an intense conflict developed between, say, the haciendas and the pueblos, the upper stratum of the Indian communities might take up the leadership of the ensuing confrontation and rely on the traditional loyalties of its commoners in order to get recruits to join its side. This type of political movement would most likely have difficulty in extending itself to wider areas, as it would imply a sort of federation of traditionally and ethnically led communities. Historical experience seems to point in the direction that highly extended and potentially revolutionary movements are more likely to be based on charismatic leadership, be it by an upper stratum of the dominated ethnic group (as in the Andes with Túpac Amaru) or by a marginal group of the dominant sectors (as in New Spain's Insurgencia).

In large urban areas such as Mexico City, a socially mobilized population was often found in large concentrations, facilitating the development of social conflict and a mobilizational type of politics. The poorer strata, semiemployed, or working in tanneries, butcheries, and other low-level jobs, were concentrated in several barrios, famous for their poverty and the violence of their streets, as well as their tendency to political eruption. The gunpowder factory and the municipal matadero were located in the plazuela de San Lucas, close to the garita of San Antonio Abad, near the barrios of San Pablo and Salto del Agua. The most typical popular barrios, to the south and southeast of the center, were San Pablo, La Palma (Santo Tomás), and the Salto del Agua, with San Sebastián, Santa María, Santa Ana, and Santa Cruz Acatlán approaching that notoriety.[4]

The canals through which agricultural produce was brought into the city converged on the southeast, where a center of transshipment developed, with the attendant congregation of muleteers, cart drivers, and warehouses. The convent of La Merced, seat of the noted Iturbidista agitator Friar Aguilar, was in that neighborhood, located between the barrios of Santo Tomás la Palma and San Pablo. To the south, a bit farther away, the Paseo de la Viga, along the canal, provided a more breathable atmosphere, but always with a predominantly popular attendance, which led some politicians to frequent that area in search of popular acclaim.[5]

It must be said that several European cities at the time had similar concentrations of extreme poverty. In one description of Glasgow in the 1830s, the author refers to his visit to the "pestilential classes . . . comprising a population of from 15,000 to 30,000 persons," crammed in lodging rooms, "sometimes 15 to 20 in number, some clothed, and some naked, men, women, and children all huddled promiscuously together . . . all employed in the minor or the major departments of plunder."[6] However, Mexico City, though not totally exceptional by international standards, occupied a very high position in the ranking of proletarianization.

Leaders of the People

Between the extremes of poverty and wealth, an important middle class existed, largely made up of small traders and shop-owning artisans, whose frontiers with the lower depths, nevertheless, were not securely delimited. A well-known representative of the upper layers of the artisan class was Lucas Balderas, who as a young man came from San Miguel el Grande to the capital. He was apprenticed as a tailor and joined the volunteer militia, the "Realistas Fieles de Fernando VII." He was too young to make up his mind about the Insurgencia (he was eighteen years old by the time Morelos was shot in 1815), but he soon joined the populist wing of the liberals, that is, the Yorkinos. He participated in the Acordada rebellion in 1828 and in other liberal revolutions. He moved between his tailor shop and his positions in the militia, in which he rose to captain in 1827 (not a full-time job) and later to that of inspector general. A less famous example of the same class was a certain barber and brilliant amateur guitar player, Melesio, whose family name has been lost to posterity, and who became Guillermo Prieto's great friend when the latter descended in social condition, due to his father's death. Melesio "had been a *cívico*, and put on military airs to make one die laughing" He was a

> friend of the *cabezones*, that is, learned men, especially if they were his partisans . . . he was an unrepentant Yorkino, and [did not] omit a letter of a half-broken volume of Holbach's Morals, which he almost knew by memory . . . He had been through dangerous adventures with the followers of Zerecero, the accomplices of Regidor Paz and the partisans of 'Gómez Furias'. . . He

knew like few others how to use a printing press . . . how to take
away the smell of ink, how to hide a tract in a loaf of bread . . .
and all the frauds applicable to love or politics.

The Regidor José Ignacio Paz, of whom Melesio had been a follower (no
relation to the Indian albañil, or builder, turned senator, Agustín Paz),
was a *maestrescuela* and *titiritero*, and thus a member of the insecure
lower reaches of the middle classes, whose profession also had a guild,
scarcely above those of the manual artisans. Paz was a pragmatic populist, who had been involved in the agitational component of Iturbidismo
and who had participated in a plot, in October 1823, to bring back the
emperor after his downfall. He then became a Yorkino and was elected
regidor. In 1827 he took advantage of that position to effect inspections
in the houses of Spaniards who were suspected of being unfaithful to the
republic. Due to his excesses, he was jailed and condemned by a judge to
lose his municipal functions and to withdraw forty miles from the capital
for four years. He nevertheless participated in the "estupendo grito de la
Acordada," about which he wrote a pamphlet. In all he was a good example of the middle-level political activists, who always found an audience among the Mexican plebs, and who oscillated between radical
populism and other probably more opportunistic involvements with leaders of a different extraction, such as Iturbide or Santa Anna, who might
appear equally capable of providing leadership for the people against the
Establishment.[7]

Typical of this intellectual group of modest origins was José Joaquín
Fernández de Lizardi, self-styled as El Pensador Mexicano, very well
known for his journalistic and literary endeavors, if not for the firmness
of his political involvements.[8] The son of a medical doctor, he entered
San Ildefonso (formerly Jesuit) college, but did not finish his studies. He
held a position as teniente de justicia in Taxco when the insurgents attacked it in 1811, and as he did not act with the necessary vigor in resisting them, he was sent to jail; he quickly got out, however, in part through
writing two diatribes in verse against the rebels, attributing to the intervention of the Virgin Mary the protection of the capital against Hidalgo's
hosts and admonishing their secret sympathizers, "insurgentes a la
sordina," to come back into the fold.[9] Lizardi (as he was usually known)
engaged in a career of journalism and short-story or novel writing, which
in time made him very well known. His novels *El Periquillo Sarniento*
(1816) and *La Quijotita y su prima* (1819) brought him popular fame
and also endeared him to the opposite sex. In 1812 when freedom of the

press was established, he started a newspaper, *El Pensador Mexicano*, getting in trouble with the authorities and going again to jail before the end of the year. He continued to publish his paper from prison, where he remained for seven months. Finally when the new viceroy, Félix María Calleja, was appointed, Lizardi took the opportunity to write an address to the public extolling his virtues and was freed, to resume a second series of his *Pensador*, which finally came to an end in 1814, when Fernando VII regained absolute power.[10] This was the moment for Lizardi to concentrate on his novel and short-story writing, publishing also the more jejune serials *Alacena de frioleras* and *El cajoncito de la Alacena*. His next opportunity came with the opening up of constitutional government in 1820, when he started *El Conductor Eléctrico*, at the same time issuing innumerable pamphlets that provided him with a meager sustenance. He then wrote a *Justa defensa del Excmo Sr. Virrey de Nueva España,* by then Juan Ruiz de Apodaca, who had replaced the "sanguinary" Calleja, in an attempt by the crown to pacify the kingdom.[11] Now, with freedom reestablished by the liberal Spanish revolution of 1820, it was logical to cooperate with the authorities, even if some unrepentant insurgentes, such as Guerrero or Guadalupe Victoria, still bore arms or remained in hiding, and some writers took advantage of the new freedom to produce covert independence propaganda or at least to antagonize the authorities. At first this was not Lizardi's attitude, and he concentrated on religious and social reform, working "from inside" the regime.

In proposing equality of rights for blacks, he used the slippery argument that it was thanks to them that New Spain was now free of insurgents. In his *Conductor Eléctrico* no. 23 (1820), he featured a dialogue between two blacks, remembering the "brave negroes of Yermo." He was referring to Gabriel de Yermo, a dynamic Spanish merchant and meat abastecedor to the capital, owner of large sugar haciendas in Cuernavaca, with hundreds of slaves whom he had freed, keeping them as wage workers and sure to rely on them when the occasion arose. He had opposed Iturrigaray's attempt at independence in 1808, organizing a coup de main using the young Spaniards who worked like mules in the capital's shops. At the same time, he had sent for his blacks from the plantations, though it was not necessary for them to become involved in the action, due to the quick success of the coup.[12] Lizardi alerted, nevertheless, against the danger that the still existent insurgentes might make use of the blacks, as had been done by Guerrero and Victoria in the tierra caliente areas of the south and Veracruz, potentially reproducing the horrors of Saint Domingue.

Later on, in 1825, in another serial, *Conversaciones del payo y del sacristán*, he would come back to the subject of the blacks, this time referring condescendingly to the "little blacks of Cuautla Amilpas and the tierra caliente," who had unfortunately fought against freedom. Now he recommended radical land reform to give them lands and win them to the cause of liberty. He was at the time expounding an ideal constitution, which is a good example of his democratic-authoritarian, or populist, mentality. He proposed, among other things, the death penalty for stealing more than ten pesos; condemning murderers who employed particularly cruel means to suffer the same form of capital punishment; putting a *celador* every four blocks "to inquire about the work and mode of living of all residents"; setting vagrants to learning a trade or else sending them to poorhouses (*talleres nacionales*); requiring all citizens to wear a blue and white ribbon on their left arm; limiting the ownership of land to four square leagues (10,000 hectares), then alloting the rest to poor farmers, who were to be helped by government with the necessary implements; teaching better skills to artisans, giving them protection against foreign ones, and helping them to set up shop; requiring votes to be expressed in an audible voice, so as to avoid the distortions produced by printed lists given to illiterates; sending indecent women to cook for the inmates of prisons; and revoking citizenship for going about dressed in rags or for not learning to read and write in the course of three years. The psychological authoritarianism that emerges from some of these proposals must be judged, of course, by the standards of the time, but still it is quite extreme and obviously addressed to a lower middle class or even popular public concerned about security but also about equality.[13]

In 1821, in yet another dialogue, *Chamorro y Dominiquín*, he attacked the recently proclaimed Plan de Iguala, asserting that it was better to be free under Spain than independent but "slaves of a few tyrants."[14] However, he declared that independence was necessary and would certainly be granted by Spain, a supposition that landed him in jail for a few days. Lizardi's "oficialismo," however tactical it may have been, involved him in controversies with others who had suffered long imprisonments for seeking independence under Iturrigaray (but who were protected by their high social position), such as Francisco de Azcárate or Juan Bautista Raz y Guzmán, fiscal agent of the Audiencia.[15] Fernández de Lizardi was held in such esteem by the royal government, that when Rafael Dávila, a liberal pamphleteer who also cultivated the popular genre, was imprisoned, an anonymous author pungently asked the Pensador to remember his sufferings of 1813 and write in favor of someone who had fallen because

of telling the truth.[16] The Pensador, while more antiestablishment or populist than such people as Azcárate and Raz y Guzmán, was prepared to
"adulate" the viceroy so as to better use existent freedoms. For this he
had to cut his links with the independent party, but his game was being
increasingly detected by foes and rivals. Hard-line supporters of the viceregal government concocted a supposed *Carta de Iturbide al Pensador
Mexicano*, in which Iturbide treated him as his friend, and in footnotes
the author asked Lizardi whether it was true what people said in the
coffee houses, that Hidalgo and Morelos had been "heroes of liberalism"
and Iturbide equivalent to them and to Quiroga, the leader of the 1820
Spanish revolution. The Pensador adeptly answered that independence in
itself was a good thing and that there were good and bad insurgents,
adding somewhat cynically that if Iturbide won he would be called a
hero, but an insurgent if he lost. Yet once he saw the writing on the wall,
he picked a fight with the authorities and decamped to the Iturbide quarters in Puebla.[17] We will follow in the next chapter his later evolution.

Lizardi, apart from his grander struggles against the conservative elements in church or government, also cultivated a clientele of small traders and artisans, about whose problems he was quite well informed. In an
early issue of the *Pensador* series, in 1813, he imagined a dialogue between a young girl and Tata Pablo, a shoemaker. The latter complained
about the high cost of becoming a maestro, which involved paying over
fourteen pesos in taxes (*media annata*), four pesos to the mayoral, two to
each veedor, and an estimated thirty or forty for the entertainment to
celebrate the title. He concluded that setting up a shop should be freed
from guild control. At the same time, he condemned the tenderos, that is,
the moneylenders who advanced small sums of money in exchange for
property (mostly clothing) that was kept as a guarantee, but which they
systematically sold when their clients fell into arrears, without returning
the excess sums thus obtained; they should be required to give at least 50
percent of the requested loan in money and only the remainder in merchandise, which is what they preferred to do for the total amount.[18]

The Pensador also supported a group of small retailers, the *casilleros*,
who had small kiosks in the plazas where they sold bread and occasionally meat, thus circumventing the "monopoly" of bakers and butchers. A
member of the casillero community thanked him in 1820 for his efforts
"during the last constitution" (before 1814) to obtain "free bread and
meat" for the people and admonished the present Ayuntamiento to resist
pressures to revise that measure.[19] Another anonymous writer, in the
same year 1820 of the blossoming of a thousand flowers, picked up the

thread, asking the Pensador, whom he highly praised, to denounce the bad treatment meted out to workers in the *panaderías*, which had labor conditions similar to those of the obrajes; he should also fight for a reduction of taxes on houses and coaches. The small vendors in the plazas and mercados were an active community, ready to press for their interests through petitions or otherwise. In 1821, after the liberation, they asked the newly established junta to stop "encomenderos" (the old regatones or abarcadores), that is, intermediaries, from waiting in the garitas for the suppliers of merchandise and to require the latter to proceed to the central plazas or mercados and sell only to vendors who had permanent shops or puestos. On the other hand, poor women who sat on the pavement selling a couple of cuartillas during the whole day might as well be allowed to proceed with their trade (apparently they were no serious competitors) and not be sent to work in an *atolería* when caught without the necessary licenses.[20]

Another friend of the Pensador sought his support for the elimination of passports and licenses for using horses, invoking the new spirit of liberty dominant in 1820. He gave the example of a poor man who had taken out a small loan (*habilitación*) to go to Chalco to buy six cargas of maize, hoping to make a profit of one peso on each one. He forgot his passport and had to pay a fine of ten pesos. Now this imaginary man was not that poor, if he hoped to make six pesos on a couple of days' work, but he certainly was a member of the modest and unstable lower middle class, to whose needs the Pensador catered. The authorities complied with the demand, and later on Lizardi would be very proud of his contribution to this accomplishment, though his critics ridiculed the whole affair. A few years later, he was still engaged in defending members of his potential public, writing a brochure against the regidor Molinos, who wanted to prohibit the consumption of alcohol in coffee houses (which needed to sell liquor to retain their clients), vinoterías, and bodegones or fondas (where food was consumed and had to be washed down).[21] Lizardi of course also cultivated the artisan public, and in his *Conversaciones del Payo y del Sacristán*, in early 1825, he made a number of proposals, including that foreigners should not introduce articles that competed with local produce, a standard demand at the time. However, toward the end of the year he moderated his position, unwilling to antagonize the British excessively by promoting a full prohibitionist policy. His friend and follower the Payo del Rosario had published a tract in 1825 whose title, *Si no se van los ingleses hemos de ser sus esclavos* is clear enough as to its contents; it earned its author a prison sentence. The Pensador posed as an impartial judge in two pamphlets, where he said that local artisans were not so destitute as they claimed and that in fact it was difficult to find oficiales. What artisans needed was to learn from foreign examples and improve their products; maybe Fernández de Lizardi was thinking of the consumers this time.[22]

Confessors to the People

The lower secular clergy, men like Hidalgo and Morelos, had shown, since the Insurgencia, their capacity to mobilize the masses. However, a special place must be allotted to the regular branch, particularly the mendicant orders: Franciscans, Dominicans, Augustinians, *mercedarios*, and Carmelites, all of them familiarly called friars.[23] They were numerous in the two extremes of the urbanization continuum: in the cities and in the outlying missions. In the latter they performed functions similar to those of the lower secular clergy, though with the support of a relatively autonomous organization, and they often administered important productive units. In the medium-size and large towns, they lived in convents, and due to their great numbers, they had an everyday presence in the streets and public places. It was easier to become a friar than a curate, as generally less instruction was needed, except for the Jesuit order. Bishops usually accused the friars of being ignorant, and from early colonial times it was remarked by critics such as father Pedro José de la Parra that many recently arrived Spaniards, sailors, pages, scribblers, and personal servants took the opportunity to enter an order and make progress there on the basis of their nationality.[24]

Some civilian authorities shared this opinion. Thus the secular cabildo of Lima, in 1587, said that people entered convents "without any serious examinations, except the nomination by [the convent's] prelate, which is easily won for love and fear of the coming *capítulo*."[25] In a controversy against the mendicant orders, in Puebla in 1640, Bishop Palafox argued that the curates were better qualified, because they knew the native tongues which they had absorbed "with their maternal milk," implying of course that they were mestizos, though of a good social origin via their fathers. The secular clergy, in his opinion, was composed of descendants of the conquistadores, while the regulars were recently arrived poor whites.[26] In a later period, the Spanish influx into the monasteries was reduced, and in many orders in Mexico there was a native majority, but always with what appears to have been a low social status.[27]

The friars' critics accused them of being idlers and therefore urged that they be eliminated, because they were a charge on the public and on the church. The church judged that they were examples of charity and devotion, building and staffing hospitals, missions, and schools, and sometimes taking charge of parishes, in which case their role was assimilated to that of the secular priests. The mendicant orders, in marked contrast to the Jesuits, elected their authorities (the prior of the convent, the provincial, and even the superior of the order).[28] The friars, in principle bound to obey the pope, clashed with the secular clergy, which were subordinated to the bishop and therefore more to the crown than to the pope.[29] The elections of authorities were a strange democratic institution in that theoretically so submissive environment. In practice they were an occasion for fights and competitions, and they created positions equivalent to those of the bishops but less influenced by civil power.[30] Mendicant friars had begun, in their origin, as the army of the pope, though this now varied according to circumstances. They formed, nevertheless, a quite distinct group, subject to their own rules of discipline, though not always abiding by them, quite separate and often antagonistic to the secular clergy.[31]

Though quantitative data are hard to come by on this subject, most qualitative evidence indicates that friars had a markedly lower social status than did parish priests.[32] For a lower-middle-class family to put a son in a convent was one way of coping with downward mobility, by partially anticipating its effects. The boy would be maintained by the community, in a frugal life-style, at the price of not reproducing himself. In the numerous cases where this norm was infringed, the children were illegitimate, for whom downward mobility was more acceptable. The enormous quantity of friars existing in Hispanic countries can be seen as a form of pruning the demographic growth of the middle classes by socially sterilizing a segment of their membership.

The total population in Spain in 1797 was 11,600,000, while the secular clergy included 70,840 persons, and the male regulars amounted to 53,098.[33] Both branches of the church thus formed 1 percent of the total population, an apparently small proportion; but this proportion should be calculated more realistically in relation to the number of middle-class males of active ages. If the middle class (urban and rural) is estimated at 20 percent of the total and that figure is divided by half to remove the women and by half again to eliminate the minors, then we have 5 percent of the total population as being made up of middle-class males of active ages.[34] In relation to them, the 1 percent of the church army is fully 20 percent. In Mexico toward 1803, the population could be estimated as 5,380,000 inhabitants, while the male members of the clergy, according to Humboldt, were between 10,000 and 13,000 individuals; that is, taking the upper estimate, 0.3 percent of the total population, a smaller amount than in Spain. However, the greater difference between the urban and rural populations in Mexico (the latter being largely Indian) suggests taking the urban middle-class population as the basis for calculation. Supposing the urban population to be 20 percent of the total, and 30 percent of them middle class, the "urban middle-class" adult males made up 1.5 percent of the total population using the same estimation method as above. Masculine clergy then would be about a fifth of the urban middle class before independence. This very rough calculation is borne out by the Querétaro figures in chapter one, where the total urban middle class was made up of 5,134 individuals (levels 1, 2, and 3), of whom 1,620 were ecclesiastics, a handsome 31 percent, and this two decades after independence. Querétaro, a high-density area, probably had more clerics than some outlying and more frontier areas, such as the north or the Tierra Caliente, but Mexico City must have been equally if not even better endowed with clergy.[35]

Individual reactions to the life prospects of becoming a friar were unpredictable, but they were sure to include resentment, agitations, and fights. To become a prior in a convent or superior of the province through the elections was a means of getting away from this inferno and was in principle open to the defter types. By contrast, in the secular branch, promotions up to the position of curate were more like those of a profession or a bureucratic career, for which a previous training had been undergone. Regarding nuns' convents, the situation was quite different, because they included women of a higher social standing. Here the unacknowledged aim was to sterilize (generally with success) a part of the upper or upper-middle classes, to keep excessive numbers from ruining them.[36]

Most friars, who lived closer to the misery of their parishioners than the priests, and who in search of alms often ended up mixing with the world of the street dwellers, were quite sensitized to popular states of mind. A Carmelite friar in the early seventeenth century complained that despite the fact that the rule said that monks had to stay day and night in their cells meditating, they were made to undergo public humiliations so as to test their faith. They "were given a bundle of alfalfa or wood . . . to sell for a very high price so that no one would buy it . . . or they were sent to eat with the poor in the *porterías* (the doors of other convents)." In

Querétaro superior authorities bent on disciplining the supposedly con-
templative Carmelites were worried at their reaction, which "threatened
to arouse the obrajeros and the local battalion."[37]

In Spain the bishop of Cuenca in 1809 expressed his concern that the
members of impoverished convents would "wander about with the pretext of collecting alms and become dissolute [thus] bringing scorn on
their calling."[38] The friars' training enabled them to become leaders of
those very masses they were supposed to assuage. They were potential
fanatics, not only religious but also social and political, and given the
unfathomable alchemy of their souls, they could easily turn into apostles
of new and strange gospels. For a friar to become an *exaltado* liberal or a
populist demagogue was, in a sense, to continue at the same trade. As for
the secular priests, they were submitted to similar pressures, though of a
much lesser intensity, as they had in front of them a more open-ended
career, involving escalating positions from auxiliary roles to the coveted
one of curate in charge of a parish, in which case they obtained a better
income, charging for the sacramental functions they performed.

The reforms ordered by the Spanish Cortes in 1820 produced an up-
heaval among the regular clergy, stimulating the formation of a liberal
group within its ranks. The monastic authorities in general rejected
changes, though in some cases they pretended to have been prepared at
first to silently obey the legislation; only later were they driven to open
protest, due to continuous excesses on the part of civilian authorities.
Right after the Spanish liberal revolution of 1820, the general, that is, the
highest authority of the Franciscans, Cirilo Alameda, resident in Spain,
inveighed against the provision that would have eliminated the provincials'
functions, giving the bishops control over the friars. He said that the rule
would be particularly inapplicable to the mendicant Franciscans, who
needed their prelates' spiritual and economic government, and who did
not belong to any convent in particular but were assigned by their superiors to various destinations according to need. A provincial in Querétaro,
Manuel Gutiérrez, who already was on record as having said in 1818
that the constitution was infernal, but who now admitted it had been
"*desinfernada*" by Ferdinand VII, addressed his parishioners along similar lines. As he was known for his scorn for Mexicans, he received a series
of critical tracts, which converted the religious issue into one between
Mexicans and Spaniards, a division typical in religious orders.[39]

Antireligious propaganda stooped to rather low levels, in Mexico as
much as in Europe, producing the reaction of some clerical writers who
alerted their flock about the introduction of obscene cards, urinals, and

the like; though Ferdinand VII was still the king, he had lost so much
power that it might be necessary to build a wall along Mexico's coasts. At
a more sophisticated level, an anonymous *"religioso liberal"* explained
his condemnation of a tract that had recently appeared, *Bosquejo de los
fraudes que las pasiones de los hombres han introducido en nuestra santa
religión*, which ridiculed all that was most sacred, invoking the authority
of such figures as Locke, Montesquieu, Voltaire, and Rousseau. Against
those heretics it could be argued that similar things relating to freedom,
but without antireligious excesses, had been expressed by Cardinal
Belarmino (who averred that though wisdom comes from God, it resides
in the people), Francisco Suárez, Cardinal Cayetano, Alfonso de Castro,
Domingo Soto, Alonso Ledesma, Diego Covarrubias, Navarro Azpilcueta,
and Juan Diedron, making an interesting list of the pantheon of traditionalist liberal Catholics. The *Bosquejo* made quite an impact, and it
was taken up by Lizardi, who supported the argument made by its author that vows entered into by friars and nuns at an early age were "rash"
(*temerarios*). After some prodding by the prior of the Oratorio of San
Felipe Neri, he had to admit that such an opinion about vows might lead
to *scandal*, a very strategic concept for the Church. No, answered the
prior, the Bosquejo was not scandalous, it was positively *heretical*.[40]
     Another irritating work introduced into Mexico at the time was the
Testamento de España, written by the famous Melchor de Macanaz, who
had been a minister in Madrid and was well known for his tirades against
the church. Immediately after independence, the fight became more intense, because one of the objects of the separation from Spanish rule was
to stop the application of the Cortes' reforms. A Franciscan friar, Juan
Rosillo de Mier Quatemoczín, defiantly published a *Manifiesto sobre la
inutilidad de los provinciales de las religiones en esta América*, maintaining that the Cortes' legislation had to be applied in Mexico and that it
was not true that Iturbide had liberated his country just to stop religious
reforms, as was muttered. He took the opportunity to recount his life,
saying that in 1818 he had fled from his convent near Mexico to avoid
getting involved in violent episodes against a tyrannical guardian. He had
been to the missions in Tampico, and having quarrelled with his superior,
he became a capellán in the army. He also added a lot of gossip about
competitions and ambitions for the post of prior or provincial, all of
which would be wiped out if those authorities were eliminated. Having
been rebuked by a *Defensor de los religiosos* and by the *Abeja*, he reaf-
firmed his position, counseling his critics to read Voltaire. He again re-

ferred to his convent's episode as illustrating the injustices in the ordinary friars' life. It may seem surprising that the authorities allowed this wandering friar to go from post to post without control; poor communications were no doubt the reason.[41]

The friars were an important component of Iturbide's structure of popular support, as noted by many chroniclers. The day of the coup that led to the founding of the empire, masses of people filled the legislative building, among them many friars and military men. In the Convento de la Merced, located near the ill-famed barrios of Santo Tomás La Palma and San Pablo, lived the noted Aguilar, "chief of the demagogues," agitating in favor of Iturbide, according to Bustamante. Aguilar was very active in the desperate last attempt by the tottering empire to strengthen its popular support, as will be seen in the next chapter. He was made colonel of some militia battalions quickly recruited among the lowermost strata of the capital's population. A few days after Iturbide's abdication, while the deposed emperor was still in the capital awaiting a decision as to his future, there was a large disturbance by léperos in the barrios of San Pablo and La Palma against the troops of the Liberating Army from Veracruz that had defeated the imperials and were entering the town. Father Aguilar was the chief of the mutiny, which cost several dead and wounded. In a pamphlet written three years after the events, another anonymous writer concerned about public peace remembered the battalions recruited by Iturbide, "with the name of the four barrios," led by Aguilar, sworn enemy of freedom. The barrios were those of San Pablo and Santo Tomás La Palma, plus the Salto del Agua, all of them constantly referred to by the literature of the times; the fourth one was probably Santa Cruz Acatlán, near the garita de San Antonio Abad in the southeast. They were the poorest in the city, with the exception of the northern suburb of Santiago Tlatelolco, which was more Indian and appears to have been less marked by Iturbidista agitation.[42]

Clerical elements involved in agitational politics were especially of two types: the small-town or rural priests, such as Hidalgo, Morelos, and Matamoros, who provided leadership for a very violent and potentially revolutionary insurgency; and the more obscure friars, operating in the larger urban concentrations as transmission belts for populist movements of the Right. All of them competed with the radical liberals such as the Pensador Mexicano or the Payo del Rosario, as well as with more pragmatic populists emerging from the ranks of the people, such as Vicente Guerrero.

Anticlericalism

The strength of the church and the friars produced the reaction of anticlericalism, which was mostly an affair of the urban middle classes, with some possibility of occasionally involving the lower strata. On the forefront of the struggle were such intellectuals as José María Luis Mora and José Joaquín Fernández de Lizardi. Mora operated at a more sophisticated and cultured level among his peers in the upper middle class, though he also produced books and periodicals for wider consumption. Lizardi argued that his writings were addressed to "viejas y gentes de capote rabón," in contrast to the more learned texts found in the pages of *El Sol*, in a somewhat exaggerated underevaluation of his readers' intellectual attainments.

Mora began as a moderate, especially in matters pertaining to the mobilization of the popular classes in politics, but he always had a definite anticlerical attitude. In 1831 he prepared a learned brochure in response to an invitation by the state of Zacatecas, where he outlined a possible program of reform. This was a preparation for the intense months of the Gómez Farías government of 1833–34, as we will see. El Pensador, on the other hand, started soon after independence (in February 1822) to attack the church, writing a *Defensa de los Francmasones*, prompted by the republication in Mexico of the papal bulls of 1738 and 1751, condemning freemasonry. The clerical reminder of the existence of those bulls was an attempt at stemming the victory, in the December 1821–January 1822 elections, of the anti-Iturbidista liberals, most of whom had political masonic connections, since they were organized into the Escocés lodges. The church thus was issuing a warning; though it could not influence the elections themselves, it was just in time to have an impact on the convening members of the new congress, which opened its sessions toward the end of February.

An anonymous author, perhaps Lizardi himself, published at about the same time a lighter and similarly titled tract, *Triunfo de los francmasones*, in which he defiantly stated that it did not matter if those who won were accused of being "francmasones, jacobinos, volterianos, liberales, libertinos, jansenistas." Other moderate liberal publishers also responded to the church with more voluminous revisions of the past history of the freemasons and their persecution by the church, which they tried to show was unjustified, because the freemasons had actually generally been very much in favor of Christianity—until a part of their organization had fallen into the hands of "the infamous Luis Felipe de Orleans," who allowed it to be taken over by scoundrels such as Voltaire, D'Alembert, Diderot, and Condorcet.[43]

The reaction of church authorities was swift: on February 20 a Carmelite friar delivered a sermon against Lizardi in the cathedral, and that same day the pamphleteer was excommunicated, motivating a protest by him to the newly inaugurated Congress. He also said that he was unjustly being victimized, since nothing was being done about other tracts recently published on the same subject. The Junta de Censura Eclesiástica, which gave its verdict unanimously, was headed by the provisor Félix Flores Alatorre and included, among others, Miguel Guridi y Alcocer and two highly placed friars, one of them the *mercedario* Manuel Mercadillo. As the Pensador could be insistent, by the end of March he had already sent a second and even a third *Ocursos* to Congress presenting his case.[44]

In April a clerical pamphleteer, who signed his name "El Papista" and whom Lizardi suspected of being fray Mercadillo, the *mercedario* who had participated in the excommunicating Junta de Censura, attacked him with *Cascabeles al gato*, which started a long series of rejoinders and responses that kept the presses and the newsboys busy. Lizardi published four *Cartas . . . del Pensador al Papista*, where among other things he complained to the public that if he had been a rich man, like the conde de la Cortina, his freemason sympaties would have been overlooked. Finally, in his fourth and last *Carta*, of August 14, which was published together with a fifth *Ocurso* to the Congress, Lizardi challenged the Papista and the whole Junta de Censura Eclesiástica to an open debate at the university. He affixed red posters to that effect in several parts of the city, which produced millings and discussions of curious passers-by.[45] A few days afterward, he also presented a *Satisfacción del Pensador al Soberano Congreso,* reminding the legislature that five months had passed and no decision had yet been made. In the special commission where the matter was debated, the Iturbidista Antonio Mier y Villagómez, who "never spoke," attacked the Pensador, as did others, except Carlos María de Bustamante, a respected old rival who, however, was silenced by the majority. Lizardi also warned the Congress that if the matter were sent to the Audiencia, justice could not be expected, because in it sat Flores Alatorre's own brother.[46]

The proposed dispute at the university was never held, but it gave rise to another wave of pamphlets, none of them very serious, as each of them was trying to appeal to a broad public in search of emotions and entertainment rather than arguments. Signed by a certain "Bachiller Esmeregildo

Fernández," an apparently voluntary ironical misspelling of the author's real name, Hermenegildo, a very well printed pamphlet issued by the Imprenta Imperial heaped scorn on the Pensador and his procuring a passport, suggesting that he was planning to go to the United States. This was soon followed by another pamphlet by the same author, this time with his name correctly spelled, announcing the untimely death of the Pensador, and by two other anonymous productions, one of them lamenting the imprisonment and travails of the Pensador, the other pretending to be a defense by his "*aprendiz.*"[47]

Lizardi could not remain silent in the face of this barrage, so he invented a fictitious character from San Pablo, who said that, being a tanner, he had gone a few days previously to buy some materials, when he heard a boy soliciting prayers for the soul of the dead Pensador; then he had a dream and saw that the author was a filthy friar. This of course was immediately followed, probably by "Esmeregildo" Fernández, who gave life to another "guapo" answering to the one that had come up in defense of the Pensador. This one said he was born and had lived his whole life in the barrio de San Pablo, famous in the art of stone-throwing; he challenged his rival to a contest in the ill-famed Plazuela de la Viña, early the next day. Lizardi retorted with a "*limonazo*" by his first *sanpableño* against the other one, where the intellectual level of discourse rose a bit higher; the imaginary tanner maintained that the excommunion was invalid, as was the latest encyclical condemning the dismemberment of the Spanish empire. Finally the Pensador made a list, in another pamphlet, of his enemies, answering each one of them individually.[48]

The dispute continued, being occasionally obscured by political events that also vehemently involved its participants. At the end of October 1822, Lizardi published a *Segunda defensa de los Francmasones*, purportedly a letter he received from a friend in La Habana and timed to appear when the Congress was about to be closed down by Iturbide. At that time, while continuing to support the empire, he was trying to express some sympathy for the oppositionists, who could be considered "freemasons," and against whose imprisonment he had written a tract.[49]

The last convulsions of the empire made the religious dispute recede, but soon after the collapse, another Carmelite friar preached against the excommunicated Pensador, who admonished him to keep to religious subjects in his sermons. Finally the matter was taken up by the Audiencia, which declared Lizardi free of excommunication. So he informed the public, with a "rotulón," or bill, which he distributed and affixed as usual.[50]

Lizardi (never out of trouble) continued to have difficulties with the inquisitors. By mid-1825 he was warned again that his writings were heretical, and he was given a week to recant. He asked for three months' time to reflect and engaged in theological discussions in further pamphlets. He also took the opportunity of some political events in Guatemala to renew his attacks on the clergy, who "are not so much to be feared for being friars, or clerics, but due to the consideration they get from the more fanatic part of the populace."[51]

Meanwhile Lizardi had become involved in a secondary fight against José María Aza, a Spaniard of liberal opinions, who had been decidedly anti-Iturbidista and who had suffered persecution because of it, ending up as an "*escribiente*" in a *fonda*, surely one of those people who wrote letters for illiterates.[52] Aza, beginning by November 1825, trying to exploit the same market off which Lizardi and Villavicencio lived, started a series of tracts called *Enójanse los compadres y sácanse las verdades*, in which he picked on both of them, though at moments pretending to be a friend of the Payo.[53] He went into the long history of Lizardi's changing attitudes, emphasizing his attacks against the insurgentes during viceregal times, as well as his Iturbidismo; in other words, publicly washing his "trapitos," in an extremely aggressive tone. Aza said that Lizardi had attacked liberalism and religious tolerance in 1813 and that now he was attacking the church, in both cases out of opportunism, thus he could not be considered a "true" (*sano*) liberal.[54] He also recalled how the Pensador had gone to Cuernavaca during the Lobato revolt of 1824, attempting to participate in the uprising, and then came back very peacefully, after the defeat of the attempt.

Aza, despite his liberalism, was also trying to cater to the clerical public, which explains some of his titles and the objects of his invectives. As Aza was using the printing press of that other cultivator of public feelings, Juan Cabrera, the Pensador answered to both in several tracts, accusing Aza of being a maromero who had worked for Manuel de la Bárcena, Iturbidista governor of the Michoacán bishopric, a noted monarchist. He soon added a very meticulous record of his sufferings for freedom, that is, the whole story seen from another perspective, attested by such prominent republican figures as Vicente Guerrero, Anastasio Bustamante, Vicente Filisola (who in March 1825 had named him capitán retirado for his past services), Miguel Barragán, José María Lobato (a fly in the ointment, but just to show who his friends were), and none other than president Guadalupe Victoria himself.[55] An overreaction, perhaps, but more was yet to come. As Aza continued his attacks, Lizardi finally went to the printing office, reportedly with a gun, to dispose of or more probably only to intimidate his enemies, but he was calmed down by the Payo, who happened to be there also.[56] Lizardi tried to belittle the whole affair, but Aza then retorted with a thorough résumé of the Pensador's career.[57]

In the latter part of 1825, Lizardi was appointed editor of the official *Gaceta*. Political tension was on the increase, with the rise of the Yorkino lodges; their activity produced a reaction from moderate circles, who were planning legislation to ban all masonic organization in politics. Though the Escoceses were also based on masonic structures, the really widespread political organization was that of the Yorkinos, whose network reached popular levels. For the more elitist Escoceses, it was easy to replace masonic gatherings with small, private meetings, so they would win with the ban.

Given these circumstances, the Pensador in May 1826 came out again in a second "salida" in defense of the freemasons. For one thing, he wrote in defense of the Payo, who was also being attacked as a heretic for his campaign for religious tolerance; he also published a *Verdadera defensa de los Francmasones* which, as usual, had a combined religious and political aim.[58] The clericals, of course, and not only the moderate-liberal Escoceses, were also in favor of lodge suppression; though the measure was aimed at a political organization of an increasingly populist character, discussion had to take theological overtones. The Pensador was able to deflect the church's attack more easily this time; to prove his orthodoxy, toward the end of the year he started a serial, *Correo Semanario de México*, devoted to recounting the lives of the popes (admittedly a risky subject), with only a few matters of current social interest. The main argument against the lodges, though, was that by planning political activities in secrecy, they were acting subversively.

Elections and Early Party Organization

Popular elections were a new thing for Spain and its American possessions at the beginning of the nineteenth century. One may wonder why the Cádiz constitution gave them such a central position and why successive regimes on both sides of the Atlantic continued to hold them, if in practice they were so often reduced to formalities, with no capacity to introduce changes in the ruling personnel. To some extent they were a concession to the spirit of the times, a ritualized but soon distorted copy of practices that were anchored in very different social conditions. The question is particularly relevant because universal (or almost universal) male suffrage was a rarity in those times.

To understand the predicament of the Spanish Cortes, it must be kept in mind that they were the expression of a revolutionary situation, in a country waging a war of national survival against foreign invasion. Under those circumstances, it was necessary to mobilize popular support, and one way of doing it was to give the people the vote. But were the people really so interested in having the vote? And how did the process of their mobilization take place? It can be hypothesized that the really strategic group that had to be given a stake in government was not the "people" themselves, but the local leaders who were capable of recruiting them and establishing with them a relationship of caudillismo, based on either traditional or modern patterns of leadership. Thus under wartime conditions, two types of what may be called protopopulist nuclei emerged: one led by the clerics and one by the more radical, or *"exaltado,"* liberals. Even the clerical nucleus had a mobilizational or populist character, as it had to inspire people to fight under conditions of a weak or nonexistent national government, when a good portion of the conservative elites had defected to the enemy. Clerical populism was not the same thing as the more traditional conservatism led by time-hallowed notables, though in more peaceful times both could converge.

The problem, after more or less normal conditions returned, was how to accommodate the middle-level or grass-roots mobilizational leaders, from the Right or the Left. If restricted suffrage were adopted, there would be no place for them, since they could not obtain the support of the better-off part of the population. With extended or almost universal suffrage, they had a good chance to compete, though it was not a totally easy contest, as the notables also had some capacity to garner popular sentiment.

The Cádiz constitution, then, adopted the prestigious but long-since-rejected French revolutionary model of 1791, giving the suffrage to all adult males descended from the populations of Spain's possessions in Europe, America, or Asia, thus eliminating blacks and mulattoes, which in Spain itself had no significance and only a marginal one in Mexico. Thus, the Cádiz constitution became the paradigm of progressivism, adopted in the Spanish-speaking world and also in Portugal and Naples, when these countries went through their liberal revolutions in 1820. The only restriction to male universal suffrage, apart from the racial one (aimed especially at colonies with large slave populations), was that domestic servants were deprived of the vote, to avoid excessive influence by their masters. Voters were also required to have a job or independent economic activity, and illiterates were given ten years to learn the alphabet, if they wanted to keep their rights. Rural workers, who in areas such as Mexico were usually called servants, were explicitly differentiated from personal servants such as cooks and other house domestics "de escaleras abajo" and were assured a vote.[59]

The constitution itself did not specify whether the vote was to be secret or open, but laws and regulations made it mandatory that the vote should be openly expressed. Again this was a widely accepted practice at the time, as it was thought that responsible citizens should be able to express their opinions publicly and that open voting was less liable to later ballot manipulation. It is not clear whether this argument was seriously believed, since it was so obvious that salaried dependents and tenants could be swayed by their employers. Probably this mechanism was preferred, because it lent some moderation and stability to popular decisions. But the people could also be influenced by agitational leaders, especially in conditions of war-induced mobilization. Moreover, not all members of the popular classes were employed dependents of the wealthy or their tenants in rural areas. There were many smallholders, independent artisans, transport entrepreneurs, and their own employees, as well as street vendors and the semiemployed, to be reckoned with. The strategic social actors, though, who have to be taken into account in order to understand the rationale behind elections with a wide potential electorate, were the above-noted phalanx of popular leaders and agitators from both the Right and the Left, who had emerged in Spain during the war of independence against Napoleon and in America under similar circumstances. They were a destabilizing factor, always ready (or easily tempted) to return to violent practices and thus participate in coups, revolutions, or other kinds of civic affrays. In order to channel them into more acceptable forms of political participation, not only elections, but also their incorporation into militias had to be legislated and carefully watched over. We will later return to the subject of militias.

The first elections held in Mexico during the revolutionary era took place previous to the Spanish constitution. The Spanish Central Junta convened them according to traditional practices, asking the existing ayuntamientos, organized by provinces, to send delegates. The erstwhile colonies had an important representation in the Constituent Cortes, though considerably less than their numbers would have warranted. The Americans were a deciding factor in many legal controversies, often holding the balance between liberals and conservatives. Once the constitution was sanctioned, orders were given to hold elections in the Americas. In Mexico Viceroy Venegas convoked them for November 1812, when the complex indirect system of representation, lasting about a month between primary and tertiary gatherings, would be started. The election of "electors" at the parroquia level gave a great majority to Americans, thus inflicting a resounding defeat to the royal authorities. Venegas, with the argument that undue "influence" via the ill-famed "cédulas" had been exerted, suspended the application of the secondary and tertiary gatherings (at the partido and province levels), while the Audiencia decided on the legality of the process.[60]

The Audiencia found no grounds for annulment, a decision it came to coincident with the assumption of viceregal powers (then defined merely as those of jefe político of the intendencia of Mexico) by Calleja, in April 1813. So the election of the ayuntamientos and the "electors" proceeded, as did the further meetings at the partido and province levels (secondary and tertiary juntas), with the foreseeable results, based on the primary elections of late November. As mentioned above, Calleja, though commanding the royalist troops, had been (and probably still was) tempted to join at least a faction of the rebels in leading the country toward a moderate form of independence. So it is not too surprising that he allowed public opinion to express itself, and as a result practically no Spaniard got elected. The majority favored the opposition criollo politicians, some of them even suspected of subversion (though at the same time with a record of past collusions with Calleja). In a sense Calleja was creating a set of acceptable go-betweens for himself, both locally and in the Cortes.

By the end of 1813, new elections for the Ayuntamiento had to be held (they took place every year). The Pensador Mexicano, a few months out of prison, due to his *proclama* in favor of Calleja, was getting ready, following his zig-zagging political strategies, to participate in the formation of public opinion, donning for the moment the mantle of moderation, advising the electorate to let some *gachupines* enter the cabildo.[61] The whole experience, however, was cut short by the resumption of authoritarian rule on the peninsula in 1814, and no more was heard about elections until a thousand flowers were allowed to bloom in 1820. This time, with the Insurgencia practically wiped out, freedom of the press was more genuinely granted, and the electoral process was again set in motion.

As mentioned above, however, the system was highly indirect, so that public opinion had a chance of being "distilled" (*alambicada*) through three levels. The basic polling meetings, or primary asemblies (called parochial), elected a number of electors proportional to the population. These then proceeded, the next week, to the *cabecera de partido*, where a secondary assembly was held and electors were selected for a general gathering at the provincial capital. There, the following week, the tertiary assembly took place; it appointed the deputies for the Cortes, as well as the seven members of the local provincial diputación (a collective executive to cooperate with the jefe político). The same system served for municipal government, as the primary electors who had been appointed by the citizenry in the parochial assemblies also had the responsibility of designating the members of the ayuntamiento. In large cities it was not possible to convene all citizens of one parroquia in one place, so smaller gatherings took place where *compromisarios* were elected, and these in turn met at the parish level, where they voted for their electors.

At that time polling was not understood, as it is today, to be an event that could take place at any time throughout the whole day. Though the booths remained open, the basic proceedings took the form of a local gathering, when most people would assemble at the same time. To create the right mood, it was mandated that in each parroquia the voting should start with a solemn mass, thus practically requiring everybody to be present, including the curate and the civil authorities (that is, the alcalde or the jefe político, in the more important places). Then people would go en masse to the polling station, where, under the direction of a member of the ayuntamiento, the gathering would select four of their number to act as controllers. Those with a right to vote (all resident adult males except blacks, castas, domestic servants, and those without a known living) then proceeded to vote, writing the names of their preferred candidates on slips of paper or bringing the slips of paper already written. The rest of the day was reserved for late-comers or those from the countryside. Local authorities and the curate were there to see that only those effectively residing in the locality (and no domestic servant or casta) were admitted to the proceedings.

In traditional Hispanic societies, public gatherings were seen as potentially subversive, unless they were held for religious purposes; even then, festivities had always been suspected of giving rise to disorders and protests, perhaps with the help of some alcohol. There was a whole body of conservative thinking that condemned the indiscriminate use of the right of assembly, unless it was strictly controlled by the state. According to an anonymous Puebla writer, the "clubs," allegedly already corrupt in the English tradition and later abused in revolutionary France and in Spain, even when "inspired by the purest and patriotic intentions," were nothing more than tumultuous assemblies made up of people of both sexes and all classes and ages, where one or more speakers rise, and address the crowd with improvised speeches . . . Who has given to a private individual the authority to harangue the people, to publicly comment on the laws, and to examine and censor the government's conduct? [In Spain] the lowest plebs was flattered, so as to rule with its support and in its name . . . [Typically speakers] refer to the unequal division of wealth, the opulence of the powerful, the misery of the poor . . . and other such cliches which lend themselves to declamation.[62]

The right to address oneself to the public, according to this theory, belonged only to the magistrates. Even private associations for the pursuit of limited goals, such as artisan guilds, literary associations, or commercial companies, were only legitimate if controlled by the government.

With such an attitudinal background, electoral gatherings could only mean trouble most of the time, especially when there was an incongruence between the sovereignty ascribed to the people on paper and their submissive role in everyday life. If the polls had been restricted to property holders, there would have been no such inconsistency between the realm of legitimate political power and that of social stratification. In later years José María Luis Mora, the noted moderate liberal thinker, derived quite a logical consequence from this perception: voting rights had to be restricted only to those holding some property or having an equivalent occupational position. He argued that at the time (the late 1820s) elections with no property requirements were only prevalent, or had been applied, in the most backward countries, such as Spain, Portugal, Naples, and Spanish America, or in the more advanced ones, such as the United States. The standards of education and public responsibility found in the United States being obviously unattainable in the foreseeable future, it was necessary to follow the British or French (Restoration) models, making electoral power more parallel to economic, social, and cultural prominence and thus capable of really influencing society.[63]

In his analysis of why these Latin countries had adopted such a wide franchise, Mora thought the cause lay in the tendency to copy prestigious models from abroad or in acting according to theories without accepting the constraints of reality. Actually, though such factors may have been present, the fact that these were societies just out of a revolutionary armed struggle should also be taken into consideration. Elections were functional alternatives to insurrection, in which an opportunity was given to those who had become leaders in armed struggle to continue practicing their capacity for mass leadership. If they accepted a minimum of rules of the game, these leaders might have a chance to compete for positions in national or local government with the traditional conservatives or the moderate liberals, both of them more clearly linked to the establishment, old or new.

In the 1820 Mexican elections, royal government, as in 1812–13, was again unable to influence the outcome. Probably this was because it was higly divided. After all liberalism on the peninsula had been established at the point of the sword, and in America as well the troops were subject to strong masonic and liberal infiltration. Attitudes toward the church were also divided, as the Spanish government was going through a confrontation with the clergy; but many officials must still have been rather favorable toward its retention of temporal privileges. The result then was that elections gave widely different results in different parts of the country. In Mexico City liberal candidates, many of them with past associations with the Insurgencia, were victorious. In other areas, such as Puebla, the clergy could organize itself to obtain a majority.

The "abuse" of distributing printed leaflets with the names of candidates, for voters to use as ballots to copy at the booths, was stigmatized by a clerical pamphleteer from Mexico City. He added the more serious grievance that house servants had been sent to vote and that some people kept returning to the poll to repeat the expression of their preferences. What is surprising is that such innocent tactics as the distribution of leaflets with the lists of candidates, pushed into the hands even of those who did not ask for them, should have been so strongly condemned. This was surely part of the slow adaptation to party politics, which also took some time to be accepted in such places as Great Britain or the United States. The prevalent idea, particularly among conservative and clerical circles, was that the influence spontaneously deriving from the notables should be left to operate without outside interference. "Outside interference," however, was very much in operation, and not only from the radical liberals, but also from certain sectors of the church itself, which were trying to imitate the new methods. In Puebla in 1820, the clericals were victorious, and there it was the liberals' turn to complain about distortions in the public will. An anonymous tract (published in the Imprenta Liberal, owned by the very moderately liberal Troncoso brothers) stated that "the right outcome of the elections presupposes . . . a free will not deflected by extraneous influences, a condition not fulfilled by the late ones . . . Comparing the three we have had, we can easily see that the bad mood, the fickle mood, has been on the increase." It added another argument that would later become commonplace: "The first selections of the people [in primary assemblies] are always healthy, but their compromisarios abuse public confidence" and in successive secondary and tertiary asssemblies end up by appointing those who influence them, even if they are unknown to the original voters. The author finally advised the liberals to refrain from participating in the next elections, so as not to legitimize them. As long as they were accused of being "impious and heretics" and the people believed such nonsense, it was impossible for them to be elected. From Michoacán as well there were complaints about the excessive organization of some political groups.[64]

The following year, 1821, starting with the Plan de Iguala, and from that time on arms, not ballots, would speak, until the liberation of the capital in September, when electoral politics once again caught everybody's attention.

Electoral Preparations at Independence

Strange as it may seem, it was not thought at the time that elections would automatically produce results in favor of the government, perhaps because the government (the five-member Regencia) was not homogeneous and therefore had no single will to impose on others. So it was important to devise methods that could help shift opinion in one's behalf. A pro-Iturbidista and clerical tract, called with the self-explanatory (though probably disingenuous) title of *El tribuno de la plebe, o escritor de los pelados*, warned against the use of printed ballots, as in the previous Cortes elections, when an organized group, presumably liberal and masonic, had done a bit of social engineering from its headquarters in the Calle de Santa Clara. The paper recommended trusting in the candidates supported by the Liberator.

One clerical writer, early in October 1821, suggested that it was unnecessary to go through the complex "distillation" of primary voters' opinions in secondary and tertiary assemblies. He was trying to respond to a certain demand for more direct elections, which was already being promoted, among others, by the Pensador. The clerical writer, who turned out to be a certain Dr. J. E. Fernández, proposed maintaining the election of *personeros*, compromisarios, or parochial electors in primary assemblies, more or less as stated by the Cádiz constitution. But once these personeros were selected, they should get together in the parroquia itself and vote directly for deputies. The results should be recorded in a list, and then sent, with two of the personeros, to the cabecera de partido, where together with the others from the rest of the partido, partial results would be added up and a composite list prepared, with the total number of votes received. From each partido two selected personeros would take these composite lists to the provincial capital, where a general summing up would be performed, and those with the most votes would become deputies. In this way, rather than having secondary and tertiary assemblies, only the additions of partial voting results would be performed by representatives sent from the localities. These, then, rather than having as in the Cádiz constitution the responsibility of collectively deciding whom to select, only had the task of controlling the accurate collection and summation of partial results. There would be less occasion for cabals and alliances between factions; political leaders well known throughout the state would have more chance of getting elected over local sons. Dr. Fernández also proposed that those found distributing printed lists of candidates or requesting other people's votes would lose their electoral rights. He also thought that only those people resident for more than five years in the locality should have the right to vote, thus reducing the role of the shifting population attracted or repelled by the many oscillations of the labor market and likely to be influenced by agitational leaders.[65]

The Pensador immediately responded, in a long series that was almost a book, called *Ideas Políticas y Liberales*. In his usual obstreperous way, he started with a proposal that people found tinkering with electoral results should be shot immediately during polling day, after being allowed one hour to make peace with their creator. This proposal was not calculated to ingratiate the Pensador with the more serious sector of the Mexican intelligentsia; it had another public in mind, a public that must have savored these flights of the imagination. Such excesses formed an integral part of what I have earlier called "democratic authoritarianism," a pattern surely widespread among the lower sectors of the social pyramid.

More to the point, Lizardi proposed direct elections, without personeros or indirect representatives of any sort. Each individual would vote for just one candidate for deputy to the Cortes, and his written vote, which had to include his own name, would be pasted on a board for all to see, so that afterwards it would be more difficult to ignore or alter the results. This system was designed to avoid intermediation, cabals, and the influence of parties or organizations bent on forging alliances behind the scenes so as to win a majority in secondary or tertiary assemblies. Lizardi gave the example of Oaxaca, where the last elections during the constitutional period had been "*canónico-mercantiles*," that is, manipulated by a combination of clerics and merchants against the more immediate expression of the popular will in the primary meetings. The idea was to enable the voters themselves to select the deputies, fixing their attention on people well known in the province, bypassing the local notables. Notables could of course get some votes from their neighbors and clients, but if they were not widely known in the state they would not be able to accumulate enough preferences. The proposed system was especially appropriate for new men who might have risen to prominence through the war or through pamphleteering or newspaper editing. These same ideas were repeated by Fernández de Lizardi in a brochure addressed to Iturbide, where special emphasis was put on the need to conduct direct elections.[66]

Fernández answered him, picking, of course, on the easy target of the shooting proposal, but claiming that one hour was not enough for repentance. He also counterargued that if direct elections were held with no personeros, rural votes would be wasted, because in the pueblos and haciendas, national or provincial figures were not well known. Only in larger urban centers, where voters would concentrate on prestigious personalities, could there be an effective summation of direct popular preferences. Thus, he continued, the Pensador's system would give undue advantage to urban votes over rural ones.[67]

Lizardi came back with a *Bombazo*, arguing for the *n*th time that the people do not normally commit mistakes; rather it was the intermediaries who distorted or sold out the public interest. In his optimistic belief in human nature, he added that it was more difficult to fool a multitude than a small number of individuals, a maxim reflected in the dictum "Vox populi vox Dei." He quoted the "philosopher of Geneva" as saying that any laws enacted by representatives were null and void, because the popular will could only be expressed directly. He admitted, however, that due to the corruption of the times, much intensified since the days of "cultivated Rome," some form of representation was necessary; that is, deputies should exist, but they should be directly elected by the people themselves.[68]

There were others, on the opposite side, who argued that a broad franchise in the elections of ayuntamientos, direct or indirect, tended to fill the councils with "sastres, tenderos o zapateros," who became haughty and refrained from paying due respect to their functional superiors in the administration of justice, the *jueces de letras*. Such alcaldes and regidores, scarcely knowing how to conduct their own private affairs, let alone those of the municipality, committed countless blunders and did not accept correction. In fact, when reprimanded, they insulted the jueces de letras "in indecorous terms, and instigated the plebs . . . to pay no heed" to authorities. The newly independent country should put a stop to those abusive practices, which had already been observed during the constitutional period under Spanish rule. A sector of conservative public opinion was thus being formed; it aimed at curtailing the powers of municipalities, which could easily fall into the hands of popular factions.[69]

Meanwhile Iturbide was proposing a system of elections that would break totally with the Spanish constitution by adopting corporatist representation. He would have had a total of 120 deputies, elected by special groups as follows:

1. 18 ecclesiastics, half of them representing the cathedral cabildos, that is, the high clergy; the other half elected by the parish curates;

2. 10 labradores, elected according to the Spanish constitution, but only including propertyholders and arrendatarios having the right to vote (this would have excluded Indian pueblo residents, except for those who rented lands in haciendas);

3. 10 miners, appointed "in the way they do it ordinarily," that is, through the diputaciones de minería;

4. 10 artisans, following the Spanish constitution, but only including masters with an open shop;

5. 10 merchants, 2 by each consulado, including two new ones to be created in Puebla and Campeche;

6. 9 military men, one from each estado mayor (infantry, cavalry, dragoons, artillery, and Campeche) and three from the navy apostaderos of Veracruz, San Blas, and Campeche;

7. 24 public officials, namely the jefe político and the intendente of each one of the 9 provinces, plus 3 from each one of the audiencias of Mexico and Guadalajara;

8. 18 intellectuals and professionals, 4 from the University of Mexico, 2 from that of Guadalajara, 2 from a Casa de Estudios in Campeche, 2 from the Colegio de Abogados, 2 from the Protomedicato, and 2 from each one of the remaining six dioceses, one of them appointed by the bishop and the other by the jefe político (there was a mistake in this sum, as the total would have been 24 rather than 18);

9. 2 members of the nobility, presumably selected by their peers; and

10. 9 representatives from the Indian pueblos, elected according to the Spanish constitution.[70]

At the time, corporatist ideas had some legitimacy, and even the Pensador, in his *Ideas Políticas y Liberales*, approved them in principle, though the electoral methods he preferred were hardly compatible with the theory. He considered society to be divided into eight branches or occupational corporations, namely, religion, militia, marine, agriculture, sciences, arts, commerce, and mining. One-eighth of the legislative seats would be allotted to each; but it was not clear how universal suffrage would produce such an evenly balanced result, as he was not suggesting that each corporation vote separately.

The liberal press, as could be expected, disagreed with the Liberator. The argument was made, in a learned and moderate vein, by Sánchez de Tagle in the *Semanario Político y Literario de México*, rejecting corporatism on principle as a method for representing national opinion. In a more direct reference to economic interests, the Puebla diputación, at that time in the hands of a liberal faction, argued that too much weight was given to the artisans in Iturbide's proposal, and that they would surely take advantage of it to impose protectionism on the nation's consumers. On a more popular level, the *Hombre Libre*, a radical liberal paper, published a jocose dialogue between a friar and his assistant (*pilhuanejo*), in which the latter complained that Iturbide did not give the likes of him an adequate representation, adding that "we are no longer now as we were ten years ago," implying that modern times had arrived and that now all were equal.[71] This attitude of course did not necessarily reflect those of the real "pilhuanejos," or common people, but rather those attributed to them by radical liberal writers. Quite a few of the common people, it would seem, did have a liking for Iturbide, but this had nothing to do with any pretensions to the right to vote; and that popular liking was not repaid by Iturbide in any constitutional provisions which would have put a significant number of congressional seats within reach of such people. The connection that was being created between the caudillo and his followers was of another sort, which involved occasional mass action and the repayment of individual efforts through clientelage, not faith in any particular type of elections.

Finally the junta decided on a system of elections that was a compromise between various proposals, only secondarily taking into account Iturbide's corporatist ideas. Basically the system adopted was very much based on the Cádiz constitution, but with the following alterations:

1. Parochial primary elections were retained, entrusted with the task of choosing electors, or personeros; but the latter, rather than

proceeding to the secondary assemblies at the partido level, elected the ayuntamiento, thus inevitably focusing their preferences on
local notables or other local people such as the "sastres, tenderos
or zapateros" about whom so many complained. But in any case,
they would be local people, whose responsibility would be en-
sured by their having to discharge municipal duties;

2. The newly appointed ayuntamientos (whatever their population) designated from among their ranks one elector to proceed to
the secondary assemblies in the cabeceras de partido; in the cabeceras the assemblies were formed by the representatives of the
parroquias' ayuntamientos, plus the members of the cabecera's
own ayuntamiento, thus giving the cabecera extra weight. Similarly, at the tertiary level, the representatives from each partido
got together with the capital city's ayuntamiento to vote for
national deputies and then for the provincial diputación, the
seven-member local authority. The process of "distillation" or
filtering of public opinion, then, gave a very strategic role to the
municipalities, which all things considered implied a conservative
bias, though of course it could backfire (as any electoral system
can unless held under a restricted franchise or a heavily corporatist adjudication of seats);

3. The number of deputies for each province would not be proportional to their population but to the number of partidos they
had (with two deputies being elected for every three partidos).
This gave overrepresentation to some geographically large but
sparsely populated provinces, such as Durango and Arizpe (later
divided into Sonora and Sinaloa), which together received 31
representatives out of a total of 162, more than the province of
Mexico, which was allotted 28 deputies;

4. All "castas" were given the vote, thus eliminating the restriction included in the Spanish constitution;

5. The vote would be openly expressed in the primary gatherings
and secretly only in the secondary ones;

6. As a concession to Iturbide's corporatist concerns, a certain
balance of professional representation was established for each
province. Thus, for example, of the 27 deputies elected by the
province of Mexico, at least one had to be an ecclesiastic, one a
military man, one a lawyer, one a miner, one a nobleman, and one
a mayorazgo; the remaining 21 would be unrestricted. These ·
proportions were to be taken into account by the rather small
tertiary assemblies of each province, where voting could easily be
attuned to the requirements.[72]

4

Popular Caesarism

Cleavage Lines

The first elections held in independent Mexico, between December 1821 and January 1822, resulted in a very heterogeneous Congress, with no single group predominant. Once again the government could not impose itself, because there was no uniform governmental will. Power was very much divided between Iturbidistas, conservative clericals (not all of them necessarily Iturbide partisans, though increasingly supporting him), liberals divided into moderates and radicals, and republicans with an Insurgente past. Criss-crossing those ideological divisions, or occasionally coinciding with them, provincial or regional interests also expressed themselves.

In the period between the liberation of the capital (September 27, 1821) and the end of March 1822, when it became known that Spain had rejected the Treaty of Córdoba, there was a testing of forces in readiness for the main alternatives, either crowning a European or American monarch or establishing a republic. On October 7 and 8, 1821, there were massive demonstrations in Puebla, engineered by the clerics in favor of crowning Iturbide. An anonymous pamphleteer who recorded the event noted that it was not the rich and the powerful who had called for Iturbide on that occasion, but rather the humble. They had carried portraits of Iturbide, and they had asked for the cathedral's bells to be tolled, which was accepted by the bishop and also by the jefe político and the commandant, so it could not be said (as surely it was by the opposition) that it had been a seditious gathering. Another author remembered that a thousand times the multitude had acclaimed Iturbide emperor, and that its being an unlettered opinion did not detract from its validity.[1] Clerical populist support was expressed in such brochures as *Yo no entiendo de estas cosas*, addressed to an uneducated public, where the previous viceregal authorities were accused of having almost destroyed religion by applying the liberal measures of the Spanish Cortes with the help of the Parián and the merchants, enemies of independence. In the same vein, an ironist published a tract in which he decried Iturbide for not establishing religious tolerance or a republic, probably mimicking some of the arguments heard in the cafes against the Liberator.

Also in 1821 two issues were published of a *Tribuno de la Plebe, o Escritor de los Pelados*, written in a popular style. It argued that the plebs was the better part of society, formed of "labradores, artisans, miners, arrieros, and all those who work for their sustenance," who were shouldering the main tax burden and had supported, in the larger cities, the armies of freedom (an overly kind historical interpretation). The pamphleteer differentiated, however, betwen the plebs and the "*vulgo*," the latter a very heterogeneous construct, as it included some rich men plus the populace of idlers, tricksters, beggars, and people with no trade. It warned against "corporations" and the excessive influx of clerics and lawyers, as well as against the strategy of distributing small leaflets (*cedulitas*) during elections so as to orient them through secret cabals. The author seems to face two enemies: on one hand clericalism, and on the other freemasonry, dominated at the time by the moderate liberals. To defeat them it was necessary to adopt an electoral system simpler than the Spanish one (a possible reference to direct elections) and to follow the guidelines of the Liberator.[2] In Puebla, as we have seen earlier, Iturbide could count on the Troncoso brothers, who though somewhat liberal favored his accession to the throne in an orderly way, and who were also concerned with the abuse of "cédula" distribution by political factions (in their case, the clericals).[3]

Iturbide, for his part, had since the beginning of his campaign against the royal government taken some measures destined to increase his popularity among his soldiers and wider sectors of the population. He had promised to distribute lands to those enlisted for more than six months, a usual procedure at the time, which also reflected the opinions of his adviser, Francisco Severo Maldonado. After the six months had elapsed, the capital having already been liberated, there was some agitation among the troops regarding the fulfillment of this promise; the general's partisans argued that it was not yet possible to do so, due to the presence of the Spaniards in San Juan de Ulúa.[4] Iturbide also tried to ingratiate the blacks, especially the royalist soldiers of Cuernavaca and Cuautla, which included the famous "negros de Yermo," who had been freed by their owner only to help shackle their brothers. The subject also preoccupied Fernández de Lizardi, who, as we have seen, thought that if they had been property owners they would have not defended the Spanish cause so consistently.[5]

Iturbide of course could not rely on most of the old Insurgente military leaders, whose memories made them uneasy in the new situation. Among them, he had placed only Guerrero in a high post in the army, as a reward for his role in the Plan de Iguala. The others were left in subordinate functions; thus men such as Ignacio López Rayón, Nicolás Bravo, Guadalupe Victoria, José Sixto Verduzco, Manuel Mier y Terán, and Juan Pablo Anaya, took to the opposition, principally the republicans. Guerrero, compelled by his official job as head of one of the five main subdivisions of the armed forces, seemed to support Iturbide's ascension, but without enthusiasm, and toward the end he was one of those responsible for his downfall.[6]

Among the civilian former Insurgentes, sympathy for Iturbide was not very widespread either, but there were important exceptions. Though Carlos María de Bustamante and Fray Servando were opposed, José Manuel de Herrera had become his private secretary during the campaign against Spanish rule and would become his main cabinet member. Something similar had happened to Andrés Quintana Roo, a well-established Yucatecan lawyer and journalist, one of the more relevant intellectuals of the Insurgencia and, in republican days, leader of the "party of progress." Like Herrera, he had come to his own conclusions about the need to curtail legislative excesses, which in the Hispanic American context were more likely to end up in a disrupting *frondisme* rather than consolidating public freedom. Thus soon after the coup of May 1822, Quintana Roo assumed the role of undersecretary of relations under Herrera, and he followed almost to the bitter end the authoritarian leadership of the emperor.

Of great significance for the future development of Iturbide's political formula was the presence in the liberating army, even before the occupation of the city of Mexico, of José Joaquín Fernández de Lizardi. His record of anticlericalism and populist politics was not designed to ingratiate him with the representative of clerical reaction, but Lizardi saw farther ahead, or had his own capacity for contradictions. He had abandoned Mexico City after trying to bore "from within" the viceregal regime. When his freedom to express himself through the press was curtailed, he decamped to the Trigarante Army in June 1821 and soon was urging Iturbide to crown himself emperor, dismissing the Treaty of Córdoba. For Iturbide this was a very important addition to his image, correcting the bad effects the former Insurgentes' ill will had on a certain sector of public opinion, a sector quite capable of taking to the streets. These were people mostly from the lower-middle-class or artisan level, who though they had done practically nothing concrete for the Insurgencia, had quite a bit of sympathy for it. Lizardi reflected their attitudes, and his entertaining pamphlets, read or listened to in bodegones, pulquerías, and cafes, enjoyed a wide audience.[7]

Another writer similar in many ways to the Pensador was Pablo Villavicencio, El Payo del Rosario, who arrived in Mexico City from a Sonoran real de minas in 1822, introducing himself thus:

> Yo no salgo a pelear escribidores
> ni a presumir tampoco de talento,
> ni ganas tengo de eso, no señores;
> que soy payo del puro tierra-adentro.
> Ansina me dijeron allá en casa
> que sus mercedes eran criticones;
> pero a mí ni cuidado se me da
> de sus mordidas y sus arañones.[8]

He immediately became a close friend of Lizardi. Carlos María de Bustamante did not like him, calling him "an abominable man . . . [who] supported every revolution in which he could get a slice."[9] He did support Iturbide during most of the latter's career, though with episodes of autonomy, criticizing his authoritarian tendencies. Immediately after independence, he argued, against a real or imaginary former insurgent who demanded recognition for his services, that the important thing was to bring matters to a successful conclusion, not just to initiate them, particularly if it had been done through "perfidious and tyrannical means." During the republic the Payo joined the populist politicians and became especially vocal in his anti-Spanish agitation.[10] The expulsion of Spaniards, of course, opened up many interesting positions for the aspiring native middle classes. The Payo also published a number of brochures and booklets on the life of the Liberator, including his *Memorias* (in 1827), apparently out of bibliographical curiosity, but surely with an eye to sales. He explained that he had edited whatever he had found about Iturbide, and he inveighed against those who scorned his memory: "Oh, Iturbide, never will my heart abandon your grave." Both the moderate-liberal *El Sol* and the radical *Correo de la Federación* considered these publications imprudent to say the least, but the Payo announced that he would return with more the following week, in a *Suplemento* to the *Memoria*. Some anonymous liberals took issue with him, pointing out that Iturbide had posed as a virtuous man and that the diffusion of his writings might again exert its "fascination [over] a fickle and ignorant people"; he should be shot again if he were raised from the dead. In an intermediate position was Luis Espino, a pamphleteer competing with the Pensador, the Payo, Rafael Dávila, and others for the attention of the public and who had followed a convoluted policy toward the regime. He considered the publication of the *Memorias* indiscreet, but the liberals' brochure venomous, since it was wrong to destroy the Liberator's reputation.[11]

Another journalist who joined Iturbide's camp and accompanied him in the adventure of the empire was Germán Prissette, a Frenchman persecuted in his country by the Restoration. It was most probably he who edited *La Minerva Mexicana* (in collaboration with Quintana Roo) and *La Sabatina Universal*, declaring in the latter that he was open to ideas from beyond the Pirenees and confident that there would be no Inquisition, thanks to "our most liberal Emperor." In the first issue of the Sabatina, started just after the May 1822 coup, he declared he was "alone," because *El Sol* had shut down and the *Hombre Libre* had followed suit like a little lamb. Both had been silenced by the government, due to their outspoken moderate-liberal position (the *Hombre Libre* being somewhat more progressive than *El Sol*). In a sense, then, Prissette (or Quintana Roo through him) was saying that he also considered himself a liberal, arguing that the other two papers had closed their doors frightened by "ghosts," an unnecessary alarm given the convictions of the "most liberal Emperor."

Prissette's support, like that of the Payo and the Pensador, was not without its nuances, because he pointed out the dangers of arbitrary power, especially deleterious for those who exercise it. But his support continued until the publication ended, before the close of 1822. When Prissette reappeared, in the *Aguila* in 1823 and especially in the *Archivista General* in 1824, he continued with a veiled defense of Iturbide. For Lizardi Prissette was a honorable patriot, while for Bustamante he was a "lunatic [*perlático*] Frenchman," a hireling of tyranny.[12] Prissette introduced himself as a "hermit [of San Cosme], a disciple of the one of the Chaussée d'Antin." In 1824 the Alamán ministry expelled him, together with other foreign radical liberals, and he died while passing through pestilential Veracruz. He probably was one of those liberals (like the irascible Julien Sorel of *Le Rouge et le Noir*) who could not overcome their memories of the time when Napoleon took the principles of the French Revolution to the farthest corners of the Old World. This authoritarian liberalism sought to impose the necessary social reforms through a strong executive, which required repressing the powerful vested interests that were sure to influence public opinion and especially a Congress made up of local notables. In contrast, moderate liberals mistrusted this proposed Leviathan and feared that it would not only infringe public freedoms but eventually also the functioning of the market and private property.

In this controversy *El Sol* took, as an example on which to peg its warnings, the *Estatuto*, or *Constitución Provisoria*, of Peru, sanctioned by General José de San Martín in his role as Protector. *El Sol* said, in its issue of January 5, 1822, that the "Statute" was in itself a good instrument; but why should it have been promulgated in such an authoritarian manner, without waiting for national representation to be convened? Andrés Quintana Roo, from the Iturbidista *La Minerva*, immediately picked up the gauntlet, stating that in times of crisis it was not possible to abide completely by formalities, because it was necessary to consolidate national power and unity, still threatened by the Spaniards in the Sierra. It was not clear to what extent this was so in Peru, but it did not matter: it was Iturbide, not San Martín, people had in mind. In Mexico there were practically no Spanish forces left, except in San Juan de Ulúa, but the possibility of a comeback was real enough. *El Sol* retorted, on January 16, with some exaggeration, that

> the Statute [was] a monument of tyranny and arbitrariness, contrary to every law and right, though, as we have already said, it may be more useful to those citizens that the laws a legitimate government could give them. . . . We agree that the meeting of a general congress would have retarded the benefits the people of Peru are receiving from the provisional statute; but it is also needful to confess that the wrongs which may result from such a usurpation of their first and principal rights are irremediable.

La Minerva responded, enlarging on its arguments, in an article signed by R. Q. A. (the initials of Andrés Quintana Roo backwards). It maintained that "the organization of representative assemblies is not the end of civil associations; it is only a means of ensuring the rights of their members . . . which supposes progress in society and the necessary lights . . . Let not your liberalism be scandalized by these maxims which are supported by a Condillac, a Mably, . . . before the degeneration of those ideas produced the sect of the false Gaditan liberals." He then repeated his earlier statement that it would have been dangerous, while Peru was still full of Spanish troops, to delegate power to a "numerous congress . . . [that] would only serve to obstruct the Executive Power, distract its attentions from the theater of war, and put in travail the passions . . . perhaps opening the doors to the expelled conquerors." In another brochure of the same time, Quintana Roo characterized monarchy as a desirable form of government, intermediate between republican democracy and absolute rule.[13]

Times of Confrontation

The months of April and May 1822 saw an increasingly open confrontation between Iturbide and the Congress, which was installed on February 24, after elections in which the executive was not able to obtain a committed majority, due to the lack of a strong enough political party or network of personal loyalties and connections. Some elements of such a network did exist, as a result of the months of war mobilization against the Spanish government (March–September 1821), but power was still very fragmented. The electoral system was indirect, with almost universal participation in theory but very low involvement in practice. In most places the local notables were able to impose their candidates. This gave great weight to the church and to the opinion that naturally emerged from the middle and upper-middle classes, which were adopting some variant of liberalism blended with concern for local issues, which also led to federalism.

Economic problems were of course paramount for the new government, though there was a great deal of optimism as to the future prospects of economic development. To reactivate the flagging mining industry, a reduction in the duties paid on silver was enacted, making the shortfall even worse. In the short run, then, it was necessary to appeal to heroic measures, such as imposing forced loans among the well-to-do, who of course were the only ones who had sizable amounts of cash at their disposal. The executive had to bear the responsibility for this measure, and it provoked a flurry of protests and demands for reconsideration. These were attended to by the junta, who tried to alleviate the impact on the taxpayers, suspending the collection of the loan and proposing that voluntary loans be obtained from the church and that funds in the estanco be diverted from crop financing to more pressing needs.[14]

When news of the rejection of the Treaty of Córdoba arrived, Iturbide, as president of the Regencia, immediately sent a circular to provincial authorities asking them what was to be done. A few days later (April 3 and 5) several sectors of the demobilized Spanish troops awaiting repatriation attempted a reaction in favor of Ferdinand VII, but they were repressed. This increased the prevalent fears about the security of independence and heated up the debate in Congress, with violent scenes between Iturbide and the opposition majority, yells of "traitor" being shouted from both sides. Vicente Gómez Farías, a Guadalajaran medical doctor and deputy from Zacatecas, played on that occasion an outstanding part in support of the generalísimo. However, the following week, on April

11, the Congress, in secret session, decided to replace three of the Iturbidista members of the Regencia—Pérez, Bárcena, and Velázquez de León—leaving, of course, Iturbide himself, in his position as president, and Yáñez, who leaned toward the liberals. The new entrants were two definite foes of the president, Nicolás Bravo and Manuel de Heras Soto, both moderate liberals, and the conservative-clerical, non-Iturbidista priest Miguel Valentín. At the same time, a commission of Congress speeded up drafting a *reglamento provisorio* that would make the command of troops incompatible with membership in the Regencia. To top it all, Congress decreed that public employees, which included military officers, had to swear allegiance to the Sovereign Congress, without mentioning the Plan de Iguala, thus giving the green light to a republic or even to religions toleration (expressly condemned by that plan and the now defunct Treaty of Córdoba).

Already in early May, a cavalry regiment, the 11th, led by Bravo, made a petition to Congress for the adoption of a republic. Iturbide, meanwhile, was preparing a demand for funds to consolidate his army, at almost thirty-six thousand enlisted men, threatening to resign if his needs were not met. Congress called his bluff; on May 17 it rejected his request, granting funds for only twenty thousand men. On May 18, in secret session, it approved the reglamento drafted by its commission, on the incompatibility between the command of troops and membership in the Regencia. This was too much; that same night the coup broke loose, with the help of noncommissioned officers such as Pío Marcha, who recruited a following from the poorer sections of the city in the south and southeast (San Pablo, La Palma, Salto del Agua), including the zone near the garita of San Antonio Abad (Santa Cruz Acatlán, Necatitlán, Matadero). The next morning Congress, hastily convoked to deliberate, validated Iturbide's proclamation as emperor, even if it did not, strictly speaking, have a quorum.[15] In that session, held amid a concourse of friars and ill-clad men who occupied all available places, Gómez Farías, the deputy for Zacatecas, played the central role in urging the decision.[16] The measure was also supported by the more distinguished members of the progressive-liberal or radical wing: Lorenzo de Zavala of Yucatán, José María Bocanegra of Zacatecas, and José Ignacio Esteva of Veracruz. Outside Congress similar attitudes were adopted by Espinosa de los Monteros and Quintana Roo, both government officials.[17]

The regionally based progressive liberals, mostly federalist, did have a preference for a republic, but they feared getting involved in any system of government where the centralist bourgeoisie of the city of Mexico would have the upper hand. To support Iturbide might be a second-best solution, contrary to some of their convictions but attractive for various reasons, among them the simple fact that it had the support of the armed forces. The church and the traditional landed aristocracy (the rural hidalgos) were powerful but declining forces, seen from the proper perspective. Therefore it was not so absurd for the federalist progressive liberals to get aboard the Iturbidista ship of state, hoping to fight for vital space once inside.

Not all members of the progressive or radical-liberal group shared these attitudes. Some, like Juan de Dios Cañedo and Prisciliano Sánchez of Guadalajara, Francisco García of Zacatecas, Manuel Cresencio Rejón of Yucatán, and Juan Bautista Ramos Arizpe of Nuevo León, remained in the opposition. Others played more ambiguous roles, like Anastasio Zerecero, while a few, like José María Alpuche, retained for life a radical rejection of compromises.[18]

The policy adopted by Gómez Farías, later to become a stalwart of anticlerical and antifeudal reform, and by many others like him, must be interpreted in terms of the social and political positions they occupied. Gómez Farías took the same tack on other occasions, notably in 1833–34 and in 1846–47, when he entered into an alliance with the military sector represented by Santa Anna. This search for the anti–status-quo military man should not come as a surprise to anyone familiar with more recent Latin American or Third World politics. Admittedly the armed forces turned out to be a much more intractable passenger aboard the ship of state than the church had been. But one could hope that what had been impossible to obtain through revolutionary violence in the Insurgencia might be accomplished by a caesarism of Bonapartist inspiration. Military force appeared in principle to be independent of the status quo and therefore available to change it, particularly if it was capable of stirring up popular enthusiasm.

The mobilization of popular support, distrusted in moderate-liberal circles, was very much advocated by the more radical ones, who hoped to reproduce the *journées* of the French Revolution, and by others of a more simply populist mentality. Fernández de Lizardi vacillated in his political allegiances, but he basically followed the emperor's fortunes. Immediately after the May coup, he published a pamphlet, *El amigo de la paz*, justifying the assumption of the crown, because otherwise the people, "who if excited are an indomitable monster," might have killed Iturbide as they had killed the Visigoth king Wamba. The only alternative was civil war.[19] In the interval between his early support and this very strategic reaffirmation, he had had some republican leanings and had been concerned about the purity of elections. In November 1821 he had published *Cincuenta preguntas del Pensador a quien quiera responderlas*, obviously addressed to Iturbide, where he demanded an early vote for Congress, with the direct election of deputies rather than the cumbersome indirect method of the Cádiz constitution. He also argued against excessive tolerance toward the remaining Spaniards and for intensifying military activity against the Castle of San Juan de Ulúa, opposite Veracruz, still in royalist hands. To these demands he added, not very consistently, a complaint about the near monopoly his rival printer Ontiveros enjoyed in the publication of calendars, plus a request that the *"caballito"* (the equestrian statue of Charles IV) be removed from public sight, and finally that women be admitted to sessions of the future legislature, probably in an attempt to expand his public to include the fairer sex. The brochure, in its attack on the "third guarantee" (union with Spaniards) was nearly subversive, joining the agitation produced by Francisco Lagranda's equally oriented *Consejo prudente sobre una de las garantías*. Both were accused by a junta of top military brass.[20]

In his defense of the coup (in the *Amigo de la Paz*), Fernández de Lizardi was conscious of its inconsistencies with some of his previous publications. He rhetorically wondered whether he might be accused of being a Proteus, and he admitted that in his "intermediate writings," he had believed in a republic; but the people did not want it. In the second number of the same publication, he said that "we have lost a dubious good and gained a concrete one." Soon after this more theoretical discussion, he wrote, for wider consumption, a few verses to be sung to the music of the popular tune of the *"trágala, trágala,"* saying that even if Iturbide were a despot, it would be better than having one from Europe, because he was "ours" and therefore would depend on "us."[21]

Already a month before the coup, Lizardi pretended to have had a dream in which he saw the country bound in serfdom under a foreign dynasty, a predicament that tended to show Iturbide in a favorable light.[22] Later on, with the empire already established, he continued to support it, but advised Iturbide against sycophancy in his *Segundo sueño del Pensador Mexicano*, where he also condemned the clericals who knew nothing about Montesquieu, D'Alambert, or Voltaire.[23] In July he professed to be alarmed by rumors that Iturbide might make further encroachments on public liberties, such as dissolving Congress and proclaiming an absolutist regime; the news must be an invention of the *serviles*. When the main opposition deputies were imprisoned in August, Lizardi accepted the fact and did not make common cause with them, but he did reveal some independence in refusing to believe they were guilty until Justice had spoken. He said that it was particularly difficult for him to accept that Fray Servando had thrown away twenty-eight years of service to the nation by plotting against its higher authority once it was independent; he and the other deputies deserved pity rather than hate.[24]

Pablo Villavicencio, the Payo del Rosario, also supported the May coup, which he referred to as "the portentous roar of the Mexican people."[25] However, he tried to avoid giving the impression of being a "servil," and when the opposition deputies were jailed, in August 1822, he said that he would incur any risk to defend the errant legislators' lives. It had been all right to crown Iturbide, as a means to stop the growth of deleterious factions, but now justice should take over the matter. Toward the very end of the regime, he turned against it, though he admitted that he had supported the emperor until recently and that the dissolution of Congress (in October 1822) had been due to the supreme law of necessity; however, the emperor should control the "incendiary" authors who goaded him to take excessive measures against the jailed deputies or innocent Spaniards. Anti-Spanish agitation was a sure means of gaining popularity, and the Payo would be far from immune to it in the future; but here he was condemning others who were already appealing to it, from an extreme agitational wing of Iturbidismo in the final weeks of the empire.[26] The more solid partisans of the empire during its final moments accused him of being a "maromero" and "*equilibrista.*"[27] Francisco Pedro Argandar, a former insurgente Iturbidista priest and member up to the end of the Junta Instituyente, also accused the Payo of "having a very large pair of boots put on backwards."[28] Others accused him (though he denied it) of having been the author of some anonymous verses published soon after Iturbide closed down Congress in late October 1822:

> Aquí bajo esta losa yace inerte
> el Congreso de Cortes sepultado
> Congreso inútil, sobre quien la muerte
> descargó el garrote más bien dado.
> Gózate, oh caminante, de tal suerte
> y al mirarlo de todos despreciado
> dale, ya que en su vida no hizo nada
> en vez de agua bendita una patada.[29]

Popular Mobilization

Classical historiography agrees on the mobilization of sectors of the lumpenproletariat that accompanied the May 1822 coup d'état. Iturbide himself was very proud of the support he had among the people. In his memoirs he said that Congress did not dare separate him from the Regencia, because "they feared being disobeyed by the army and the people, among whom they knew the regard I enjoyed." Afterwards, when he marched into exile, he maintained that the government had him go through remote places, from hacienda to hacienda, avoiding large concentrations of people, in spite of which he was received in the pueblos with the pealing of bells, and the chief of the victorious Ejército Libertador, the marqués de Vivanco, had to endure hearing his own soldiers cheering the exile. Iturbide claimed to have abdicated to avoid bloodshed, "not because I had lost regard in the mind of the people or [because] I lacked the love of the soldiers." On the other hand, in those same memoirs he mentioned several times the support his enemies had among blacks and castas. Thus he commented that when Santa Anna rebelled against the empire, he "intimidated the pueblos near Alvarado and Antigua, and those of color of the immediate racherías," and that he put two hundred *pardos* under the orders of Victoria at the strategic position of the Puente Nacional.[30]

Iturbide's enemies almost unanimously pointed to the popular aspects of his support. The liberal pamphleteer Rafael Dávila divided

> the common people, who would still like to see Iturbide on the throne, into two classes: one which is not convinced by arguments, who after having listened to many and very convincing ones only answer: . . . if he was bad, why did they proclaim him emperor . . . if he did not cut short many lives it was because he did not want to do it and because he was a saint, why didn't those who now speak against him open their mouths when he was on the throne; with this class of men I do not speak because they act as irrationals, only by instinct; I do talk with those who give a place to reason and can be convinced with the truth.

The same author continued analyzing the contraposition of interests in this way: "Only the greater part of the middling sort and a small number of the other estates aspire to liberty; [Iturbide] associated with the more ambitious ones of the upper and middle classes and with the vilest of the inferior ones."[31] The author of *Muerte y entierro de Agustín Primero* (Mexico, 1823), probably José María Guillén, friend of the Pensador and the Payo but somewhat differentiated from them in politics, included among the bereft relatives a great number of clerics, old women, monks, fanatics, a multitude with a candle in their left hand and a razor in the right, and a great number of "small léperos [with a weathercock] carrying a drum, but instead of weapons, bearing a sea of canes with *rotulones*," which referred to the habit, already present in those days, of carrying banners in public demonstrations. Among others in that imaginary procession there was "a mercedarian friar, surrounded by *leperuscos*," surely father Aguilar of the Convent of La Merced, classed by Bustamante as "chief of the demagogues," who was also a colonel of the battalion of militia raised by Iturbide among the lower barrios toward the end of his regime. Guillén also identified, "dressed as a Trinitarian, a certain mixture of tailor and colonel," a clear reference to either of the brothers Mariano or Manuel Barrera, both colonels at the time, who had profited by making uniforms for the Trigarante Army, as they would later leasing the city garbage collection; they were also among the main leaders of the makeshift militia, with such other characters as Luciano Castrejón (better known as the "marqués del bodegón)," Pío Marcha and his sergeant companions, and several other improvised colonels.[32]

In another *Testamento*, this time of Judas, reference was made to "a watchmaker, tailor, and military man, who with Apodaca dressed the troops," which throws new light on the political and business ventures of the Barrera clan. The list includes "four caudillos of the barrios," of whom one was an obscure mountebank, another lame and thin, a third one a fishmonger, and finally the already mentioned "*bodeguero examinado*, late lieutenant colonel," and the inevitable "*mercedario*, or mercenary friar, commandant whose prelate overlooked his faults." Four little orphans remained, "a small hunchback Indian, a tall and unhealthy captain of gay life, a beardless colonel adept at tight-rope dancing, and a little old man who was very glad when they ordered the liberal hieroglyphs destroyed in the Plaza de Toros, believing they were masonic signs," not to forget poor Sergeant Marcha, who "was content with two stripes when for much less the tailors and bodegueros got two or three silver braids." All these small fry in these pamphlets were mixed in with more exalted personalities, such as "a powerful count who from 1810 spent a lot to enslave us and Mina took 300,000 pesos away from him" (the conde de San Mateo Valparaíso), a "minister of the altar who was a Persa in Spain" (Pérez of Puebla), a "player, whom they call calavera" (a play on Cavalieri, also mentioned in other tracts), and many more, especially members of the conservative-clerical sector, and including Minister Herrera, "my po-

litical first-born, who gave me bad advice but fell on his four paws . . .
apprentice of everything and *oficial* of nothing," plus the Payo del Rosario,
who was depicted as battering Herrera in the dissensions they had during
the last days of the empire.[33]

The progressive-liberal sector that supported Iturbide was generally
spared in these pamphlets, either because the majority had already converted by the time they were written, or probably also because the clergy,
the léperos, and their leaders provided better copy, with less cognitive
dissonance, so to speak, for the anti-Iturbidista public that bought these
productions. There were those in verse, listing as satellites of the deposed
emperor "Marqueses, condes bobones, los militares tunantes, usureros
comerciantes . . . las simplonas *reverencias* de la *toca* turbulenta . . . los
léperos de arrabales, las mujercillas livianas, los hipócritas ancianos y los
pillos inmorales."[34]

In another tract, entitled *Nuestros sacerdotes malos fraguaban nuestras
cadenas*, it was stated that Iturbide's lies had found reception among "the
ignorant simple Americans and even among ecclesiastics of the highest
rank."

After the coup of May 1822, Iturbide tried to allay the concerns of the
wealthier segment of the population regarding the unruliness that had
accompanied his accession to power. On June 3 the emperor issued a
proclamation addressed to "his comrades and citizens," belittling a rumor launched the previous day, that soldiers would now assault the shops
of Spaniards; he also had Pío Marcha jailed in July on the basis of allega-
tions against him and his followers.[35] Congress continued in session, and
though some oppositionists ceased to attend, still Iturbide did not have a
sure majority. Toward the end of July, Congress passed a bill granting an
amnesty to all "*delitos de opinión*" incurred since the events of May, thus
benefiting several oppositionists. The executive did not agree with this
leniency, but rather proposed an opposing bill, establishing special tribunals to deal swiftly with acts of rebellion or criminality, passing it on to
the Consejo de Estado. The latter sent it to Congress and proposed a
compromise solution: namely, to promulgate the pardon for past mis-
deeds, but to enact the new severer law proposed by the executive, which
had been earlier rejected by Congress.[36]

The incapacity of Iturbide to dominate the legislature through a committed majority led to a major confrontation by the end of August. At
that time the government claimed to have uncovered a plot by former
Insurgentes and moderate liberals. Several deputies and their sympathizers were arrested, among them Fray Servando Teresa de Mier, Carlos

María de Bustamante, Eulogio Villaurrutia (Jacobo's son), José Cecilio del Valle (a moderate Guatemalan liberal), José Joaquín de Herrera, Francisco Manuel Sánchez de Tagle, José María Fagoaga, and quite a few others. Some of the accused were able to go into hiding.[37]

From this moment on, Iturbide's support among progressive-liberal circles started to dwindle, suffering notably from the withdrawal of the disillusioned Gómez Farías. Even so Congress continued to be intractable, and finally Iturbide, on October 31, dissolved it, though not without previously consulting his friends. Zavala and Bocanegra participated in the concomitant lobbying, and Espinosa de los Monteros and Quintana Roo continued to occupy high government posts. Among pamphleteers, both the Pensador and the Payo approved the measure, though their oscillations must have confused a certain sector of public opinion. An official *pasquinista* published another *Epitafio* against the now defunct Congress, saying that "el sol fue su padre, su madre la Junta. Fue su funeral el dos de noviembre, iba el Pensador de primer doliente." Obviously the clericals wanted to corner Fernández de Lizardi, who by that time had serious problems with the church due to the excommunication he had suffered because of a paper on the freemasons. He quickly answered with another tract, in which he performed a bit of "equilibrio," lamenting the errors of the congressmen but also the excessively harsh measure of imprisoning them. In general, though, he said he approved of the emperor's act, taking into account his moderation and the validity of the criticisms about congressional intransigence.[38] As for the Payo del Rosario, near the end of the regime he admitted, as we have already seen, that he had supported it until recently, and that Iturbide would have remained on the right course had it not been for Minister Herrera, who "knew how to deceive the most worthy man of Anáhuac."[39]

Having dissolved Congress, Iturbide organized the so-called Junta Instituyente, with only two representatives for each province, hand-picked from the existing deputies. In this minicongress, nicknamed "*juntilla*," some of the more loyal partisans of the emperor were included, and positions were also given to the progressive-liberal group, men such as Zavala, Bocanegra, and Esteva, though Gómez Farías had already opted out.[40] According to Bocanegra in his memoirs, this indicated the openness of the government, because he for one was already in the opposition after his temporary flirting with authority. But memory was betraying him when he wrote these recollections, because he had actively participated in the cabals organized to plan the reduction of Congress to a manageable size. On October 16 and 17, Iturbide gathered in his home a large number of committed (or at least reasonable) deputies, along with members of the Consejo de Estado. After ten hours of discussion, the emperor's idea of reducing the number of deputies to two per province was approved, as well as that of creating military tribunals to examine accusations of conspiracy and special corps of gendarmes to keep public order. This package was not accepted by the majority of Congress, providing an excuse for closing it down and replacing it with the Junta Instituyente.[41]

The next day, November 1, popular groups rampaged through the city, cheering the "absolute emperor" to the sound of drums and preparing the inauguration of the "juntilla," presided over by Bishop Castañiza.[42] By chance during those days, Joel Poinsett, special envoy from the United States, arrived in the city of Mexico. Apparently Minister Herrera had tried to prevent him from entering the country, fearing his intentions and his past responsibility in "the destruction of Chile and Buenos Aires," and sent a circular to port authorities on October 5, 1822, which, however, was not effective. Poinsett did not get a good impression of the emperor, but he established excellent contacts in the country, which he used a few years later, when he returned as representative of his country and became involved in internal politics, on the side of the radical liberals of the Yorkino lodges.[43]

The Gathering Storm

It was commonly observed at the time that the emperor had been supported, from the beginning, by the upper classes and the clergy, but this was changing as a result of economic policies that threatened to put an excessive burden on the commercial and high-income sectors. The Quai d'Orsay, after the downfall, received information of this nature, attributing the loss of prestige among the better off to the usurpation of institutional functions, persecutions, and bad administration. The informer was registering correctly the waning of support among the upper classes, though attributing it only to moral or political reasons, a disputable hypothesis. The financial situation of the empire was extremely difficult, as income had deteriorated after the changes brought about by the liberal Spanish interlude and the Iguala insurrection. Minister Medina, in a report prepared at the end of October 1822, stated that the very solid tobacco income, which during the last years of the colony had yielded some 7.5 million pesos (including costs of acquisition and elaboration), was now down to less than 2 million, mostly due to cosecheros selling privately and illegally, as the funds with which the Renta used to buy their products had been swallowed up by hard-pressed governments. Silver and gold income was also reduced from a historical level of almost four million pesos to about 1.5 million. Some forced loans had been established to confront the deficit, but stronger measures would be necessary, even at the risk of antagonizing some wealthier sectors of the population.[44]

These measures included a *contribución directa*, which would have taxed away up to 10 percent of incomes, and an issue of paper money, with the obligation to accept one-third of all payments, including government salaries, in that currency. The drop, or rather spurt, that overflowed the cup of upper-class tolerance was Iturbide's desperate decision to forcibly appropriate all the specie in a silver *conducta* (with the promise of repayment in due time, of course); this silver was mostly owned by Spanish merchants. The bourgeoisie's liberal convictions and concern for due process and division of powers soared to unprecedented heights.[45]

The international setting, meanwhile, was darkening, as the Holy Alliance decided to intervene in Spain to put a stop to the liberal experiment, under which a relatively dovish policy toward the Indies had been followed. At the end of November 1822, Austria, Russia, Prussia, and France agreed to send an armed force to the peninsula to reestablish Ferdinand in his full rights. Though the decision was secret, something still filtered out to public opinion. While it was possible to pin some hopes on British interference or on the more theoretical decision of the United States to keep America for the Americans, the prospects of Spanish reconquest were rekindled, opening up new fields of action for politicians with an eye to mass sentiments.

The month of December 1822 started with bad news from Veracruz, where the fortified island of San Juan de Ulúa, fronting on the port, was still in Spanish hands. Santa Anna, chief of the local garrison, had been trying without success to expel the last vestiges of foreign rule. In November Iturbide paid him a visit and was disgusted with his behavior, so he decided to remove him from his post. Santa Anna immediately responded, on December 2, 1822, with a pronunciamiento to reconvene Congress so as to decide on the constitutional future of the country, counting on the support of his fellow Veracruzano Guadalupe Victoria, which he soon got. After a few weeks, Bravo and Guerrero, in the south, joined the cause, thus inaugurating the last convulsive months of the regime.[46]

In view of the situation, the Junta Instituyente convoked new elections for a Congress that would really be representative, unlike the previous one. In the primary polls, only those with property, industry, or occupation would participate, while those expressly excluded were "servants from escaleras abajo," which referred to domestic servants, but left some doubts as to rural or urban laborers or the city unemployed. It was also established that voting should be done verbally, so as to avoid the use of printed lists (cédulas) as on previous occasions, which apparently was thought to favor the well-organized opposition, mainly the masonic lodges, though the method could also be used by the church if it set itself to it. If nobody received an absolute majority, a second round was to be held. It may be noted here that the mobilizational nature of Iturbide's regime (in the capital and a few other large urban places) was not incompatible with a basic preference for limited participation. There were actually different factions within the regime, and Iturbide himself, or his immediate entourage, did not always see eye to eye with the junta, where an opposition also developed, partly among the remaining liberals and partly among the more conservative clerics, who were alarmed at the increasingly mobilizational traits of the regime.[47]

Next the junta started considering a reglamento provisional for the empire, designating a commission for that purpose. When the project was read to the whole body the following month, the discussion was intense. The radical liberal group, led by Zavala, was opposed, but it lost by a vote of 21 to 6.[48] Zavala wanted elections to be held right away, in order to regain legitimacy, but the government procrastinated, because it no longer controlled large areas of the country. Zavala insisted, pursuing an ideal of formal government, or maybe because he was already passing to the opposition.[49] It was exactly during those days that Guerrero and Bravo, in Chilapa, in the southern "hot lands," proclaimed their support for the Santa Anna revolt. However, Iturbide was not prepared to admit weakness. Since the junta had approved the reglamento, he could consider himself constitutional emperor, and as such he organized a public oath ceremony for the corporations on January 24, coinciding with news that the rebels were being routed. He had sent his friend José Manuel Zozaya Bermúdez (who would later become an innovative industrialist) as representative to the United States to negotiate recognition. Stephen Austin had also just arrived, seeking land grants in Texas.[50]

Minister Herrera, to bring calm to the population of the beleaguered city, announced that Guerrero had been killed in combat by the loyal Epitacio Sánchez. This false piece of news was immediately countered by the Payo del Rosario, who said that in any event it would be a pity if either of the two died; Guerrero because of his past services to the cause of independence and Sánchez because he was obeying his monarch. The Payo warned his readers not to come to hasty conclusions, classing him as a Guerrero partisan. This confused argument (probably intentional) got him a battering from the Iturbidista hard line, who accused him of being an equilibrista and a maromero.[51] Fernández de Lizardi, on the other hand, was still supporting Iturbide, arguing that it was better to have an absolute government, if it made the kingdom happy, than allow it to be destroyed in pursuance of a kind of government that was unknown in this part of the world. Moreover, he thought that Agustín did not wish to be absolute, but it was necessary to be unified in supporting him, because "it is not easy to reunite a divided opinion, nor are there Napoleons in France or Iturbides in America every day."[52]

The conservative and clerical wing of Iturbidismo was concerned that there might be changes in the direction of republicanism or religious tolerance, particularly with such people as Zavala still aboard. In a pamphlet they recounted the history of the scarcely more than one year that had elapsed since independence, pointing to the prevalence of Spaniards among the enemies of Iturbide since the early days of the provisional Junta Gubernativa. The Congress had been elected under the influence of cabals, with the result that a large number of unknown personalities had gotten in, and the emperor was finally forced to replace it with the new Junta Instituyente. It was necessary to avoid the pitfalls of tolerantism and a "democratic" (that is, republican) constitution.[53]

Meanwhile the Veracruzan skies darkened once again. The government had sent General Echávarri, a Spaniard with liberal sympathies, to put down the rebels, but after a sucessful campaign that cornered Santa Anna within the walls of Veracruz, Echávarri and some of his fellow officers joined the opposite side. While the Spanish chief of San Juan de Ulúa suspended hostilities so as not to jeopardize the rebels' prospects, on February 1 the leaders of the imperial army signed the Plan de Casa Mata, demanding the election of a new Congress. This new body would decide on the future of the regime, meanwhile leaving administration in the hands of the Diputaciones Provinciales. Soon other prominent military men joined the plan; some, like José Morán, were from the moderate liberal group, whereas others, like Anastasio Bustamante, were close political friends of the emperor and probably joined in order to "work from the inside" in the new constellation of power, a tactic only too well known in Latin American coup experience. General Negrete, principal military figure of the empire and captain general of Guadalajara, also ended up joining the victorious cause. By March 1823 Iturbide only controlled the capital and its surroundings, and he confronted difficult negotiations in Puebla with the Liberating Army led by the marqués de Vivanco.

The Final Spasm

On February 10 Iturbide instituted a change of cabinet as a last attempt to stem the oncoming tide. In Justicia he dismissed his old friend Domínguez Manso, loyal but ineffective, and appointed his compadre Gómez Navarrete, a man of resources and with some prestige, who afterwards would become his attorney and the editor of *El Aguila*.[54] Meanwhile popular groups led by the friars and the improvised militia chiefs in the barrios agitated in favor of the "emperador absoluto." However, and in order to control these activities, which might jeopardize his position, Iturbide made a risky move. He discarded José Manuel Herrera, his "firstborn son," and took José Cecilio del Valle, the liberal Guatemalan, from his jail in the Dominican convent, making him minister of Relaciones, that is, chief of the cabinet. This early example of *cohabitation* was the equivalent of what in a more established parliamentary system would have been a shift of coalitions, with a new prime minister under the same president or monarch. To complete his new team, Iturbide searched the Dominican convent-prison again and picked the moderate-liberal General José Joaquín de Herrera (no kin to the discarded minister) and made him chief of staff, to cooperate with Gómez Pedraza, the only relevant military figure who remained on his side. He also promised to mend his ways; what else could the opposition demand? At the same time, in an address to the people entitled *El Emperador a los Mexicanos*, of February 15, he tried to calm apprehensions about sacking by popular or military groups, ridiculing the fears that had spread the day before when merchants saw one of them moving his belongings from one storehouse to another, which was wrongly attributed to his having information about the oncoming massacre. However, when news came of Negrete's defection, closer to the end, his house in Mexico City got a wholesome hail of stones.[55]

Quintana Roo, the "sotaministro" of the discarded Herrera, now took the opportunity to regild his liberal blazons, or in other words, to do what the people who did not love him called a "voltereta." Asked by the new government whether it was appropriate to go ahead with the announced congressional elections, he said that it was not, because the subject was being discussed with the "new caudillos" who controlled a great part of the country. He proceeded to state that it was ridiculous to set limits on the subjects that could be treated by a reinstalled Congress, as the juntilla wished, such as to prohibit changes in religious toleration or monarchy: the representatives of the people should decide this with complete freedom. He finally recalled that religious intolerance was an evil practice, one which "progressive countries" had already abolished. The clerical Right pounced on him, airing some of his dirty linen, surmising that he was scared because his fellow Yucatecan Manuel Crescencio Rejón, a non-Iturbidista radical liberal, was coming with the Liberating Army, promising to make him pay for his opportunism and for having thrived in the shadow of tyranny. Disunity was spreading in the imperial camp.[56]

The new ministerial-military duo of Valle and General Herrera tried to change things "from the inside," but it was a bit late. They concentrated for the moment on getting a cease-fire from the rebels camped in Puebla and on launching the elections for a new Congress, whoever might dominate militarily in each area. Even this was not accepted by the "new caudillos," who insisted on a simple reconvening of the old Congress, where it was known that Iturbide lacked a majority. Inside the regime hard-liners were not happy with the turn of events. On March 1 a group of military men signed a manifesto urging repression for the enemies of the system. No one of any relevance was included, except the old insurgente Ramón López Rayón. The hard core of the Iturbidista Right was strongly represented, by the marqués de Salvatierra, his uncle Juan Cervantes y Padilla, José María Azcárate, son of the lawyer Francisco Azcárate, and José Antonio "Cartuchera" Andrade, captain general of the capital. Neither General Herrera nor Gómez Pedraza, representatives of the more liberal wing of the government, appeared among the signatories. According to Carlos María de Bustamante, the authors ought to be confined to the Hipólitos lunatic asylum, and the Payo took the opportunity to attack them and then pretend that his life was threatened.[57]

At the same time, popular demonstrations were being prepared to proclaim Iturbide emperor once again, but this time "absolute"; at least this was the intent of the instigators of these mobilizations, which did not have the support of the new coopted authorities. The government again had to publish an announcement to calm down public apprehensions "regarding yesterday's conspiracy, which was attributed to the barrios . . . The word [had] been spread that the poorer people of the periphery were all armed, with the intent of again proclaiming the emperor" and that several well-known "liberals of the Veracruzan band" were going to be assassinated. The announcement heaped scorn on the fad of attributing every alarmist piece of news to the barrios. Pío Marcha, on the other hand, responded to Guadalupe Victoria's revolutionary manifesto, in which he had accused the sergeant of "having mobilized the barrio of Salto del Agua and several military men of [his] class." Marcha asserted that not only those people, but the whole nation and army had supported the movement of May 1822. In a contrary direction, the Pensador warned Iturbide not to follow the example of Ferdinand VII, who in 1814 had also received the acclaim of the friars and the populace, to no avail in the long run, because what matters is "to have the favor of the middling estate." If he lost it, what he had to do was to abdicate and cover himself with glory. The Payo was also trying to extinguish the fire of excessive popular agitation, an art at which he was outmaneuvered at this juncture by the combination of clerics and military men of low rank who made up the unreformed populist Right of Iturbidismo, and who might get out of control. A rival pamphleteeer, Luis Espino (who signed himself Spes in Livo) had tried to take advantage of the agitational atmosphere by hurling some additional threats at the already frightened Spaniards, commonly thought to be favorable to the Veracruzano rebels. The Payo regretted these excesses, because they might produce "an explosion of the plebs."[58]

On March 4 Iturbide decided, surely on Valle's advice, to reinstall Congress and liberate the still imprisoned deputies. Negotiations with the rebels, concentrated in Puebla, were protracted, because they did not wish to have the Congress meet in Mexico City, where pressures could be exerted against it. Meanwhile the clerical hard liners in the Iturbidista camp were planning a reaction, using their own mobilizational resources. The friars moved between convents in the capital, Puebla, and Toluca. In Mexico City militias were formed, as usual with "the dregs of the people," who were ready, according to the worried Carlos María de Bustamante, to start sacking the Spaniards' possessions. Several pamphleteers stirred up hatred against the foreigners, among them Luis Espino, as we have already seen. Despite his earlier vacillations regarding the emperor, Espino was now well advanced in his later career as an anti-Spanish *ultra*. This agitationism did not suit the government, bent as it was on trying to curb the excesses that alienated many sympathizers. Espino's paper had been signed publicly by José Menocal (a man from Iturbide's entourage and a member of the Sociedad de Amantes del Emperador) and abetted by Judge Bernardo González Angulo, but it was impugned by the press jury, and the author was condemned to four years' imprisonment as a result of pressure, we may assume, from the moderate wing of the government.[59]

There were two possible policies the government could have adopted to cope with the situation: one was conciliation with its enemies, and the other was an appeal to mobilizationism. The conciliatory strategy was supported by whatever liberals still remained in the government, including the recently coopted ones (Minister Valle and General Herrera) and Gómez Pedraza, as well as by some moderate clericals. Among the lower strata of that same clergy, especially the friars, and among the organizers of popular militia, on the other hand, the opposite, mobilizational policy was preferred. They were determined to use the weapon they knew or were learning to use, namely, popular agitation under traditional *encadrement.*

The more verticalized sectors published a proclamation entitled *Voto de los barrios de la Capital,* where they declared that they represented the Salto del Agua and were determined "at the slightest indication from His Imperial Majesty to [change] their docility and sufferance into fury and irreconcilable hatred toward the enemies of the Nation's happiness, without distinguishing whether they were born in this or another region."

Bustamante, in his *Diario,* has left an interesting though biased description of the organization by the government of a militia under the title of Batallones de la Fe. They had

> their clubs, publicly presided over by Cols. Mariano and Manuel Barrera, with whom the lame Tamariz, one of the immediate satellites of Iturbide, is intimate. Sixto Paredes has his meetings in the house of the Risco, street of Santa Catalina Mártir. The marqués del Bodegón, in the Callejuela. Pío Marcha in the Alcaicería, etc. They can be seen roaming the streets in groups and with uniforms, assuming an air of importance . . . They can distribute promotions, as Iturbide has put in their hands a portion of blank designations.[60]

In one of the several testamentos published during the last days of the empire, reference was made to "some meetings held in the barrios of this capital, with the object of entering and sacking the Parián and other shops."[61] When the city of Mexico was finally occupied by the Liberating Army, the club activists were rounded up, and the Barreras fell, but they were pardoned by judge Bernardo González Angulo, who came from the previous regime. This provoked a condemnatory pamphlet and a reply by the judge, who claimed that the two brothers he had freed were not guilty of such bad behavior as was commonly supposed. To this an anonymous author retorted, appealing to "the testimony of thousands of neighbors of all classes . . . who witnessed the repeated scenes of consternation seen in Mexico due to the Barreras' influence in the barrios."[62]

Already from the end of February, according to Bustamante, weapons were being distributed in the barrios, though the chronicler had the hope that they would all end up on the black market, sold by their supposed users to the nobler members of the Liberating Army. A group of Meco Indians arrived in the capital, well armed and offering great quantities of hides, causing a terrible impact on the population. Dionisio Moctezuma, erstwhile governor of the parcialidad of San Juan Tenochtitlán, whom Bustamante calls "an Indian fruiterer from Chalco" (the place where Iturbide had his rented ex-Jesuit hacienda), offered to recruit Indians for military service, according to another rumor.[63]

Meanwhile Iturbide assumed an attitude of disinterest, duly rejected by those bound to him. He pretended to abdicate the crown in front of the army, but it would not accept such a gesture. He presented himself in the popular Paseo de La Viga (near the southeastern barrios, where his supporters were organized), with the object of receiving some *vivas*, while the Barreras with 15,000 pesos tried to get people from the outskirts. A regidor from San Agustín de las Cuevas (Tlalpan) was also accused by an oppositionist pamphleteer of "seducing and alarming the nearby pueblos to join the barrios of this Court in their depraved movements."[64]

The moderates who still supported Iturbide were becoming increasingly alarmed about the agitation promoted by some sectors of the regime. In another pamphlet, *Las autoridades duermen mientras la patria perece* (possibly of March 5), they condemned the "anarchic" distribution of arms "to men about whose habits the worst opinion is justifiably held." They petitioned the Diputación Provincial and the Ayuntamiento to ensure that a national militia be organized "according to the liberal system," that is, including only people of a certain economic or educational level.

On March 10 there was another political show: Iturbide installed the old Congress (still without its complete number of members, many of whom feared returning to the capital) and forthwith attempted to retire to Tacubaya, where the main corps of his troops was stationed. The barrio militia did not allow him to leave the city, however, unharnessing the horses from his carriage and returning him to the palace. This Varennes in reverse reminded Bustamante of the Aranjuez mutiny in favor of Ferdinand; "mangas de léperos" passed near the chronicler's house screaming "Long live the absolute emperor and down with despotism," a logical contradiction that he did not miss registering for posterity. That same day Colonel Cela, of the infantry regiment stationed at Guadalupe (to the north of the capital) received orders to move to Tacubaya (in the southwest), passing through the central part of the city. En route great numbers of men from the poorer sectors mingled with the soldiers, talking to the troops and disorganizing their lines, which it became necessary to recompose at swordpoint. For Bustamante, who recounted the events a few days afterward, this was part of the plan to cause a popular commotion.[65] On March 12 Bustamante registered the rumor that the government was not going to pay their weekly earnings to the eight thousand tobacco workers, faulting the rebels for the lack of funds and throwing all these people into the streets.

Finally, on March 19, Iturbide abdicated, apparently for good, in the presence of his friend Gómez Navarrete, who apart from being minister of justice was the head of the Consejo de Estado, and who left the decision of accepting or rejecting the gesture in the hands of the reinstated Congress. Iturbide added an address to Congress, stating that though he knew he still enjoyed widespread popular support, he preferred to avoid bloodshed. The rebels, concentrated in Puebla, were trying to come to terms with representatives of Congress and of the Mexican Diputación Provincial. The rebels argued that they could not accept laying down their arms and obeying a Congress that still was not in a position to act freely. Government representatives informed them that measures were already being taken "to disarm those who were assembled in the barrios . . . and to dismiss from the Capital's political government and Captaincy General Mr. Andrade ["Cartuchera"], who even if he did not foment those excesses, did not seem determined to stop them."[66]

Finally it was agreed that Iturbide would withdraw with a small guard to Tulancingo, some sixty miles from the Capital, awaiting decisions about his future. His enemies still feared he might try to recoup his fortunes; in order to avoid this, it was crucial to quickly form a national militia, to which citizens would flock in order "to defend their property, their equality, their representation, and the freedom of the fatherland." Opponents of Iturbide published a *Proclama de un sanpableño desengañado*, where a supposed inhabitant of that barrio addressed himself to his "compañeros" to persuade them of their mistakes. He admitted that he "had been seduced, like so many others, to go and shout against Congress, . . . run with [his] torch and attack respectable bystanders . . . [because] the low station to which we belong does not allow us to discern, nor can our caudillos P. M., P., C., B., C., etc., enlighten us." Finally, addressing himself again to his "compañeros," he rebuked them for the "wrath and animosity which you have shown our liberators . . . Follow the example of one like myself, who also, seduced, ran to unharness the carriage and prevent the retirement of the emperor . . . but who today, repentant of such a serious crime, wishes to die in defense of the Sovereign Congress."[67]

On March 25 and 26, before the Liberating Army entered the capital, there were some disorders, provoked by the confusion of publications against or in favor of Iturbide, accompanied by a rain of small papers with the words "Long live religion, long live the Emperor." Iturbide tried to stage a harangue to the troops, informing them of his retirement, which was followed by the expected opposition to such a move. On March 27, while the Liberating Army was passing through the garita of San Antonio Abad (near the poor neighborhoods of Salto del Agua, San Pablo, and La Palma), there was an exchange of fire with a group of people shouting vivas to the "Emperador absoluto." The officer in charge wanted to ignore the disturbance, but "noticing that the number involved increased incessantly, ordered a volley which dissipated them, with two dead." The following day was Good Friday, an occasion the friars could not miss. On Saturday there was a commotion in San Pablo and La Palma, but the barrios "suffered a great loss, because they have been thoroughly defeated, the grenadiers occupying the tops of the nearby houses, from where they opened fire. It is said that the mutiny was led by the well-known friar of the Merced, Aguilar, who escaped being jailed together with fifty léperos, by taking refuge in his convent." A few days later, Pío Marcha was detained, with 200 pesos and a few gold ounces, in the Salto del Agua, where he had sought refuge under the protection "of the followers he has had in that place."[68] There were seven dead, thirty wounded, and fifty jailed. According to the author of the *Testamento de Judas*, this happened to them for not heeding the advice of the Sanpableño Desengañado.

Iturbide, who feigned illness to await the results of these actions, finally went into exile on March 30, while the new government dissolved the so-called Batallones de la Fe and those of the police, arresting the "foremen and rascals who lead them."

On March 31 Congress elected a provisional executive formed by three people: Generals Bravo, Victoria, and Negrete. Negrete was a Spaniard and therefore not a very appropriate choice for discharging his responsibilities, which in practice he declined. Bravo and Victoria represented a balance between moderate and radical liberals, both of them being former insurgentes. As alternates there were two appointments: Mariano Michelena, a liberal of old proindependence convictions, who in practice led the tripartite executive, due to the military men's need to attend to their duties; and Miguel Domínguez, a man also with insurgente associations, who had been corregidor of Querétaro. Only after another three months could Congress make up its mind as to the third alternate, General Guerrero.

The price the liberal bourgeoisie had paid for getting rid of Iturbide was a high level of participation by selected old insurgents. Of the six members, including the alternates, there were three moderate liberals (with differing shades of opinion among them): Bravo, Michelena, and Negrete, to whom Domínguez, with a long viceregal bureaucratic career behind him, could be added. The radical minority was formed by Guadalupe Victoria, quite moderate within his group, and the more removed and menacing Guerrero. The ministry was put temporarily in the hands of a moderate-liberal sympathizer, García Illueca, who at first concentrated all posts, then slowly distributed them to their final holders.

This tripartite and therefore weak Executive Power would have to confront serious difficulties in guiding the transition. Provincial interests, favoring a federal organization and reluctant to being controlled from the capital, would have to be dealt with. On the other hand, the church was not very happy under the new circumstances, and the remnants of Iturbidismo were capable of provoking more than one headache for the authorities. The international situation, also, kept worsening: on April 7 a French army invaded Spain to liberate it from the liberals, without finding too much resistance. This time the priests and the whole of traditional Spain were on the side of those who came to reinstate Ferdinand in the full exercise of his authority. The next stage might well be a more serious attempt to recover part of the Americas. The nativist struggle against the Spanish merchant colony (and the more modest small shopkeepers and employees) would offer ample scope for new popular agitations.

5

The Transformation of *Iturbidismo*

The Breakup of Iturbide's Coalition

Iturbide's attempt at establishing a strong government failed, due in part to the contradictory elements he had to encompass in order to consolidate his coalition and in part to the mobilizational nature of one of its components, which made it difficult to combine with the rest. The core of his support consisted of four major groups: the army officers, the high clergy, the old nobility with its entourage of hidalgos, and the big miners. The high clergy was well connected, despite occasional differences and some stray individuals, with most of its lower secular rungs (the parish priests), who had influence among a sector of the middle and lower strata. The military officers also had some access down the social scale, via their noncommissioned dependants. Within this Iturbidista Right, one could distinguish, then, one strong economic actor (the miners), plus a more decadent one (the old nobility), and two institutional ones (a clerical and a military caesarist variant). The whole formed a very powerful coalition, almost a winning one.

The main opposition, the moderate-liberal, or Escocés, faction, centered on international merchants and financiers, together with professionals, administrators, and some affluent intellectuals.

These two coalitions covered most of the upper and upper-middle sectors, except for some regional forces, which formed the bases of a potential federalism: the middle-sized miners, entrepreneurial and often indebted; the equally middling regional landowners, oriented toward the internal market; and finally the new tierra caliente entrepreneurs, a group with future prospects but not yet very powerful. These groups had a tendency toward some progressive form of liberalism, at odds with the wealthier and more centrally minded Escoceses, while shunning the extremes of social agitation indulged in by the populists.

Lower down on the social scale, in a band characterized by ideological or political commitment (though somewhat heterogeneous in social origins), we find four strategic groups: the friars; the Jacobins, or radicalized intellectuals; the former insurgente chiefs; and a host of low-status aspirantes, the people who got involved in organizing the Iturbidista and later Yorkino militias. The friars and the Jacobins were highly sensitized ideologically, and the former insurgente chiefs had staked a lot on a political career. The low-status aspirantes were usually of humble extraction, bent on social mobility by any means.

The Jacobin intellectuals, with quite a few stray friars and most of the old Insurgentes, could call on a good popular following, both urban and rural, forming the liberal-populist faction, which would later be known as Yorkino. The friars, together with many aspirantes, were quite capable of arousing a sector of the urban masses, forming what can be called a traditional populist force, closely linked with the military-caesarist faction. I have differentiated the two, because it was not so simple for the military to become populist agitators, however traditional they might have been. That was rather the task of individual innovators within the military, who did not always enjoy support from their colleagues.

The basis of Iturbide's power was its Right, creating, for good reason, his image for posterity and even for many contemporaries. But that coalition was only almost winning. It needed something else, due to the high degree of social mobilization existing in the country as a result of the structural traits of Mexican society, plus the very important and longlasting effects of the Insurgencia.

To understand the political strategies of the times, it is instructive to consider the relative strengths of the various social actors and their coalitions. Though it is not possible to assign numbers to each one of them, qualitatively one may say that without social and political mobilization, the dominant classes would have had more political weight than the middle and lower ones together; but with an intense mobilization of the latter, the opposite might be true. The danger of a fully mobilized antioligarchical alliance was certainly present, and the Insurgencia was the closest thing to that nightmare. But seldom, if ever, would the whole of the middle and lower classes form a united front against the rest. Alliances were usually more complex than that during this period.

The upper classes were deeply divided, due to their different reactions to the prospect of opening up the economy to the world market. During the time of his ascendancy, Iturbide was supported by a very powerful group, including nothing less than most of the church and the military, plus a very large part of the big miners and landed interests, centered around the old nobility. This group was quite possibly stronger than the moderate-liberal or Escocés group, with its merchant and financial connections and its predicament among professional, administrative, and affluent intellectual groups. But there was a large remaining group of social actors, as we have seen, namely the regionally based economic interests leaning toward a pragmatic form of federalism; the traditional populist forces, put together by friars and other low-status aspirantes; and the liberal populists, led by Jacobins and former insurgentes. The latter two shared between them the sympathies of the politically active lower-middle and popular classes.

Given the fact that there was a division among the dominant sectors, even the strongest group needed some additional force in order to impose itself. The eventual alliance of the Escocés moderates with the federalists and the populist liberals would muster greater power that the Iturbidista Right. The early months of congressional proceedings showed that something like this was in the offing, since for tactical reasons the Escoceses and the former insurgent chiefs were coming together in opposition to Iturbide, with the federalists remaining more undecided. But it was not easy to bring about such a convergence, even if the three groups could be considered to be branches of liberalism. To counteract that eventuality, the most promising line for Iturbide was to initiate a mobilizational strategy of his own, with the hope of keeping it within bounds. On the one hand, there was the possibility of exploiting (as many ancien régime governments had done in Europe) the potential strength of the traditionalist popular faction, closely associated with the noncommissioned officers of the army. This was done, and the May 1822 coup was its result. But there was also the riskier adventure of establishing contacts with the liberal populists. This was also done, and the support obtained from such important Jacobin activists as Fernández de Lizardi and Pablo Villavicencio is evidence of this tactic. The former insurgentes were more reluctant to enter into this alliance, though as we have seen earlier, such relevant figures as Francisco Severo Maldonado, José Manuel Herrera, and Andrés Quintana Roo came to Iturbide's side; the majority, however, did not. Some allies, such as Gómez Farías, were also found among the regionally based federalists.

However, Iturbide's populist overture, though it gained him some friends, irritated many of his early supporters among the conservative classes. His overthrow was not simply the result of a successful military revolt; what happened to make that revolt very difficult to stop was that

Iturbide's mobilizational policies, and the presence in his entourage of such liberal populists as Zavala, weakened the sinews of the regime. The clerical Right either abandoned Iturbide or became less adamant in his defense; and the armed forces split, concerned with the menace of social disorder and also influenced by some regional interests. Tierra caliente entrepreneurs, especially, were beginning to look to Santa Anna and an alternative economic model, not so linked to the ancien régime as Iturbide's was.

The fact that the rebellion was based in Veracruz can of course be explained by the ambitions of Santa Anna, whose contradictory personality is a very tempting candidate to take the place of more complex social causes. Veracruz's role was linked to its strategic position, so that it helped throttle any government that lost access to its port. This fact goes a long way toward explaining Santa Anna's apparently neurotic tendency, later on during the republic, to leave the presidency in charge of someone else and retire to his hacienda, which happened to be near where the troops had to be stationed if they were to defend the country, close to the port.

After the overthrow of the empire, there was an upsurge of anti-Iturbidista tracts. In Veracruz a brochure entitled *Conducta del Sr. Iturbide* was particularly prominent. It was reprinted in Mexico by Juan Cabrera, who had named his shop "Oficina liberal del ciudadano Juan Cabrera" and who became a well-known figure among exaltado pamphleteers, though he specialized in publishing other authors' productions. An anonymous "Liberal juicioso" responded, searching for a middle ground in judging Iturbide's career, not forgetting that he had contributed to liberating the country. At the same time Fernández de Lizardi, who had been one of the last to abandon the imperial bandwagon, was now forecasting a new revolution, even bloodier than the one begun in 1810. In his opinion, after what had happened to Iturbide only a republic could fit the nation's needs. In that republic, which in a show of moderation he envisaged as a mixture of aristocracy and democracy, religious toleration would be established, the contents of sermons supervised, and citizens' militias quickly organized. The conservative clericals jumped at the challenge posed by this "impious pamphlet" and accused the Pensador of following in the steps of Pío Marcha, whose same "comparsa del Salto del Agua" he was now trying to agitate. They also pointed out that the type of popular pressure exerted in the capital could be more successful under a centralized government; to stave off its effects, it would be wise to adopt the Puebla delegation's proposal that only legislation approved by two-thirds of the states' legislatures would be sanctioned. This was an extreme example of conservative federalism, which was indeed also present in the country; but most federalist forces finally took on a more liberal color.[1]

Separatist Tendencies

Between Iturbide's overthrow, at the end of March 1823, and his departure for exile from Veracruz, on May 11, there were some attempts at reaction, particularly in the Bajío and in Guadalajara, where Quintanar proclaimed the Free State of Jalisco, which under cover of federalism attempted to become a strong point of Iturbidista resistance. Several *tapatío* deputies in Mexico were of that persuasion, among them the erstwhile commandant of the city of Mexico, José Antonio Andrade, and the Cuban writer Antonio José Valdés, who was in the staff of *El Aguila* and, according to Fray Servando, belonged to the "mountain."[2] Fernández de Lizardi commented on the events in Guadalajara, which by chance occurred the same day as the deposed emperor was leaving the country, saying that a crowd gathered, proffering shouts of "Long live religion and Agustín I," but that they were dispersed after the death of eleven "fools," adding that "it was a pity that they died, but it is necessary. There is no other alternative to make them enter into their duties." The commotion, he thought, had been the work of a few ignorant ecclesiastics rather than of the léperos themselves. A few weeks earlier, he had already approved the Easter Saturday firing on the Mexican barrio crowds, saying that "these events show how insolent the scum of the people are and how necessary it is to repress them with more serious laws," among which he proposed the death penalty for stealing over ten pesos and sending vagrants to forced labor for one year, two measures that he would later include in a constitutional project.[3] To counteract a potentially strong Guadalajara, pressures were exerted from the capital to force Colima to secede from that province and become a national territory under direct central control.[4] Toward the end of May, the friars in Mexico City spread the rumor, according to Carlos María de Bustamante, that Iturbide had not departed and was actually heading toward his stronghold in Guadalajara. Friars were usually considered to be Iturbidistas, but opponents tried to influence them and cultivate a more liberal faction within their ranks, to whom the argument was put that after all, religious orders were "republics" and thus had to support a republic in civic affairs.[5]

In June 1823 Santa Anna joined the federalist agitation, moving to

San Luis Potosí and declaring himself "Protector of the Federation," though without much success.[6] Proclamations of autonomy by the provinces quickly followed each other, creating a very serious problem for the centralist Poder Ejecutivo triumvirate. Yucatán was managing its own affairs since adhering to the Plan de Casamata, and soon declared itself autonomous, holding elections and instructing its representative in Mexico, Crescencio Rejón, that only under a federal regime would it remain united. At the same time, Chiapas decided to join Mexico, but on its own terms, breaking away from Guatemala, which was also deciding on which attitude to take (it had been incorporated in the empire earlier on).

In June Oaxaca convened its own constituent congress, while Zacatecas composed a provisional plan of government. Also in June the municipality of Querétaro seceded from the province of Mexico and joined with Valladolid (Michoacán) and Guanajuato in a league to defend their own rights, proclaiming Miguel Barragán as their common military commandant. Though the declared purpose was to support the central authorities (while they established a federal constitution), the league entered into relations with the two warring factions from San Luis Potosí (Santa Anna and Armijo), signing together with them a common declaration in Celaya.[7] The mounting pressure forced Congress to declare itself in favor of a federal system and to call for elections for a new constituent legislature. During these elections, held in September 1823, papers extolling Iturbide's return were distributed at the University.[8]

Jalisco, in combination with the Bajío, had a high separatist potential. Economic interests linked to traditional internal circles, agricultural and artisan or industrial, had important roots in the zone that recognized Guadalajara as its political center, with an international outlet through the Pacific. Guadalajara not only had its own consulate but also an audiencia, and in earlier times had been the capital of the Kingdom of New Galicia, separate from that of New Spain until 1786, though under the same viceroy. Its influence could extend to the north, to the provincias internas, and to the intendancies of Zacatecas and San Luis Potosí.[9] The latter was located astride one of the main entrances to the country, Tampico, second only to Veracruz, and which might be increasingly developed in the future. An economic calculation, made in 1822 to allot to each region a fair share of the direct tax, estimated the "wealth" of each province. Giving to each geographical unit a weight proportional to its wealth, we get the figures reproduced in table 3.[10]

The potential separatism of Jalisco and the Bajío nucleated an economic force equivalent to the state of Mexico (with the capital included).

**Table 3. Provinces of Mexico, with Percentages
of Total National Wealth 1822**

Mexico-Puebla-Veracruz axis	*47*
Mexico (including capital)	28
Puebla and Tlaxcala	12
Veracruz	7
Potential Jalisco-Bajío coalition	*31*
Jalisco	9
Guanajuato	7
Querétaro	3
Michoacán	5
San Luis Potosí	3
Zacatecas	4
Others	*20*
Oaxaca	5
Yucatán	4
Tamaulipas	2
Nuevo León	3
Northern provinces	6

Note: Figures do not add up to 100 due to rounding.

Source: *Guía de Hacienda . . . 1826.*

The conflicts we have just described were an expression, among other things, of this phenomenon, which repeated itself several times in the ensuing years. Thus in 1829 Jalisco proposed a coalition to Michoacán, Guanajuato, Zacatecas and San Luis Potosí, with the purpose of resisting the domination of the Yorkino faction after the Acordada revolt. A similar convergence was attempted soon afterward with the ostensible purpose of taking into their own hands the defense against foreign aggression, in case Guerrero's central government did not act promptly enough. Carlos María de Bustamante, in his chronicle of the second government of his namesake Anastasio (1837–41), claimed, with his usual exaggeration, that in Tampico the smugglers always arranged for two revolutions each year, one to unload and the other to load the ships with contraband. The Jalisco-centered coalition only lacked a port to the Atlantic, which it could easily get in Tampico, with which San Luis Potosí had close connections. This would have required incorporating Tamaulipas, or having the port secede from it.

The alternative potential coalition of Mexico with Puebla and Veracruz would be stronger, but it was not so easy to organize it, due to the differences between a liberal and export-oriented Veracruz and a conservative Puebla, bent on protecting its industry and its religious beliefs.[11]

Iturbidista Plotting

In August the deposed emperor arrived in Leghorn, Italy, where he was required to fix his residence, but he immediately started planning his return. In Mexico, responding to rumors of this plotting, Congress approved a decree permitting the detention of suspects, and forthwith, on October 2, a score of Iturbide supporters were imprisoned, beginning with José Antonio Andrade ("Cartuchera"), the count of San Pedro del Alamo and other military men, plus several civilians, such as the schoolmaster and "titiretero" José Ignacio Paz, one Maximiliano Vargas Machuca (probably related to the former governor of the Indian parcialidad of Santiago Tlatelolco, Manuel Santos Vargas Machuca), and the Barreras.[12] This was just a part of a broader Iturbidista plot, organized by Manuel Reyes Veramendi, who was planning to pass on the leadership to José Antonio Andrade, if it proved successful. He had a following among sergeants and prepared proclamations and wrote instructions for an Ejército Restaurador de la Libertad, with the motto "Religion, Independence, Freedom Well Understood, and the Hero of Iguala."[13] In connection with this conspiracy, there is an anonymous letter stating that several Iturbidista projects were going on and urging the addressee to expedite matters so as not to remain behind. Another letter, by Vicente Manso to a certain Don Faustino, explains that "we federalists now have an armistice with the Iturbidistas."[14]

In December 1823 Iturbide abandoned his forced residence in Leghorn, pretending that he was menaced by the Holy Alliance, which had just invaded and occupied Spain, reestablishing Ferdinand in his full absolutist functions. He proceeded to London and prepared an expedition to Mexico, supposedly to offer his help in the defense against a foreseeable attempt to recover Spain's colonies. He informed Congress of his moves, but the beneficiaries were not prepared to welcome his services and declared (even before receiving the letter) that if Iturbide returned, he would be considered a traitor.

Meanwhile, just before Christmas 1823, a tumultuous junta in Puebla declared in favor of federation, condemning the excessive introduction of foreign merchandise, which was ruining the artisans.[15] The Puebla rebellion was quickly suppressed in January, by central troops under the command of Gómez Pedraza, who despite his support for the emperor until the very end, had reemerged as an important military and political figure in the provisional government. That same January of 1824, destabilization reached the city of Mexico, where José María Lobato, a colonel of liberal-populist convictions, staged a pronunciamiento to force the Poder Ejecutivo to expel the Spaniards, so as to deprive an invading army of local allies.[16] He had previously written to Gómez Pedraza to try to incorporate him into his project, asserting that the aim was the reinstallation of Iturbide. He resisted for a very short time, receiving support from Reyes Veramendi, who later went into hiding.[17] At the same time, another unsuccessful plot burst out in Cuernavaca. Both the Pensador and the Payo were involved in this anti-Spanish agitation.[18]

Reyes Veramendi continued his Iturbidista plot underground, seeking reassurances as to the loyalty of his sergeant friends and receiving from the administrator of Iturbide's hacienda in Chalco news about the return of the "*amo*," who ought to be in Guadalajara before the end of the month. Some desperadoes were planning to get money by attacking a conducta, no doubt inspired by the master's example, though having fewer resources at their disposal. They were encouraged by hearing "in the pulquerías and streets [of some villages] officers and troops shouting vivas to Iturbide."[19]

The authorities were unable to take a hard line against subversive attempts, and on March 9 Congress approved an amnesty for those involved, especially applicable to the Lobato mutiny. A few days afterward, on March 12, billboards (*"rotulones"*) were stuck to the city's walls, announcing Iturbide's return. The Payo del Rosario, who had fled the capital as a result of being indicted for two anti-Spanish pamphlets probably written in connection with the Lobato attempt, was found and jailed. He was going to be sentenced to deportation to Alvarado, but a very highly attended trial (with a public of some five hundred people) found him not guilty. At the beginning of April, Germán Prissette, the French journalist who worked on *El Aguila* and had cooperated with Iturbide and Quintana Roo during the empire, was expelled from the country.[20]

Lobato was unsuccessful, but Congress hastened to sanction an *acta constitutiva de la federación*, to calm down the provinces. Iturbide's partisans in Mexico joined the federalist agitation, taking into account that one of their bastions was Guadalajara. By doing this they were further irritating their more moderate (and centralist) early supporters among the well-to-do. Iturbide's empire and his whole philosophy, of course, had been centralist, but the frantic search for allies forced this turnabout. Here Iturbidismo was venturing into unfathomed waters and was liable to lose more than it would gain. However, it is probably the case that business support was already lost, and therefore it was necessary to seek new allies in order to survive. From the city of Mexico Gómez Navarrete, Iturbide's personal friend and attorney, founded *El Aguila*, just two weeks after the abdication, to guide public opinion and attack the government. Quite a few elements among the military (especially Anastasio Bustamante and Luis Quintanar in Jalisco), the church, and the old nobility were still on Iturbide's side, however. Eventually they might provide the basis for a recovery of support among the upper classes, once Iturbide was back in power, even if this happened through popular mobilization and federalist agitation. Of course an empire reborn in such a way would be very different from the earlier version, but it was not to be. Among other reasons this was due to the fact that the tactical support Iturbide had obtained from many populist and progressive liberals had evaporated. So he had to rely only on his traditional populist mobilizational capacity, mediated by friars and other elements, such as the Barreras.

Finally in May 1824, Iturbide left England by ship, with arms and a printing press. That same month, on May 7, the letter sent by Iturbide offering his services was read in Congress and widely published.[21] Meanwhile in Jalisco Bustamante and Quintanar continued to defy the central executive, trying to mobilize popular sectors in their favor, though engaging in a confrontation with the liberal-federalist majority in the local congress, led by Prisciliano Sánchez, who would later become a very progressive governor of the state.[22] The legislature in early April warned Governor (erstwhile jefe político) Luis Quintanar to control the "ferment in the lower populace, no doubt seduced by some aspirantes" and to apply the laws condemning expressions of support for the deposed ruler. The governor answered that the matter was trivial, based only on "some small meeting of plebeyan and idle people," and similar reassurances were given by the military chief, Anastasio Bustamante. As disturbances continued, by the end of the month the local congress again requested preventive action, because "who does not know that the lower populace, due to their ignorance and immorality, are susceptible . . . [to] becoming a blind instrument of the factious, when these acquire the means to pay and corrupt them."[23] In Mexico journalists such as Fernández de Lizardi did not support the separatist tendencies in the province, though he admitted that the authorities in that state were his friends. While he felt the national government "smelled of centralism," the excesses of provincial "little sovereign congresses" were dangerous and would degenerate into a "cena de negros."[24] This was not the attitude of his friend the Payo, who went to Guadalajara to participate in that fight against the "tyranny" that the Alamán faction was establishing in the capital.[25]

Tension in the city of Mexico mounted, and by June several Iturbidistas, including Reyes Veramendi, Juan Antonio Andrade, Luciano Castrejón (the "marqués del Bodegón"), and two dozen others were found and arrested in the calle de Celaya and other meeting places, prompting the government to take sterner measures. Three of the plotters, Reyes Veramendi, Hernández, and Santoyo, were condemned to death, but afterward were reprieved, "due to the government's weakness," as Carlos María de Bustamante recorded.[26] Finally that same month the Executive Power sent an expedition under the command of Bravo and Negrete, who in June occupied Guadalajara without too much resistance. In the aftermath of the repression of the regional Iturbidista dissidence, Bravo ordered the execution of Eduardo García and Baron Rosemberg, two military chiefs who had not surrendered in time and had fled to rugged Tepic to organize resistance.[27] Somewhat earlier, in April, a young officer, Basilisio Valdés, had also been shot for allegedly participating in an Iturbidista conspiracy.[28] Repression was harsh, probably denoting a very real sense of danger on the part of the authorities.

After being "liberated," the Jalisco legislature was of two minds as to how to deal with the new situation, since it did not wish to associate itself with the Iturbidistas, but neither did it like the possibility of the demise of federalism. It argued in a manifesto that everyone had been happy with federalism and that the central powers had overreacted by sending General Bravo to crush a few, isolated disturbances. It admitted having been ignorant of the fact that Generals Quintanar and Bustamante were part of the "factious" (Iturbidistas); now what was important was to prevent any panic from leading to a concentration of authority in a despotic national "director" or single executive, with the power to control the state militia.[29]

The Guadalajara rebellion was most probably programmed to coincide with Iturbide's arrival in the country, which took place at about the same time (early July), on the coast of Tamaulipas. After an apparently successful first encounter with the military commandant Felipe de la Garza, who owed him his life (as he had been pardoned by the emperor after his revolt in 1822), Iturbide confronted the local legislature, which was adamant in the application of the death penalty. In Mexico this time there were no protests, but Congress finally sanctioned the federal constitution and advanced by a few months president-elect Guadalupe Victoria's accession to office, to keep a power vacuum from developing.

Iturbidismo was dismembered, but its tradition remained alive, even if divided into its two main components. The element on the Right, after attempting to take on a federalist and provincial hue, finally became incorporated into clerical conservatism, or it acted more pragmatically, searching for a new caudillo. First this was Anastasio Bustamante, twice president of the republic (1829–32 and 1837–41), who had the honor in 1838 of bringing back from Tamaulipas the mortal remains of Iturbide.[30] Later on the caudillo was Santa Anna, who developed into a fine art the strategy of entering into alliances with the most radicalized liberal-populist sectors, only to confront and persecute them soon afterward. As for the other component of Iturbidismo, the popular one, promoted by the friars and the "*capataces*" of the marginal sectors, it languished as a potential force, increasingly difficult to control from the Right. Neither Bustamante nor Santa Anna ever obtained any solid popular support of their own, except through occasional alliances with the exaltado liberals. In this they differed from the Argentinian Juan Manuel de Rosas, who was capable of incorporating as his own the urban following he inherited from his ally the liberal populist Manuel Dorrego. In Mexico, by contrast, radical liberalism remained a very important force, and through it the mobilizational tendencies latent in various sectors of society were channeled, finally erupting with great violence in the civil wars of 1858–60 and in the resistance to foreign intervention.

The Centralist Bid for Power

After the overthrow of the empire, the provisional three-man Poder Ejecutivo was dominated by the centralists, despite having Vicente Guerrero as one of the alternates and the more moderate Guadalupe Victoria as one of the three principals, outnumbered by Nicolás Bravo and Pedro Celestino Negrete. The other two alternates, Miguel Domínguez (former corregidor of Querétaro) and especially Mariano Michelena, had centralist convictions. Due to the military obligations of the others and the more retiring personality of Domínguez, Michelena was at first the moving figure in the triumvirate. More important, however, was the fact that after a first short interval, during which José Ignacio García Illueca was named universal secretary, the first ministerial designation fell upon Lucas Alamán, in Relaciones, the most coveted position in the cabinet. At the same time Francisco Molinos del Campo was made jefe político of the province of Mexico, thus gaining control over the capital's police.[31] In that same month of April 1823, the recently reconvened Congress decided that it was not necessary to elect new representatives until the legal term of the old ones had run out (at the end of the year). The reaction from the provinces was immediate, particularly from a cohesive group formed by Guadalajara, Michoacán, Guanajuato, San Luis Potosí, and Zacatecas, joined by Oaxaca. These populous and economically dynamic areas did not have much confidence in the representative responsibility of many of their deputies. The system by which they had been elected was too traditional, and the vote was not proportional to population, but to the number of partidos in a province.[32]

In the city of Mexico as well, populist pamphleteers such as the Pensador inveighed against the continuation of the Congress. He published a brochure entitled *Si dura más el Congreso nos quedamos sin camisa* (signed Cogitator). When the public prosecutor accused him of being subversive, he responded with another tract, arguing that he had referred to an imaginary "congress" of léperos and drunkards in the barrio de San Pablo, adding sarcasm to insult, but getting away with it after a jury declared him innocent.[33]

Finally in May Congress accepted that new elections had to be held as soon as possible. That decision was made by 71 against 33 votes; among those rejecting the idea, on the grounds of not changing an existing legal arrangement, were Carlos María de Bustamante, Fray Servando Teresa de Mier, Jose María Fagoaga, and General Manuel Mier y Terán, eminent representatives of the moderate-liberal faction, of which Fagoaga was the leader. As party lines were not neat, if they existed at all, and there was a large number of fluctuating deputies, it was not obvious as a result of the decision that the centralists were in the minority, but matters were tending in that direction.

This time the convocation followed more neatly the Spanish constitutional method, allotting deputies according to population, and the same criterion would be used to determine the number of electors at each stage of the indirect process. All adult permanent-resident males would be allowed to vote, except for personal servants. It was expressly stated that rural peones, vaqueros, and jornaleros were not to be considered personal servants. A discussion took place in Congress as to whether the vote should be verbally cast or not. Juan de Dios Mayorga thought it was better to have it given by secret ballot, as many people would prefer not to become compromised by public knowledge of their preferences. But a very solid battery of moderate-liberal worthies (José Cecilio del Valle, José María Cabrera, and Carlos María de Bustamante) replied that if votes were not cast verbally and in a clear voice, for all to know, the recording or scrutinizing of secret ballots might lend itself to interferences; also, illiterates having to fill in a written ballot might be duped by scheming intermediaries. In other words the influence of public opinion and social hierarchies should be allowed a free hand. It was not so obvious, however, how public opinion would react in the event, as it could also be organized in a manner contrary to the dominant classes. The law incorporated the openly expressed vote, but with a contrary provision for second-level juntas, to be held by primary electors at the partido head towns. There the balloting would be secret, probably to prevent influence by organized pressure groups.[34]

At the level of the Poder Ejecutivo, Lucas Alamán, already the dominant figure, completed the formation of the cabinet by bringing in Francisco Arrillaga in Hacienda, Pablo de la Llave in Justicia, and General José Joaquín Herrera in War. Francisco Arrillaga was a Spanish merchant from Veracruz, a member of that ayuntamiento in 1808; he had made money and bought an hacienda but suffered financially as a result of the wars. He was highly appreciated by Carlos María de Bustamante, who believed he was a "vizcaíno de gran talento," and by the editors of the *Mensajero Comercial de Méjico*, a business-oriented liberal paper.[35] Pablo de la Llave, also a Veracruzano, was a canon in Morelia and a priest and botanist who had been to the Cortes. According to Zavala he changed his earlier liberal and freemason ideas into conservative ones; his proclericalism was excessive even for the Catholic Carlos María de Bustamante. He was later elected senator for Veracruz, was a member of the Escocés faction, and was close to Alamán. As for General Herrera, he too was Veracruzano, his father having been in charge of the mail in Perote. He had a distinguished military career in the service of the Spanish government against the Insurgentes, and later opposed Iturbide, who jailed him. Despite that, at the very end of the empire, when a change of guard was attempted by Iturbide, Herrera had emerged from prison to cooperate with the liberal Guatemalan José Cecilio del Valle to take up the responsibility of defending the institutions against the rebels led by Santa Anna. He was a moderate liberal and one of the few to complete a constitutional presidency, after the war with the United States.

Veracruz predominance in the executive body was very obvious, as was that of centralist interests rooted in the city of Mexico. This Mexico-Veracruz axis, with a conservative-clerical and moderate-liberal convergence, was quite powerful but, again, as in the case of conservative Iturbidismo, was not enough to rule the country, even with the support of most of the armed forces. While the ministry was being constituted (April—July 1823), the provincial rebellions were raging. Congress was again forced to make concessions, declaring on June 1 and again on June 12 that it was in favor of federalism but was not making a formal proclamation of that system, in order to let the future legislature decide freely. It was also at about this time that, as a sop to the potential opposition that was being generated in the provinces and in the capital, General Vicente Guerrero was appointed to fill in the third alternate position in the executive body.

In the new structure of alliances developing as a result of the breakdown of the Iturbidista formula, the centralists occupied a dominant position. Their base was the old moderate-liberal coalition, which absorbed some elements of the Iturbidista Right (the miners and soon the newly emerging industrialists) and some potentially federalist groups from Veracruz (the tierra caliente interests). Both the church and the military, despite harboring Iturbidista minorities, basically supported the centralist attempt at this juncture.

Conservative Iturbidismo retained its hidalgo and old nobility component, along with sectors of the upper clergy and military. These military men (symbolized by Anastasio Bustamante) incorporated, via their lower rungs, some of the remnants of the popular mobilization attempted in the late days of the empire, while losing quite a bit of it to the newly consolidating Yorkino faction. Two actors, the regional miners and the local market-oriented landowners, remained as the bases of federalism. The liberal-populist faction, in the process of becoming organized into Yorkino lodges, expanded, absorbing traditional popular-authoritarian elements inherited from its Iturbidista connections. Being highly mobilizational, Yorkinismo could channel the residual power of the urban and rural masses, thus challenging the Escocés group supported by most of the church and army. In a contest between the more upper-class Escoceses and the popular organization slowly taking the form of the Yorkino party, the Iturbidistas and the federalists could perform a function of balance.

It was very difficult to establish a solid governing coalition of the dominant classes without including Iturbidismo, that is, elements from the ancien régime and protectionist corporatism, mixed with some popular mobilization. But both the protectionist-cum-corporatist and the mobilizational features of Iturbidismo made it increasingly unacceptable to a bourgeoisie bent on establishing modern institutions and opening up the internal market to the winds of world trade. Nevertheless, a return to Iturbide's formula was attractive to some groups, especially once the expected prosperity deriving from the international market did not materialize.

Presidentialist Federalism as a Compromise

Popular elections for the Second Constituent Congress were held during September 1823, when a large part of the country had become practically independent from the central power in Mexico, and many provinces were declaring themselves sovereign states and developing their own institutional structures. Despite these yearnings for autonomy, they did participate in the national elections, and the new Constituent Congress was inaugurated in November 1823. Many Iturbidistas entered the new Congress in the guise of federalism, which was the currently acceptable form of expressing opposition to the government. Many genuine federalists, as well as populists and clericals, also got elected, despite official pressure in favor of centralist moderate liberals. The government could not control the electoral process, which was in fact in the hands of local elites, though with an element of popular mobilization in the larger centers.

Accepting the inevitable, supporters of the centralist idea veered toward a toned-down form of federalism, which they thought might not endanger national unity, as would happen under an extreme decentralization. As in other Latin American countries, there were some who believed that the guarantee of freedom lay in curtailing the powers of the executive or in making it plural, to avoid personalism. An extreme case of this was Venezuela, under the constitution of 1811, which despite war conditions vested the executive in three people. Simón Bolívar was a well-known opponent of this type of system, and during his career he veered toward the opposite extreme, a strong life-long presidency. Though these ideas were especially articulated in 1826 in his proposed constitution for Bolivia, they had been expressed by him in various forms for some time. This produced a reduction of his prestige among radical liberal politicians and earned him support from the moderate liberals, though the latter had reasons to fear his possible tendencies toward dictatorship. *El Sol* was a frequent defender of Bolívar's positions, which became an ideological and political token in the Mexican debate. Bolívar's stance against federalism and utopian constitution making was extolled, while his self-proclaimed disciple Bernardo O'Higgins's attempt at personal rule in Chile was condemned. *El Sol* had praise for the centralist-minded though in practice provincially based government led in Buenos Aires by Bernardino Rivadavia as dominant minister, which had recently snuffed out a plot in favor of "patria y religión."[36] The discussion as to the form the executive power should take in Mexico became intense; federalists wished, among other things, to make sure it would not control the states' militias, deemed to be the guarantee of their autonomy and of public liberties in general. Such Iturbidistas as Prissette maintained that the need for a dictatorship was being aired in government circles. He condemned such proposals, going to the extreme of claiming that even the idea of vesting executive authority in one man was inimical to freedom, thus probably trying to cancel memories of his past colaboration with the emperor.[37]

This position regarding the executive was not shared by all or most liberal populists, who on the contrary had a penchant for a strong presidency as a bulwark against oligarchical rule. Fernández de Lizardi argued that occasionally a dictatorship could be useful, as in the Roman practice under Cincinnatus and others. At the time he was writing this, there were rumors, which he contributed to spreading, that Iturbide was about to return. It is not impossible that the Pensador was preparing himself for a radical change of circumstances.[38]

Fray Servando, in a speech that became famous, and which he called *Profecía Política*, expressed his fears of national disintegration if an excessively decentralizing constitution were adopted. He proposed, however, a modified federal system, since he thought a centralist one was unacceptable to the country.[39] Between December 1823 and January 1824, Congress approved an *acta constitutiva de la federación*, trying thus to assuage fears from the provinces as to its intentions. However, regional rebellions continued and exploded in December in Puebla and in January in the capital (the Lobato mutiny), both being suppressed by the central authorities.

The government, having come out on top after these serious challenges to its authority, strengthened its hand by replacing Herrera in the War ministry by Manuel Mier y Terán, a clearly committed centralist. The agitation in favor of Iturbide's return went on, some rotulones again appearing in the city of Mexico by the end of March, depicting Iturbide with a crown disbanding his enemies Echávarri, Vivanco, and Santa Anna. The Iturbidista editor of *El Archivista General*, the Frenchman Germán Prissette, was jailed and deported, and the editors who continued his work for a few more issues stated that the need for a dictatorhip was being openly discussed, adding that they thought it would be inconvenient. A few days later, in their final appearance, they again reported that Congress was considering the appointment of a director, or chief executive, and that they would always be against this, as they were against rule by any one man.[40]

One important issue associated with the federalist insurrection was the division of taxing powers between the center and the states, which was settled in April of 1824. The federation retained import duties and the levies collected for the export of specie (in coins or bars), most of the tobacco monopoly, the minting dues of the Mexican Casa de Moneda, and other minor items; it also enjoyed preferential access to loan funds. The states would get the alcabalas, the mining levy at production (reduced since independence to 3 percent), the civilian share of the church tithes, the monopoly on cigar elaboration in their territories, and the minting dues of their casas de moneda. The states were so generously treated, that in order to compensate the central power, they were to pay to it a *contingente* of some 3 million pesos per year, in installments due every fifteen days.[41]

This contingente payment proved to be largely theoretical; most often it was in arrears or simply forgotten. Silver exports, on the other hand, were at very low levels, but slack vigilance was also responsible for the small amount of revenue collected from that source. Fiscal recovery would be gradual but persistent; it rose from some 3.7 million pesos in 1825 to 5.8 million the next year, almost 10 million in 1827, and over 12 million in 1828. These were the results of the British reactivation of the mines and of the relative stability the country enjoyed during those years.[42]

But in 1823 these developments were as yet in the future, and in order to make them a reality, it was necessary to consolidate the institutional system, for which the need for a one-person executive was becoming evident. The example of the dictatorship offered to Bolívar in Peru was publicly discussed, as a fact from which diverse conclusions could be derived. It could be argued that in an early stage of state formation it was necessary to concentrate power in the executive; or alternatively, that it would easily degenerate into strong-man government.[43]

In July Iturbide arrived in Tamaulipas and his execution took place, rendering the consolidation of legitimate authority more urgent. At the same time, it was necessary to widen the regime's basis of support. This took the form of a weakening of Alamán's monopoly of influence. In August Arrillaga was replaced in Hacienda by another Veracruzano, José Ignacio Esteva, who, however, was of a very different orientation. He came from a modest background, usually being called "chocolatero" and known as the owner of a bookshop in his native city. According to reports in the hands of the Quai d'Orsay, he was a small merchant of the old style, a prohibitionist with little knowledge of finance. He had been elected alcalde of the port city in 1821 and became in 1825 the founder, with Lorenzo de Zavala and Miguel Ramos Arizpe, of the Yorkino liberal-populist lodges. He was a radical liberal, of the group that had cooperated with Iturbide, and a good friend of Guadalupe Victoria, who was becoming prominent as a transactional candidate for the presidency.[44]

Meanwhile Congress had finally enacted the federal constitution, in October of 1824. The president was to be elected by the votes of the state legislatures during September, and the choice was Guadalupe Victoria, over Nicolás Bravo. To avoid a vacuum of power, Victoria was made to assume office in October, earlier than the normal date of April 1 and also earlier than the newly elected national Congress, which was convened on January 1, 1825.

Before the end of 1824, to consolidate the transactional nature of Mexico's federalism, the city of Mexico was nationalized, thus giving greater financial resources to the central government through its Aduana, where an important sum of alcabalas was collected. This was a serious blow to the state of Mexico, which would have preferred to retain its valuable capital city and, as in the North American case, create the federal capital in some smaller town. There was an attempt at resistance by the state legislature, which in order to forestall the measure tried, in October 1824, to force the national Congress to leave its capital city. Fernández de Lizardi referred to this attitude, which he equated with the one adopted earlier by Guadalajara, when it became autonomous and expelled the centrally designated financial commissioner in charge of tax collection. But resistance was easily overcome, with no serious prospects of armed confrontation. The issue was completely different from the one that loomed so large in Argentina from about 1825 to 1880; what was at stake in Mexico, of course, was only an internal aduana, collecting sales taxes, and not control of an international port.[45]

In the Mexican case, also, the nationalization of the city was undertaken by a government that represented a coalition between Veracruz and Mexico City interests, a coalition that, while not totally dominant, was very powerful. It was not carried out in opposition to political groups based in the city and state, as was the case in Argentina in 1880. The ayuntamiento of Mexico was very much in favor of separation from the state, and it argued, against those who said that the national Congress had no authority to make this decision, that similar discretion had been exercised when Colima was cut off from Jalisco or Coahuila joined to Texas. The Ayuntamiento's only concern was that by becoming the federal capital, the city might be treated as a territory and lose its vote for the presidency (which was cast by the state legislatures) and would thus lack representation in the Senate.[46]

Coalition Government under Guadalupe Victoria

Guadalupe Victoria, who also came from Veracruz, owned lands in Papantla, near the northern coast, and had been a determined insurgente who never surrendered to the Spaniards but rather went into hiding when the cause was lost.[47] Born Félix Fernández, he had adopted his name as a token of revolutionary "Guadalupista" fervor, but he had become more moderate and tried to bring the various factions into government. For that purpose he retained Alamán in the important post of Relaciones, and Pablo de la Llave and Esteva in Justicia and Hacienda, respectively. The latter's presence involved an alliance with the populist sector, soon to become the Yorkino party, and was thus an attempt to gain solidity and a predominant political position for the ruling coalition, even at the expense of making it excessively heterogeneous. Equally important was the incorporation into the ministry of War of Manuel Gómez Pedraza, a military man who had served the empire up to its end. He continued to be a prestigious figure among his comrades-in-arms, perhaps because he represented a more "professional" ideal, if such a concept can be applied to the times. However, given his Iturbidista connections, this was also a move calculated to reassure that faction, even if it was not more directly represented in the new system. Gómez Pedraza, who was originally from Querétaro, also had mining connections through his father-in-law, the lawyer Juan Francisco Azcárate, in turn related to the powerful Valenciana–Rul–Pérez Gálvez clan.

As a result of the policy of opening up the economy, British capital flowed into the semiparalized silver mines. During 1823 and 1824, two loans were also transacted in London, with Mariano Michelena and Vicente Rocafuerte, moderate centralist liberals, as main agents for the government. A total sum of almost 22 million pesos was obtained, and though later on one of the banking firms where the balance was deposited failed, the inflow of that money, plus the funds from the mining companies, occasioned a short era of prosperity; the peso even held a premium over the pound, given the need for many foreign companies to make payments in Mexico. This abundance of financial resources was responsible for the greater comparative tranquility of these years. The flow would start drying up by late 1827, giving rise to the renewed political violence of the following year.[48]

Foreign recognition was being negotiated, and the British loan was an important symbol of success on that front. In France the more liberal sectors in the government might recognize the fait accompli of independence, but the "ultras" were opposed. Even the Spanish government, it was said, would follow suit if a monarchical system were adopted.[49]

In Mexico factional conflict went on, though for the time being in a peaceful way. In September 1825 a group of radical-liberal deputies, Juan de Dios Cañedo from Guadalajara, Lorenzo Zavala and José María Alpuche from Yucatán, and Vicente Gómez Farías from Zacatecas, entered a charge against Alamán, for alleged irregularities in the Mexican legation to the United States. This might have been backed by the American representative in Mexico, Joel Poinsett, who was becoming involved in local politics, siding with the radical and populist liberals. Alamán had to resign, and his post fell to Sebastián Camacho, yet another Veracruzano from Jalapa, a moderate liberal who was a friend of Victoria and whose ideas were expressed in *El Oriente*. The director of the French Rhenanian mining company in Mexico considered him an acceptable local notable and right-thinking journalist, contrasting with the arrogant parvenu Esteva.[50] With this appointment Guadalupe Victoria attempted to compensate for the bad effects of Alamán's forced resignation, and by the way he strengthened the cohort of his personal friends in the cabinet. Veracruzano dominance, however, was excessive, and could produce ill will among other provincials. The latter were to some extent assuaged by the presence of Gómez Pedraza, however, who had the interests of the Bajío at heart.

At this moment a military event provided the opportunity for Esteva to make some political capital. The fort of San Juan de Ulúa, which faced Veracruz and where the Spaniards retained a foothold, was about to surrender. Esteva left his ministerial position temporarily to go to the coast to participate in the negotiations, in which General Miguel Barragán, a moderate liberal from San Luis Potosí, also took part. Santa Anna missed the opportunity, because since his failed attempt at becoming protector of the federation in 1823, he had lost favor and was trying to recoup his fortunes by getting involved in Yucatecan politics, envisioning the liberation of Cuba. This was one way of keeping the military forces active, idled as they were by the end of hostilities on the continent; international conflicts might provide a justification for continued budgetary largesse. Moderate opinion, of course, considered the Cuban project impracticable, and it was common wisdom at the time that it would provoke a slave insurrection in the island and was therefore to be condemned by civilized nations. But there were always political innovators who would dream of glory and propose plans for starting a caste war by stimulating the slaves to seek their freedom with the help of Mexican arms. The French sent their congratulations to the Mexican government for the reconquest of San Juan de Ulúa, but added that it would be a mistake to proceed now to the invasion of Cuba. The Mexican authorities answered in March 1826 that they had renounced such a project, but there was always the possibility that it might be revived. More likely, though, was the prospect of a Spanish invasion to reconquer the country, which actually materialized, though only in 1829.[51]

Broad coalition government under Guadalupe Victoria was a fragile construct, made possible by the temporary balance between factions. Soon Yorkino pressure would put an end to it, but for the moment the country was relatively calm, and even foreign opinion was impressed by the order and prosperity Mexico had achieved under its new institutions. But funds were running short, and the calm would not endure.[52]

6
Political Polarization, 1826–1828

The year 1826 started with an instruction from the president to the customs offices that beginning January 1, half the proceeds of tariff collections would be set aside for the repayment of the British debt. The debt had been incurred during the years 1823 and 1824, and the lending houses had already discounted the services for the first two years from the principal, so up to now there had been no burden on the treasury. The problem was going to start immediately, introducing tensions in a government that was still of a coalitional nature, though dominated by Minister of War Manuel Gómez Pedraza, a man of Iturbidista origins who had veered toward a relatively moderate liberalism without, however, becoming identified with the Escoceses. The latter had as their representative in the cabinet Sebastián Camacho in Relaciones (replacing Alamán, who had been forced to resign), but the Yorkino faction had been able to put José Ignacio Esteva in Hacienda and Miguel Ramos Arizpe in Justicia.

The presence of the British could not fail to produce nationalist reactions among the political class. The Payo del Rosario started in early 1825 with a few tracts and reached the limit in November 1825, with one defiantly entitled *Si no se van los ingleses hemos de ser sus esclavos*, addressing them as "monsters . . . who live off the sufferings of their slaves, tyrants of humanity whose greatness is based on the work of their wretched colonies," and who "have covered with rags our artisans with the introduction of their merchandise." The following day he was detained and sent to Acapulco, where he had to remain for two months until a jury absolved him. Fernández de Lizardi (who as a friend harbored Villavicencio's family in his home) joined the battle with an ambivalently titled tract, *Consejo de guerra a los ingleses*, where, however, he came to their defense, saying that despite some ill effects on the artisans, their presence was beneficial to the country. When the Payo came back from

Acapulco, he continued with his war of pamphlets against foreigners, publishing an unintelligibly titled *Se va a descubrir la facción de gachupines que sedujo al Payo del Rosario para escribir contra los ingleses*. With that title he was alluding to the accusation levelled at him by his enemies, that his anti-British ardor had some interested backers among the other immigrant community. He of course denied this, and gave to the presses three tracts regarding the return of the coyotes, culminating in a *Plan de desgachupinar si vienen los de la liga, o sea tercera parte de Los coyotes de España*. In it he proposed to concentrate all Spaniards in a centrally located city, where they would be guarded and their numbers and properties listed. If found outside the "depósito," they would be shot. He explained that this was not an oppressive system, as it was the result of the state of war that still technically existed, though there had been no hostilities since the surrender of the fort of San Juan de Ulúa. The potential threat of a Spanish expedition was the justification for the government having special authority to deport people or transfer them from one area of the country to another. Fernández de Lizardi, proving again to be somewhat more moderate in these affrays, recommended calm, in a tract in which he adopted the garb of a "converted" coyote telling the hens (that is, the Mexican people, supposed victims of its savage instincts) that it was an exaggeration to say that no Spaniard could be a good person.[1]

Meanwhile the problem of common criminality was becoming very serious and taking on political overtones, as law-and-order stalwarts harped on it as an example of the weakness of existing institutions. To counter this, Governor Molinos del Campo (an Escocés), beginning the previous year, had been hauling suspects to the securer old Inquisition jail, where recently enacted special legislation allowed military justice to be applied, rather than going through the laxer procedures of the Cárcel de Corte, under Ayuntamiento control. This produced conflicts between the expeditious governor and some of the members of the municipality who were concerned with human rights issues for those arrested, said to be crammed by the dozen where there was room for just one.[2]

Despite these measures, the crime wave hit the foreign community. European legations were concerned, and the government reacted by clamping down on the culprits so as to set an example. On March 6, 1826, a group of four people who had earlier that year stolen 6,000 pesos and 250 ounces of gold from foreign residents was condemned to death. They were a cobbler, a bizcochero, an "operario" (guardian of the house that was broken into), and a gunmaker, who was the brains behind the operation. They had as accomplices a porter and two mine operatives. Originally an army council of war had condemned them to six years hard labor, but General Filisola, the military commandant of the capital, changed this to the death penalty, despite the aggrieved parties' appeal for clemency. The following day some *Amigos de la igualdad ante la ley* expressed concern, not for the fact that a severe penalty had been applied, but because of the difference in treatment when foreigners were involved. Summary justice, however, was also meted out to those victimizing nationals, as progovernment pamphleteers tried to show.[3]

Economic Problems

Esteva, as minister of Hacienda, had the responsibility of finding funds for all the various financial demands, mainly from the military. At the beginning his task was facilitated by the availability of the British loan money, but at the same time he had to reassure Congress and public opinion that in the future there would be resources not only to cover current expenses but also to repay the international creditors.

At the opening of Congress in January 1825, he reported to both houses on the state of the public treasury, with which he had been entrusted only a few months before, in August 1824, toward the end of the triumvirate Executive Power. The funds of the first London loan had been almost totally spent, but the second one, for 3,200,000 pounds (16 million pesos), was still intact, as it was in the final stages of implementation, thus providing a respite. Using values for the previous year or two, Esteva forecast a federal income for the coming year of 1825 of just over 9 million pesos, against expected disbursements of almost 18 millions, of which two-thirds were military. The main item on the income side was provided by the customs houses, which were projected to yield almost 4.4 million; it might be necessary to reduce the authorized ports of entry in order better to control them.

Tobacco, which before the Insurgencia had yielded a net income of almost 4.5 million, now was reduced to 1 million, from which one-third had to be deducted for the states. The monopoly had been abolished as one of the first measures of Congress in 1822, when many deputies thought they might endear themselves to public opinion by such a measure; Esteva admitted having been one of them and now recognized his mistake. However, pressed for money, that same Congress had renewed the application of the estanco for two years, in October 1822. But in June 1823, soon after the demise of the empire, the elaboration of cigars had been opened up, thus inevitably relaxing controls over the primary producers. Protests from some states (Michoacán, Guanajuato, and Querétaro) had contributed, in February 1824, to the reestablishment of the full estanco, with the states receiving the industrial part. However, contraband continued, and it would take a strenuous effort by the government to recover that source of revenue. Esteva recommended prompt reconstruction of the estanco's liquid capital, which was used to finance the producers, thus stopping them from using illegal outlets. The participation of local states in the monopoly (at the cigar-elaboration level) should be eliminated, he thought, because it contributed to disorder and contraband; they might be compensated by being allowed to run their own lotteries, or to reduce the "contingentes" they were supposed to send to the central treasury. Mining did not give any resources to the central government except at the moment of export of specie, already included under import and export duties. The much reduced levies paid at the place of production were now collected by the states, and coinage duties were so low that the Casa de Moneda operated at a loss. Esteva urged the reconstitution of the Casa's liquid fund of some 2.6 million pesos that it had had in colonial times, now reduced to a paltry 100,000 pesos. That cash was used to pay the miners delivering their barras to the mint, without having to wait for the coining process. When the money was not available, the temptation to go to private merchants who might export the barras illegally was too high and was responsible for a reduction of the amounts coined. Esteva proposed a return to the traditional colonial regime in silver taxes, accepting, however, that the states would collect the amounts awarded to them under the accepted distribution, but the increases necessary to return to colonial levels should be retained by the federal government.[4]

As a result of his proposed measures, Esteva thought he might collect an extra 3.3 million pesos in tobacco and 3.4 million in silver (two-thirds in increased production charges and one-third in minting). With this and the remaining unused 1.3 million of the first London credit, the budget would be balanced.

The Senate's Finance Commission took the report to pieces, demonstrating that the government, especially its Yorkino sector, did not have a majority there. Its five members were Juan de Dios Cañedo, Francisco García (both noted federalists, from Jalisco and Zacatecas, respectively), Antonio Medina (a Spaniard from Veracruz who had been a low-profile minister, first of War and then of Hacienda under Iturbide), José Loreto Barraza (from Durango), and Juan de Dios Rodríguez (from Querétaro). They scrutinized the much-inflated list of proposed War Ministry expenditures, which had been reported by Esteva (see table 4).

Table 4. War Ministry Budget for 1825

Administrative staff and military salaries for permanent army and navy	7,894,281
Active Militias, in the interior of the country and on the coasts	7,313,907
Construction of seven war ships and one arsenal	1,482,097
Extraordinary expenses	2,256,238
Total	18,946,523
Total after reductions due to unfilled posts	14,934,533

The senators first of all rejected the validity of the exceedingly large "extraordinary expenses" item and thought the number of ships constructed should be smaller. But they were particularly concerned at the idea of "activating" such a large number of militias. The militias were normally the responsibility of the states, commanded by their governors, unless mobilized and paid by the central government in order to be used for national purposes. The senators rejected this item almost in its entirety, leaving only some forces on the coasts; as an alternative they proposed that the federation distribute seventy thousand rifles and thirty thousand swords to the states for use by their militias. This proposition of course would have given added teeth to federalism and was tantamount to asking the central government to commit suicide. It was not accepted, mainly through the intervention of the lower house. Perhaps it was based on an idealistic view of what a genuinely decentralized federation would be like, but conditions at the time in Mexico did not allow for this type of proposition to be acceptable.

With the cuts proposed, the senators thought money would abound rather than be wanting. They thus resisted the proposal to return the states' part of the tobacco estanco to the central government, they ridiculed the idea of reducing the ports of entry, which should instead be increased, since trade was bound to pick up; and they wanted the silver taxes to be left as they were, because otherwise mines would stop production. They also proposed that the *internación* tax collected by the federation in the ports in lieu of alcabala be abolished and alcabala on foreign products be reinstated, collected, of course, by the states. Finally, with an eye on the international financial community, they reminded Esteva that the public debt (national and foreign) had to be serviced, or entire families would fall into misery, and this would require another 4 million pesos. In this item they professed not to understand how Esteva had earmarked half a million from the British loan to repay some credits (mostly belonging to Spanish merchants who had migrated) and was going to designate another amount for similar purposes. These funds, if they existed, should help defray the next year's current expenses, including the repayment of all creditors, not just arbitrarily privileged ones.[5]

The lower house also had a commission to examine the minister's report, and though it was less incisive than that of its colleagues in the Senate, it also remarked that War expenses were too high, but concentrated on what it considered an excessive underestimate of customs receipts. If before the war it was usual to import 20 million pesos, and now everybody knew that imports were much higher, with an average tariff of 25 percent, why was the forecast for less than 3 million (not counting the 15 percent internación)? If to that 25 percent the 15 percent internación was added, the total should be much higher; it was necessary to reorganize the collection structure, and by the way also set up a special office in the lower house to control accounts.[6]

The mining industry, of course, reacted to the threat of being taxed as in colonial times. The Tribunal de Minería had recently published a report explaining that mining needed fewer and not more taxes. These arguments were taken up by *El Sol* and by some brochures, which repeated the very well known arguments that production had increased when in 1716 the Spanish crown had reduced taxes on production from 20 percent to 10 percent, and that if the Provisional Junta had not reduced them still further, to 3 percent in 1822, there would have been no more silver in the country. According to *El Sol* it was not true, as some people said and the minister repeated, that only foreigners benefited from these reductions; they were not owners but only financiers of the mines, under temporary contracts, and it had been demonstrated that for every peso they took out, fourteen were put into circulation.[7]

The issue had repercussions abroad, especially among the liberal Spanish community in exile in London, which included the famous economist Canga Argüelles. These people wrote in a monthly called *Ocios de Españoles Emigrados*, which was financed indirectly by the Mexican minister in London, Rocafuerte. They signalled for attention the fact that Esteva had not made provisions for paying the foreign debt and that the Senate had insisted on the priority of that item. The Spanish liberals thought that sums destined to service the foreign debt should be the first item in the budget, so as to rebuild public credit. They put their hopes on customs receipts, though with a moderate tariff and no prohibitions; they also favored a cautious use of the direct tax, or contribución directa, but avoiding the mistakes committed during Iturbide's application of that levy.[8]

Esteva defended his figures in a brochure published toward August of 1825, where he countered the estimates of his critics as to increases in customs receipts, which were much slower to come than some people believed. The merchant community, in expectation of some reductions of the tariff, was keeping business at a low level. He also took care to justify his proposed payment of some debts with monies derived from the British loan. The latter did not have any provision as to the way it should be used, and it was necessary to meet some recently incurred obligations in order to bolster public confidence. He said he had obtained some reduction from the minister of War, but more was very difficult to implement. The Senate's commission came back with another analysis, concentrating now very decidedly on the issue of the credits paid with the British loan money. The issue is too intricate, and it is unnecessary to follow it here in any detail. Basically in the case of a state that was not a good debtor, it was very important for creditors to establish degrees of precedence, as well as to earmark special income items for the repayment of certain debts. Esteva had given priority to some local (Spanish or native) victims of forced loans, including the tobacco growers of his native Veracruz, who were owed funds by the estanco, and the *manilos*, or Manila merchants, whose conducta had been taken by Iturbide to finance his Trigarante Army.

The Senate was averse to this preference, the legality of which depended on an intricate reading of several laws and decrees promulgated since independence; it preferred to suspend as much as possible all payments till everyone could be included, or a renegotiation and consolidation publicly established. One of the things that Esteva was criticized for was that he had exchanged the government's drafts in pounds against London (where it had the loan funds) for a combination of cash and old (worthless) credits. Esteva's not very convincing explanation was that given the great need for Mexican specie on the part of the mining companies, they were prepared to pay high premiums against their own British drafts, thus diminishing the latter's market value. In other words, the Mexican government found itself in possession of undervalued foreign currency (up to 15 or 20 percent) that it had no use for, as it had to pay its expenses in Mexican pesos. So Esteva argued that it was better to avoid the extra payment necessary to obtain the relatively scarce Mexican specie, and to this end it was all right to accept up to one-third in local credits. His argument was easily destroyed by his opponents, as of course the debased local paper was practically worthless in the market; in order to avoid a loss of 15 to 20 percent, the government was incurring a penalty of practically 30 percent.[9]

Finally no change was made in the tax structure, and the senators' proposals were dismissed by the House as not being within their authority. However, Esteva's projects were not approved either, so things remained as they were, with silver duties low, and only hopes of returning the tobacco monopoly to its previous splendor.

The new year, 1826, would see a continuation of the Senate's battle against Esteva, who also came under attack for his active participation in the electoral campaign. Toward the end of 1826, he was preparing his papers to leave the ministry, in which he was replaced by another Yorkino, Tomás Salgado, in March 1827. He wrote a report on the state of the public funds since August 1824, when he had taken on the ministerial responsibility, until December 1826, including some instructions for his successor. He explained that the internal public debt incurred in the fight for or since independence had been almost entirely repaid. This included the tobacco producers, the manilos, and the paper currency and forced loans imposed by Iturbide. By mid-1826 the federation had received from the state of Mexico its aduana, where mostly alcabalas and some other consumer duties were paid, and income was steady from that source. The second large London loan was being used to cover deficits, and military expenses had somehow been kept down, but the expected miracle in customs receipts still was not occurring. There was great hope centered on the current congressional discussions of tariff reduction from the relatively high levels established in early 1822, which were thought to deter foreign merchants from engaging in commerce with Mexico.[10]

The Search for a Strong Executive

In November 1825 Yorkino pressure had succeeded in replacing the moderate Pablo de la Llave in Justicia with the radical federalist Miguel Ramos Arizpe, from Coahuila. In July 1826, while Esteva continued his fight with his Senate and *solero* critics, the lodges obtained another victory at cabinet level: the government decided to send Sebastián Camacho on a mission to Europe to seek formal recognition, on the basis of reports that opinion was becoming more favorable.[11] It was difficult to fill his post, which in a sense was morally still Alamán's. In any event, as his mission was temporary, the office was left in charge of his *oficial mayor*, who happened to be Juan José Espinosa de los Monteros, a liberal with an Iturbidista past, close to the Yorkinos. That month of July was already disturbed by the coming congressional elections, which would begin with primary meetings of voters in August and finish with tertiary gatherings of electors in the state capitals by October.

The Escoceses had already earlier in the year begun a move to have secret societies (that is, primarily, Yorkino lodges) rendered illegal, which prompted the Pensador to write a *Verdadera defensa de los Francmasones*, playing on the similarly titled tracts he had published since independence. He continued with other tracts such as *Se acercan las elecciones, cuidado con los Borbones*, where he warned against the excessive influence the priests had over the electorate in small towns or villages. The radical-liberal Italian exiles Claudio Linati and Florencio Galli, who with the similarly minded Cuban poet José María Heredia published the literary and artistic periodical *El Iris*, also came to the defense of secret societies, explicitly defending the record of the Italian *carbonari*.[12]

The authorities feared violence during the elections and suspected the more radical members of the intelligentsia to be the possible instigators. One of these was an exiled Neapolitan nobleman Orazio de Attelis, baron of Santangelo, persecuted in his country after the liberal interlude of 1820–21 for his radical ideas. Earlier he had collaborated with Murat and then was one of those who, combining Jacobin and Napoleonic memories, recommended taking the revolution abroad in international warfare as a means of consolidating it. In Mexico he became a close friend of Zavala and Quintana Roo and was associated with the latter in the inauguration of an Instituto Nacional, as a new center of higher studies, free from the clerical control still dominant in the university. He wrote an analysis of the international situation, in the form of proposals to the coming Congress of Panamá, where Mexico would soon participate, sending as delegates José Mariano Michelena and José Domínguez Manzo. The gist of his position was that Mexico had to prepare itself for international war, as it could not rely on the permanent protection of the British, who if pressed by the Holy Alliance might allow it to establish monarchies in the Americas, as long as their trade was not hindered. As a matter of fact, the British might even become Mexico's enemies, if they felt the development of the new nation might endanger their industrial monopoly. North American support was more reliable, but it was jeopardized by those in the Mexican Congress who insisted on giving preference in commercial treaties to other Spanish American republics, as though the United States were not a part of the Americas.

Santangelo also believed that resistance to granting Britain reciprocity in religious matters (which would have implied tolerance for Protestants) cooled the determination of the London cabinet to come to Mexico's rescue if necessary. After referring to Napoleon as a genius who had envisaged universal monarchy, he stated that Spanish America would have done better in 1808 to accept Joseph's rule as a means to cast off the shackles of "those ridiculous and venomous Spanish customs, which stupefy the person, degrade the soul, chain reason, numb the body, smother great and generous passions, corrupt taste, befoul the national name, obscure merit, hinder all happiness, destroy all hope . . ." This long litany reflects Santangelo's scant regard for Mexico's inherited Spanish culture, which he hoped to transform through shock treatment, including mass participation in war. He scorned Riego's refusal to take the 1820 revolution to its limits, because "in this sort of situation prudence requires impetuous actions rather than an ill-understood moderation." The opportunity had been lost "to purge Spanish soil of all its monsters, lead one hundred thousand men accross the Pyrenees, and proclaim the freedom of the universe." It was necessary to wait for Karl Marx in the 1850s for someone to be so sanguine about the possible international consequences of revolution in Spain.[13]

The subject of dictatorhip as a necessity in order to confront the combination of internal turmoil and foreign threat became a matter of public discussion, as it had two years earlier, during the crisis of the autonomist rebellions in the provinces. At any rate several radical writers expressed concern about the likelihood of authoritarian rule being established. Fernández de Lizardi predicted that if things did not change before the end of the year, "we would not have a homeland any longer." The radical editors of El Iris also treated the subject, but in an ambiguous manner, which probably reflected the Napoleonic leanings of their friend and compatriot Santangelo, who might also have been inspired by some trends in Bolívar's own thinking. The Neapolitan professed, however, to believe that the Venezuelan Liberator (to whom he dedicated his book) would never follow in the steps of an Alexander, a Caesar, or a Napoleon. Claudio Linati wrote two unclear articles on dictatorship, where he admitted that in difficult conditions it might be justified, as illustrated by Roman history, to which he added the dubious example of Washington and the more real one of Bolívar. In the following issue, Santangelo took up the pen to defend the editors against the barrage of abuse they had been submitted to in response to Linati's article. He also maintained that in times of external danger, such an extreme measure might be necessary;

his book, translated and extolled by Zavala, happened to be a protracted argument that the country was in fact in that situation. A polemic with *El Sol* followed, and finally the *Iris* editors inserted in the semiofficial *El Aguila* (which had a wider and more influential readership than their own paper) a communiqué attempting to clarify their position, still insisting that under conditions of foreign threat, it might be convenient to have recourse to authoritarian rule.[14]

It was not easy to tell who might benefit with a legitimation of the idea of dictatorship. The more radical liberals hoped that the popular agitation that would accompany the resistance against foreign intervention might facilitate their accession to power; they also felt confident of being able to exert it as a weapon for social change. The realities of the military situation, though, showed that the strongest man, a man in control of the military forces, was for the moment Gómez Pedraza.

Both Pedraza and Minister of Relaciones Camacho (still in office at the time of publication of Santagelo's book) were concerned about the possible effects of this type of press campaign. The official government paper attacked the foreigner who was meddling with such effrontery in Mexico's business, endangering the good relations that should exist with Great Britain. In July 1826 Santangelo was arrested and ordered to leave the country, this being one of the last measures taken by the departing minister of Relaciones, the moderado Sebastián Camacho. The Italian revolutionary headed for New Orleans, where he arrived after losing his son on the trip as a result of crossing Veracruz at the time of the plague. The crackdown became a cause célèbre and produced a lot of sympathy for the old man, who was made to pay for Zavala's scheming. The two Italian editors of the *Iris* were also deported, while their Cuban partner, Heredia, remained in the employ of the official *Gaceta*, after having parted company with them as a result of the crisis.[15]

The Elections of 1826

The primary elections were held, in the city of Mexico, on Sunday, August 20, 1826, and throughout most of the country in that same or the following week. Esteva, Alpuche, and Zavala organized the Yorkino forces and took advantage of the friends they had in government, where they controlled three out of the four ministries: Esteva in Hacienda, Ramos Arizpe in Justicia, and Espinosa de los Monteros, temporarily in charge in Relaciones. Gómez Pedraza, in War, held a somewhat independent position between the Yorkinos and the Escoceses, but he was still considered to be nearer to the Yorkinos, where many of his old Iturbidista friends were also active.

Carlos María de Bustamante witnessed the elections, which he took to be a parody of free civilized practices. In a dialogue between a barber and his customer, he depicted the barber (who spoke with many grammatical mistakes) as a Yorkino activist, commenting on the previous day's victory. The barber acknowledged that they had money to distribute and weapons, just in case. At a certain moment the léperos who had gone along with him pointed toward Esteva, who was passing coiffed with a white band, which he usually donned on great popular events, to check whether they had got hold of all voting booths, or casillas. The barber's customer, alter ego of the author, equated these scenes with those of the Iturbidista coup of May 1822. He told the barber that the pope condemned associations (of a masonic kind) and that even if he was wrong, as Fernández de Lizardi and Cañedo maintained, public opinion rejected cabals. In a special twist to the dictatorship argument, the customer admitted that associations (probably interpreted as popular mobilizational agencies) might be necessary when there was a foreign threat, but not in peacetime. The barber, once finished with his work, admitted he had to go to the barrio del Salto del Agua, where it seemed that six times as many votes had been cast as citizens were registered.[16]

The following Sunday primary elections were also held in the state of Mexico, which was controlled by the Escoceses, with the old insurgente Melchor Múzquiz as governor and a legislature where José María Luis Mora had passed some progressive legislation. Zavala, however, was attempting to extend the action of the Yorkino lodges to that state also. He quickly bought a house from his brother in San Agustín de las Cuevas, to be able to stand for the legislature and later for the governorship. He was present at several primary and secondary (partido) juntas, but he was reserving his forces for the later meetings, especially the last, or tertiary, one, when about a hundred electors were to congregate in Toluca to choose the legislators; many would surely come undecided, and they had to be influenced in various ways.

By early September secondary meetings in the main towns of partidos were held, while, acting at another institutional level, the old legislature of the state of Mexico selected the Escocés Agustín Paz for the national Senate. This was one of the peculiarities of the constitution adopted in 1824, which diminished the legitimacy of the authorities and of some of the representatives: senators and presidents were elected by the state legislatures (in the president's case this required sending ballots to the national Congress). The indirect nature of the process was criticized by some as excessively deflecting, rather than reflecting, the popular will. It also seemed to many observers that, given the personalist traditions prevalent in the Iberian world, a direct appeal to the voters would be more appropriate. However, the weakest part of the Mexican constitutional mechanism was that balloting was by the old, not the new legislatures, and right at the moment when elections were being held to renew their members. In this way the constituents had attempted to ensure that changes brought about by the electoral process would be slow, allowing new majorities time to acquire experience, or lose their impulse, before they could make major decisions. The unexpected snag was the loss of legitimacy of the system, when public opinion changed in important ways from one electoral period to the next. Equally serious was the fact that for presidential elections, each state had an equal number of votes.[17]

The role of ayuntamientos in influencing elections and in creating independent sources of power in the countryside, especially in the Indian pueblos, was widely seen as quite pivotal. The Spanish constitution, in its article 310, ordered that every town with over one thousand population should have an elected municipal authority. This generated a lot of small-town (in fact rural) politicians, as the number of posts to be filled was high in comparison to the availability of people with at least some education. It was also difficult for the system of social control to reach down to the smallest villages and prevent them from electing representatives capable of discussing working conditions and land titles with neighboring haciendas. The state of Puebla, for example, had seven departamentos (each one ruled by an appointed prefecto) and twenty-five partidos (headed by subprefectos). Each partido in turn might have as many as four or five ayuntamientos. Already in 1824 (December 13), after a national armed intervention headed by Manuel Gómez Pedraza against federal rebels, the new authorities had enacted legislation reducing the number of ayuntamientos, thus closing "the door to the entry into those corporations of those who did not have a regular subsistence in some farm, capital, or branch of industry." It was argued that it had become usual for day laborers to occupy those posts, and even "maintain themselves at public expense," thus withdrawing many hands from agriculture. In fact what concerned these observers was not so much a diminution of the supply of labor as an increase of the availability of local protest organizers, based on the empowerment structures of municipal government. The extension of a net of social control down to the smallest social units, especially after years of agitation and revolution, was no easy matter, though with time and a few authoritarian governments in between, it would be managed. The new system of social control demanded, among other things, the development of the skills of mobilizational caudillismo, which channeled into safer conduits what could have been a tempestuous popular torrent.[18]

Following the same inspiration, in 1826 the moderado state government enacted legislation to reduce the number of ayuntamientos still further. Only those in the cabeceras de partido, or in congregations with over three thousand inhabitants, or where a permanent curate was stationed, would be allowed to continue in operation, that is, those that could be closely surveyed. Only alcaldes in cabeceras de partido could distribute permits for carrying arms. The political group making these reforms in Puebla saw itself as moderate liberal and admonished its constituents against the twin perils of the serviles, who whipped up religious sentiment, and the liberal exaltados, who also played on mass sentiments.[19]

In most parts of the country, the 1826 elections were disturbed, and in some areas they gave rise to violence, the main factions indicted being those of the radical Yorkinos and of the clericals. In Oaxaca there had been a popular mobilization led by the clergy, good competitors of the Yorkinos in matters of street agitation. Fernández de Lizardi published a tract against them, which was condemned by the Ayuntamiento for saying that the "*populacho*" and the clergy had abused their rights; he had only accused the populacho, not the pueblo, he soon retorted in another brochure. The Payo also referred to these Oaxaca elections, remarking that the clerics had prevailed

> using the influence they have on an ignorant and fanatic people; they go around in the barrios preaching . . . to nightly meetings held at the home of some pious man owning a standard and a few lanterns, who thus becomes the *capataz* of fifty or sixty others, in whose company he comes out praying the rosary through the streets and singing the Ave María, coming back home at about eight thirty, after which the meeting is dissolved and everybody gets drunk. Of such processions there are as many as twenty-five or thirty, without including those praying the viacrucis and the cofradías, among them especially that of the Holy Ghost.

For the Payo this segment of the population was "mean and stinking . . . brutal . . . voluble, ill-tempered, humble, thankless, grateful, blind, inconstant: they are children, old, judicious, and mad." But they could change suddenly, so he warned the clericals: "Beware, you must not abuse them, because soon they can turn against you, and if today you have their applause and acclaim, later on you will have to suffer all the weight of their rage and indignation." A whole program of political alchemy was implicit in these lines.[20]

The fact was that the clerics or factions of the Right could also put the people in the streets. But in most states, with the main exception of well-known conservatively inclined Oaxaca and Puebla, the Yorkinos emerged triumphant in the primary juntas, occasionally by allying themselves with the Iturbidista variety of ancien régime populist agitators.

As a reaction against these events, by mid-September, when the tertiary and final elections had not yet been held, Manuel Ceballos, senator from Coahuila y Texas, demanded from the government a list of all masonic associations existing in the country. Though in the Senate there was a large moderate group, the proposal was not accepted. When the moment arrived for the tertiary and final electoral meeting at Toluca, to form the local state legislature and select the national deputies, tempers ran high. Zavala came to Toluca with a large following, including Zerecero from Mexico City, and arranged to lodge and even in some cases dress the electors at his expense. Most of his folllowers took quarters at the local Franciscan convent, and all of them took their meals there. When the first session was held, Zavala got himself elected secretary, so as to control the proceedings, and immediately insisted that the vote should be open and verbal, so as to know where everybody stood. This his opponents interpreted as an attempt at intimidation, though the regulations did not provide for secret balloting at the tertiary level.

Among Zavala's followers were several priests, including in a prominent position Epigmenio de la Piedra, a friar who served the parish of Yautepec in Cuernavaca, an area where conflicts between sugar haciendas and pueblos were particularly intense. Piedra had already been used by Iturbide at the time of Iguala as a contact with Guerrero, and later on would become a promoter of anti-Spanish legislation. In 1834 he participated in a local revolt in the south, signing the Plan de Chicontla, which proposed an Indian monarchy headed by a descendant of Moctezuma, with special privileges for religion. He was an excellent example of that type of friar who combined some religious functions with radical politics, and who was not bound in his ideological convictions by apparent logical contradictions. In the meetings, when some violence erupted, he and others were heard shouting "viva la religión, viva el Sr. Zavala," an apparently incongruent combination but sensible to many listeners. It so happened that the Escocés-controlled Mexico legislature had passed some anticlerical legislation, under the prodding of José María Luis Mora.[21]

The events in Toluca triggered a complicated process of intervention by different branches of government questioning the validity of the proceedings. First of all, early in November, a special commission of the lame-duck legislature of the state of Mexico, where the anti-Zavala sector held a majority, invalidated the electoral process, on the basis of a petition by ten of the ninety-six electors who had taken part in the junta. Mora, who was a member of the commission, proposed that the legislature leave the city of Mexico, where it was still holding its meetings, arguing lack of freedom to conduct its proceedings. Later on that same month, the legislature accepted its commission's report and declared the elections void. This decision, though, was overturned by the national Congress in December, on the grounds that it was its duty, not the local legislature's, to pass upon the validity of elections of its members, thus creating a constitutional conflict of national and state prerogatives.

Labor Unrest

The year 1826 saw the beginning of a wave of labor unrest in the mines, stimulated by the introduction of British capital and corresponding innovations. At Vetagrande, near the capital of Zacatecas, relatively minor confrontations took place, but in Bolaños (in the north of the state of Jalisco) there was a major though short-lived strike, whose development illustrates the operation of local leadership and authorities in such conflicts.

The local manager, Robert Auld, tried to impose controls on the barreteros' use of candles, gunpowder, and pickaxes. There was resistance and protests, but it seemed that the new regulations would be accepted. However, on October 29, 1826 (a Sunday), when the barreteros had to go as usual to the tienda to retrieve their equipment for use the following day, they said they would only work under the traditional system, and "went out in groups marching through the town, uttering threats against [Auld] and the main tendero." When the administrator heard about this, he mounted his horse to inspect the site, and while passing by the pueblo

> amid the seditious . . . [he] listened to many threats [though he] was not the object of any direct insolence. That night the miners organized two fandangos with the explicit intention of *assembling*. The alcalde, far from trying to calm the people, seemed to give his support to those proceedings by his presence. During the

whole night there were groups marching down the streets, and many thronged near the almacenero's house, but there was no violence." [emphasis in original][22]

That Monday at dawn the manager, together with the man in charge of the almacén, went to the despacho and noticed that only a dozen barreteros or so were prepared to go down the shaft; even they showed signs of fear of the reprisals of the rest. After an interval a messenger informed him that one of the barreteros who had taken the tools had been attacked by the others and was enclosed in the despacho and in serious danger to his life. The manager ran to urge the alcalde to make his authority felt, but not getting a favorable answer, he armed himself and went with the almacenero to try to free the scab and identify the leaders of the disturbance. He found the man wounded and the despacho surrounded by some two hundred miners. The latter, in Auld's words, "pushing and milling around me, and well provided with stones, tried to intimidate me into adopting the old method. I listened to what they said, and answered that if they did not wish to work under the new terms they were free to go. They declared then that *no one* would work and threatened to kill the first man who would pick up his tools."[23]

At this juncture (it was already ten in the morning), Auld sent a written request for help to the alcalde, while the protests continued through the whole day. The written answer of the alcalde was disconcerting.

In answer to [your] paper . . . I say that the patience with which out of pure condescension I have acted till now has been the cause of these extremes, because if since the beginning I had required that company to comply with the . . . ordenanzas de minería . . . surely there would have been no cause for the grievances of the hapless workers, who justly complain about [the] aberrations which can be seen every day at the site . . . So in the future, as director of the company, you will see to it that what is ordained in the above mentioned ordenanzas be observed without further ado . . . because those infractions committed by the English company can have fatal consequences.

He added that he would make provisions regarding those who might have committed crimes, "doing the same with your dependants who have had the insolence of showing themselves armed . . . , against whom I am preparing a summary proceeding so as to stop their unbearable behavior and premeditated alarms." Auld then decided to appeal to the jefe político of the district, who resided in Colotlán, a quite distant locality, where he sent two of his employees, and meanwhile, to avoid further conflict, he shut down the mine. He sent another message to the alcalde, telling him about the interruption of work and his appeal to the higher authorities, adding that he would go to the highest power in the republic in defense of his rights. With tongue in cheek he asked the alcalde to "please inform me . . . in what manner must I work the mines, whether as the operatives see fit or as I consider they should, following the Ordenanzas, which I am sure do not force me to condescend with anybody." The alcalde inmmediately retorted that "as for not working the mines, you can do whatever you wish; as for working according to the operatives' or your own taste . . . it will have to be according to the Ordenanzas de Minería, because neither you nor anybody else is authorized to [infringe] them or much less to impose new rules in this continent."[24]

During the night of that Monday, the uproar continued. According to Auld the alcalde gave firearms to the seditious, and a group of fourteen of them mounted guard in front of the gates of the Hacienda Grande, with others in front of the almacenero's house. Possibly what was happening was a call to service to the local militia, which quite logically attempted to protect the installations of the company and the unpopular almacenero's house. But admittedly there may not have been much difference between "protecting" and "threatening," and the same people who appeared as miners during the day may have showed up as militia members at night.

It is necessary here to establish an important difference between the two lower echelons of local authority. The municipal system was quite widely established in Mexico at the time, even in the smallest pueblos, where the main authority was the ayuntamiento with its executive chief, the alcalde, who also had judicial functions. Both were elected, and the electorate most of the time included in theory almost all adult males, without restrictions of literacy or property. This was the tradition of the Spanish Cádiz constitution of 1812, adopted in Mexico. Voting was indirect and not secret; nevertheless, if the legal pattern had been respected, a strong popular participation in the formation of the public weal would have been involved. Despite distortions, popular pressure could somehow be expressed through the ballot box, supported by street agitation. The system of elections allowed a legitimation of these pressures, and in turn was a result of them.[25]

Being popularly elected the alcalde had to be sensitive to popular demands, especially in places such as the mining reales, where violent reactions were likely as a result of upsetting that peculiar combination of popular and intermediate strata forming the "people." In contrast to the alcalde, the jefe político (sometimes also called prefecto), was an officer designated by the higher authorities of each state. He depended on the governor, who though elected, had come to his office as the result of a highly indirect and filtered process of opinion formation. Below the governor there were a number of jefes políticos, or prefectos, who often had under them tenientes, subjefes or subprefectos, practically always appointed, not elected, who formed the eyes and ears of the state executive. They were responsible for the maintenance of order and control over the local ayuntamientos and alcaldes. They were in charge of the militias, delegating some of their functions to the alcaldes. There was usually a tension between the jefes políticos, sensitized to the authoritarian aspects of order maintenance, and the alcaldes, more concerned with the consensual elements of that same order or occasionally responding more directly to pressures from below, with which they might sympathize, if only as a result of facing a common antagonist.

On the same Monday when the strike and the lockout began, many barreteros went to Colotlán to see the jefe político, in a move parallel to the one adopted by the manager, while others sought the "licenciado" in Tlaltinango. There is some ambiguity as to who this licenciado was. He might have been simply a lawyer, whose advice the workers were trying to obtain, but more probably he was the local juez de letras. The latter, in contrast to the alcalde, who also had judicial functions, was a magistrate of a higher level, appointed by the state authorities. He was not a part of the executive but of the judical power, so he might have a more independent point of view, theoretically more impartial (or at least different) from those of the jefe político and the alcalde. There was no particularly favorable response, however, in any of these instances.

On Tuesday everything continued the same, in an "impressive and ominous silence." On Wednesday, which happened to be November 1, the day of All Saints, a fair was normally held in Bolaños, but the arrieros did not dare come with their merchandise. The jefe político, called by the manager, had not yet showed up. The coincidence of the strike with the holiday season was probably no chance happening, as ethnohistorical studies increasingly show the association between popular festivities and protest. On Thursday Mr. Auld again called for the jefe político, who finally arrived by midmorning. He installed himself in an "independent" house, made his inquiries, and finally publicly reprimanded the alcalde for his permissive behavior. The miners decided to return to work, and the ringleaders left Bolaños. Mr. Auld showed himself an optimist in his final report on the events, saying that "now everything is better than before the disturbances. The barreteros blame the alcalde, who will be demoted, after the preparation of a sumario against him."[26]

The Militia and the Maintenance of Order

We must consider here the fact that of the major mining centers operating at the time, Guanajuato was the one with the fewest reported labor confrontations; at any rate the British legation, always careful about these matters, did not register any serious incidents. Paradoxically this may well have been due to the fact that the situation in Guanajuato was more explosive, because of its greater size; thus it was more carefully controlled by the authorities. These authorities happened to be positioned right above the real: the governor, the better regular troops, and the more select militia, resided in the capital, among whose barrios and peripheral townships the mines and the workforce were located. The control mechanisms can be seen in operation in a minor episode, in July 1827, when two employees of the Anglo Mexican Company were returning to the city from the Valenciana Mine, followed at some distance by a Mexican servant. They had to pass by the post that guarded the entrance to the city, which performed security as well as fiscal functions for the receipt of the alcabala tax. The local militia, or cívicos, served in this place. The English passed without any problem, but their servant was held, and in the ensuing discussions they were all detained, receiving "without the slightest provocation" merciless blows. En route they were seen by the vice-governor, who happened to know them and who ordered them back home. The representatives of the British company, in passing the information on to the chargé d'affaires, remarked that the situation was extremely delicate, "the custody of the city [being] in the hands of the Cívicos, because there are no troops; the greater part of these Cívicos come from the lower rungs of the people, because anybody capable of paying three reales gets himself excepted; and these soldiers have been seen frequently in [taverns] even during service hours . . . It is impossible to see the future without alarm and fears, [because] these men are capable of committing acts like the above and much worse ones, which cannot be controlled by a more respectable force."[27] In this particular case in Guanajuato, the "abuses" of the militia were compensated by the closeness of the social tissue, with the superposition of different levels of authority in the same city, and the promptness of the vice-governor's intervention, even if the conflict of jurisdictions retarded compensatory measures.

This lack of confidence in the militias (seen more as a menace than as a protection) was endemic at the time. Another example took place at El Oro, in the state of Mexico near Michoacán, where the United Mexican Company conducted a middle-size operation. In March 1828, after a request by the company's manager, transmitted by the chargé d'affaires, the national government sent regular troops to the real to stem the "riotous disposition" of the mining population. As long as the troops remained, everything was peaceful, but when they had to be withdrawn toward the end of April, "excesses began to be committed, and the property of the company, consisting of minerals of the highest content, [was] in imminent danger," and a new detachment was asked for. The national minister answered that twenty men would be installed there permanently, and meanwhile he would instruct the governor of the state of Mexico to deploy the militia of El Oro to cooperate with the national troops. Asking the intervention of the governor, Lorenzo de Zavala, was like jumping from the frying pan into the fire, or at the very best it was an ineffective cure, because he was one of the more adept practitioners of the art of mobilizing the masses and using the militias for his own ends. The militias, when they had to be used to repress popular protests, often refused to act, especially if they had personal relations with the people involved. Belonging to the militia was not a full-time job, like serving in the regular army. In theory all able-bodied citizens between certain age limits had to enroll in the militia and be ready for the call of duty. When they were called they received a certain payment, which was attractive for the poorer ones. The better off simply excepted themselves through a small payment. When there was a major alteration of public order, not only the minimum skeleton forces in almost permanent service were called up, but also some of the others, who because of their usual occupations maintained close ties with the laboring mass of the population. Thus in the mining reales, when it was unavoidable to call up the militias, they were brought from other places, so that they might act in a more "objective" manner.[28]

In 1830, after the Jalapa conservative pronunciamiento was victorious, the Puebla authorities dismantled the profuse structure of militias created by the previous liberal administration, whose "barbarous" policies had led them to establish no less than twenty-four battalions, incorporating, of course, the "dregs of society." From then on, only two battalions would remain: those led by "Colonels" Esteban de Antuñano and José Antonio Ibarrarán. The title of colonel was in their case mostly honorific, based on a part-time occupation that was seen as reflecting civic conscience on the part of its holder.[29] By contrast populist ideologues, liberal or otherwise, had a lot of confidence in the role of the militia, "whose very name terrifies [the serviles] . . . and this is the reason why they try to oppose their organization."[30]

The Radicalization of the Populist Faction

As a result of the 1826 elections, the Yorkinos came out triumphant practically everywhere, with the main exceptions of Puebla and Oaxaca. The
grip they thus acquired on state legislatures boded well for their presidential prospects two years hence, because it was those recently elected bodies that would have to cast their ballots in 1828. At Mexico City's
municipal level, in elections held at the end of 1826, the Yorkino victory
was reproduced, with no opponents contesting their preeminence at the
polls. The list of "electors" selected at primary voter assemblies showed
the mixture of new radical elements and old Iturbidista hands, both from
its more conservative and its populist wings. From the barrio of San Pablo,
the ill-famed Colonel Manuel Barrera was elected and then made *alcalde
de sexto voto*. Santa Cruz y Soledad sent Agustín Gallegos, Zerecero's
uncle, a man of all trades who had been a Guadalupe in 1813 and lived in
one of the barrios, where he milked a few cows and had a starch "factory" combined with a metal kiln and a coach-repair shop. Antonio
Galicia, from a family that had had the Indian governorship of San Juan,
represented Santa Cruz Acatlán, while the tailor Lucas Balderas and the
"titiritero" José Ignacio Paz obtained positions as regidores, and Manuel
Reyes Veramendi became an alcalde. On the other hand, a few prestigious personalities were included, mostly from the Iturbidista Right, such
as Miguel Cervantes, former marqués de Salvatierra, representing the
better-off neighborhood of San José, while Juan Wenceslao Barquera was
made *alcalde de primer voto* and Francisco de Azcárate síndico.

The editors of *El Aguila*, reflecting the government's position, had pretended to expect from the electors a more reasonable roster of appointees, taking into account that these municipal positions, not being paid,
were not appropriate for poor lawyers or artisans. Now they commented
that the appointees, except for three, were all unknown people, and one
of them lived on the borders of indigence (probably José Ignacio Paz).
Sure enough the new representatives of the people were not prepared to
incur the cost of buying the ridiculous "gothic" uniforms required for
their ceremonial functions, and this produced some tensions among them.[31]

The agitationist way in which the popular faction had won its objec-
tives caused divisions within its ranks and antagonized the executive power,
notably War Minister Gómez Pedraza, who until shortly before had been
considered an ally. A moderate sector within the Yorkinos themselves
was trying to put some brakes on the mobilization of their followers, but
as M. Alex Martin, the French representative in Mexico, observed, "they

have sought support for their ambitions among the multitude . . . and they will realize only too late that the multitude can only be led by those who follow it, and that in a revolution there is a death penalty for parties that try to put a halt to it."[32]

Attacks began against Ramos Arizpe, who was thought too moderate. The goal the Yorkinos were setting for themselves was the expulsion of the Spaniards, with a possible first step being simply to bar them from official positions. In this they met the opposition of Ramos Arizpe, and against him they aimed their press during the months of November and December 1826.[33] The new year, which opened with the sessions of the renovated national Congress, would witness an event that heated up the already active tempers. On January 18 and 19, 1827, General Ignacio Mora, governor and military commandant of the Federal District, denounced proposals made to him by a Spanish friar, Joaquín Arenas, to participate in a plot to bring back King Ferdinand's rule to Mexico. The first inquiries did not lead to suspects more important than low-life individuals such as the friar himself, but this might have been just the tip of a greater conspiracy.

Arenas was one of those members of the religious orders who were in permanent conflict with the authorities, both civil and ecclesiastic, and whose lives fed the stereotype of the dissolute friar. He belonged to the Dieguino, or "strict observance," branch of the Franciscan order, though he did not take its precepts very seriously. Back in 1820 Arenas, who was then capellán real in Chihuahua's military hospital, ran into trouble with his bishop, Francisco Castañiza, who got wind that the friar was living with a woman. The bishop had him sent under custody to Mexico City, where Arenas pleaded his constitutional rights and issued a tract stating his position. Three years afterward he became involved in the discussions about secular intervention in the control of religious orders. He was of the opinion that provincial priors should not exist and that the best policy would be to disband the orders. He disappeared from public attention for some time, but according to reports that surfaced when he came back into public eye, he had maintained a double life, occupying a cell in a convent but at the same time running a liquor-distilling outfit where chinguirito was produced and other "chemical operations" conducted. On one occasion those installations accidentally caught fire, causing the death of two workers and almost killing the friar, who apparently was then reduced to opening up an establishment for betting and card playing.[34]

Later on in January, the Puebla government detained two Spanish priests who were allegedly part of the Arenas conspiracy. Alpuche, the radical Yorkino senator, proposed that all Spanish priests who had not been clearly in favor of independence be expelled from the country, and Zerecero added that Spanish haciendas be registered for possession of weapons. In early February General Gregorio Arana, a Spanish Escocés with an important military career, was suspected of being associated with the Arenas plot and jailed.

The search for accomplices was intense, and it produced some excesses, such as those by regidor Ignacio Paz (the Iturbidista titiritero and school-teacher turned Yorkino), who was jailed for entering into Spaniards' houses without being legally empowered. He had to remain in prison for several months and got involved in a long litigation, in which he argued that the only way to get at the culprits was to be expeditious in looking for them. Fears of possible popular support for the plot led to stern proposals, such as the one that Deputies Tames, Cañedo, Llano, and Escandón put forth, which would have meted out the death penalty to anyone uttering vivas to Spain. The proposal smacks of hysteria, caused by the proverbial image of the friars' and priests' ability to influence the lowermost strata of the population.

This attitude was also reflected in quite a few tracts that came out on the occasion of Arenas's execution, in June. Luis Espino had published, with the usual ambiguous title, a tract with the original plan of the conspiracy, signed by one Juan Clímaco Velasco, who would have become the king's representative if it had succeeded. It involved organizing an "Ejército Restaurador de la Fe" and giving back to the Indian communities their traditional privileges and exemptions from certain taxes. When the friar was condemned to death, Espino thought the government was showing signs of weakness by ordering the execution to be held at night and away from the town, when it should have been done publicly, in the light of day and at the Plaza Mayor. Pedraza, he stated, wanted the decapitation to be effected in the Plaza de Mixcalco, in the poor eastern area of the city, where criminals were usually punished; but Ramos Arizpe, with the excuse that the culprit was a man of the robe and that the church should not suffer humiliation because of its erring son, ordered otherwise. Fernández de Lizardi was also of the opinion that the execution should take place in as visible and public a way as possible. Doing it in the dark of night, as when General Bravo had the "unhappy patriot" Basilisio Valdés shot in the Plaza de la Paja, would start people whispering about why the government was not prepared to confront the public.[35]

In a more ferocious mood, an anonymous A. F. A. inveighed against friars and priests who, he acknowledged, had a lot of influence; they should not be feared, but rather the people enlightened, and for this "a bit of holy blood spilled in time [might] save that of millions . . ." Other anonymous pamphleteers joined this barrage, adding a new dimension: an attempt at rehabilitating Iturbide in the face of this sudden reappearance of the Spanish threat. One of them favored the confiscation of the Spaniards' haciendas in Cuernavaca, "those lairs of the enemies of freedom, those castles strengthened by a numerous, conceited, and insolent *negrería*"; mindless of the economic consequences, he would have all the blacks working there sent abroad to countries where slavery was allowed. He contrasted the delays in Arenas's trial with the expeditious manner in which the "immortal" Iturbide had been dispatched by the Tamaulipas. Another tract along these lines expressed a very militant Yorkino position, at the same time heaping praise on Iturbide, who was depicted as being in the Elysium, due to his civic virtues. Arenas had invented, the author thought, the sect of novenarios to get support among the ignorant people. This, though wrong, was a sideswipe against the new political faction organized in groups of nine (whence their name), which might be confused with a religiously inclined group resorting to novenas as a political weapon.[36]

The detention in March of Generals Negrete and Echávarri, both Spaniards, on suspicion of being involved in the Arenas plot, added fuel to the flames of Iturbidista rehabilitation. Luis Espino branded those two generals as traitors to Iturbide, "Casamatistas," and went on to indict five prominent Escocés senators as well. As Iturbide's son, living in Philadelphia, had become for some a potential symbolic figure around which to build a comeback, the state of Veracruz, which was the main center of Escocés resistance to the federal government, banned him explicitly from returning to his homeland. The Payo picked up the gauntlet, with a *Defensa del hijo de Iturbide ante el Congreso de Veracruz*, where he said that he "would not tire of repeating that the Iturbidista party exists only in the heads of our enemies." However, he took the opportunity to reprint Iturbide's memoirs, and to counter those who thought it was improper at the time, he added a supplement, where he denied that all Iturbidistas were Yorkinos, as was said in Veracruz, nor was the faction a creation of Poinsett. Fernández de Lizardi, who was ill and would die that same year, published a *Testamento y despedida*, where he pinned his hopes on a continuation of the struggle against obscurantism and clerical influence, extolling a recent proposal by Alpuche for strengthening the role of the state in the exercise of the patronato. He also encouraged President Victoria to assume a more active role, avoiding the influence of his ministers and showing himself more often to the troops and regaling them with refreshments—in other words, cultivating the role of a Bonapartist leader, for which the man was not very well adapted.[37]

Finally the lower house acted. Already in February it had decreed, by thirty-six votes to nineteen, that no Spaniard could be employed in the strategically vital Post Office and in the Customs. But this was only the beginning, and in May, after long discussion, a law against Spaniards was passed, eliminating all peninsulars from federal government posts, though (as a result of senatorial insistence, led by Molinos del Campo) they would continue drawing their salaries. A rather mild disposition, given the existing high emotions, that did not satisfy anyone.[38]

The Yorkinos, however, tried to stage a mass celebration and got only small numbers of the usual léperos on the streets. *El Sol*, admittedly a biased source, reported the excesses on May 15 but at the same time noted the scant resonance these rowdy celebrations had among the population, by comparison to the fateful events of May 18–19, August 26, and October 30. These were the three major days in the Iturbidista canon: the proclamation, the celebration of the arrest of the opposition deputies, and the closure of Congress. The French minister concurred, reporting that most of the laboring artisans had remained quietly at their work and that only a few hundred ill-clad people had followed some officers of the worst reputation to assault the cathedral's and other churches' belfries, forcing the pealing of bells. When they came to the national palace, asking for General Victoria to appear on the balcony, they were told that the president had other business and could not appear. After being repeatedly denied the firing of some cannon, they dispersed without further disorder.[39]

Perhaps the lack of enthusiasm reflected their disappointment at the very mild measures taken against the coyotes. The Payo lamented that similar lenience had not been exerted toward protesters in the south, or earlier toward Lobato and his supporters "in the calle de Celaya," or the expatriates, or the Jalisco heroes. The references were clear for those who had any memory; they mixed federalists with the exiled Iturbide family and with a recently imprisoned Colonel Mangoy, who had tried to involve the Acapulco garrison in an armed demand for Spanish expulsion and was stopped by Commandant Juan Alvarez, who despite his Yorkino sympathies had acted with moderation. An anonymous "Enemy of slavery" took issue with *El Sol* for its critical description of the popular celebration and warned it that these days the nation's generals were not dupes, as in 1823, when they were seduced by the Escocés opposition to overthrow Iturbide. In the same line of argument, Luis Espino considered the editorial an incitement to a military coup and denounced *El Sol* as seditious. Another pamphleteer signaled the main enemies of the people in the Senate as being the Escoceses Agustín Paz and Florentino Martínez, together with the clerical Manuel Ceballos; while in the lower house they were led by the clericals Rafael Berruecos, José Ignacio Espinosa (no kin of Espinosa de los Monteros), and José María Couto Ibea, plus the Escocés Sánchez de Tagle. Under the pressure of social confrontation, the secularist theme was losing its relevance, and there was a tendency toward coalition-formation between moderate Escoceses and conservative clericals.[40]

Fragmentation of the Governing Front

Within the ruling coalition, freed since the middle of 1826 of the Escocés presence, fissures began to appear as a result of different approaches toward the policy to be taken regarding the Spaniards. Ramos Arizpe adopted a moderate stance and suffered increasing attacks, but he managed to survive for the whole year of 1827. On the other hand, Esteva was under heavy pressure from the opposition, due to the complication of his accounts in Hacienda, and had to leave his post, but he was replaced by another Yorkino stalwart, Tomás Salgado, in March.

The state of Veracruz, governed by Miguel Barragán, now became one of the main contenders for power against the national executive. The Escoceses, having lost their foothold in the cabinet, dug themselves in in the coastal state. It was widely recognized that control of the port town could be vital in the event of a conflict.[41] The Santa Anna brothers, Manuel and the well-known Antonio, who since the days of the Casamata revolt against Iturbide had mostly cooperated with the Escoceses (despite Antonio's short-lived attempt at becoming "Protector of the Federation" in San Luis Potosí in 1823), supported the Veracruz state authorities. The local legislature passed in April 1827 a very controversial law prohibiting the existence of secret societies, penalizing their members with five years of banishment. The next month Esteva arrived in his native state, where he had been sent by the federal government as finance commissioner, after he had been relieved of his duties in the ministry due to pressure from the opposition. His appointment was one way of actively maintaining him in the public scene and having him oversee the proper collection of federal funds in the port. A few days afterward the state legislature applied the new law to him, as a well-known *logista*, and he was sent back to Mexico. To explain matters the same legislature by mid-June published a manifesto, stating that all Yorkino lodges were dangerous, because they were in accord with Poinsett and with the Iturbidistas. But the expulsion of Esteva was an unacceptable affront, which also created a conflict of authority. People could imagine a repetition of the situation that occurred at the end of the empire, when a revolt nurtured in Veracruz toppled the national government. The scandalous elections of the state of Mexico could provide an issue.[42]

To counteract this possibility, José Rincón, commandant of the city of Veracruz, decided to act on his own and produce a pronunciamiento in favor of the central powers. He belonged to a Veracruzano military family, with a good record of service to the emperor; he was a rival of the Santa Annas. His brother Manuel, also a Yorkino sympathizer, was well placed in the capital, where he had replaced Pedraza for two weeks during a temporary absence; he was soon to be designated chief of staff in Mexico, after the forced retirement of the Escocés José Morán, marqués de Vivanco.

Seeing that the campaign against the lodges was orchestrated by the *Veracruzano Libre*, José Rincón sent a group of officers to destroy its presses on July 25, 1827, and declared that he would only obey orders from the federal government. Again this was a conflict of authority, because his immediate superior was Governor Barragán, who was also commandant of the state of Veracruz. Barragán ordered hostilities against the rebels and appointed Antonio López de Santa Anna as commandant of the port city, replacing Rincón. The federal government could not accept Rincón's service, and sent Guerrero, designated as commandant of the state in lieu of Barragán, to pacify the area. This was accomplished and matters returned to normal, Guerrero later leaving the equally Yorkino Ignacio de la Mora in his place. The local legislature soon afterward designated Antonio López de Santa Anna as vice-governor, to reward him for his support against the Rincón attempt at what was called "central intervention." The fire kept smoldering in the coastal state.

Gómez Pedraza, who was the real power behind the presidency of Guadalupe Victoria, did not wish to become a tool of the Yorkinos nor of the provincial federalists, who were close to the Yorkinos ideologically, though somewhat less mobilizational in their tactics. His mouthpiece, the semiofficial *El Aguila*, by June 1827 started condemning the secret societies' intervention in politics, declaring itself "impartial" among the warring masonic lodges. This was aimed at anti-Spanish agitation and in practice also against the overt political parties.[43]

The Yorkinos resented this apparent abandonment by Gómez Pedraza, which, however, was not yet clear or inevitable. Their organ, *El Correo*, tried to explore the federalists' feelings, as the latter held a pivotal position and were capable of giving victory to the candidate of their choice.[44] If the lodges' nominee were too radical or too distrusted by established opinion, like Guerrero, the federalists would demur from supporting him. Alternatively both the Yorkinos and the federalists might continue to be in favor of Gómez Pedraza, wresting him from the embrace of the establishment. But he was set on an ambitious project and was tempted to organize his own connections and achieve the presidency with few obligations to independent factions.

Ideological Battle Lines

The threat against the Spanish community was very serious for those involved, which included some of the wealthiest people in the country, and also for criollos in similar positions, who might feel menaced by an extension of the popular fury fanned by ravenous aspirantes. For the country as a whole, the emigration that already had started at independence and was picking up as a response of those who envisaged worse to come implied a colossal loss of capital, which some estimated to be as high as 40 million pesos.[45]

To defend the Spaniards, and in general to influence public opinion in a moderate-liberal direction, several Escocés notables got together in June 1827, including Molinos del Campo, Florencio Martínez, Juan Nepomuceno Quintero, and José M. Cabrera, along with the clerically inclined Sánchez de Tagle and the more radical and federalist Manuel Crescencio Rejón, to publish a theoretical journal, *El Observador de la República Mexicana*, under the direction of José María Luis Mora.

On the opposite side two of the more intellectual Yorkinos, José M. Bocanegra and José M. Tornel (the latter a life-long friend and supporter of Santa Anna) launched in August 1827 *El Amigo del Pueblo*, a name inspired by Marat's organ of the same name. They got the cooperation of José Manuel Herrera, the former Insurgente who had been the chief minister under Iturbide; Agustín Viezca, who was soon to become grand master of the Yorkino lodges, succeeding Esteva; José Ramón Pacheco; and José Dominguez Manso, another friend and minister of the empire. The *Amigo del Pueblo* quoted profusely from Locke, Rousseau, Condillac, and the "geniuses" Bentham and Constant. It criticized Bolívar for his attempts at one-person rule and his *código disparatado*, the Bolivian constitution, also condemning any idea of dictatorship. In an attempt at conciliation, it expressed its relief at the fact that Mexico had three heroes—Victoria, Guerrero, and Bravo—not just one. If Bolívar was not careful, he might meet the end of Napoleon or Iturbide.

However, the *Amigo del Pueblo*'s image of Iturbide was not totally negative (signaling the presence among its editors of some noted collaborators of the empire). In defending Gómez Pedraza it portrayed his career, remembering that he had supported the emperor even after the Plan de Casa Mata, which was commonly considered among Yorkino circles to be a creation of the Escoceses and the Spaniards. It dwelt on the sorry sight of erstwhile anticlericals joining the obscurantists in the new Novenario sect. It welcomed the pressures the state of Jalisco was exerting in favor of Spanish expulsion, going to the length of claiming that it had saved the federation a second time, the first one being in 1823 and 1824, when it resisted the centralist bid of power of the triumvirate. At the same time, though, it did not approve of the extreme federalists of that state, who published *El Tribuno* and pretended that the states were practically slaves of the central power, because they were required to harbor national military units headed by centrally designated commandants. From the beginning the *Amigo del Pueblo* maintained a defense of political parties, denying that the present agitation in the country was their making, or that it was critical; it resembled similar occurrences in the United States or England. In early 1828, when the law expelling Spaniards had been sanctioned and had produced the Escocés armed reaction known as the Plan de Montaño, which was repressed, the *Amigo* concentrated its fire on the defeated faction, which was still entrenched in the Senate.[46]

For a time the *Amigo del Pueblo* hoped to convert Gómez Pedraza into its mouthpiece, but it soon realized this was impossible, because the general had already organized his own network, the so-called imparciales, taking with him some relatively moderate Yorkino elements and receiving the tactical support of the Escoceses. Carefully the journal, whose main editors were Tornel and Bocanegra, would steer toward a more independent position and finally, when presidential elections by the legislatures were about to take place, in August 1828, it declared in favor of Guerrero, after which it soon ceased publication, probably because of losing a government subsidy.[47]

The ideological and political line of these progressive liberals is quite interesting to follow, as they were always trying to maintain a certain "equilibrio": shunning the moderate-liberal position associated with the interests of commerce and mining, cultivating popular support and even agitation, while condemning excesses. In various articles they attempted, however, to justify the use of weapons in "popular demonstrations" (that is, military pronunciamientos), as a result of the fact that the right of petition was not yet established in Mexico. Thus it was, they went on to say, that in various strategic circumstances, popular petition had degenerated into armed intervention, starting with the Spaniards' coup against Iturrigaray, then the destitution of Apodaca by Novella, the undoing of the emperor, and the widespread rebellion of the states that led to the adoption of the federal system. Now the demands for the expulsion of the Spaniards were of a similar type, and it was not true that they had everywhere been accompanied by a show of arms. People like Tornel and Bocanegra, who had cooperated with the Iturbide regime, would repeatedly try to influence "from the inside" some military strong man, particularly Santa Anna during his more liberal periods, or even during some of his more dubious ones, though Bocanegra shunned his clearly reactionary episodes.[48]

The more radical Yorkinos continued to express themselves through the pages of the *Correo*, which also came out very expressly in favor of political parties, an issue that had obviously become symbolic of opposition to the hegemonic efforts of Gómez Pedraza. Conditions were being created for a new bout of coalition making, and the fire of factionalism would prove itself stronger, for yet a few decades, than any attempt at general integration of the dominant political class.[49]

7
Guerrero and National Popular Politics

The whole period of Mexican history from independence up to the wars of the Reforma was bedevilled by the issue of protectionism, which divided the dominant classes. Opening up the economy to the world market was attractive for silver producers, who could expect cheaper imported equipment. It was also dear to the hearts of some provincial groups, especially the Veracruzano and Yucatecan real or potential exporters. But some tierra caliente interests were doubtful about their capacity to compete internationally and felt a need to be treated as an "infant agriculture," threatened by imports of American cotton or tobacco. For the country at large, the changeover to an export-import economy meant following a pattern that would impose itself ever more strongly in Latin America in the following decades. But the late-colonial Mexican economy had developed in many directions to fill the demands of a wealthy elite and a populous country under the protective mantle of Spanish legislation; it was not so easy to change, as vested interests associated with protectionism were very strong, stronger than in most other parts of Latin America.

Among the lower strata the artisans would be the foremost losers, though if the economy were to pick up, they might also benefit, but that would be in a very hypothetical second stage. The difficulties of the transition, added to the political weight of the popular classes, forced the independent governments to enact protective legislation that allowed the formation of large-scale industry. The financiers or agiotistas, searching for new areas in which to invest their money, selected this as a possibly promising one, so as to diversify away from the highly risky business of funding the government.

Industrialists and Agiotistas

Several noted individuals were at the same time, or in succession, agiotistas and industrialists. This was the case of Cayetano Rubio, owner of a modern factory in Querétaro in the forties, who though intent on prohibiting the importation of textiles, made every effort to be allowed a free hand in bringing in raw cotton. As this was often also prohibited, special concessions were sought, in return for some help to the needy central government. Thus Rubio, in his personality as an agiotista, had obtained in 1844 a permit for the importation of 20,000 quintals of cotton, promising to pay in advance the 120,000-peso import duties.[1] He also diversified into salt mines, acquiring control of the very important Peñón Blanco salinas on the border between Zacatecas and San Luis Potosí, taking advantage of his centralist connections.[2]

Perhaps the most prominent personality in this field was Esteban de Antuñano, a Veracruzano merchant who, after receiving a costly education in Spain and Great Britain, established himself in Puebla, making it the main seat of his activities, which included not only the founding of textile factories but also an abundant outflow of pamphlets and essays. He also engaged in politics and in the organization of militias, which he financed and directed personally, having had some military experience. Like most other industrialists, including Alamán, he supported the Jalapa regime after the coup of December 1829 and the longer centralist presidency of Anastasio Bustamante from 1836 to 1841. He was also associated with Santa Anna in some of the latter's episodes of government.[3]

José Manuel Zozaya Bermúdez, a lawyer from Guanajuato and a member of Iturbide's entourage, who was sent by the emperor to the United States to try to obtain recognition, came back with artisans and installed a paper factory in Tizapán, near the capital.

Antonio Haro y Tamariz, from Puebla, was also a heavy investor in the textile industry, having on occasion leased Antuñano's factory La Constancia Mexicana. His brother Luis was associated with Iturbide's son, whose royal aspirations he would support by the fifties.[4] Another agiotista who looked for new areas of investment was Felipe Neri del Barrio, a Guatemalan who married into the Fagoaga family. He and his brother Rafael were already by 1831 considered important members of the Escocés faction, veering toward "legal opposition" to Bustamante. When the radical liberals came back in full force in 1833, the Barrios were expelled from the country, by application of the "ley del caso," but soon returned. Mora considered Felipe "the most pernicious man in the country," which reflected the parting of the ways of people who had been politically close in earlier times. Mora had moved to the left, so to say, while Barrio to the right, as had several other erstwhile Escoceses. Barrio in 1835 was close to Santa Anna and profited from the general's victorious campaign against the federal resistance of the Zacatecans, entering into an arrangement to take up the tobacco estanco of that state now become a department.[5]

Manuel Escandón, born in Orizaba, was also actively dedicated to financial and industrial affairs, venturing into transportation and mining. Together with his brother Antonio, he was one of the most powerful capitalists of his day in Mexico, and when the British company of Real del Monte ran into insurmountable difficulties in 1849, he bought them out. He owned a company offering the coach service from Mexico to Veracruz, contracting in 1834 the maintenance of that road; he later started construction of a railroad, which only began to operate in 1873. He also founded a textile mill in Guadalajara in the 1840s, together with Manuel Olasagarre, who became finance minister in the final Santa Anna regime of 1853–55. Escandón strongly supported the general financially during his time in office during the American war. Another of his partners, Anselmo Zurutuza, involved in the Veracruz road-transport venture, also had a ship company and diversified into sugar production.[6]

All these people and quite a few others, prominent among them Lucas Alamán, who was less financially secure but more connected politically, were a very dynamic entrepreneurial class, which did not have many ideological commitments but basically thrived on government support and protection for business expansion. They needed protectionism but were not consistently in its favor, as in some instances they needed cheap imports of some staples produced by others. Together with the artisans struggling at the other end of the social pyramid, they provided an important pressure group for pragmatic, often protectionist policies.

Economic liberalism, both in internal matters and in opening up to the world market, had to overcome serious resistances before it could be accepted more widely, which only happened during the Porfiriato. On the Mexico-Puebla-Veracruz axis, the dominant force in the country, attitude towards protectionism were quite contradictory. Puebla was clearly on the protectionist side and Veracruz mostly against it, but the latter state had some textile activities also, and even some of the potentially exporting tierra-caliente interests, such as cotton and tobacco producers, often feared foreign competition. In order to create a winning coalition, and given the many crisscrossing cleavages that tore at Mexican society at all levels, it was often necessary to combine, or assuage, both protectionist and free-trader interests, a next to impossible task. Only the violent decade of the wars of Reforma and Intervention would clear the panorama and set the stage for a new beginning.

The generation of liberals who came to power with the Reforma, who had some opportunities of acquiring experience in state and federal governments during the forties, were in general opposed to protectionism, repeating the argument that it involved losing vital customs receipts. However, the exercise of official responsibilities gave some of them doubts about the appropriateness of extreme attitudes. Thus Guillermo Prieto, having a position in the liberal administration of president Herrera (1848–51), published a report on the state of the treasury, in which he cautioned against copying the theories of European economists who, unaware of the "restrictive laws which English commerce works under . . . [or of the] open contradiction between the doctrines of Rossi, Blanqui, and Chevallier [and] the French tax system," recommended opening up the economy. He admitted that "leaving aside the lessons of experience, and heeding only the theories of European economists, we have called constantly for the reduction of tariffs, but without seeking a proportional quota, and forgetting [about] the necessary measures to stop contraband." He also thought a "navigation act" protecting national shipping should be adopted, but prohibition of textile imports was not appropriate, as it stimulated a noncompetitive industry.[7]

Protectionism, however, was only one possible component of a *desarrollista* economic policy. We may call *desarrollismo* the idea that government was responsible for taking an active participation in setting the conditions for economic growth or modernization. It included a defensive strategy, mostly protectionism, but it also had a more aggressive one. This involved such programs as immigration from overseas, colonization with land subdivision, the building of canals or other types of infrastructure directly by the state or foreign companies, and extending education. These latter lines of action, which required a nondormant state but not necessarily a very interventionist one, and certainly not protectionism, were more palatable to liberals.

Desarrollismo, in a sense, was a continuation of the traditions of the Enlightenment, particularly in its version of so-called enlightened despotism, which did not believe blindly in the virtues of the market, though it was of course prepared to use it as yet another tool. Jovellanos and Campomanes were among the main Spanish theoretical figures of this spirit of development and progress, which on the peninsula and in many

Hispanic American countries was channeled through the Sociedades de Amigos del País. In Mexico a society of this type was organized immediately after independence, under Iturbidista inspiration, representing the most intellectually oriented members of the future emperor's entourage, together with other prestigious personalities. Prominent places were given to Juan Francisco Azcárate, Juan Wenceslao Barquera, José Manuel Zozaya Bermúdez, Mariano Primo de Rivera, Basilio Arrillaga, Diego García Conde, Andrés Quintana Roo, Manuel de la Peña y Peña, Mariano de Almanza, and Juan Bautista Arechederreta (his brother Lucas Alamán was in Europe, otherwise he would also have been included), as well as to less intellectual but well-positioned figures, such as the marqués de Aguayo and the marqués de Salvatierra.

Moderate liberals of the Escocés faction were not very well represented, except for the Conde de Heras Soto, probably because the issue of industrialization and protectionism was particularly divisive. This desarrollista line of thought accepted the tenets of economic liberalism to a point, but it was preoccupied with enabling the state to become an engine of change, particularly necessary in a backward nation where many traditional structures had to be overcome in order to set free the forces of competition, both nationally and internationally. More radical free traders, by contrast, were less concerned with state-induced changes, because of a greater belief in the capacity of society to channel itself in the right direction if left alone. They had as one of their main pundits Víctor Foronda, a Spanish economist much valued by some liberals in Mexico.[8]

One example of desarrollista thinking and practice was the Jalisco-born Tadeo Ortiz, an early economist. Typically, he wrote a book about Mexico's problems, treating a mixture of political and economic matters. He introduced himself as having been favorable to the Morelos regime, which he represented in Buenos Aires in 1814. Earlier he had gone to Europe in 1808 with Iturrigaray's family, in charge of the education of the deposed viceroy's children. He expressed criticism of Iturbide's role, even though the emperor had sent him on a secret mission to Guatemala, which he forgot to recount in his book. He lived for several years in the Tehuantepec region, planning colonization projects that caught the attention of the French minister. The state of Veracruz was proposing to colonize those lands with local Indians and foreigners, and the prospects of an interoceanic canal had been aired, only to be abandoned due to their cost. To further the scheme Tadeo Ortiz, who was politically quite adaptable, obtained from the Guerrero government an appointment in 1829 as consul in Bordeaux. This made him suspect to Alamán, when the latter was at the helm of state after the Jalapa coup, and almost lost him his job, but he survived. He hoped to use his foothold in Europe to inform the governments, the public, and potential investors as to the prospects offered by Mexico. The Tehuantepec canal was never to be, but it was one of those projects that inflamed the national imagination, and at some point it was even the basis for the formation of a special department carved out from Veracruz and Oaxaca, so as to expedite matters. Another such project was the colonization of Texas, which attracted many aspiring politicians wishing to combine national development with some private gain.[9]

Coalition Making: Gómez Pedraza Versus Guerrero

Political battle lines were being drawn more sharply by the latter part of 1827. The issue of how to deal with the Spanish threat was paramount, but it covered a deeper social division within Mexican society, split along several cleavage lines, especially those dividing the haves from the have-nots and the protectionists from the free traders. The have-nots, it is important to bear in mind, included many middle-class sectors and most aspirantes, people of an extremely insecure or downwardly mobile status, who needed the mediation of politics to redress their life prospects. Some aspirantes, though, could not by any means be classified among the have-nots, but their unsettled economic circumstances also made them turn to public activity. Often they would try to get on the bandwagon of a popular movement (or lead it), because the majority of the more established dominant classes preferred to defend their existing interests rather than extend solidary support to those who had fallen from grace. Though these high-status aspirantes had always existed, their numbers and straitened circumstances were becoming more critical as time passed and the country did not recover from its decline. Many came from the ranks of the impoverished hidalgos and were very abundant in Iturbide's camp.

One important change had occurred among the propertied classes since independence, namely, the incorporation of new, foreign interests. One was the mining companies, controlled from abroad, and the other was the large-scale international merchants, mostly resident, even if some might return to their countries of origin. Because of their recent arrival, their involvement in politics was less than that of their native or Spanish counterparts, though in cases of crisis they would participate like anyone else.

Another new actor, which would be growing in stature, was the agiotista or financier, who took the place of the traditional merchant, much weakened by foreign competition. There were close ties between agiotistas and industrialists, as we have just seen, the latter having grown in importance and destined to become even more influential in future years.

As we have seen earlier, the intensification of social conflict was producing a rapprochement between the clerical Right and the moderate liberals, or Escoceses. This was expressed in the formation of a new political group, the novenarios (so called because of their organization in groups of nine), to replace the more masonically tinged Escocés lodges. The moderate liberals had already obtained a good part of what they wanted, as international trade had basically been opened up, despite some protectionist restrictions (not yet as consolidated as they later became). The tariff sanctioned for the year 1826 had met with a very good reception in European commercial circles, and so had Camacho's mission. In May 1827 he signed with the French foreign minister, Baron Damas, a "joint declaration," to be renewed every year, in lieu of the treaty Mexico desired, as a basis for trade and diplomatic relations; by September of the same year the first direct commercial packet line between Bordeaux and Veracruz began operating.[10] Many corporative restrictions were crumbling, including civil entails, artisan guilds, and trade associations of the Tribunal de Minería or Consulado type (as far as their monopolic legal status was concerned). Breaking up the Indian pueblo communal landholdings was still far away, but this was secondary in comparison to other sources of worry. The church, on the other hand, was becoming adapted to coexisting with a republican government, and practically none of the moderate liberals would insist on such things as religious tolerance to irk the clergy. Most upper-class elements were joining this conservative front, where room could be found for the miners, the merchants, and the Veracruz tierra-caliente interests. The main exception were the industrialists, who had to fend for themselves after the departure of Alamán; the agiotistas, always on the lookout for new connections; and some provincial sectors, who feared excessive control from the center.

The military did not form an organic component of the conservative alliance. Some of its members had come close to it, at the moment of confrontation with the last desperate attempts of Iturbide to maintain himself in power through popular agitation. But many Iturbidistas retained positions of importance in the army, notably Anastasio Bustamante and Luis Quintanar, after a short period of being furloughed.[11] Even Gómez Pedraza could be considered a part of the Iturbidista connection, though he had become more independent; in any event the faction was slowly disappearing. It was becoming reabsorbed into a sort of "military party," prepared to uphold order against extreme mobilizational attempts, but at the same time conscious of the need to come to terms with the representatives of the masses, perhaps even establishing an alliance with them, so as to acquire a solid governing base. One may wonder why they should have been preoccupied with these matters, when they could have established an alliance with the Right (clerics and moderate liberals) and thus simplify the political scene, by creating an overpowering front of the ruling classes. As argued before, however, this was easier said than done, because of the schisms among the various business interests, especially in connection with protectionism and federalism. If the middle classes and the lower strata were left to their own demagogues, they could become threatening, as they did have a lot of weight, especially if united with some upper-class aspirantes. This is, actually, what was going to happen before the end of that fateful year 1828.

The army, then, preferred a more independent stance, relatively pragmatic and in a sense "centrist," but in contrast with other such groupings, it was a strong and armed participant in the political game. Despite its strength, which was more apparent than real, it had constant changes of opinions and strategies, as befits a center faction. These indecisions, these shifting alliances, personified a few years later by Santa Anna, had much to do with their position in the social system and their greater awareness, in comparison to the upper classes, of the dangers of not taking into account the pressures from below. In other parts of Latin America, the situation had some common elements, but many contrasting ones. Thus in Brazil and other slaveholding societies such as Cuba, the potential threat from the masses, that is, from a slave insurrection, was such that it kept most of the upper and middle classes quiet and solidary among themselves. Elite politics and monarchy, or the maintenance of colonial status, was the result. In a sense Mexico occupied a very special, almost unique situation on the continent. The level of threat coming from its popular classes was quite high, but not high enough to dissuade ambitious aspirantes or middle-class ideologues from arousing them.

The group forming around the leadership of War Minister Gomez Pedraza could be interpreted as having two wings. One was civilian, based on sectors of the "progressive" professionals, administrators, and intellectuals, plus quite a few people who could be classed as high-status aspirantes with a pragmatic ideological orientation and a sizable middle-class following. The other Pedrazista wing consisted of the armed forces, including their Iturbidista sector. The "centrist" position assigned to Gómez Pedraza's political stance is congruent with its members' self-designation as imparciales, a sort of lodge to eliminate all lodges. Adding up their civilian and military wings the imparciales had a considerable political base on which to build, but not enough (even taking into acccount that they included the armed forces) to rule the nation without some extra alliance.

Among the lower sectors of the social pyramid, the Yorkino party collected a large following, much of it mobilizational; that is, only transformable into political capital through intense confrontations. There were also some vestiges of traditional populism, still with Iturbidista resonances but increasingly integrated within Yorkinismo. The latter, despite the loss of some of its members to Gómez Pedraza, was still the strongest individual force, though also incapable of exerting power on its own.

As for the upper classes, despite a certain tendency to coalesce when faced by a common enemy, there was still a maze of conflicting interests concerning protectionism and clericalism, and coexistence with the foreign sector was not always easy. The new novenario entente between Escoceses and clerics was a sign of hope, and if augmented with the foreign merchants and miners and the loose industrialists and agiotistas, a solid front could be formed, overpowering the Yorkinos, even without counting on the military. This union, however, was not yet formed, and Pedraza attempted another strategy. For one thing his "progressive" image allowed him to take some middle-class sectors away from the Yorkinos. Following that same policy, he might try to bring in the federalists, thus getting closer to the Yorkinos' strength. With some valor and good fortune, along with scattered support from other sources, for example old-style Escoceses dissatisfied with their party's turn toward the Right or elements of traditional populism attracted by his Iturbidista image, his might have become the strongest of all the existing coalitions. But this was not to be.

Intensification of Conflict

The Yorkino party opted for a policy of increased mobilization and intensification of attacks against Spaniards, banking on the widespread resentment against the relatively privileged positions even poor whites from Spain had enjoyed for such a long time during the colonial regime, and which still they had at each social level considered. In the provinces too, anti-Spanish feeling might force the federalists to antagonize the Pedraza-oriented government, which tried not to employ extreme measures so as to avoid international complications. The Spaniards having already been banned from government posts at the federal level, it was almost automatic to do the same in each state, but pressures mounted to expel all or most of them. The state of Jalisco passed such legislation in early September 1827, quickly followed by a more "barbarous" law adopted in the state of Mexico under the prodding of its governor, Lorenzo de Zavala. Though this law was immediately declared invalid by the national Senate, the lower house took its time to treat the subject, thus allowing the measure to produce its effects. Other states followed suit, some more or less voluntarily, some pressed by armed gatherings in the streets, in which the civic militias played a strategic role.[12]

The furor against the Spaniards moved from the states to the capital, where Yorkino congressmen Zerecero, Alpuche e Infante, and Berduzco proposed a bill to require all Spaniards except especially handicapped ones, or those married and with Mexican children, to leave the country within sixty days. Even Escocés-controlled Veracruz sanctioned a law of expulsion, if an extremely mild one, just to forestall sterner measures or to avoid being accused of doing nothing against the national enemy.

On December 5, 1827, a commission of the lower house approved a bill of expulsion, which was quite inclusive, though in practice loopholes remained and were taken advantage of by the wealthier peninsulars.[13] The chamber approved the measure in general by 42 to 13 votes the same day, a majority that gives an idea of the number of allies the more extremist faction had obtained, or of the need the more moderate sectors felt to comply with some form of open persecution against what was considered to be a threatening Trojan horse. The law was finally signed on December 20. Three days later the expected armed revolt of the Escoceses exploded in Otumba, a rural area of the state of Mexico, apparently led by a local hacienda administrator, Manuel Montaño, from whom the "plan" took its name. The Montaño plan demanded the abolition of all secret societies, a change of cabinet, and the expulsion of American representative Joel Poinsett. A few days later Nicolás Bravo, the vice-president, joined the rebels, but he could not pull much of the army with him.

Some observers thought that the plan also had some monarchical intent. From Paris the Mexican envoy, Tomás Murphy, Jr. (who had replaced his father, dismissed because of his nationality), reported suspicious moves by Mexicans in Europe in early January 1828, including José Francisco Fagoaga, marqués del Apartado; the marquesa de San Román; the dean of the Valladolid cathedral, J. M. Gil; and Juan de Novoa. The issue of monarchist plots became entwined with the competing proposals of J. García del Río and Gabriel Ouvrard, representatives of European banking houses proposing a new loan to Mexico to repay the previous ones and provide more fresh money. There was a protracted polemic, including the publication of pamphlets, between Murphy and the new Mexican envoy to Rome, Luis Gordoa. Apparently the latter supported García del Río's financial proposals and accused the Murphys of interest in the rival banking house of Ouvrard, while Murphy considered that García del Río, who years earlier had represented the Peruvian government in search of loans and a king, was at it again. These dealings were coupled with others centered in Bordeaux, where the Spanish merchants exiled from Mexico were talking openly about the coming expedition of reconquest.[14]

The military part of the Montaño insurrection was quickly resolved, through a campaign by Vicente Guerrero. The rebels, Nicolás Bravo and others who had joined him, including Miguel Barragán (erstwhile governor of Veracruz, dislodged after the Rincón disturbance), were jailed. In Congress some Escocés representatives proposed an amnesty, as had been done before in similar cases, such as the Lobato revolt. The more radical Yorkinos, in and out of Congress, demanded the death penalty, and the capital city was "inundated by incendiary pamphlets and its walls covered by posters equally wild." Finally Zerecero proposed to commute that penalty to one of banishment for ten years, which was effected. The Payo del Rosario and others protested this weakness of the authorities, deeming that only death could clear the affront to the republic; after all, Bravo had shot several rebels during his campaign of 1824 against "heroic" Jalisco.[15]

The country was in a state of turmoil, with an empty treasury incapable of servicing the foreign debt and facing the clear prospect of a Spanish invasion, which would drain resources even further. In fact that expedition arrived only a year later, but reports of its preparation were already known. To add fuel to the existing fires, soon presidential elections had to be held. Though they did not involve direct popular voting for the president, they were part of a complex process, developing throughout August and September. It started with primary voting for national congressmen, and in most states for local legislatures, beginning in August and finishing in third-level juntas by late September or early October. Before that each of the old local legislatures had to convene on September 1 to cast ballots for president and vice-president. Their preferences, which obviously would be known to everybody, would be officially counted only in the first days of the next year, when the newly elected Congress would convene. That new Congress would have to decide as to the validity of the polling, and for doing this it would have to sit "by states," that is, the representatives of each state would cast a single vote. Still more important, the responsibility of electing a president would fall upon it if no absolute majority emerged from the state legislatures' votes.[16]

Social agitation was stimulated by the prospect of a radically reformist or even revolutionary government coming into being. In many parts of the country, armed groups were taking justice into their own hands, and peasants were occupying Spanish-owned lands, sometimes prodded by Yorkino governors. In Mexico a well-publicized confrontation between a large hacienda and its neighboring Indian pueblos, lasting for several months, allows us to see the interplay of factors involved in the maintenance of order in the countryside. The hacienda was located in the district of Toluca, partido of Tenango, some hundred kilometers to the southwest of the capital, and it was one of the oldest established in the country. Its owner, the conde de Santiago, being a minor, it was administered by his grandfather, Martín Michaus, a Spanish merchant of great wealth. The neighboring Indians complained that the hacienda had encroached on their lands, moving the boundary posts up to their own homes and graveyards, and that it maintained a permanent armed force of two hundred mounted men.

Governor Lorenzo de Zavala, who had replaced the Escocés Melchor Múzquiz earlier in 1827, visited the zone in July, determined to effect justice or extract some political capital, depending on one's perspective. When he arrived at the town of Mexicalcingo, "over a thousand Indian women came over to him in the church's patio, kneeling and weeping and lifting up their children, clamoring to the governor: father of the people, look here so many innocents who will die of hunger, because the hacienda de Atenco has taken away our lands and left us with absolutely nothing to eat." As the scene repeated itself, he left instructions to the jueces de letras of the partidos of Tenango and Tenancingo to request the hacienda owners to show their titles and, if they could not find them, to restore the lands to the communities. The Tenango judge fulfilled his instructions and requested the hacienda to withdraw its *mojoneras*, which was done by the Indians. Michaus then appealed to the state supreme court, which ordered matters back to their earlier state, dismissing the judge and replacing him with his colleague from Tenancingo.

The Tenancingo judge hastened to the place with a great number of attendants, to force the pueblos back to their reduced limits. He had so little sense as to undertake this action during Easter week, April 1828, with the subprefecto of Tenango and the commandant of the militia, who had recruited a few hundred horse and infantry men. This was being done against the wishes of the governor, under the protection of some of the old personnel of the judiciary, "corrupted by Michaus's gold." As soon as they arrived at the pueblo, they found about a thousand Indians, who soon trebled their numbers, led by the ayuntamiento. The judge and the subprefecto, after vainly trying to persuade the crowd, using the good offices of the local alcalde and síndico, ordered the troops to charge. Immediately the gathering dispersed, leaving five dead in the field. In the confusion the alcalde and the síndico had disappeared. The repositioning of the mojoneras was thus undertaken with no further problem, and preparations were made for doing the same in other pueblos, some quite distant.[17]

During the affair the commandant, José Ignacio Pliego, noted that a sector of the militia, that of infantry from Santiago and Capuluac (surely made up of Indians), had been very hesitant in obeying orders, so he sent them back to their homes, under their captain.

Governor Zavala, on hearing of these events, instructed the prefecto of Toluca, who was in charge of the subprefectos, to suspend the proceedings. On April 11 both the subprefecto and the juez de letras of Tenancingo, who had directed the operation, received the order but did not obey it (probably because they considered it unconstitutional), but continued with their work. The same day (according to the chronicler of the *Correo*), Zavala went out incognito to the place to get direct information, but he was immediately recognized and followed by a crowd that numbered three to four thousand people by the time he arrived at the actual location of the combat. Immediately he summoned the two disobedient officials and sent them to jail in Tlalpam, the state capital. *El Correo* celebrated this decision, which even if of doubtful constitutionality, had averted worse consequences, since the fugitive Indians had probably gone to fetch arms and join the sector of the militia that sympathized with them. *El Correo* added that "in all the pueblos of the Toluca valley the symptoms can be seen . . . of a land revolution that will be disastrous. The thoughtful man cannot but be impressed by the unequal distribution of properties . . . Agrarian laws given in time may equalize property holders as much as possible, and thus the convulsions that agitated the Roman Republic would be [avoided]."[18]

In the mining centers, labor unrest also exploded, stimulated by political agitation and by the withdrawal of regular forces or militias when order broke down in other places. In Real del Monte, a very important strike erupted, apparently encouraged by the local priest, José Reyes, a friar of "bad life," inclined to share a drink with his parishioners, if we are to believe the company's reports, and condoned by José Rodrigo de Castelazo, the agent of the conde de Regla (who as owner of the mines was a partner to the British). Castelazo, a state legislator, was a political friend of Governor Lorenzo de Zavala. The conflict, which has been studied by Robert W. Randall, lasted from July to August 1827, and reignited again in August 1828, with scenes similar to those seen earlier in Bolaños.[19]

To the usual combination of alcaldes, jueces políticos, priests, and local leaders, now there were several additional figures: the local legislator and the equally local representatives of the miners' guild (the diputación de minería), probably connected with the smaller mining entrepreneurs. At one point the juez de letras at Pachuca, Lic. Juan José Rosales, reminded the company that "in our country it is not considered criminal for operatives to advise their companions against continuing work, so as to obtain a partido, . . . of which not without reason they consider themselves deprived by the company."[20] After the end of the first conflict, which was won by the men with the help of Castelazo's mediation, the company made several demands of the government. First the friar should be transferred to "some far-off part of the country," which was duly implemented by the government. Second regular troops should be permanently stationed at the real, because the "mining population is so numerous, that it is easy for it to defy the civil authority in moments of altercation such as the present ones." This was also carried out by the minister of War, who ordered that the detachment sent provisionally during the first skirmishes remain permanently. The minister also added a recommendation to the governor of the state of Mexico, who was responsible for the militia, not to call out those forces, because the company preferred to do without them. Third the "magistrate" (juez de letras) should be located in the real and not in Pachuca, to expedite decisions in times of conflict and "decide with impartiality, . . . because the present alcaldes, or local magistrates, being more or less connected to the miners, nobody could expect from them an impartial administration of justice."[21]

Peace lasted for about a year. Toward the end of August 1828, the national political scene had become extremely tense, due to the obvious preparations of a pronunciamiento by Santa Anna, who was trying to convince several ayuntamientos of the state of Veracruz to invalidate the recent election of Gómez Pedraza as successor to Guadalupe Victoria. This was the last act of the drama that would lead in three months' time to the Motín de la Acordada, which succeeded in annulling the election and designating the popular Guerrero in his place. The troop movements necessary to thwart Santa Anna's rebellion (already declared by mid-September) threatened to leave the mines defenseless, as they had been before.[22]

Already on August 26, when it became known that the troops would leave (they actually left on September 19), the barreteros stopped work in one of the mines, "with the greatest insolence, pretending that they, and not me [reported the manager] would nominate the administrator of the mine," adding that "it was useless to ask help from the authorities. The alcalde already quite some time ago informed the governor that he cannot rely on the cívicos because, without the presence of a regular force, he cannot take responsibility for the maintenance of calm . . . Probably it will be necessary, in order to preserve our lives and property, to arm the British subjects." Regular troops, however, finally arrived, and peace with them. But a while afterward, with the prospect of those troops being used in other theaters, agitation resumed. The usual chain of requests for protection to the chargé d'affaires went into operation. The British representative wrote to the minister of Relaciones that he understood the difficulty in keeping regular troops at the mine, given the critical circumstances of the country, but at least he should summon "the nearest militia . . . because experience has shown that the militia of the place itself can not be relied upon, due to its connection and daily intercourse with the very persons from whom the aggressions are feared."[23] In fact regular troops abandoned the real in November, and when they were leaving, which was on a Saturday, payday, there were some provocations, with shots, stones, and wounded on both sides. Finally Governor Zavala, his power already consolidated at a national level after the Acordada, and with Guerrero designated as president-elect, had federal troops sent to the real, and peace returned.[24]

In Vetagrande, Zacatecas, another episode took place during that same year 1828.[25] An electoral campaign was under way, because the state legislatures (elected two years earlier) were to meet on September 1 for the presidential election. Zacatecas was a very prosperous state, the main silver producer in the country, and a solid base for a liberal variety of federalists who, though they had some populist sympathies, avoided supporting Guerrero and leaned instead toward Gómez Pedraza, to whom they gave one of the state's votes.[26]

During that April a violent miners' movement resisted the usual innovations by the British management. Soon the alcalde arrived, argued the barreteros' point, and made a deal that apparently calmed everybody down. But that same evening Mr. Kerrison, the manager, got news that new disturbances were being planned and that some people were going to the main shaft with the intention of setting fire to the surface structure, or *galera*, as well as to the engines used for pumping water. Kerrison sent another note to the alcalde and got ready to sell his life dearly. The crowd increased incessantly, reaching some fifteen hundred people; they began forcing the gates to enter the house where the British employess were staying, hurling stones and receiving some shots in response. Incensed by this reaction, they proceeded to burn the galera, accompanied by songs and laughter, destroying in a few instants the work of two years, according to Kerrison, or only producing a few damages, "una friolera," as reported by the semiofficial Mexico newspaper, *El Aguila*.[27]

Meanwhile the alcalde did not appear, impeded by the barreteros, in *El Aguila*'s version, but really due to his ill will, if we are to believe the company. Kerrison sent two of his employees to the state capital (two leagues distant) to ask for help. The governor received the request at eleven in the evening, and immediately gathered the cívicos, sending two hundred of them under their commandant. They arrived in the first hours of the following day and found everything quiet, but they remained a few days so as to reestablish confidence.[28] The governor then sent a special report to the central government, telling the story from a perspective that must not have been very favorable to the company. When the minister of Relaciones, Juan de Dios Cañedo, received the news on April 16, he immediately wrote to the chargé d'affaires (without waiting for the usual British complaint), in uncommon terms. He said that the president had been informed that

> the company has displeased the workers, and that as a result of having removed a foreman and replaced him with another one, whose dealings the operatives deem prejudicial, things became worse, to the point that some employees of that company opened fire on the miners . . . The undersigned has the honor of communicating to you the disgust with which H. E. the President has learned about these events . . . requesting you to take the necessary measures in relation to individuals from your country so that nothing will disturb the good order and harmony which must prevail between Mexicans and the subjects of His Britannic Majesty.[29]

His Britannic majesty was not accustomed to receiving this type of warning, and his chargé d'affaires quickly answered that he had received the official note while he was preparing his own, complaining about the ill will of the local authorities and about Cañedo's supposition that there had been provocation from the British employees, probably due to distorted reports from the state authorities. He insisted that it "was most essential to the success of the company's operation that it have the freest and most uncontrolled power to designate the superintendents of the works." During the two following days, the official mouthpiece *El Aguila* and the Yorkino *Correo de la Federación* published notes highly favorable to the workers and to the alcalde and flattering to the Zacatecan governor, José María García Rojas, who obviously had friends in the capital.[30]

The controversy was settling down. However, a few days later *El Correo* published more notes on the events, and to save the national honor it recalled to its readers that "all countries of the world have known the vengeance produced by the abuse of power . . . witness to this, the Manchester revolt against machinery, and the effort it took to appease the rebels . . . We must remind the '*mandones*' of the prudence and style with which it is proper to treat dependents, and especially the operatives in the strenuous work of the mines."[31]

Gómez Pedraza's Search for Allies

With the backdrop of this type of social agitation raging in various parts of the country, already in November 1827 Gómez Pedraza was trying to consolidate his ruling coalition by bringing in Francisco García, the prestigious federalist from Zacatecas, to replace Salgado in Hacienda. But mounting pressures from the Yorkinos produced a cabinet crisis in February and March 1828, after the demise of the Escocés revolt. They no longer wished to tolerate the presence of Ramos Arizpe, who had a soft position on Spanish expulsion, in Justicia. They also wanted to bring back Esteva to his old job in Hacienda. This meant displacing García, which would be a serious problem, especially if it were coupled with the dismissal of Ramos Arizpe, a noted federalist. So the solution was to compensate by putting Juan de Dios Cañedo, another well-known federalist from Jalisco, in Relaciones, the main ministry. Espinosa de los Monteros, who was covering it as *oficial mayor* while Camacho was abroad, passed on to Justicia to take Ramos Arizpe's place. Camacho, still in Europe, was of course not taken into consideration. Moderate opinion, however, sighed in relief, seeing that Relaciones had not fallen to the intriguing Espinosa de los Monteros but to a more trustful provincial worthy, Cañedo, a federalist turned moderate. The new cabinet, then, retained a coalitional character, dominated by Pedraza in War, flanked by a federalist in the formally preeminent Relaciones, and a Yorkino (Esteva) in Hacienda, plus the sinuous Espinosa de los Monteros in Justicia. But both Esteva and Cañedo had become wary of agitational politics, so the new cabinet was not to the liking of the more extreme Yorkinos; by contrast the Escoceses rose to the occasion and became more favorable to the government.[32]

Gómez Pedraza was a very strong candidate, backed as he was by a large part of the military, the commandants in each state being his "creatures." Against him the Yorkinos put up Esteva and Guerrero. Esteva had become more moderate, and it was even said that some Escoceses, who could not field any credible candidate after the armed rebellion, might support him. Apparently he had resigned the leadership of the lodges to Guerrero some time before. At any rate the race soon became defined as a contest between Gómez Pedraza and Guerrero. Guerrero had the larger part of the popular classes with him but also a considerable sector of the army, which had been antagonized by Gómez Pedraza's disciplinarian attitudes.[33]

The primary elections in the city of Mexico were held amid scenes of violence and popular mobilization on August 17, 1828, a Sunday. These were contested elections, in which the power of the state, especially its War minister and the army, could not be fully exerted because of the deep divisions within the cabinet. The Yorkinos had a number of friends in high offices, starting with Esteva, and were also well connected to President Guadalupe Victoria. Cañedo and Espinosa were ambivalent, because though they would not relish a Guerrero victory, they were not full adherents of Gómez Pedraza either. As a result, on one side there was the unimpaired functioning of the populist mobilization machine of the Yorkinos, while against it the influence of the Pedrazista sector of the executive was blocked by ministerial dissension. Of course in these elections only the new members of Congress and of the legislatures were being selected, but though the responsibility for selecting the president was not theirs, they would have to pass on the legality of the process. Besides if the balloting of the legislatures did not generate any absolute majority, it would be up to the new Congress to elect the president (allowing each state delegation one vote). As we have seen, the electoral process was very indirect, progressing through the old provincial legislatures, but popular pressure could always be expressed. The results of the primary juntas would of course be very influential in determining the legitimacy of the whole package.

Popular pressures were not long in appearing. In Veracruz, the heartland of the Escocés resistance, a change in the political attitudes of Santa Anna was taking place. During the Montaño revolt, he had abstained from joining his Escocés friends, though his brother Manuel did participate and was sent into exile together with Bravo, due to the determination of War Minister Pedraza. Now the Veracruzano opted for the radical camp, which happened to contain the enemies of Pedraza; so he became a supporter of Guerrero's candidacy for the presidency. Santa Anna had his agents organize popular gatherings in various places, forcing the ayuntamientos of Jalapa and Orizaba (two of his main bastions, reflecting the rise of the new tierra-caliente producers) to make, late in August, petitions to the state legislators to give their votes to Guerrero. The legislature rejected the pressure being exerted on it and proceeded to vote for Pedraza. Two days afterward, on September 3, popular disturbances took place in the state capital, Jalapa, but the lawmakers responded by removing Santa Anna from his position as vice-governor. He forthwith entered into armed rebellion, marching with his troops from Jalapa to the nearby fort of Perote, determined to resist what he termed impositions of the local senate, which had intimidated the wavering deputies. He demanded a change of vote by the legislature and declared Guerrero president-elect, on the basis of his own count of the states' balloting.[34]

This swift change by Santa Anna, who until shortly before had been classed among the Escoceses' supporters, brought an unexpected ally to the Yorkinos' cause, though militarily he was initially unsuccessful and had to withdraw to Oaxaca, where he retained a foothold. The semiofficial Pedrazista mouthpiece, *El Aguila*, denounced plans by the Yorkinos to support Santa Anna's revolt with arms in hand; it went on to condemn the "anarchists" who were unwilling to accept electoral defeat. The Yorkino *Correo de la Federación*, which under the editorship of Lorenzo de Zavala was the "official organ of the democratic party," according to the French minister, blasted back, accusing the "parianistas" of attacking the nation's integrity. Congress was prevailed upon to declare Santa Anna a rebel and "beyond the law," which meant that he would be shot if caught. There were plans to give special powers to the president, but these did not pass Congress, mainly due to the joint opposition of the Yorkinos and of the moderate Senate. The government was more successful in introducing a law restricting freedom of the press. Lists of potential jury members (drawn by lot for each case) were compiled by the ayuntamientos; they were therefore full of Yorkinos, thus making the oppositionist press untouchable. To correct this an amendment was introduced requiring a capital of four thousand or an income of one thousand pesos as a condition for being included.[35]

In early October Zavala himself was accused, first by the executive and then by the Senate, of abetting subversion. Tornel, Santa Anna's alter ego in the capital, was demoted from the governorship of the city, because of his failure to take decisive action against a militia unit led by the popular agitator Severiano Quesada, who had had a violent encounter with the gendarmes, a police force directly dependent on the Federal District governor. He was replaced by the moderate José Joaquín de Herrera. The government moved to arrest Zavala, to make him face his Senate accusers, and sent troops to nearby Tlalpam, the state's capital, where he resided officially as governor; but he escaped and went into hiding. The national Congress, yielding to moderado pressures, finally enacted the law against secret societies that had been demanded so strongly by Escocés sectors. Soon the Puebla legislature followed suit. In the same defiant mood, Veracruz lawmakers annulled the local elections for national deputies, which had been won by José María Tornel and Ignacio Basadre, both of them intimate colleagues of Santa Anna and prominent Yorkinos. It also annulled elections for the local legislature and hurriedly held complementary ones in December; since they were conducted under the "Pedrazista terror," they returned a majority for the Escoceses, represented in the government of the state by Sebastián Camacho. Widespread protests and armed revolts in the countryside were a response to these tactics.[36]

The Popular Explosion

The main armed revolt, however, occurred in the capital, led clandestinely by Zavala, with the help of such experienced plotters as José María Lobato, Anastasio Zerecero, and Lucas Balderas, joined by the unlikely José Manuel Velázquez de la Cadena, Iturbide's friend who had been ennobled by him.[37] The revolt was started by a group of artillery cívicos led by Balderas, who quickly took control of the jail of the Acordada, demanding prompt implementation of a stricter law against the Spaniards, closing the many loopholes and exceptions the previous one had. In the provinces many "armed petitions" had succeeded in forcing, convincing, or otherwise cajoling the legislatures into sanctioning local laws of expulsion. Now the cívicos who had taken control of the Acordada were demanding similar legislation at the national level. From the late hours of November 30 until December 4, the city of Mexico was the scene of a prolonged confrontation, with the participation of civic militias hastily convened for the occasion by their elected commanders. Soon large crowds of the ever-present "léperos" gathered, apparently quite spontaneously, giving the affair the prospects of a major rebellion, or alternatively, of a general sack of the wealthier shops. Tornel, who participated in the events trying to induce moderation, but clearly on the side of the rebels, explained a few years later that there was a high possibility of a "repetition in Mexico of the scenes of horror which in similar circumstances have been seen in other countries, notably France." Zavala was called to lead the rebels and at the same time seek a negotiated solution, given his connections with the president. Victoria tried to be firm in resistance, but finally yielded to the demands. More strangely, Pedraza was not capable of organizing a serious repression of the movement; this was surely due to the fact that a large armed popular force was concentrated in the central area of the city, and some sectors of the regular army must have been doubtful as to their ability to counter it.[38]

Gómez Pedraza's attempt at organizing a political connection of his own, with a progressive-liberal character and army support, had failed. His alliance with the provincial federalists had not been solid enough, and as for the Escoceses and novenarios (that is, the liberal-cum-clerical Right), they did not really believe in him. So much so, that quite a few conservatives were said to have preferred, from the start, a Guerrero victory, gambling on the inevitable excesses the insurgente hero would commit and the equally unavoidable and salutary reaction that would sweep the country.[39]

So Pedraza opted for an early flight, resigning his position as minister of War, and went to Jalisco, where he could rely on the traditional animosity of that state against the central powers and on his friends among mining circles in the Bajío, to organize resistance. Vicente Filisola, an Iturbidista general who had been a member of the Yorkino lodges and then sided with Pedraza, was commandant of the city of Mexico and as such was in charge of repressing the mutiny. He was overwhelmed by events and sidestepped by the negotiations; he finally withdrew to Puebla, to join Melchor Múzquiz, the local governor, who was considering putting up a fight. The victors organized a campaign to convince Filisola to agree to the fait accompli and sent a mission to Puebla formed by three men, among whom was Gómez Navarrete, the noted Iturbidista, probably with friends on both sides of the battle lines. Poblano resistance was overcome when the local militias and some regular troops were tempted to mutiny and reproduce the scenes of the Acordada, but this time they attacked a silver conducta, rather than the Parián.[40]

Gómez Farías, whose progressive federalist group had been close to Pedraza, left the capital also and headed toward his native Guadalajara, earning from the Correo editors the appellation of "rabid dog," sure to plot in favor of the fallen tyrant, as he had already done in the service of Iturbide.[41] The vigilant *Correo* repeated a rumor (though professing not to believe it) that Anastasio Bustamante was planning a resistance from Jalisco against the victorious popular party. In passing it recalled that Vicente Guerrero, minister of War since the Acordada, was in Puebla (where he had gone in order to reestablish federal authority after Filisola's procrastination) and was ready to march wherever he might be needed. Only Veracruz was still enslaved to the Escocés faction, but soon Santa Anna would turn on his state from Oaxaca and set things right.[42]

Actually Jalisco had become the hub of a series of moves by that region's states to organize resistance to the impositions coming from the capital. Local authorities made declarations arguing that surely president Guadalupe Victoria and the Congress were not free to make decisions, as they must be coerced by the mutineers, so it was necessary to organize civil and military resistance. For this a defensive league was formed, but it was of short duration.[43]

As prospects for successful protest diminished and conditions became more normal in the capital, the potential provincial rebels realized their mistake and acknowledged that the national authorities, given Pedraza's formal resignation of his candidacy, had been correct in designating Guerrero president.[44] However, it was necessary for the government to use troops against the Bajío, where Pedraza had initially taken refuge. The central government's action was focused on Juan José Codallos, commandant of Querétaro, who managed another Acordada-like eruption, an easy task according to Carlos María de Bustamante, due to the large unemployed population in that state, created by the decadence of its erstwhile prosperous textile obrajes. The demise of Filisola and Múzquiz at Puebla helped bring the Bajío to heel. However, the new government sent Lobato there to impose the new order of things even more decisively, and he moved his military force between various of the region's capitals, as a self-styled "Defender of the expulsion of Spaniards." At the same time, he was arousing the Indian population, to which he promised lands, and some of whose occupations of neighboring hacienda properties he supported. As a part of the victors' attempt at consolidating the new regime, Father Vidal, Indian vice-rector of the Colegio de San Gregorio (where Yorkino lodges were thoroughly "implanted") wrote a tract entitled *Los indios quieren ser libres y lo serán con justicia*. Their opponents feared the beginnings of a "caste and color war."[45]

The Yorkino victory had been achieved with external support, notably that of Santa Anna, who was not a reliable recruit of that faction, even if some of his friends, such as Tornel and Basadre, had solid connections with the winning party. The tierra-caliente interests, increasingly represented by Santa Anna, could be interpreted as having broken their connection with the Escocés party, which in any event was in the process of dissolution, some of its members being very determined anticlericals, like Mora, and others all too ready to reconcile themselves with the church, like Sánchez de Tagle. For the more pragmatically oriented tierra-caliente interests, it was not easy, however, to come to terms with the Yorkinos, as the latter depended very much on their artisan base and thus were prone to enact protectionist legislation. In fact one of the first measures of the new Congress was to decree a total prohibition against importing coarse textiles (that is, those more widely consumed), which were produced locally.

In the capital the victors, having acceded to power a few months before the inauguration of Guerrero (which was to take place on April 1, 1829), proceeded to push aside some of those who had tried to remain above the struggle, such as Cañedo, who was attacked by Zavala and had to leave his position at Relaciones.

Guerrero, of course, was the real power behind the lame-duck Guadalupe Victoria, who had been overcome by events. The other emerging main figure was Zavala, who had quite a lot of influence over the president-elect, despite rivalries for preeminence. Zavala, trying to cultivate an image of moderation (not a very easy thing for him), published a manifiesto condemning the looting and the unleashing of popular wrath, laying some of the responsibility on Guerrero's lack of determination to avoid the excesses and on his disappearance from the capital before the end of the journées. This was an indicator of tension between him and the more stalwart Guerreristas, which would surface after a few months, producing his removal from the cabinet. To aggravate this potential conflict, the opposition launched rumors that a temporary dictatorship was being prepared, to be exercised by Zavala so as to clear the ground before Guerrero's inauguration; this was repeatedly denied by the *Correo* and was considered to be a lie aimed at discrediting the victory of the "national party." The contraposition between a "national party" and "antinational" elements or policies became a password in the Yorkino press, especially *El Correo*.[46]

The new cabinet, formed already during the last few months of the moribund Victoria presidency, was very heterogeneous, as was remarked by several of its supporters.[47] In War was appointed the rather faceless Francisco Moctezuma, who declared himself friend of both Bravo and Guerrero, his comrades-in-arms during the Insurgencia, and remained throughout the approximately one year of the Guerrero presidency. Perhaps he was singled out so as not to reproduce the Pedraza syndrome of a powerful War minister overshadowing the chief executive. Relaciones was taken by the Zacatecan federalist José María Bocanegra, who had cooperated with Tornel in editing the *Amigo del Pueblo*, and who also lasted until the end of the Guerrero administration. In Justicia Espinosa de los Monteros had no trouble continuing to take care of the office, but when Guerrero assumed the presidency, he was replaced by José Manuel de Herrera, who had been the main minister practically throughout the period of the empire. This surprising resuscitation of a political cadaver was a very significant signal to the Iturbidistas, always strong in the army and among some sectors of the upper classes and the clergy. Another signal was the proposal by newly elected deputy José Domínguez Manso, who had been minister of Justice during the empire and was a childhood friend of Iturbide, to allow the latter's family to return to Mexico. This was rejected by the House, José María Tornel taking the responsibility of arguing in favor of the proposal. Another move in the same direction was a gesture toward Judge José Manuel Zozaya Bermúdez, who had been suspended by the previous authorities and persecuted by the noted anti-Iturbidista federalist Juan Bautista Morales. However, people such as the Payo did not like the return of this "maromero."[48]

The vice-presidency fell to Anastasio Bustamante, who had come in third in the polling by states for the presidency. Thus another noted Iturbidista was placed near the highest positions of power, representing the mentality of many an army officer. In Hacienda Esteva, who had been growing increasingly critical of mass- mobilizational methods, was replaced first by the old Iturbidista judge Bernardo González Angulo and then more permanently by Lorenzo de Zavala when Guerrero fully assumed the presidency. On the other hand, Tornel was reinstated as governor of the Federal District, which he had been forced to resign by the Senate at the time of the Santa Anna rebellion. As Tornel was still under scrutiny by the Senate, to reinstate him was tantamount to an open disregard for the upper chamber; it was done, nevertheless, as a necessary emergency measure.[49]

Guerrero inaugurated his presidency with a manifiesto indicating that the days of free trade were over, because "the spurious application of economic principles, and the inconsiderate latitude given to foreign commerce, aggravated our wants, and the outcry . . . against it is overwhelming." Passing on to a more philosophical level, he compared himself with Napoleon in such an inmodest way that the text could only have been penned by a ghostwriter, probably Zavala or Tornel, with a political object in mind, even at the cost of making the president sound ridiculous:

> Napoleon Bonaparte, no less accomplished a politician than able general, wrote that [during a crisis] society apparently seeks the man capable of steering the ship of State . . . An immense nation, according to the illustrious prisoner of St. Helen, always has within itself that tutelary spirit, though there are occasions when his coming onto the scene is delayed . . . But if this hoped-for liberator signals his existence in whatever way, the national instinct will . . . call him to its aid and a whole people will exclaim, coming on to him: this is the one! If I was destined by Providence to contribute to the aggrandizement of my fatherland, I will consider myself happy, and even happier because I will follow in the footsteps of my friend General Guadalupe Victoria.[50]

The idea must have been to convince the public that (if French revolutionary images had to be evoked) Guerrero would not become an American Robespierre but at most a replica of the more reassuring Napoleon.[51] In any case, the new government team was the expression of a strange coalition, more nuanced than the usual interpretation of it as the rule of the people or of the Yorkinos. In addition to "the people" and the Yorkinos, there were also the tierra-caliente interests represented by Santa Anna and the Iturbidistas who claimed José Manuel de Herrera among their numbers.[52] Protectionism also extended a hand to the industrialists, and the new situation could also attract the agiotistas, though for the latter the popular pressure and the anti-Spanish campaign were unsettling. But the agiotistas were a new group, made up of people who had been going through a whirlwind of changes in their fortunes (some of them were severely hit by the competition of foreign merchants) and thus were prepared for new political combinations. They were foxes richly endowed with the spirit of coalitions, to use Pareto's simile, in contraposition to the steadier lions of the rentier, mining, and large-landholding groups. In the same scheming category, the ever-alert pretendientes must be classed, among whom there was a good breeding ground for the new regime, as many abandoned the sinking ship of Pedrazismo.

The "national-popular" coalition was clearly the stronger one, particularly due to its dual capacity to act in a mobilizational way and yet to attract allies from sectors of the upper classes, available as a result of the propertied groups' failure to build stable coalitions. The presence of some foreign investors, not yet incorporated into political life but responsible for wreaking havoc among sectors of the local bourgeoisie, was a per-

turbing factor. The unsettled and insecure character of the property-hold-
ing and entrepreneurial groups was behind their contradictory strategies
and alliances, which weakened them considerably. One sector entered
into an alliance with the popular classes and their middle-class
mobilizational leaders. This alliance was unstable, however, because the
very strategies that were necessary to stimulate the masses were a cause
of alarm for their better-off partners. On the other hand, if the coalition
leaders dropped their mobilizational policies, their strength would be severely diminished and their preponderance over their enemies jeopardized.

The Breakup of the Guerrero Coalition

President Guerrero had difficulty controlling the complex coalition that
had brought him to power. Financial difficulties endangered the loyalty
of the troops, and in order to collect funds it was necessary to raise taxes
and to ask for loans from the local agiotistas, as foreign sources could no
longer be tapped. Raising taxes, though, was difficult, because the support received from various social groups had to be repaid, and this involved losing revenue. Import taxes would fall as a result of the prohibition
against importing certain coarse textiles produced in Mexico, a decision
the lower house made in February and which finally became law in May.
Customs receipts, which had been recovering from 1825 to 1827, had
already started falling because of increased tariffs in force during the last
two years of Victoria's presidency. From a high value of just over 8 million pesos in 1826–27, annual customs receipts had already dropped to
6.7 million for 1828–29; they went down even further, to less than 5
million, for 1829–30. The tobacco monopoly was also scrapped in May,
in response to tierra-caliente pressures. Though cigar elaboration remained
under government control, planting was now free; this gave an almost
mortal blow to an already ailing item that had been the fiscal mainstay of
colonial times. Zavala tried to compensate with a tax package that was
considered by the French representative to be in line with the most modern practice in Europe. He established a 5-percent direct tax on annual
incomes higher than 1,000 pesos and a patent for all businesses, even the
small ones. The direct levy, however, did not yield much money, while it
antagonized the rich; and the fee on shops of all kinds produced great
concern among the lower middle classes.[53]

The long-awaited transformative increase in exports and imports, which
was supposed to come as a result of opening up to the world market, was
slow in materializing. For one thing, protectionist measures in the textile

area put a brake on it; on the other hand, tierra-caliente production was not picking up as had been expected. The snag was that in order to stimulate it, some unburdening of taxes was necessary (as in tobacco, or earlier on in mining) thus creating a vicious circle, or rather a trough, that would be difficult and costly to pass through. So money had to be requested from the agiotistas, at rates of interest that, being a function of confidence, shot up to unprecedented levels. Or so it was on paper, as often both sides of the ledger had a lot of air in them. The government acted as though it believed its bonds and promissory notes were valuable, and it occasionally accepted them at par as payment of duties, or at a higher than market value in other transactions. When it had to pay the interest or give back the capital, it did so with a combination of cash (very little if any), more promissory notes that everyone knew would not be redeemed, and special favors such as lifting import prohibitions for specific transactions. It is next to impossible to determine the real rates of interest involved in financial transactions between the agiotistas and the government, but though they must have been high, they were not in reality as overtowering as they appear on first inspection. At any rate they created a very heavy burden for the government and transformed the agiotistas into a powerful actor in the Mexican scene as they diversified into other activities, notably the textile industry and agrarian projects.[54]

On a more personal level, Zavala, who had obtained a land grant from Coahuila y Texas in May 1828, asked his colleague Bocanegra to confirm it before the end of December, a necessary action because the lands were near the American frontier. Bocanegra acquiesced but reminded the grantee that the general regulations had to be complied with, regarding the Catholic origin of the settlers.[55]

As the army was suspected of not being totally loyal to the regime, an impetus was provided for the formation of militias with wide bases of recruitment, thus providing a structure for the arming of the popular followers of the party in power, if a crisis were to develop. The subject was very controversial, and in the aftermath of the Acordada, the members of several of the hastily convoked civic battalions were sent back to their homes, as there was no longer any need for their services. This was the usual practice with militias, though a somewhat longer period under the colors might have left them with more positive martial memories and more help for their pockets; but their commandants (elected by the enrolled men) would never make the offensive supposition that they had come to the call of duty only for economic reasons.[56]

However, as the threat of foreign invasion became more realistic, it was necessary to reactivate several militia units, the artillery corps under

Lucas Balderas being among the most important both for its military potential and its political convictions. The Spanish expedition finally appeared at the end of July near Tampico but was quickly defeated by the converging forces of Manuel Mier y Terán from Tamaulipas and Santa Anna from Veracruz, the glory falling mostly to the latter, as a result of the action of September 10, 1829.

In August Guerrero, in order to be better prepared to resist foreign aggression, had been granted special powers by Congress, which immediately afterward went into recess. During that recess, and using his new special powers, the president abolished slavery, a very important symbolic measure that would also have concrete repercussions, especially if applied to Texas, the only place where the institution was still in widespread use. The concerned editors of the *American Annual Register* commented, reviewing events in the world during the years 1829–30, that Guerrero's abolition of slavery "had not benefited the slaves, whose condition was scarcely inferior to that of freemen, but had displeased the rich."[57]

Conservative pressure to expel Poinsett, seen as a promoter of the Yorkino lodges, increased and in August almost passed the lower house, where it lost by a narrow margin. He finally left in January of the next year, after a request by Guerrero to the United States president, who transferred him to another diplomatic destination. The same pressure was exerted to oust Zavala from his grip on the country's finances. Demands for his dismissal came from the state legislatures of Puebla (usually quite conservative) and of Mexico (where there was a balance of forces with a wavering center). Technically Zavala was governor of Mexico with leave, so the legislature first withdrew his permission and then, when he actually resigned the ministry and wanted to resume his functions, barred him from doing so. Here we may notice the change of position of some members of the legislature who had earlier supported him as governor and were now displeased with his role in the cabinet. Guerrero replaced him with the trusted Bocanegra, whose job in Relaciones was taken by another Yorkino, Agustín Viezca.[58]

José María Tornel, the Yorkino with close ties to Santa Anna, had been one of the main supporters of the Guerrero regime, though he later professed not to have agreed to its excesses, while accepting them out of mere governmental solidarity. When in the final months of the regime a strict press law was enacted, he applied it, as governor of the Federal District, to an anonymous libel, apparently without knowing it was by a member of the more radical faction, the "camarilla," thus incurring the displeasure of that group. The camarilla then prevailed upon Guerrero to send Tornel on an impossible mission, as commandant general of Yucatán, which had for all practical purposes separated itself from the federation, after a centralist-oriented military takeover. Guerrero finally decided to send him as minister plenipotentiary to the United States, which he accepted. When he passed through Veracruz to embark, the Jalapa army pronunciamiento had already been issued, apparently only asking for a change of ministry, which Tornel deemed sensible enough. Despite (or because) of the uncertainty as to who was master in Mexico, he proceeded to New York, probably in accord with Santa Anna, with whom he had had a short interview.[59]

The second expulsion bill against the Spaniards, which despite Senate resistance was steamrolled through Congress before Guerrero's formal assumption of power, continued to irritate both rich and poor among the immigrant community. The friars were among the worst hit, because exceptions tended to benefit married men or, within the clergy, the secular priests. The mendicant orders, after having had a last moment of political activity during the Iturbide mobilizational episode, began a long decline from which they never recovered.

The reaction of the opposition and the socially more established members of the ruling coalition created a vacuum around the government. The provincial federalists were fending for themselves, and a few weeks before the Barradas invasion, they were planning yet another defensive coalition led by Jalisco and including Guanajuato, Michoacán, Zacatecas and San Luis Potosí.[60] This league of states had no place under constitutional law. Its stated aim was to second the national government or to take its place if it were overthrown, but separatist potentialities could always materialize. Gómez Farías, though not a supporter of the Guerrero government, was entrusted by the president with a mission aimed at pacifying the states, but the provincial federalist sector was not happy with the conduct of affairs at the center.

To assuage opposition from the Escoceses, Guerrero decreed an amnesty for the exiled leaders of the Montaño Plan; thus by November, Bravo, Barragán, and Facio were back in the country and already participating in the plotting. The radical wing of the government, with *El Correo* (edited by Zavala) as its main mouthpiece, initiated an analysis of the constitution, proposing among other things the acceptance of religious tolerance, and direct elections instead of the complicated indirect system, which overly "filtered" public sentiment. As the opposition was very incendiary in its publications, a decree (passed by the executive branch through its special powers) applied severe penalties for all those who advocated the destruction of existing institutions or who slandered the authorities. Immediately the most scandalous opposition journalist, Francisco Ibar (also a painter by profession) was jailed.

One of the means used to counteract the feared Spanish invasion was to send José Ignacio Basadre, a hot-headed Yorkino, to Haiti with 10,000 pesos and the mission to interest that government in a campaign against the neighboring island, with the intent of freeing the slaves. Predictably Carlos María de Bustamante thought the real intention was to recruit black troops to form a praetorian guard around Guerrero, to whom they would be loyal through ethnic solidarity.[61]

Finally the armed forces, very much influenced by conservative public opinion, took the initiative in toppling the government. First in early November there was a coup in Yucatán, where the local commandant replaced all the existing governing powers and declared the state's intention not to remain united to Mexico unless the centralist system was adopted. A few weeks later, on December 4, the armed forces in Jalapa (the main cantonment near the gulf coast), under the direction of Ignacio Inclán, José Antonio Facio, and a few other officers of middle rank, presented their plan, theoretically in defense of federalism against centralism, but demanding a change of cabinet, the recall of Congress for extraordinary sessions, and the suspension of the executive's extraordinary powers. Santa Anna and Bustamante were offered the leadership of this movement. Santa Anna wavered but finally rejected participation, while Bustamante accepted.

Guerrero took to the field, leaving behind Bocanegra as acting president. But in a matter of days the capital's garrison rose under the leadership of Luis Quintanar, who asked Pedro Vélez, the head of the Supreme Court, to head a provisional executive, flanked by Lucas Alamán and himself. The signatures in the garrison's declaration are a good representation of the military Iturbidista Right: besides Quintanar himself, there were Pedro de Terreros (the former conde de Regla), Miguel Cervantes (former marqués de Salvatierra), and Ramón and Ignacio López Rayón, old insurgents who had changed their views for quite some time. There was a short-lived armed resistance by loyalist forces that mobilized the militias, but it was unsuccessful. Crescencio Rejón and Lucas Balderas were involved in that attempt, but according to Carlos María Bustamante, so was Carlos Beneski, the Polish military man who had accompanied Iturbide on his return to Mexico. Though Bustamante's information must always be treated with caution, if true it would confirm the mixture of Iturbidista and Yorkino forces behind the Guerrero regime. However,

Guerrero's support was rapidly falling apart, and many had already changed sides, notably the Iturbidista Right. By the new year, Anastasio Bustamante was sworn in as constitutional president by a recalled and somewhat overpowered Congress, where he had a solid two-thirds majority in the Senate, thus dominating the lower house.[62]

The national-popular coalition had been undone, not only by the opposition of the armed forces, but by the solid congregation of all or most of the dominant sectors against the mobilizational and secularizing threat his administration presented. It was significant that the two main military officers participating in the coup, Bustamante and Quintanar, were the representatives of Iturbidismo in the army from the days of the Jalisco resistance against the triumvirate, in 1823–24. Similarly Santa Anna, with tierra-caliente interests always in mind, in practice also defected, his defense of the Guerrero regime being very mild; until the end it was rumored that he was also one of the rebels. Probably his more exalted role as hero of Tampico and his rivalry with the other Jalapa plotters convinced him to wait for a better opportunity.

Both Tornel and Santa Anna acted in 1828–29 in a fashion that would later become systematic: a first stage of collaboration with a popular or reformist government and then opposition (or perfunctory defense) of it when radical pressure became excessive. This pattern is very well known for the two Santa Anna–Gómez Farías episodes (1833–34 and 1846–47). Less known and more complex in its mechanism was the Santa Anna–Bocanegra–Rejón episode of 1841–44, to which we shall later return. To these one may add this earlier differentiated cycle, in which Santa Anna played a more distant role.

The inauguration of Guerrero, with Bustamante as vice-president, soon after the Acordada, can be interpreted, then, as the coming to power of a national-popular coalition, with the participation of Santa Anna and sectors of Iturbidismo, in which the popular element was given pride of place at first. When "excesses" materialized, the rightist component of the alliance struck back. The distribution of roles between president and vice-president was the opposite of that in the Santa Anna–Gómez Farías alliances but it reflected similar coalitional tendencies, even if the elements combined were of course not identical.

This revision of Bustamante's role also helps explain other attempts by him, during various crises during his second presidency (1837–41), to recompose the national-popular formula, notably when he pretended to proclaim a return to the federation in 1841, in the face of the challenge by the combined forces of Santa Anna, Paredes, and Valencia. Seeing the Guerrero-Bustamante sequence from the perspective here proposed helps to delimit a distinct pattern that was something more than a sequence of opportunistic moves, a pattern rooted in the social conditions of the times. These conditions basically derived from the confrontation between the protection-oriented interests and those more open to foreign commerce, and they lasted until the major civil and international wars of midcentury dealt the cards in a radically different way, after the destruction of the corporative rural and urban sectors of the economy.

One may wonder why it was necessary to give such prominence to the popular component of the alliance. In the Guerrero-Bustamante case there is an obvious answer: it was the hero of the south who had been elected president, and he also had considerable support among sectors of the army. But this can not be argued for the Santa Anna–Gómez Farías episode: this time it was Santa Anna who had been elected. I would hypothesize that if Santa Anna preferred in 1833 not to directly take over the helm of office, it was not because his leg was aching but because any national-popular alliance in early independent Mexico was of such a nature that its popular element had a great deal of power and had to be treated with great care if it was to be of any use. This was seen quite clearly by the British representative, who reported home that "[Guerrero's] popularity with the lower orders is such, as might make it dangerous to take any measures against him."[63]

One of the strategies to be used by the Right in the alliance was to allow its more radical partners to overreach themselves and alienate centrist public opinion. Then it would be easy to strike at them. Of course this was a dangerous game, rendered necessary by the cross-cutting contradictions among sectors of the elites, which systematically led one of them to seek the support of the popular classes. For the "national" component of the national-popular alliance, the situation was worthy of a Shakespeare to dramatize it: it could not govern without the popular sectors (because in that case it would fall prey to the free-marketeers, hegemonic among the upper and upper-middle classes), but neither could it easily rule with them, because the necessary mobilizational tactics generated a backlash from conservative circles.

8
Cycles of Coalition Making under Santa Anna

Having seen in some detail the dynamics of the formation and destruction of populist alliances under Iturbide and Guerrero, we will examine in this final chapter the pattern of politics during the later part of the prewar republic. We will focus especially on the well-known Santa Anna–Gómez Farías partnerships of 1833–34 and 1846–47 and refer more briefly to the complex Santa Anna–Bocanegra–Rejón sequence of 1841–44 and to the decidedly marginal attempts by Bustamante in 1838 and 1841.

The Right, Unified Under Bustamante

Bustamante, or rather the threat from below, accomplished the miracle of unifying most if not all the warring sectors of the dominant classes: conservative clericals, moderate liberals, military professionals, Iturbidistas, and pragmatic desarrollistas (increasingly being represented by Lucas Alamán). The upper-class components of the national-popular coalition, made up largely of Iturbidistas and desarrollistas, abandoned their popular allies and rejoined their class. The foreign investors can also be seen at this point to have become involved in the political game more directly, giving their support to the new Jalapa administration. On the other hand, the popular coalition, after losing such weighty allies, became more tinged with populist radicalism, though some components of mobilizational Iturbidismo still remained within their ranks. The former Pedrazistas and the Federalists occupied an uneasy middle ground as progressive liberals, shunning the increasing conservatism of the Escoceses as well as the populist tactics of the Yorkinos.

In this description of political cleavages, we should keep in mind that people classifiable as liberal could be found on all three main fronts. As examples of moderate liberals supporting the Bustamante administration (at least at the beginning and for some time thereafter), one can mention Mora and the Fagoagas. In the extreme opposite position, working within the Yorkino fold, liberals of a populist or radical persuasion included such men as Lorenzo de Zavala, Alpuche e Infante, Esteva (though with increasing doubts), Pablo de Villavicencio, and others following in the steps of the recently deceased Fernández de Lizardi. In the middle there was a group that can be characterized as progressive liberals, at some times becoming more radical and at others diminishing their reformist ardor, including Ramos Arizpe, Gómez Farías, Juan de Dios Cañedo, and Rejón.

Conservatives (though the word was not yet in common usage) were at this moment mostly in the Bustamante coalition. They could be either clericals, such as Becerra or Bishop Pérez; Iturbidistas, such as Anastasio Bustamante himself; or pragmatic desarrollistas, such as Lucas Alamán and Esteban Antuñano.

The Bustamante government tried to maintain legal fictions, considering that Guerrero had become incapable of exercising the presidency so that the vice-president had to take his position. Congress was maintained, and when it first convened, on January 1, it defiantly elected none other than Alpuche e Infante as its president. The election was by a small majority, against the Iturbidista José Domínguez Manso, who had, as was true of most others in his faction, abandoned the populist alliance. Alpuche e Infante immediately attempted to become the head of a resistance movement with military connections, but his papers were seized and he was jailed and exiled, the same happening to Zerecero, also a member of the lower house. Zavala, who was under judicial investigation as a result of Senate accusations regarding financial matters, decided to leave the country, and soon his *Correo* ceased publication. *El Atleta*, another opposition paper that had been started recently, was silenced through heavy fines, and so was Quintana Roo's short-lived *El Federalista*, in April 1830.

By that time, with several members of the House in exile, opposition was reduced, and many wavering deputies joined the government or muted their dissent. In the states local legislatures in several cases were considered to be invalidly elected and thus were either replaced by their predecessors, as in the state of Mexico, or elected anew. Changes were implemented through Congress, where the Senate's two-thirds majority could overrule the House. Decisions were then imposed with the help of regional military commandants in charge of regular troops. As had happened on other occasions, regional resistance was led by Jalisco and

Zacatecas, San Luis Potosí proposing the convening of a convention in León, to oppose centralist inroads into their independence. After discussions with the new national authorities, the autonomy of some of these legislatures was recognized, attempts at changing their composition were abandoned, and peace was restored on that front.[1]

The cabinet was centered around Lucas Alamán, in Relaciones. He had as his colleagues Rafael Mangino in Hacienda, José Ignacio Espinosa in Justicia, and Antonio Facio in War. Mangino, a Poblano, was a bureaucrat who had started his career in public administration in colonial times and continued it under the republic. He then became a Bourbonist, a friend of the Fagoagas, with whom he had been to Europe, and in general was a very hard working and unassertive man. He had joined rather early the Plan de Iguala and had been forced to take a leading role in Iturbide's coronation, because of his official position at the time, but he was not an active partisan of the emperor. He was known as a good friend of the Spaniards and was very much opposed to their expulsion.[2] José Ignacio Espinosa (no kin to Espinosa de los Monteros), the choice for Justicia, was a determined clerical, who according to Zavala gave the appearance of being austere but was in fact faithless, avaricious, and hypocritical. Perhaps the perception was slanted, but it helps to locate him in the factional struggles. José Antonio Facio, the minister of War, was a hard-liner, who had been exiled for his participation in the Montaño revolt and had recently returned. General Miguel Cervantes, the former marqués de Salvatierra, was made governor of the Federal District.

With the solid upper-class support the new administration enjoyed, it is no surprise that it could put order in the administration, collect more taxes, and make the government meet more of its bills than it had grown accustomed to. Alamán favored a dynamic program of developing industry through official banking, with funds collected from tariffs on textile imports. The prohibitions already enacted were temporarily cast aside for some and then for all types of imports, until enough money was collected to form the capital for the bank, to finance large-scale industrial projects, and also promote artisan modernization. The artisans, always in need of tariff protection or actual prohibition, had stood to gain a great deal from Guerrero's policies and were now spared a policy of total opening to international trade, which would also have put the newly forming industrialists at risk.[3]

The government, though quite authoritarian in its treatment of the opposition, was not excessively powerful, because its support among the upper classes was mixed, and due only to their common fear of what could have happened under a prolonged Guerrero presidency. Social revolution was in the air at the time, and a few months after the Bustamante administration was inaugurated, it exploded in France. On August 11, 1830, the Mexican representative in Paris reported the orderly way in which the event had taken place, the result being that those in favor of recognizing Mexican independence were now in office. But three months later he was alarmed at the "disasters" that had taken place in Lyon, which were serious enough to cause the new king's own son to march there at the front of an army of forty thousand men; he was hopeful that the situation would come under control, but the resistance of the national guard, which had sided with the rebellious workers, would undoubtedly be quite strong. The motive of the uprising, Murphy thought, was the great reduction in the salary of silk workers and "to proclaim the republic with Napoleon as supreme chief." This was an interesting reading of the situation, a premonition of classical Bonapartism twenty years before it happened, which recent Mexican experience made quite intelligible to the envoy.[4]

Yorkino resistance was suppressed, and freedom of the press was practically abolished after fines were systematically levied on journalists considered subversive. In defeat the Yorkinos were abandoned by people who had been close to them or even their leaders; but many of them had already cut their connections some time earlier, as in the case of Esteva and Ramos Arizpe. Several others were in exile, such as Alpuche e Infante, and some had made an about-face. This was the case of José María Tornel, appointed ambassador to the United States by the previous government and who remained at his post, probably also reflecting Santa Anna's attitudes.

Resistance against Bustamante

Resistance against Bustamante took an armed form, led by such people as Francisco Victoria, brother of the former President, and José Trinidad Salgado, governor of Michoacán, both of whom were imprisoned and then escaped, due to Salgado's influence among the local cívicos.[5] Victoria was captured and shot and so was Juan José Codallos, while attempting an uprising in the southern tierra caliente. Gordiano Guzmán, Juan Alvarez, and Guerrero maintained an almost impregnable resistance in their local strongholds. However, in January 1831 Guerrero was caught by deceit, by a mercenary Italian ship captain and delivered to the federal authorities, who after a quick military trial had him shot in Oaxaca.

Later that year an apparently minor episode was blown out of proportion by repressed public opinion. On September 16 the patriots were preparing to celebrate the Insurgencia, but they were deterred by a prolonged rain; someone proposed moving the festivities to September 27, the day the Trigarante Army had entered the city of Mexico, which was rejected. The Iturbidistas decided to hold the celebration on their own, which the president would have preferred to avoid, so as not to create occasions for conflict. The gathering took place, however, with a few vivas to Iturbide at the end, thus giving rise to suppositions about the existence of a faction. The event worried the authorities enough to prompt Alamán to send his representative in Paris an official account of the events, diminishing their importance, but alerting him as to their possible use by interested parties.[6]

During the early months of the new administration, the Yorkinos attempted to influence popular opinion through a campaign against the many recently arrived foreigners who owned or managed shops dedicated to retailing.[7] Of course there were also those, mainly the British, operating on a larger scale. But others, especially the French, were beginning to compete with locals. So the energy that had gone into the campaign against Spaniards found another vent for Mexican nationalism. The lower house (where most of the old deputies were still sitting, as there had been no new elections but only the exile of a few of its members) passed a bill to prohibit foreigners from engaging in retail trade; it also increased import duties by ten percent for merchandise coming from countries that had not yet recognized Mexican independence. The Senate, always more conservative, under government pressure voided the lower-house decision on the subject of retail trade. Alamán, reporting this fact, feared that the matter might soon be brought up again and that it would be impossible to resist it, given the intensity of public sentiment.[8]

Church support also had to be accommodated, and the government opted for a compromise solution regarding vacancies of positions in the cathedral chapters and the ordainment of priests. If relations with the Holy See had been normal and the right of patronato accepted, appointments would have been the result of joint action by church and state. But Rome had not extended recognition to the new regime, so that it was not possible to come to an agreement. So the Bustamante administration proposed that "for this time," as an exception to be admitted without being considered a precedent, the bishops themselves, or in their absence the existing members of the cathedral chapters, could fill in the positions. This was resisted by the opposition, which, though stripped of a daily press, could still resort to pamphleteering. The measure was delayed but was finally adopted in May 1831.

On the anticlerical front, Vicente Rocafuerte, the moderate liberal who had been in London negotiating the loans in 1823 and 1824, published a tract in favor of religious tolerance. This was enough to indict him. He was in fact detained, and he could have ended up either in jail or with a stiff fine, had it not been for a very widely attended jury meeting, in which he was absolved. His stance reflected the position of some people who were very far from solidary with the downfallen regime, but who objected to the increasingly repressive measures being adopted, especially the punishment meted out to Guerrero.[9]

Other abuses contributed to this feeling, notably several violent attacks against the press. Manuel Crescencio Rejón, a federalist liberal from Yucatán, who had accused the sergeants of the permanent army corps stationed in the capital of preparing a centralist coup, had his press destroyed, and he himself was severely beaten, in November 1831. Carlos María de Bustamante, in his chronicles, thought that this episode would provide the necessary excuse for Yucatán, always restive in the federation, to secede, which in fact occurred. This was topped by an intemperate reaction on the part of Ignacio Inclán against an attack in the press. Inclán was a rather unstable soldier who had had Yorkino sympathies (and would espouse them again in the future) but was now identified with the regime. In November 1831, as commander of Guadalajara, he detained the printer Juan Brambila, accused him of subversive publications, and was about to have him shot, when local clerics intervened. This was a scandalous event, generating a widespread reaction, and the government had to relieve Inclán of his duties.[10]

Meanwhile the economy was for the first time in years functioning in a more acceptable way. Mining had recovered with the infusion of British capital, state revenues were picking up, and though servicing the foreign debt was always a problem, things appeared to be under control. Textile mills were being constructed, mainly in Puebla, but also in nearby Orizaba, later to spread to Querétaro, Guadalajara, and the national capital. The early mills concentrated on yarn production, displacing the mostly home-working hand spinners, and were not yet in competition with the weavers.

By the end of 1831, after two years of conservative rule mixed with authoritarianism, and despite economic success, some opposition began making itself felt among sectors that had been at first either neutral or even supportive. Thus a "legal opposition" was formed, taking that name to differentiate itself from the more violent one that had arisen in several parts of the country and had been bloodily repressed. In this legal opposition converged some of the moderate liberals who were not happy with the conservative orientation of the bulk of the Escoceces, plus the federalists and the remnants of Pedrazismo.

The religious issue was an easy target for the opposition. Congress had accepted a papal bull entrusting the bishop of Puebla with the task of reforming the regulars in his province. This involved admitting Vatican intervention in internal Mexican affairs, without requiring previous recognition of the country's independence nor any agreement as to the exercise of patronato. Zacatecas, always a center of federalist resistance and now very well administered and rich because of its revived mines, requested that the central authorities deny the bishop the power to inspect the friars. Vicente Rocafuerte started *El Fénix de la Libertad* in December and followed with a campaign against the ministry, who had accused him of wrongdoings in connection with the British loans.[11]

The next year would start with a familiar event: on January 2, 1832, Santa Anna made a pronunciamiento against the ministry, asking for its collective resignation, and began to recruit militia among his trusted *jarochos*.[12] War Minister Facio, who was not very happy with the extreme clerical orientation of the government, immediately resigned, and his duties were provisionally covered by the top official of the secretariat. By the end of January, troops departed from the capital headed for Veracruz, and the remaining ministers also tendered their resignations, which were not accepted. The solidarity between Bustamante and his cabinet, however, remained impaired.

In March 1832 military fortunes appeared to be on the government's side. Its troops defeated Santa Anna and forced him to withdraw to Veracruz, which was besieged toward the end of the month. Meanwhile in Tampico, Santa Anna's allies had taken control of the port and had won the support of the governor of Tamaulipas, but they were confronted by Manuel Mier y Terán, commandant of the federal troops in that region.[13] So now there were two types of opposition: the legal one, strong in the city of Mexico and in some federalist provinces, and the armed one, led by Santa Anna. This armed opposition was, however, very different from the previous guerrilla-type resistance that had been stamped out with Guerrero's execution, and which only lingered in small pockets in the south.

The government, to prevent Yucatán joining the armed camp, had Congress sanction an amnesty for all those involved in its attempt at separation. Zacatecas now demanded changes in the cabinet and so did the legislature of the state of Mexico, prompted by its liberal Escocés governor, Melchor Múzquiz. By the end of April in Toluca, the new state's capital, a popular agitation in favor of Santa Anna was organized by Quintana Roo, Lucas Balderas (the Yorkino tailor from Mexico), and surprisingly, the volatile Inclán, of Brambila fame, who was performing a "voltereta." The governor repressed that movement, but without too much energy.[14]

Finally the expected cabinet crisis occurred: in May 1832 Alamán and Espinosa resigned, their posts being provisionally covered by the head officials of their staffs. Meanwhile the approach of the murderous hot weather forced the army besieging Santa Anna in Veracruz to withdraw to healthier Jalapa, and in June an armistice was arranged. Now pressures from Santa Anna himself and from the very active Zacatecas legislature (having now obtained the removal of the hated ministry) concentrated on one major objective: the return to "normalcy," as it existed before both the Acordada and the Jalapa coups. In other words, what was being demanded was the return of Gómez Pedraza, to fill in the few months still remaining of what should have been his legal term in office.

In the country at large, the situation was increasingly chaotic. San Luis Potosí was loyal and was preparing its militia to defend against a possible attack by Zacatecas. In Guadalajara, on the other hand, a military officer, José Cuesta, through an armed pronunciamiento, declared himself "Protector" of the state and in favor of Santa Anna. This added another complicating element to the pattern of opposition to the central powers, because what he was overthrowing was a rather independent-minded federalist local government, part of the legal opposition formed during the previous year.[15]

In August President Bustamante finally undertook a risky restructuring of his political base: probably inspired by Iturbide's strategy as he tried to save his tottering empire, he offered to share power with the legal opposition, which was accepted. Francisco Fagoaga (brother of the marqués del Apartado) was asked to head the cabinet in Relaciones; Ignacio Alas, a man who had held top administrative positions in the Treasury during the empire, took charge of Hacienda; and Justicia was entrusted to Juan Ignacio Godoy, the financier and industrialist from Guanajuato, who early in 1829 had proposed to sell on credit to artisans a large number of simple mechanical looms, if only he were licensed to import some textile grades "which even in the United States are allowed."[16] The Ministry of War continued under the provisional responsibility of its top official, José Cacho. Bustamante then left the capital for the Bajío at the head of a federal army, to confront the Zacatecans, and Melchor Múzquiz was elected by Congress as interim president.[17]

The loyalists seethed, believing this was a thinly disguised coup against the president, and wanted Congress to order the return of Bustamante to cancel the move. In fact the whole operation had been engineered by Molinos del Campo, and it gave pride of place to the more liberal Escoceses, among whom Molinos himself, Múzquiz, and Fagoaga could be counted as major luminaries.[18]

In a state of increasing national chaos, with armed uprisings spreading all over the country in favor of a change of government, Bustamante confronted the Zacatecan troops in the undecisive battle of Gallinero. Despite the uncertain result, Bustamante realized he could no longer maintain control of events, and he resigned the presidency, withdrawing to friendly San Luis Potosí to reorganize his forces.

In the capital the usual "end of regime" fears spread like wildfire among the propertied classes. The conde de la Cortina paid from his own pocket for the formation of a dependable militia, the nearest thing to a personal guard for the upper classes. The raising of a more formal one, along the lines of the old Batallones del Comercio, was also begun. In nearby San Agustín de las Cuevas, a large crowd of léperos declared for Santa Anna, but they were dispersed by troops led by Eulogio Villaurrutia. Again later that month, a similar mob formed in the capital and was bloodily repressed by the energetic governor of the Federal District, Miguel Cervantes, the former marqués de Salvatierra.[19]

Progovernment pamphleteers focused their attention on the fact that Santa Anna was accompanied by foreigners (many expelled from their countries because of being troublemakers) and by the léperos from the despised "plebe poblana" and from Veracruz. In an interesting series of four tracts, an appeal was made to property holders and to artisans, whose antiforeign instincts might have made them rally to the defense of the existing order. The memory of Iturbide (after whose death things were said to have gone from bad to worse) was invoked, as was the example of the "wise and brave" Napoleon, with whom Santa Anna vainly pretended to be compared, while respect was expressed for Guerrero, who had been misled by the Yorkinos. The author condemned freemasonry in general, but spared the Escoceses somewhat, probably reflecting recent convergences and the détente with well-known representatives of that faction. He was obviously worried about the prospects of popular insurrection in the capital, so he constantly addressed himself to the "plebe mexicana," an excessively abstract word betraying a writer with little experience in cultivating a really popular audience. Reference was made to the agitators active in some barrios, prepared to welcome the invading Santa Anna forces (the usual San Sebastián, San Pablo, Salto del Agua, Santa María, and Santa Ana), but their capacity to deliver results was belittled. The author was proposing the formation of a citizens' militia, with the careful selection of members, to keep order in the capital, freeing the regular army to face the enemy. When faced with the charge that in his proposal to arm public employees he was putting weapons in the hands of people well known to be favorable toward the rebellion, he answered that office chiefs would know to whom they could entrust the weapons.[20]

Carlos María de Bustamante, who also contributed with his prolific pen to the defense of the government, argued that the cabinet having been changed in order to appease the opposition, there was no longer any reason for revolt. Along this path, Mexico would soon descend to the depths of Central America or Colombia, where "every man is a soldier, every city a fortress, each house a trench." On the other hand, from Veracruz a revolutionary tract branded Anastasio Bustamante as a man who had been a tool of the viceroys or of Iturbide and who was now the representative of an "oligarchic military-ecclesiatic nucleus," intent on putting power in the hands of "a few privileged classes," by which terms the military and clergy were commonly known, due to their fueros; but there was also here a jab at the "oligarchy," or simply rich people.[21]

By bringing in the legal opposition, the government had accomplished one aim; namely, to avoid its combining with Santa Anna and some of the provincial pronunciamientos. But the forces unleashed by the Santa Anna initiative proved to be stronger. The Veracruzano general, after considering the armistice no longer valid, sent troops to Toluca, where they declared Zavala, already en route from exile, the rightful governor. Santa Anna then moved to Puebla, which he occupied by early October, declaring that he was going to avenge the wrongs done to Iturbide and Guerrero. The government sent commissioners to arrange a cease-fire, which was accepted. The decision was then made, on October 13, 1832, to recall Gómez Pedraza from New York.

Before the end of the year, Gómez Pedraza was occupying the presidential office, and a new cabinet was formed. Relaciones was put in charge of a rather second-rate figure, the old Iturbidista judge Bernardo González Angulo, probably revealing a lack of coordination as to what should be done in that area. More significant were the appointments of Miguel

Ramos Arizpe in Justicia and Valentín Gómez Farías in Hacienda, while War was given to the old insurgente Juan Pablo Anaya and then to Joaquín Parres, a general who had been governor of Jalisco and was earlier a partisan of Iturbide's accession to the crown. Pedraza had made a determined effort to obtain the cooperation of either Gómez Farías or Francisco García, the governor of Zacatecas, considering them interchangeable in terms of his coalition building.[22] Pedraza returned to the capital in the first days of January. Tornel had arrived already a year before, leaving his post in New York but taking up another commission from the Bustamante government, purportedly as a civil servant, which did not involve political support. Tornel, short of funds at the end of his stay in the United States, had to ask the widow of Iturbide for a loan of 1,000 pesos, which was not given without hopes of some return. In fact Gómez Pedraza while in exile had also cultivated that important friendship. One of the first private requests the new Congress received was from the erstwhile empress, asking for her pension to be increased, among other things.[23]

Elections for state and national legislators were held during February and March 1833. The law of July 12, 1830, approved by insistence of the Senate during the Jalapa regime, had required a preregistration of voters, so that by having to show a paper on polling day, they could not vote more than once. This in practice severely diminished the number of people capable of participating in elections. In some states the distribution of printed bills with lists of candidates was also prohibited. Now these regulations were not strictly applied, so that in some places, such as Puebla, so many "stupid and descamisado" people came up as primary or secondary electors that even their mentors were frightened, or so the opposition maintained; the Yorkinos with their allies won practically everywhere.[24]

By the end of March, the new Congress convened and checked the legislatures' votes, which made Santa Anna president and Gómez Farías vice-president. The national-popular coalition, or some variety of it, was again back in power. Apparently it had Santa Anna as its head, but during its first year, the vice-president was the chief executive most of the time, as the general had to take to the field to combat local rebellions or withdraw to Jalapa to restore his health. This time the coalition included the federalists and the remnants of Pedrazismo, that is, the progressive liberals. The wavering industrialists and agiotistas could not have been happy at the demise of the Bustamante administration, which had been very supportive of their needs, but some of them also participated in the new regime.

Santa Anna and Gómez Farías, or Who Uses Whom?

When the moment came, on April 1, 1833, for the new executive team to take over, Santa Anna found that he could not come to Mexico City. He would countless times in the future repeat the scene of refusing to take office or that of resigning soon afterward. As suggested earlier, conditions in Mexico City were extremely unstable and difficult most of the time, both from the point of view of finances and maintaining order. So Santa Anna preferred to hold to his power base in Veracruz, where the army was, and whence he could hope to throttle the country into obedience, in case a civil war erupted. As the oppositionist *El Mono* said, Santa Anna wished the disrepute to fall on someone else's shoulders, and he accepted being reduced in effect to the position of commandant of Veracruz, in order to thwart any attempt at revolt against him.[25]

Gómez Farías, in taking over the provisional presidency, had to abandon his Hacienda portfolio, which he passed on to the trusted José María Bocanegra, the federalist from Zacatecas. For the important post of Relaciones, Bernardo González Angulo was replaced by another man with an Iturbidista past, Carlos García. García had early supported the Plan de Iguala and had been designated governor and intendant when Iturbide entered Puebla; he was later to become alcalde of that town. Ramos Arizpe continued in Justicia, and in War Parres was replaced by the more trustworthy General Herrera.

A letter from Minister García, still in Puebla in May 1833, to Gómez Farías throws light on the attitude some cabinet members had toward Santa Anna. García informed the vice-president that finally Santa Anna was making preparations to go to Mexico City, alone, and jokingly told him to take good care to prepare him a bed, "in addition to the one we are thinking of." The problem, however, was to see who would make whose bed.[26]

The new government, under Gómez Farías's leadership, started a program of reform, attacking the church first, which happened to provide also a welcome source of funds. The new popular coalition, by comparison to the one headed by Guerrero, was more ideologically oriented and somewhat less populist. One of its more sensational measures was to close down the university (controlled by the clerics), establishing in its place a new institute of higher learning, dependent on the ministry, and divided into sections. Typically José María Luis Mora was named director of the section of Ciencias Ideológicas y Humanidades and was the spirit behind the whole plan.[27]

This was a major attack against the corporatist educational and religious structure of the ancien régime, and as such it revealed a basic contrast with the Iturbidista type of national-popular coalition (to which Guerrero's was closer). But convergences existed, as usual, forming highly heterogeneous intersections of interests and factions, with whom it was very difficult to govern. The radical sector of the coalition was represented, among others, by Crescencio Rejón's *Columna de la Constitución Federal de la República Mexicana*. Rejón had been associated earlier with the more moderate *Fénix*, written by Rocafuerte, Pedraza, and Rodríguez Puebla, who also supported the reforms while trying to add an element of moderation and condemning some of its methods. Rejón started *La Columna* by mid-1832, still under the Jalapa regime, and now engaged in permanent polemics with the *Fénix*, attacking it from a more radically federal and populist position. These attacks intensified to the point that the *Fénix* decided to stop answering the invectives of this new version of the ill-famed Cardillo.[28]

In a special supplement, in November 1833 (just before the last frantic period of radical reform under Gómez Farías was begun), a petition for the official burial of Guerrero, described as "Iturbide's colleague," and Iturbide himself, that "immortal caudillo," was signed by a group of "lovers of freedom." They explained that there had always been two parties in the country, one made up of aristocrats and fanatics, and the other, the "only national one," supported by the "immense majority." Among the score of individual signatures, one could find those of Manuel Reyes Veramendi, Ignacio Basadre, José Antonio Mejía, Ignacio Inclán, and Antonio J. Valdés, a good sample of agitational politicians who combined radicalism with Iturbidismo.[29]

However, in this version of national populism, the lower-middle-class Jacobin element was more evident, and the lépero-mobilizing friars were almost absent. The budding industrialists could not see the predominance of Veracruzano interests without alarm, but as noted earlier, many tierra-caliente producers had second thoughts about free trade.

One important individual combining Veracruzano with agiotista and entrepreneurial interests was Antonio Garay, a partner with Zurutuza and Escandón in the coach-transport business. He became very influential in the new government and by June 1834 had obtained the contract to repair the Veracruz road, charging a toll. In colonial times the consulados took charge of the road and its revenues and paid interest to a traditional group of creditors, which included the Fagoagas. Now the concession no longer provided for the preferential payment of those creditors, who thus joined the hapless mass of state creditors.[30] The Fagoagas, main rivals of Garay in this operation, had fallen into disgrace, due to Francisco's participation in the previous government. They, together with several dozen others, were expelled from the country, by the application of a vaguely worded law that came to be called the "ley del caso."[31]

When Santa Anna finally arrived in the capital, six weeks after Gómez Farías's inauguration, he assumed office, though only for a few days, because he had to leave at the head of his troops to suppress a rebellion of the Michoacán local garrison, seconded by others in the outskirts of the capital. The rebels opposed the radical measures being taken by the administration and supported Santa Anna, urging him to assume the reins of office. The general, shortly after leaving the capital, suspiciously fell prisoner to the rebels, who had been joined by Santa Anna's assistant, General Arista. Apparently this piece of theatrics was planned by the general, with the aim of putting the blame for the coup on someone else's shoulders and still allowing him to benefit from it. But back in Mexico, Gómez Farías reacted promptly, taking advantage of the small number of regular troops remaining there. He assembled the militia and soon was in command of six thousand armed men, "the very dregs of the people, without discipline or subordination, and ready to take advantage of any opportunity to plunder and commit excesses."[32] This was enough to dissuade Santa Anna, who realized that the odds were not so clearly on his side. So he managed to escape from his "prison," returned to the capital, and started out again shortly afterward. This time he was successful militarily, after almost four months of campaigning, and imprisoned his opponent-supporters. He then came back, apparently to assume his official position, on October 27, 1833 (he would last almost a month and a half this time).

During all these early months of the joint Santa Anna–Gómez Farías regime, the radical forces had been very active, both at the federal level and in some of the states, notably Zavala-led Mexico. Gómez Farías, as a result of the military rebellions, had been granted extraordinary powers by Congress. The states of Jalisco, Guanajuato, Michoacán, Zacatecas, San Luis Potosí, and Durango, following an already familiar pattern, organized a federal league to defend federalism against any threats. A similar one was set up by Puebla, Oaxaca, and Veracruz. These regionalist movements were apparently supported or even instigated by Gómez Farías.[33] In the state of Mexico, the lands of the Philippine Missionaries were confiscated and distributed to small cultivators in family-size parcels, and later the same was done with the lands of the absentee duque de

Monteleone (whose administrator was Lucas Alamán) and also with his real estate in the city of Mexico, while Indian pueblos were authorized to occupy nearby fiscal lands.[34] Citizens' militias, whose role had been downplayed during Bustamante's rule, were reorganized so as to be under radical-liberal control. This was aided by the introduction, in barracks and jails, of progressive experiments in teaching and manual-work experience for inmates and soldiers.[35]

The already-mentioned restructuring of the University was accomplished, the legal obligation to pay tithes and to enforce monastic vows was annulled, and plans were set for the expropriation of all church lands, only a small part of the proceeds to be used to sustain the clergy. The progovernment *Monitor del Pueblo*, to obviate the danger of civil war, urged the establishment of a "political system such that by levelling the conditions and fortunes of all its members . . . [it would put an end to] two belligerent nations [the so-called "hombres de bien" and the sans-culottes] which sooner or later are going to destroy each other."[36]

When Santa Anna resumed office (on October 27, 1833), he tried to stem this tide, with little success. The radical majority in Congress threatened to go ahead with anticlerical legislation and to dissolve the military units which had been disloyal, which meant in effect reducing the strength of the president's partisans. Finding himself in difficult circumstances, Santa Anna informed the public that he was ill and retired to Veracruz. This was quite obviously a strategy to put responsibility on the radicals' shoulders, or to force the more moderate among the reformers to act as a brake against the rest. When he left (on December 15, 1833), the final four and a half months of radical reform were inaugurated.

At this juncture Garay stepped in. Together with Zurutuza he offered to finance the government, by tendering 300,000 pesos in cash plus 3 million pesos of public debt to be recognized at par value and repaid with drafts on the customs houses during the coming years. This was a significant offer, justifying in the eyes of its proponents the astronomical rate of interest involved, because parting with those 300,000 pesos with the hope of recovering a larger sum someday at the aduanas (most probably to be paid in public-debt papers) required a lot of confidence in God's protection.

Bocanegra resigned, probably in opposition to this proposal, and the ministry was temporarily under the care of its oficial mayor, Juan José del Corral, also a strong foe of Garay and the agiotistas around him.[37] The government, pressed for funds, gave in and finally appointed to the vacant Hacienda post none other than Antonio Garay himself, who came in on January 2, 1834, with a full package of regulations suited to the lenders' interests. This was the price Gómez Farías had to pay for the money his government needed badly in order to survive.[38] Others at the time were proposing such pragmatic ideas as selling Texas for 10 to 12 million pesos and using that money to develop California.[39]

Regarding the confiscation of church property, there were two factions among the liberal reformers. Zavala, always the more practical but also playing into the hands of speculators, proposed to sell everything at public auction, with the inevitable drop in prices. Gómez Farías preferred a much more moderate solution, granting ownership to the present occupiers in exchange for a fee practically equal to the rents they were already paying. This would have avoided any danger of evictions by new owners, but would have left the state only with a not easily collectable yearly income and no lump sum of cash, in contrast to Zavala's solution. Zavala's links with the agiotistas were very prominent and gave rise to countless accusations against him, dating from his period at the Treasury during Guerrero's presidency. The connection in fact was so close between some agiotistas and the liberals, that it has prompted a recent scholar to argue (somewhat exaggeratedly) that the "Liberal party [was] a coalition of native creditors, import merchants of mixed nationalities, and disgruntled regional concerns."[40]

At this moment, when the tempo of reform was increasing, divisions set in among the liberals in charge of the government. Ramos Arizpe, too much inclined to contemporizing, resigned in August 1833 and was replaced by the hard-liner Quintana Roo. As we have seen before, Bocanegra was removed from Hacienda in December, and at about the same time, Carlos García was replaced by Francisco Lombardo, a man of strong anticlerical tendencies, despite his moderate origins.[41] The commission in charge of public instruction became almost a junta for promoting revolutionary measures. Its members were José María Luis Mora, who had exchanged his earlier moderation for a determined anticlerical ardor, expressed in the columns of his new publication, El Indicador de la Federación Mexicana; Andrés Quintana Roo and José Espinosa de los Monteros, who had been strong supporters of Iturbide's empire and had also evolved along more progressive lines; Juan Rodríguez Puebla, of Indian descent and oriented toward the emancipation of the aboriginal race; and Manuel Eduardo Gorostiza and José Bernardo Couto, also clear-cut liberal reformers.

At a more popular level, experienced mass agitators met at Ignacio Basadre's house in Mexico. Basadre had been personal secretary to Esteva and Guerrero and was a dominant force at the War Ministry during the latter's accession to power. Now he joined José Antonio Mejía, a Cuban military officer close to Zavala, with whom he would later share the ill-starred Texan adventure. According to Mora they promoted the persecution of members of the fallen regime and committed all sorts of excesses, being able to influence to a high degree Gómez Farías himself.[42] Santangelo, who had returned to Mexico after the downfall of Bustamante's administration, was also part of this group, and he was later accused of being the instigator of the new police "espionage system," an allegation he of course denied.[43] Governor García of Zacatecas, on the other hand, was growing increasingly restless at Gómez Farías's incapacity or unwillingless to control the hotheads among his ranks.

Bishop Vázquez of Puebla was considered to be in rebellion, because of his resistance to accept governmental involvement in matters of patronato without papal agreement. While Gómez Farías's version of the bill for church-property confiscation was debated in Congress, bishops who opposed the validity of the forced sale of church property were threatened with expulsion and in fact were preparing to leave the country. To avoid resistance from the Supreme Court, Congress impeached its members for having cooperated with the illegal Jalapa regime, replacing them with their alternates.[44]

In the country at large, resistance was widespread and from various sources. In the south General Bravo attracted guerrillas of a conservative nature, and in Chicontla, near Cuernavaca, Father Epigmenio de la Piedra, an old Iturbidista who had sided with Zavala in 1826 (against the moderate liberals' secularizing measures), now declared himself in favor of an Indian monarchy, in practice being used by Santa Anna.[45] Epigmenio de la Piedra's trajectory, combining clericalism with Yorkino involvements, was typical of a certain sector of Mexico's political class. In 1827 he was still included (together with several Iturbidistas such as José Ramón Malo) in a list of some two hundred Yorkinos and their allies, surely in recognition of his active pro-Zavala role in the Mexico state elections of 1826. Now, even if acting in favor of Santa Anna, his movement was described by Relaciones minister Lombardo as aiming at a "war between Mexicans of different colors."[46]

After four and a half months of this, Santa Anna finally decided the time was ripe for his return, so he rose from his sickbed and took over his full powers, at the end of April 1834. His return was accompanied by popular demonstrations engineered by the chiefs of the barrios and the clergy, according to Zerecero, who knew about this type of agitation but happened to be on the other side now. In fact there were two types of populist mobilization, of which the dominant was the Yorkino, or radical-liberal, while the other one, employed by Santa Anna after his break with Gómez Farías, was a diminishing asset, based on old-regime practices. These included

> carriages surrounded by some léperos with canes and banners, while the most prostituted friars, dressed in their habits, went about mixed with the populace, leading the scenario . . . A certain Juan Acosta, who had a winery in the Puente de Monzón and a pawnshop in the calle de Corchero; a Don Juan Chavarría, also a wine vendor, and others who had access to barrels of liquor, were the chiefs. The revolution did not enjoy popularity, but *popula-chería.*[47]

This time the break with Gómez Farías was final, and the vice-president soon left the capital heading north, presumably for exile, but en route passing through Zacatecas, where resistance to the new regime was likely to develop and give him a foothold for returning to power with greater strength. Santa Anna retained Lombardo and Quintana Roo in Relaciones and Justicia, and put Juan José del Corral, the *oficial mayor* of Hacienda who had resisted the Garay loan, provisionally in charge of that ministry. Not that Santa Anna was averse to such transactions, but he did oppose this one and wanted to gain some political capital at the expense of the ill-famed Garay, a fly in the liberals' ointment.

Soon Santa Anna also brought his friend Tornel into the cabinet, to head the War Ministry. He dismissed the special commission in charge of public instruction, reestablished the clerical-dominated university, suspended the "ley del caso," and disbanded several cívico units, giving positions once more to Bustamantista officers. Congress, whose ordinary sessions were coming to an end, was closed down after a procedural discussion as to when exactly it was to stop meeting; some oppositionists considered (somewhat exaggeratedly) that Santa Anna had dissolved Congress. What he actually decided was not to reconvene it and to anticipate elections for a new legislature, which would meet on the first day of the next year. This would give him over half a year of executive rule without congressional interference. In addition the members of the Supreme Court who had ben purged by the liberals a few months earlier were recalled.[48] The confiscation of church property was annulled, and in exchange for this the church offered a generous loan.

Quintana Roo, despite his capacity for understanding the need for a strong executive, did not last long under the new regime and joined the opposition, for which he published *La Oposición*, to replace Rocafuerte's *Fénix de la Libertad*, and Mora's *Indicador de la Federación*, both of which suspended publication, their editors heading for exile.

A few weeks after Santa Anna's resumption of governmental powers, military and civilian petitions in many parts of the country demanded the total repeal of the legislation enacted by the reformist Congress and the banning of its deputies from reelection. This movement peaked in the Plan de Cuernavaca, of May 25, 1834, which for years was considered the basis for constructing a new regime under a centralist constitution.

Despite the expected resistance from the federalist league centered on the Bajío and Zacatecas, Santa Anna consolidated his position, overcame a Pueblan attempt at reaction, and ordered new congressional elections. Among moderate or middle-of-the-road liberals, Santa Anna had some supporters, convinced that a stop had to be put to reform in order to avoid civil war. Among them were Gómez Pedraza, Guadalupe Victoria, and even Francisco García, who was embarrassed by his friend Gómez Farías's excessive reformist zeal.[49] The Escoceses were also on Santa Anna's side, notably Gutiérrez Estrada, who took over in Relaciones. Clerical influence was thus to some extent controlled, and some reforms, such as the abolition of the legal enforcement of tithes, were retained.

The new Congress, meeting in January 1835, had a centralist and clerical majority. Santa Anna, after having governed for fully nine months, decided that the time to retire had come. Congress passed a special disposition depriving Gómez Farías of his post, and elected Miguel Barragán provisional president.[50] Next it legislated a drastic reduction in the number of men each state could keep in its militia. This was aimed particularly at Zacatecas, whose governor decided to resist the measure. Santa Anna then took command of his troops once again and headed north, to impose control on Zacatecas, Coahuila, and Texas. In Zacatecas he was successful, after a bloody battle that signaled the end of federalism. In Zacatecas several foreigners participated in the resistance, and three of them died in battle, a fact magnified by rumors and government propaganda so as to stimulate popular sentiment. The British consul general, Charles O'Gorman, was particularly supportive of the Zacatecans, and his expulsion from the country was demanded by Santa Anna. When the general returned to Mexico City to celebrate his triumph, the crowd interspersed its rejoicing with cries of "mueran los ingleses."[51]

In Congress, according to the British representative, there were now three "parties": one still trying to save the federal constitution, another advocating a republican centralism, and a third one proposing a radical change in the direction of absolutism and unrestricted executive predominance. The liberal opposition was muted or reduced to cryptic and ironic expressions.[52]

One of Santa Anna's first measures upon conquering Zacatecas was to transfer ownership of the large state-run mining concern at Fresnillo to the central government, leasing the operation to a private company made up of Mexican agiotistas and other midlevel investors.[53] But despite his military success, he was incapable of imposing his will on Congress, which was preparing the bases of a constitution with conservative guarantees against personalist power (the so-called "Siete Leyes"). These included a "Poder Conservador," patterned after Benjamin Constant's idea of a monarchical moderating force. This five-man body was empowered to intervene occasionally in the constitutional process, when it became mired down or unforeseen complications arose, and to decide just what "the will of the nation" was. The French minister, acting as an *esprit fort* toward his superiors in Paris, claimed that such an institution, "elected by the aristocracy . . . had not been seen since the days of the Council of the Ten of the Venetian Republic." But he remarked that the conservative majority was stronger than Santa Anna, particularly due to the latter's need to head his troops to continue his interrupted Zacatecan campaign farther north.[54]

Law and Order under Bustamante (1837–41)

Santa Anna's disgrace in Texas is well known; as a result he had to retire to his hacienda, this time for good. After the enactment of the new constitution, Bustamante was elected president, for a period that should have lasted eight years and that in fact did last for almost five, beginning in early 1837. His second presidency was a conservative, law-and-order regime, with considerable upper-class support. Economic policy was oriented toward industrialization, with protective tariffs and the stiff repression of regional resistances.

During this period a conflict arose with France, stimulated by discussions as to indemnities to be paid by the Mexican government to French citizens who claimed damages due to local actions, the Guerra de los Pasteles. This was only an excuse, resulting from a bellicose stance on the part of the French, some of whose diplomatic corps favored armed intervention and the establishment of a protected friendly government, monarchical if possible. The episode began in February 1838, when a French fleet appeared off Veracruz to demand the payment of indemnities due individual citizens; hostilities broke out in November, with the bombardment of the port. Santa Anna rose to the occasion and had the good fortune of losing his leg in the defense, thus recovering his political capital. In March peace was achieved, with British mediation.

During the crisis the liberal federalists took the opportunity to step up regional revolts, so much so that they were dubbed "Frenchmen" by their opponents.[55] Some of them adopted this policy more openly or more decidedly than others. José Urrea, at the same time that the French were menacing Veracruz, was leading an insurgent "army of liberation" in Tampico, which included the noted radical federalist José Antonio Mejía. Bustamante, in order to dispel the threat to his regime from this "armed opposition," attempted a cooptation of the moderate liberals, those led by Gómez Pedraza and called "the philosophers."[56] In other words he attempted another power sharing, as he had done in 1832. After August 1838 Pedraza had been proposing the convocation of an assembly, elected with a restricted franchise and banning the participation of those associated with the several illegitimate regimes in existence since the Acordada.[57] The radical federalists opposed this, ridiculing Pedraza's attempt to return to the federation "with only himself" aboard.[58] Bustamante could exploit these differences between the two branches of "legal" liberalism and between them and the "armed opposition" of Urrea and other rebel generals in the provinces. He offered Relaciones to Pedraza and Interior (the former Justicia) to Rodríguez Puebla in early December 1838, when hostilities against the French were at a maximum. The pair accepted, with the condition that their "plan" be adopted. As this was impossible, the whole affair ended up in the short-lived "Ministerio de los tres días." All things considered, this turned out to be just a diversionary strategy by the hard-pressed Bustamante.[59] In such cases the coopting strategy had to overcome not only the natural diffidence on the part of the potentially coopted, but also the resistance of the regime's hard-liners to losing their positions of dominance.

Revolutionary tensions again broke out in the capital in July 1840. Both Gómez Farías and Alpuche e Infante were back from exile, and both had been imprisoned as a result of attacks on the government and presumed plotting. At a certain point, the combination of insurgencies in the provinces plus ill feelings in the capital caused an armed rising with cívico and popular support, which could easily have ended like the Acordada. At the beginning the rebels were successful and were able to imprison

Bustamante and liberate both Alpuche e Infante and Farías, the latter taking over the leadership of the movement. There was also an attempt to obtain support from the moderate sectors, represented by Pedraza, but this was unsuccessful. After a few days of gunfire and shelling, with several hundred dead, the government recovered control, and the rebels were sent into exile.[60]

During another crisis, in September 1841, Bustamante found himself at the end of his tether, facing a regionalist revolt combining the insurgencies of General Mariano Paredes y Arrillaga (a conservative in charge of military forces in Guadalajara) and Santa Anna (as usual based in Veracruz and with some liberal support). To top it all off, General Gabriel Valencia, in charge of the armed forces in Mexico City, joined the pronunciamiento. Before surrendering Bustamante tried a desperate gambit: to rally in his favor the most feared forces of popular agitation and extreme federalism. The strategy was well known. Already in 1837 an anonymous correspondent had told Gómez Farías that forces of revolt were seething in Mexico, threatening the social order, and that the only hope for Bustamante to control them was to put himself at their head.[61] This time Bustamante actually tried to follow that advice, deciding to proclaim the federation officially, thus attempting to remove any legitimate motive for armed action.

A nephew of Bustamante, recently returned from France, where he had been in touch with modern ideas, published a serial, *El Vigía*, during the last few days of the regime, attempting to rouse public enthusiasm. In it the chances for the reestablishment of the federation under Bustamante were extolled.[62] On September 30 and October 1, 1841, respectable citizens gathered in the main plaza, under governmental prodding, and signed a petition, that included the signatures of the governor and the prefect in charge of the city of Mexico, along with such other well-known Yorkinos as Anastasio Zerecero and Manuel Reyes Veramendi, demanding the reestablishment of the federal constitution. In the barrios similar declarations in favor both of Bustamante and of a return to federalism were initiated by some old hands at popular organization from above, the Barreras, of Iturbidista fame.[63] Lucas Balderas was said to have participated in the federalist proclamation, but a denial purportedly signed by him appeared in the pages of a *Boletín de la Ciudadela*, published by Valencia's rebel forces. Tracts alerting the "real" federalists against the government's gambit appeared, denouncing the presence of people such as the Barreras and others, whose federal convictions were highly suspect.[64] Finally the attempt failed, after a minor military confrontation, in which Bustamante's forces were overcome. Santa Anna's Bases de

Tacubaya, annulling all centralist authorities and convoking a new Congress, were accepted.[65]

Political Turbulence under Santa Anna

The rebel forces occupied the capital and hand-picked a self-styled junta of representatives of the departments, which designated Santa Anna president. Santa Anna was supported in the War Ministry by his trusted Tornel, who from this time on would become an unavoidable component in any Santanista coalition. But in Relaciones, after a short appearance by Gómez Pedraza, Bocanegra was put in charge, thus giving a voice to the progressive-liberal element. Justicia was also given to a liberal, from Jalisco, Crispiniano del Castillo. In Hacienda Ignacio Trigueros brought connections with the financial community and a good technical knowledge of affairs, which was later praised by Guillermo Prieto, even if the latter lamented that it was used during Santa Anna's regime.[66]

This was a de facto government, attempting to legitimize itself through the flimsy formality of a junta of representatives of departments (the earlier states), who had been all appointed by Santa Anna himself. But soon relatively free elections were held, which Santa Anna was unable to control, and a moderate-liberal majority was formed, with the high likelihood of adopting a federal constitution. To avoid this eventuality, Santa Anna performed his usual disappearing act, in October 1842, leaving responsibility on the shoulders of Nicolás Bravo, who toward the end of the year dissolved Congress and appointed a Junta Nacional Legislativa, made up of notables, two per department, along the lines of the Junta Instituyente that Iturbide had established in 1822. This Junta adopted a document called *Bases de Organización Política de la República Mexicana* (better known as *Bases Orgánicas*) in lieu of a constitution, maintaining the centralist system. Elections were held to form a new Congress, where again Santa Anna could not rely on a safe majority. The French representative commented on this, expressing his belief that Santa Anna's lucky star might be abandoning him. Opposition from the upper classes was becoming very clear, according to the same observer, who remarked on the disrespectful behavior of the people at the theater in his presence. He also thought that if Santa Anna were persistently scorned by electors and elites, he might need to have recourse to another coup.[67] Popular pressures had succeeded in forcing the government to prohibit the exercise of retail commercial activity by foreigners, though the process was slow and controversial. In any case it prompted serious efforts by the French representative to organize a "dossier" to justify armed intervention and the imposition of a foreign-supported monarchy.[68]

In early 1844, in line with the procedures detailed in the *Bases*, the newly elected Congress began its sessions and counted the departmental assemblies' votes for president; the post fell to Santa Anna. The general then came back to Mexico City, to take up his constitutional role. But opposition was increasing, and it included a pronunciamiento by General Mariano Paredes y Arrillaga in Guadalajara. Santa Anna left the capital once more, delegating authority to Canalizo, and prepared for another armed confrontation.

Meanwhile the ministry had been remarkably stable, though heterogeneous, during these years of Santa Anna's supremacy (1841–44), which have been called his "dictatorship" because of the repeated acts of nonrecognition of legislative bodies, but which in practice never witnessed the thorough predominance of his supporters. In the final period, before leaving affairs in the hands of Canalizo, Santa Anna coopted the radical Manuel Crescencio Rejón in Relaciones, to replace Bocanegra; toward the very end of Canalizo's provisional functions, the War Ministry was taken over by Ignacio Basadre, the radical populist who had been, together with José Antonio Mejía, one of the main anticonservative agitators of the 1833–34 period.

Rejón was conscious that his involvement with Santa Anna at the very end of the regime needed some explanation. Gómez Farías had reprimanded him for his gullibility in believing that it was possible to work with Santa Anna, recalling the latter's betrayal of the progressive cause in 1834. Rejón (after his downfall) responded that in the long run, his grand strategy of using Santa Anna would be understood.[69]

Santa Anna's 1841–44 regime, at first provisional, afterward fictitiously constitutional, was rather repressive and faced increasing opposition, mostly of a moderate-liberal nature, despite or rather because of the radical liberals' inclusion in the cabinet. Civic revolt finally erupted on December 6, 1844, prompted by an arbitrary act of the executive canceling any further meetings of Congress, which was accused of being soft toward Texas and national rearmament. There was the usual combination of a mortal threat at long distance, from Guadalajara, by Paredes y Arrillaga, with gatherings in the main plaza of the capital. This time, though, the mass included more young intellectuals and enlightened members of the bourgeoisie, inspired by the ideology of freedom versus dictatorship, rather than the usual national-popular combination. Popular wrath discharged itself by toppling Santa Anna's statue and unearthing his leg, which had been buried in advance of the rest of his body, in commemoration of his exploits against the French.

There is a marked contrast between the Acordada revolt of 1828 and this one. This time the crowd was less rowdy, less set against the rich and powerful, and more opposed to authoritarian rule. It embodied more an educated middle class rather than a populist mob. Consequently official liberal historiography has only good words for this episode, and none for the Acordada. Carlos María de Bustamante, a participant in the affairs, despite his dislike for large gatherings, this time observed many "young men who had organized themselves" and many "lindas mexicanas" waving their handkerchiefs from the balconies. A large number of supportive participants showered him with "undeserved praise" and practically carried him into the sessions of the reconvened Congress. He was so excited that he forgot the contents of a speech he made there, so that later he could only recall the Latin verses with which he ended it. He thought that "the immense crowd surrounding us gave a new proof of its talent and docility." There were of course a few léperos, those who had toppled the Santa Anna statues and unearthed the dictator's leg, but they had not harmed anyone else. Rejón and Basadre were imprisoned, but they soon freed themselves.[70] As for Santa Anna, his armed forces deserted him, and he had to escape toward Veracruz; this time, however, he was caught and imprisoned in Perote castle, awaiting trial on the very serious charge of subverting the constitution, which was punishable with a death sentence.

Admittedly the Santa Anna–Bocanegra–Rejón episode is more complex than the Santa Anna–Gómez Farías or the Guerrero–Bustamante ones. The centralist dominance of the second Bustamante presidency, with its protectionist policy and respect for church and social hierarchies, was replaced by a combination of peripheral interests and popular agitators. However, some variables continued unchanged; for example protection could not be dismantled, and Lucas Alamán had an important say in economic policy during those Santa Anna years, through his position as Director of Industry.

The "glorious revolution of December 6" inaugurated a moderate-liberal regime presided over by José Joaquín de Herrera, which lasted for practically one whole year (1845), with support from the center of the political spectrum and some agiotistas, such as Pedro Echeverría. One of its first measures was to raise a special militia, different from the traditional *cívicos,* because "a sad experience has shown us what these kinds of troops were capable of." The new corps was called the Voluntarios

Defensores de las Leyes, which came to be called the Cossacks; it was made up mostly "of strong and honest peasants, who know how to use the pike and the machete."[71]

However, the Right feared that not enough control was being exerted over the popular forces. The correspondence of General Mariano Paredes y Arrillaga, now stationed in San Luis Potosí, with his colleagues, especially Arista, who was in Monterrey, throws some light on how the popular threat was perceived by top military officers. Both were supposed to be preparing for a war to reconquer Texas, or alternatively for a defense against an American invasion. In fact they were more concerned with what was going on in Mexico City and a few other places in the country, which supposedly were threatened by "sansculotismo" and the agitation of "descamisados" intent on "undermining the government and the army."[72] From Guanajuato Teófilo Romero reported that there had been a popular mutiny, instigated by the old hand Lucas Balderas, who now was decrying the "fraud" of December 6 and plotting with Gómez Pedraza to convince the local garrison to proclaim a return to federalism.[73] Toward October elections were held, with victories for the liberal federalists, for the moment apparently under the joint leadership of Pedraza and Gómez Farías. The "leperócratas" threatened to gain the upper hand in that unstable liberal coalition, but finally the more moderate ones prevailed, though still determined to fight for the readoption of federalism, which implied opening the doors to more agitational politics and uncontrolled civic militias.[74]

By this time a friar, Manuel de San Juan Crisóstomo, had become an intellectual advisor to General Paredes. He informed him that the "plebs, both the naked one and the ill-clad which wears costly coats and cassocks . . . [control] the House," while the "Mexican nation" (that is, conservative or moderate forces) had apparently triumphed in the Senate. The cleric thought that it might not be a bad thing for the democratic party to dominate one chamber and the aristocrats the other, if executive power were in monarchical hands. He recommended that the general read Simonde de Sismondi to clarify these concepts. This should probably be understood as prompting a semilegal coup, replacing the executive body but leaving the legislative branch as it was.[75]

Political convolution reached an unprecedented peak when a letter arrived from Vicente Gómez Farías himself, marked "muy reservada," seeking a meeting with Paredes to discuss the means for allowing the real will of the country to express itself.[76] At the same time, José María Tornel, who had been ill and in retirement since the revolution of December 1844, told Paredes he was the only hope of the country to stop such excesses as the formation of the new civic militias, one of which was headed by a famous thief from the barrio de la Palma. Anonymous letters poured in, some of them supporting the rumor that Congress was preparing to sell Texas for 12 million pesos.[77] By the end of 1845, the centrist Herrera administration was defenseless against the plotting from the Right and the continued attempted popular outbursts from the Left, or populist, side.[78] When in December Paredes proclaimed his plan for a "government of the propertied classes," and the Mexico City garrison joined him, no resistance was possible.

Paredes's government was short-lived, despite the fact that during it the war with the United States began. This event, rather than unifying the nation, further divided it, adding to the government's weakness and thus facilitating its overthrow. The national-popular coalition took shape again, carefully stitched together by correspondence between Havana and New Orleans.

Ignacio Basadre, in exile in Cuba together with Rejón and Santa Anna, created the theory that it was necessary to flatter Santa Anna and convince him that it was the clericals, the moderates, and the appeasers who had betrayed him and the nation in causing his downfall in December 1844. Rejón, in March 1846, resentfully informed his Yucatecan friend Crescencio Boves that Santa Anna would already have sanctioned a federal constitution, if he had not been deposed by the likes of Boves in the ill-conceived December affray; now Rejón was working closely with Basadre and Santa Anna to prepare the Veracruzano's return. In a similar vein, Rejón commented to Gómez Farías that Santa Anna had been overthrown by a "comparsa de serviles," supported by Paredes from Guadalajara, implying that the liberals involved in the December revolution were dupes of the Right. Both Rejón and Gómez Farías included among their enemies the moderate liberals such as Herrera and Gómez Pedraza, especially after the latter's lack of support for the July 1840 federalist revolt against Bustamante.[79]

By early 1846 Santa Anna himself was writing to Gómez Farías proposing joint action and claiming that he had been deposed by monarchist and proappeasement forces. He also informed him that his agent in Veracruz was Joseph Welsh, a strong merchant who had been British consul. He later sent Fermín (Gómez Farías's son) a letter to Cayetano Rubio, asking the agiotista to provide Don Valentín with the necessary funds so that he would not be in need.[80] Finally in August 1846, a military pronunciamiento in the ciudadela of Mexico City proclaimed a return to the federal constitution and recalled Santa Anna.

History repeated itself in an uncanny fashion. Since Santa Anna, in exile in Cuba, took some time before arriving, General Mariano Salas first assumed the provisional presidency and convoked a new Congress, which declared Santa Anna and Gómez Farías elected to the two top executive posts. During Salas's provisional government, which lasted three months, Gómez Farías occupied the Hacienda Ministry for a short while, flanked by Rejón in Relaciones. Gómez Farías was a major force in the Salas cabinet, due to the strength of his connections with the radical element in the capital, which included a militia recruited so as to incorporate the radical-populist activists. A new element of political mobilization sprang up at the university, where continuous "meetings," inspired by American practice, caused great alarm, if Carlos María de Bustamante's reaction is any indication. He saw in them a copy of Protestant sectarian practices and a harbinger of religious tolerance. Between August and October 1846, there were popular movements aimed at putting Gómez Farías in the presidency, but these were thwarted by Salas, who used an alternative militia recruited among the relatively better-off sectors of the population and organized by the conde de la Cortina, governor of the city.[81]

Resistance against the radicals' influence soon emerged, and Salas dispensed with the services of the Gómez Farías and Rejón, but Gómez Farías soon reemerged, because Santa Anna needed him to take the responsibility for extracting money from the church. So from the end of December 1846, when the new executive was to be empowered, Gómez Farías replaced the hard-to-find general. The period before the arrival of Santa Anna lasted for over six months, and during it the forces of radical change and antichurch legislation were again unleashed, with the purpose of milking the ailing but still wealthy giant corporation.

Resistance against Gómez Farías expressed itself again in a protracted demonstration and rioting (from February 26 to March 23, 1847), known as the revolt of the Polkos, by a combination of civilian and military units, into which the better-off sectors of the population had been recruited as part of the preparations against an eventual American invasion. The rebellion was financed by the church and also had moderado support, ranging from that of old hands such as Pedraza to that of new militants such as Mariano Otero and Guillermo Prieto.[82] Santa Anna, who was busy preparing the army to resist an invasion, thus had an excuse for returning quickly to the capital to take over his position for a few days, so as to stop Gómez Farías. Then after convincing Congress to eliminate the vice-presidency, he delegated his functions to a trusted nonentity, Pedro María Anaya. The church was grateful and repaid the favor with further loans at modest rates of interest. The whole contorted operation of the Santa Anna–Gómez Farías alliance and breakup was necessary only because of the peculiar relation of the forces in Mexican society, because otherwise it would have been much easier just to establish a Santa Anna regime from the beginning.

After the war a moderate-liberal government under President José Joaquín de Herrera (1848–51) was inaugurated. This time American reparation payments allowed it to function for a complete term, to be succeeded by a similar one headed by Mariano Arista. By then funds were again running short, and conditions for another bout of extreme confrontation were coming to a head. Santa Anna returned again (1853–55), this time leading a clearly conservative and protomonarchical regime, but only at the cost of generating yet another national-popular outburst, in 1854.

Conclusions

The aim of this chapter has been to suggest that the pattern of coalition formation and dissolution, studied in greater detail for the 1820–30 period, repeated itself afterward in broad outline. One of the strategic factors in creating this kind of cycle was the presence in Mexico of a large popular mass (including downwardly mobile and insecure sectors of the middle classes) that threatened the stability of the existing sociopolitical order. The terrible explosions of the Insurgencia and of the wars of Reform and Intervention, with their enormous losses of life and property, delimit the period under consideration. During that period a solid system of domination was never established. Social cleavages produced by opposing attitudes toward tariff protectionism and the role of the church created divisions that were compounded by contradictory strategies aimed at avoiding the danger of popular insurrection. The protection-oriented sectors (both at the industrial-entrepreneur and the artisan levels) were potentially strong, due to the number of their supporters, but they were weakened by their difference of interests and because rousing their popular components intimidated the dominant classes.

The result was a surprisingly nonhegemonic polity: neither a solid dictatorship, such as that in Argentina, nor a powerful civilian regime, as in Chile or Brazil, could emerge. The repeated attempts by a minority sector of the upper classes to coopt the masses and use them as a battering ram in the political struggle was the source of what may be called a national-popular type of politics. This alliance was systematically undermined by the very strength of its popular component, which grew to threatening proportions even in the eyes of those who had conjured it up.

The final rebellion, in 1854, against Santa Anna's conservative regime, however, would prove stronger, longer-lasting, and more intractable than the previous ones, so much so that it survived a long civil war and a war of intervention. Having passed through these ordeals, it changed and degenerated into a new dominant structure. In a paradoxical outcome, almost like that of the later Mexican Revolution, the erstwhile outcasts, or at least some of them, became the new masters. Massive and continued violence had allowed them to build a new system of social control, which remained stable for several generations, thus signaling the end of the period of political cycles that had seen the rise of the popular movement in Mexico.

Chronological Outline

1820 May–June: Return to constitutional rule in Mexico; elections for representatives to Cortes begin.

1821 Feb.: Plan de Iguala.

1821 Sept.: Iturbide enters Mexico City; he appoints a provisional junta and a five-man Regencia.

1821 Dec.–1822 Jan.: Elections for ayuntamientos and for deputies to a Constituent Congress.

1822 April: Congress makes changes in the membership of the Regencia, creating an anti-Iturbidista majority.

1822 May: Military coup with popular support proclaims Iturbide emperor.

1822 Aug.: Several members of the opposition, including deputies, are imprisoned, accused of plotting.

1822 Oct.–Nov.: Iturbide closes down Congress and replaces it with a pliable Junta Nacional Instituyente.

1822 Dec.: Santa Anna starts a rebellion in Veracruz, soon supported by Guerrero and Bravo.

1823 Feb.: Imperial troops join Santa Anna and sign the Plan de Casamata. Iturbide changes his cabinet, incorporating opposition moderate liberals.

1823 March–April: Abdication and exile of Iturbide and his replacement by a three-men Poder Ejecutivo, dominated by Lucas Alamán as minister of Relaciones.

1823 April–Sept.: Most provinces become sovereign states through local pronunciamientos by their civilian or military authorities, including Santa Anna's self-proclamation as "Protector of Federalism" in San Luis Potosí.

1823 Sept.: Elections for a new Constituent Congress, to meet in November.

1824 Jan.: Attempts by radicals and Iturbidistas at forcing state autonomy and/or expelling Spaniards in Puebla, Cuernavaca, and Mexico City (Lobato), are foiled.

1824 June–July: National forces under the command of Bravo occupy Jalisco. Several Iturbidista military leaders are shot, and so is Iturbide, when he lands in Tamaulipas.

1824 Oct.–Nov.: The federal constitution is proclaimed, and Victoria is elected by state legislatures. A coalition government is formed with Alamán and Esteva, soon under the hegemony of Gómez Pedraza. Mexico City is made federal capital.

1825 Sept.: The recently formed Yorkino lodges obtain the ouster of Alamán from the cabinet. He is replaced by moderate-liberal Camacho.

1826 July: Elimination of Escocés influence in cabinet; Espinosa de los Monteros replaces Camacho.

1826 Aug.-Oct.: Yorkino victory in agitated legislative elections, except in Puebla and Oaxaca.

1827 Jan.: Arenas conspiracy, supposedly in favor of a return to Spanish rule.

1827 May: Law suspending Spaniards from public positions.

1827 June: Gómez Pedraza starts campaign in favor of an "impartial" orientation opposed to both Escocés and Yorkino lodges. Escoceses form new "novenario" organization, together with some clericals.

1827 Dec.–1828 Jan.: Law expelling Spaniards. Plan de Montaño, led by Bravo and Escoceses, attempts to repeal the anti-Spanish law and put a stop to Yorkino influence.

1828 Aug.–Oct.: Legislative elections again create a Yorkino majority. In September the old legislatures elect Gómez Pedraza president over Guerrero by a narrow margin; Santa Anna rebels in Veracruz, claiming vote was not free.

1828 Dec.: Motín de la Acordada, popular and military uprising against Gómez Pedraza, who flees. New administration established, with Yorkino predominance and Iturbidista participation.

1829 March: Second, stricter law expelling Spaniards.

1829 April–May: Guerrero assumes office, and Zavala takes over Hacienda. A law prohibiting the importation of coarse textiles is enacted.

1829 July: Spanish invasion led by Barradas is resisted by Santa Anna and Terán.

1829 Dec.–1830 Jan.: Army declares against government (Plan de Jalapa). Bustamante assumes its leadership and takes power in the capital, with Alamán heading his cabinet.

1830 Feb.: Armed resistance against the new government begins, mostly in the south. The national government intervenes in several states to replace authorities.

1830 April–Oct.: Prohibitive legislation relaxed, Banco de Avío created to finance industrialization.

1830 July: Law controlling voter registration and setting income requisites for secondary electors.

1831 Feb.: Guerrero shot in Oaxaca. Armed resistance continues, though somewhat abated.

1831 Oct.–Nov.: Abuses against the press. Formation of a "legal opposition" by sectors of Escoceses and moderate Yorkinos.

1832 Jan.: Pronunciamiento by Santa Anna starts "armed opposition" to Jalapa regime. Civil war begins, increasingly involving the as yet undecided federalists from Zacatecas.

1832 Aug.: Bustamante organizes reform ministry with members of the "legal opposition."

1832 Dec.: Civil war finished by Convenios de Zavaleta, recalling Gómez Pedraza to complete what would have been his legal term, until April 1833. New cabinet includes progressive liberal federalists headed by Gómez Farías. New elections, ordered to be held to renew state and national powers, are won by Yorkinos.

1833 April: Santa Anna, president-elect, unable to assume office; delegates authority to vice-president Gómez Farías, who forms a radical reform cabinet with some Iturbidista participation.

1833 May–Dec.: Santa Anna heads troops to stem military rebellions purporting to defend religion. When he comes to reassume office in October, he finds himself unable to control his more extreme liberal allies and asks for leave.

1834 Jan.–May: Gómez Farías heads the administration in a last period of radical reform, accompanied by popular agitation.

1834 May: Responding to new military pronunciamientos, Santa Anna reassumes the presidency and closes down Congress, a few days before the official end of its sessions. He is supported by Escoceses and clericals, who compete for influence.

1834 Aug.–Oct.: Legislative elections, with conservative majority, independent of Santa Anna, who soon asks for leave.

1835 Jan.: Conservative Congress elects Barragán as provisional president.

1835 June: Successful campaign by Santa Anna to overcome Zacatecan resistance to laws limiting the role of states' militias and undermining federalism.

1835 Oct.: Bases for new centralist system established by Congress.

1835 Dec.: Santa Anna begins his campaign in Texas, which ends with his imprisonment and disgrace.

1836 Feb.: José Justo Corro named provisional president, to replace the ailing Barragán.

1836 Dec.: After long deliberations lasting over a year, Congress finishes the enactment of the so-called "Seven Laws," which perform the function of a centralist constitution.

1837 April: Bustamante elected president by the departmental assemblies.

1838 Feb.–Dec.: Conflict with France over demand for compensation to its citizens, backed with threat of intervention. Federal revolts are widespread throughout the country.

1838 Dec.: French attack on Veracruz, defended by Santa Anna, who loses his leg and recovers his reputation. Bustamante seeks to incorporate moderate federalists Gómez Pedraza and Rodríguez Puebla into the cabinet, without success ("Ministerio de los tres días").

1839 March: Treaty of peace with France. Bustamante heads army to confront federalist rebellions and leaves presidency provisionally in charge of Santa Anna.

1839 July: Bustamante reassumes presidency.

1840 July: Gómez Farías leads an unsuccessful but bloody popular revolt, with federalist José Urrea, in Mexico City. He does not obtain the concurrence of Gómez Pedraza and fails after prolonged fighting.

1841 Aug.–Oct.: Pronunciamiento by Paredes in Guadalajara, later supported by Santa Anna in Veracruz and Valencia in Mexico City. Bustamante attempts to mobilize popular support for a return to federalism, but without success. He is displaced, and a new system is organized by the Bases de Tacubaya, with Santa Anna as provisonal president.

1841 Oct.: Santa Anna forms his cabinet, including the progressive liberal Bocanegra and his friend Tornel.

1842 April: Constituent Congress is elected, in which moderate liberals are dominant; they start preparing a federal document.

1842 Oct.: Santa Anna, unable to control Congress, asks for leave and is replaced by Bravo.

1842 Dec.: Bravo closes down Congress and establishes in its place a Junta Nacional Legislativa, formed by hand-picked notables.

1843 March: Santa Anna reassumes office.

1843 June–Oct.: The junta sanctions the Bases Orgánicas, as a provisional constitution for the republic, maintaining the centralist system; legislative elections are held, which do not yield a Santa Anna majority but give a dominant position to the liberals.

1843 Oct.: Santa Anna asks for leave, and he is replaced provisionally by Canalizo.

1844 Jan.–June: The new Congress registers the departmental assemblies' votes and declares Santa Anna constitutional president. He assumes office in June.

1844 Aug.: Opposition from conservatives and liberals alike mounts against Santa Anna. He replaces Bocanegra with the radical-liberal Rejón.

1844 Sept.: Santa Anna asks for leave and is replaced provisionally by Herrera and then Canalizo.

1844 Dec.: The pronunciamiento of the local garrison, in support of a similar move by Paredes in Jalisco, triggers a revolt in Mexico City, with middle-class and moderate-liberal participation. Herrera, as president of the Consejo de Estado, assumes the presidency, and Santa Anna is jailed and then exiled to Cuba.

1845 Aug.: Departmental assemblies designate Herrera as constitutional president. Radical-liberal agitation increases, preparing for a new bout of reform.

1845 Dec.: Revolt in the Ciudadela of Mexico City deposes Herrera and entrusts the presidency to Paredes, who organizes an authoritarian system.

1846 April: Hostilities begin between Mexico and the United States.

1846 July: Paredes entrusts the presidency to Bravo and leaves to confront an armed revolt by Santa Anna supporters, combined with progressive liberals such as Gómez Farías and Rejón.

1846 Aug.: A revolt, also started in the Ciudadela, overthrows Paredes, puts Salas provisionally in power, declares the federal constitution reestablished, and recalls Santa Anna. Gómez Farías and

Rejón lead the radical-reform faction within the cabinet. A new Congress is elected.

1846 Sept.–Oct.: Salas forces Gómez Farías's and Rejón's resignations from the cabinet.

1846 Dec.: Santa Anna and Gómez Farías elected president and vice-president by the states' legislatures. Santa Anna delegates authority to Gómez Farías, who takes the brunt of confrontation with the church.

1847 Jan.–March: Revolt of the "polkos," supported by moderate liberals and clericals, with some militia participation, to stop reform measures.

1847 March–April: Santa Anna returns, immediately obtains the suppression of the office of vice-president, and delegates authority to Pedro María Anaya, to resume his role as leader of the army.

List of Abbreviations

BSMGE: Boletín de la Sociedad Mexicana de Geografía y Estadística (in early issues called *Boletín del Instituto Mexicano* . . .). Unless otherwise stated, the 1a Epoca is referred to.

BMMT: British Museum Mexican Tracts. Catalog number given only when the name of the tract is too short to identify without this reference.

Embajada Mexicana: Archivo Histórico de la Embajada de México. Paris.

HyD: Hernández y Dávalos Manuscript Collection, University of Texas. Austin.

FO/50: Public Record Office: Archives of the Foreign Office, Mexico. London. Referred to as FO/50, plus volume number and folii.

Q.d'O.: Archives du Ministère des Affaires Etrangères: Mexique. Paris.

VGF Archive: Archive of Valentín Gómez Farías University of Texas. Austin.

Notes

Introduction

1. Luis Chávez Orozco, *Historia de México (1808–1836)*, pp. 252, 256.
2. Henry Ward to George Canning, October 25, 1826, in Public Record Office (London), Archives of the Foreign Office, Mexico (hereinafter FO/50), vol. 25, ff. 24–27.
3. See for example Stanley C. Green, *The Mexican Republic: The First Decade, 1823–1832,* especially pp. 90–94, and his characterization of Zavala as an organizer of the masses, p. 174, which I believe to be correct, if interpreted within the parameters of the time. A contrasting view is held by Michael Costeloe, in his introduction, "The historical background," to Colin Steele and Michael Costeloe, ed., *Independent Mexico: A Collection of Mexican Pamphlets in the British Library,* where he maintains that "no political party or leader, either civilian or military, attracted any significant degree of active popular support" (p. xxvi). Eric Van Young, "Islands in the Storm: Quiet Cities and Violent Countrysides in the Mexican Independence Era," *Past and Present* 118 (Feb. 1988), emphasizes the greater role of the countryside in the genesis of violent confrontations, probably underestimating the social turmoil originating in the urban sector.
4. Ciríaco Iturribarría, "Memoria geográfica y estadística del Departamento de San Luis Potosí," *Boletín de la Sociedad Mexicana de Geografía y Estadística (BSMGE)* 7, p. 301; Mariano Otero, *Ensayo sobre el verdadero estado de la cuestión social ye política que se agita en la República Mexicana,* p. 57. According to Manuel Abad y Queipo, "there are no graduations or middling sort, they are all rich or miserable"; see "Escritos del obispo electo de Michoacán," in José María Luis Mora, *Obras sueltas,* p. 205. On the other hand, some highly placed observers did see the existence of a middle class, such as the British minister Henry G. Ward, who in his *Mexico in 1827* did include among the "middling classes" the "lawyers, the curas. . . , the artizans, the smaller landed proprietors and the soldiers," few of whom, in his view, could prove themselves exempt from some Indian blood (vol. 1, p. 29). More recent

observers, such as the noted positivist Francisco Bulnes, interpreted the war of independence as being "a struggle of the middle class against the rich privileged class," but his definition of middle class was probably nearer to Otero's. He characterized the Latin American "famelic" middle class as being "of bureaucratic rather than industrial origin," thus excluding the small urban or rural producers, or minimizing their numbers. See his *Las grandes mentiras de nuestra historia,* p. 338, and *Juárez y las revoluciones de Ayutla y de Reforma,* p. 109.

5. "El populacho de México," unsigned article in *El Museo Mexicano,* vol. 3, 1844, p. 450, most probably by Prieto; *Discusión habida en la Sala de sesiones del H. Congreso de la Puebla,* in *Colección de documentos para la historia del comercio exterior de México,* ed. Luis Chávez Orozco, 2d series, vol. 1: *El comercio exterior y el artesano, 1825–1830,* pp. 182 and 195. For an early self-perception of maestros as members of a middle class, see "La clase media," in *Semanario artístico para la educación y progreso de los artesanos,* Sept. 3, 1845. For the deterioration of their living standards, Luis Chávez Orozco, ed., *La agonía del artesanado mexicano,* in *Colección de documentos para la historia del comercio exterior de Mexico.*

6. Rafael Durán, "Memoria sobre el Censo de la República Mexicana" (read in 1863), *BSMGE,* 9; *Representación que las maestras, oficialas y demás . . . dirigen al Supremo Gobierno.*

7. Francisco López y Pimentel complained against educated Indians, particularly lawyers, who condemned white and landowner domination, becoming conceited and arrogant, forgetting that "the greatest tyrants of the Indians had been those of their own stock, when they were raised even to the level of *alcaldes.*" See his *Memoria sobre las causas . . .* p. 233.

8. Tutino, *From Insurrection to Revolution,* pp. 24–37.

9. José Iturriaga, *La estructura social y cultural de México,* pp. 44, 52; Frank Tannenbaum, *The Mexican Agrarian Revolution,* p. 27.

10. Nathan L. Whetten, "El surgimiento de una clase media en México," in Miguel Othón de Mendizábal et al., *Ensayos sobre las clases sociales en México,"* p. 51; Green, *The Mexican Republic,* p. 55; Frederick Shaw, *Poverty and Politics in Mexico City, 1824–54.*

11. John K. Chance and William B. Taylor, "Estate and class in a colonial city: Oaxaca," *Comparative Studies in Society and History* 19 (1977); John E. Kicza, *Colonial Entrepreneurs: Families and Business in Bourbon Mexico City;* Guy P. C. Thomson, *Puebla de los Angeles: Industry and Society in a Mexican City, 1700–1850;* Richard Salvucci, *Textiles and Capitalism in Mexico,* p. 10. See also Fred Bronner, "Urban Society in Colonial Spanish America: Research Trends," *Latin American Research Review* 31, 1 (1986).

Chapter 1

1. Pedro Rodríguez de Campomanes, *Discurso sobre la educación popular,* pp. 183–184.

2. *Ordenanzas de gremios de la Nueva España;* Manuel Carrera Stampa, *Los Gremios mexicanos,* Rodríguez de Campomanes, *Discurso sobre el fomento de la industria popular;* Antonio de Campmany y de Montpalau, *Memorias históricas sobre la Marina, Comercio y Artes de la antigua ciudad de Barcelona;* Héctor Humberto Samayoa Guevara, *Los gremios de artesanos en la ciudad de Guatemala (1524–1821);* Frederick J. Shaw, "The artisan in Mexico City."

3. Dawn Keremitsis, *La industria textil mexicana en el siglo XIX;* Robert Potash, *Mexican Government and Industrial Development in the Early Republic: The Banco de Avío;* Salvucci, *Textiles and Capitalism.*

4. Dorothy Tank de Estrada, "La abolición de los gremios," in Frost et al., eds., *El trabajo;* Manuel de Segura, "Apuntes estadísticos del distrito de Orizaba" (1839), BSMGE 4, p. 32.

5. Rodney Anderson, *Guadalajara a la consumación de su independencia,* table 17, p. 102; Jorge González Angulo, "Los gremios de artesanos y la estructura urbana," in Alejandra Moreno Toscano, ed., *Ciudad de México,* p. 34.

6. Carlos Contreras Cruz and Juan Carlos Grosso, "La estructura ocupacional y productiva de la ciudad de Puebla en la primera mitad del siglo XIX," in *Puebla en el Siglo XIX,* p. 137, refer to "fabricantes" as salaried workers, generally living near the large factories where they worked, often in rural areas not far from cities.

7. Manuel de Segura, "Apuntes estadísticos," p. 30; José M. Naredo, *Estudio geográfico, histórico y estadístico del Cantón y de la ciudad de Orizaba,* 2: 248–67.

8. For the stages of protectionist legislation see Keremitsis, *La industria textil,* pp. 83–84; Salvucci, *Textiles and Capitalism,* pp. 163–64.

9. María Amparo Ros, "La real fábrica de puros y cigarros"; Susan Deans-Smith, "Compromise and Conflict: The Tobacco Workers of Mexico City and the Colonial State, 1770–1810"; José Antonio del Raso, "Notas estadísticas del Departamento de Querétaro," in BSMGE 3, especially pp. 198–200 (I have corrected some data on p. 198 in view of the totals given on p. 199); David A. Brading, "Relación sobre la economía de Querétaro y de su Corregidor Don Miguel Domínguez, 1802–1811," *Boletín del Archivo General de la Nación* (Mexico) 2a. serie vol. 11, nos. 3–4 (1970), where several documents are published.

10. See Archivo Histórico de Hacienda, *Colección de documentos publicados bajo la dirección de Jesús Silva Herzog,* vol. 1: *La libertad de comercio en la Nueva España en la segunda década del siglo XIX,* espe-

cially the introduction by Luis Chávez Orozco, pp. 3–8; Banco Nacional del Comercio Exterior, *Coleción de documentos para la historia del comercio exterior de México,* 1st series, vol. 2: *Controversia que suscitó el comercio de la Nueva España con los países extranjeros, 1811–1821,* ed. by Luis Chávez Orozco; John Lynch, "British policy in Latin America, 1783–1808," *Journal of Latin American Studies* 1, 1 (May 1969):24–30.

11. The Consolidación was in effect in New Spain from 1805 until early 1809, when international considerations counseled its annullment. See Asunción Lavrín, "Execution of the law of consolidación in New Spain: economic aims and results," *Hispanic American Historical Review* 53, 1 (Feb. 1973); Romeo Flores Caballero, *La contrarrevolución en la independencia,* pp. 46 and 63, and his "La consolidación de vales reales en la economía, la sociedad y la política novohispanas," *Historia Mexicana* 18, 71 (Jan.–March 1969).

12. Alamán, *Historia de Méjico* 1:152; Zerecero, *Memorias,* p. 35

13. Contreras Cruz and Grosso, "La estructura ocupacional," p. 145. These authors analyze in detail the occupational structure of the city of Puebla and environs in the 1830s and 1840s and distinguish three sectors among the laboring classes: (a) factory hands, (b) dispersed salaried workers in small and medium units, and (c) independent workers still owning their means of production (p. 113).

14. "¿La voluntad general puede errar?" in *La Abeja Poblana,* Jan. 25, 1821; *Testamento de Iturbide.*

15. Seven numbers and a supplement appeared, starting by early June or late May 1820, immediately after freedom of the press had been established. The author did not disclose his identity, but he engaged in a polemic against more liberal-minded pamphleteers.

16. Miguel Quintana, "Papel histórico de Puebla en el progreso industrial de Nueva España y México," *BSMGE* 5ª Epoca, vol. 62, 2 (Sept.–Oct. 1946); Alberto Carabarín Gracia, *El trabajo y los trabajadores del obraje en la ciudad de Puebla, 1700–1710;* Miguel Quintana, *Estevan de Antuñano, fundador de la industria textil en Puebla,* who reproduces several of Antuñano's pamphlets; Manuel Payno, "Un viaje a Veracruz en el invierno de 1843," *Museo Mexicano* vol. 3 (1844):163–64.

17. Frederick Shaw, *Poverty and Politics,* pp. 38–42 and Appendix E. One problem with Shaw's percentages is that they do not add up to 100 percent; this is probably due to the existence of an important residual group (approximately 15 percent) of adult males who failed to declare their occupations.

18. Rodney Anderson, *Guadalajara a la consumación de su independencia*

19. José M. García, "Breves noticias estadísticas de Guadalupe Hidalgo," *BSMGE,* 7. The following is a corrected calculation from the

one I made in my "Dangerous classes," pp. 103–04. See also Delfina E. López Sarrelangue, *Una villa mexicana en el siglo XVIII.*

20. Luis M. Servo, "Apuntes estadísticos de Mazatlán," *BSMGE,* 7.

21. José Fernando Ramírez, "Noticias históricas y estadísticas de Durango (1849–50)," *BSMGE,* 5.

22. Arturo Shiels, "El Partido del Carmen. Breve reseña histórica, geográfica y estadística," *BSMGE,* 2ª Epoca, 2.

23. Joseph Antonio de Villaseñor y Sánchez, *Theatro Americano;* Francisco Antonio Navarrete, *Relación peregrina de la agua corriente . . . . de Querétaro;* Carlos de Sigüenza y Góngora, *Glorias de Querétaro (1680) reescritas por José María Zelaa e Hidalgo;* Juan Agustín de Morfi, *Viaje de indios y diario del Nuevo México;* Luis Berlandier and Rafael Chovel, *Diario de viaje de la Comisión de Límites;* Juan María Balbontín, "Notas formadas para la geografía y estadística del Departamento de Querétaro," *BSMGE,* 7; *Reglamento para la Compañía Queretana de Industria.*

24. See his "Notas estadísticas," especially pp. 204, 205 and 214, and his complementary *Estadística del Departamento de Querétaro;* also Juan María Balbontín, "Notas . . . del Departmento de Querétaro."

25. José Francisco Bustamante, "Apuntes estadísticos relativos al Departamento de Querétaro," (1854) *BSMGE,* 7.

26. Lucas Alamán, *Historia de Méjico,* vol. 1, p. 108. Rafael Durán, in his "Memoria sobre el Censo de la República Mexicana," written in 1863, also attributed proletarianizing effects to "modern and scientific industry."

27. William B. Taylor, *Landlord and Peasant in Colonial Oaxaca;* John K. Chance, *Race and Class in Colonial Oaxaca;* Brian R. Hamnett, *Politics and Trade in Southern Mexico, 1750–1821;* Elías Trabulse, ed., *Fluctuaciones económicas en Oaxaca durante el siglo XVIII;* Nicolas Joseph Thiery de Menonville, *Traité de la culture du Nopal,* vol. 1, pp. 118, 124, 129, 132, 137; José María Murguía y Galardi, "Estadística antigua y moderna de la provincia hoy Estado libre, soberano e independiente de Guajaca" (1826–27), *BSMGE,* 7.

28. Delfina E. López de Sarrelangue, *La nobleza indígena de Pátzcuaro en la época virreinal;* Wayne S. Osborn, "Indian Land Retention in Colonial Metztitlán," *Hispanic American Historical Review* 53, 2 (May 1973).

29. Delfina E. López de Sarrelangue, "La población indígena de la Nueva España en el siglo XVIII," *Historia Mexicana* 12, 48 (April–June 1963); José Miranda, "La población indígena de México en el siglo XVII," *Historia Mexicana* 12, 46 (Oct.–Dec. 1962).

30. Paul S. Taylor, *A Spanish-Mexican Peasant Community: Arandas in Jalisco;* David Brading, *Haciendas and Ranchos;* Luis González, *Pueblo en vilo;* Jean Meyer, *The Cristero Rebellion;* Francois Xavier Guerra, *México: Del Antiguo Régimen a la Revolución,* vol. 2, annex 5.

31. "Primer Reglamento," in *Reglamentos de Policía para la observancia de las ordenanzas municipales,*included in a collection of *Ordenanzas Municipales . . . del Depto de Guanajuato*, pp. 27–32; Pedro García Conde, "Ensayo estadístico sobre el Estado de Chihuahua," *BSMGE*, 5; José Agustín de Escudero, *Noticias estadísticas del Estado de Chihuahua*. For a recent discussion of this subject see Jean Meyer, "Haciendas y ranchos, peones y campesinos en el Porfiriato. Algunas falacias estadísticas," *Historia Mexicana 35*, no. 139 (Jan.–March 1986).

32. R. Vera Quintana, "Noticias estadísticas de la ciudad de Salvatierra. Año de 1865," *BSMGE*, 2ª Epoca, vol. 1, especially pp. 585–86; "Preámbulo," in *Integración Territorial de los Estados Unidos Mexicanos* (1952). Donald Brand, *Quiroga, a Mexican Municipio*, describes the municipio of Quiroga as being composed of the villa, or cabecera, plus six dependent ranchos and three Tarascan pueblos. Here obviously the six ranchos are also territorial subdivisions rather than individual properties.

33. Morfi, *Viaje*, pp. 145, 146, 189; Luis Berlandier and Rafael Chovel, *Diario de viaje de la Comisión de Límites*, pp. 183, 186, 202, 214–16, 233–34, 238; Isabel González Sánchez, *Haciendas y ranchos de Tlaxcala en 1712*. Manuel Payno, "Memoria sobre el maguey mexicano y sus diversos productos," *BSMGE*, 10, gives a list of the twenty-one more important haciendas and the twenty foremost ranchos in pulque production for the last century (pp. 428–34). The average value of the ranchos in that list was almost 50,000 pesos, a very large sum, which would have made its owner a member of the upper middle class, if not higher, and thus in a different category from the common rancheros.

34. Marcos Esparza, *Informe presentado al gobierno superior del Estado . . . de la visita que practicó en los partidos de Villanueva y Juchipila*.

35. Alejandro Villaseñor y Villaseñor, *Memoria política y estadística de la prefectura de Cuernavaca*, pp. 19–20.

36. Jan Bazant, *Cinco haciendas mexicanas*, pp. 88–90, and "Peones, arrendatarios y aparceros en México, 1851–1853," *Historia Mexicana 23*, 90 (Oct.–Dec. 1973); David A. Brading, *Haciendas and Ranchos*, p. 5; Brian Hamnett, *Roots of Insurgency*, p. 7; Eric Van Young, *Hacienda and Market in Eighteenth-Century Mexico*, p. 231. Van Young, in contraposition to the usual idea that the burden of debt reflected a peon's wretched condition, asserts that the fact of having a large debt was an indicator of a high, not a low, status, as it revealed the effort the landlord had to make to retain the services of his personnel (p. 249).

37. James Taylor, *Socioeconomic Instability*, pp. 52–54, who, however, hesitates to call the medieros a middle class. He reports very interesting occupational data for various districts of Guanajuato, which, however, are not arranged by homogeneous status groups. If this rear-

rangement were made, an urban stratification profile with a large middle class would emerge.

38. Guillermo Prieto, *Indicaciones sobre . . . las rentas generales de la Federación Mexicana*, pp. 386–87 and 439. Prieto was contrasting those more emancipated Indians with the miserable majority, including those who brought agricultural products to Mexico every day.

39. Bazant, *Cinco haciendas*, pp. 103–12.

40. Any qualms about calling the better-off arrendatarios "middle class" can be assuaged by the knowledge that Viceroy Manuel Guirior of Nueva Granada also referred to them in that way. See Mario Góngora, *Origen de los "inquilinos" de Chile central*, p. 109.

41. For Chile see Góngora, *Origen de los "inquilinos,"* who considers that peones derived in their greater number from people settled in the outskirts of the hacienda (thence the name), whose situation was similar to that described by Bazant for the less secure "arrendatarios."

42. *Relaciones del siglo XVIII relativas a Oaxaca*. For other situations in the tierra caliente and the slopes of the mountains, where conditions were favorable for small-scale squatter activities involving the collection of natural products, see Carlos Casas, "Raíz de Jalapa," *BSMGE*, 2ª Epoca, vol. 1; David Ramírez Lavoignet, "Arroyo Hondo," *Historia Mexicana* 12, 47 (Jan.–March 1963).

43. Eduardo Fages, "Noticias estadísticas del departmento de Tuxpán," *BSMGE*, 4. See especially the statistical annexes at the end of the monograph.

44. A similar situation, though with some haciendas, could be found in other areas of Veracruz state: Casamaloapan and Papantla. See "Partido de Casamaloapan, Departamento de Veracruz," *BSMGE*, vol. 4; and José M. Bausa, "Bosquejo geográfico y estadístico del partido de Papantla," *BSMGE*, 5. For the society and economy of a wood-export center in present-day Tabasco, see Shiels, "Partido del Carmen."

45. "Noticias estadísticas del Departamento de Aguascalientes, correspondientes al año de 1837," *BSMGE*, vol. 1; Secretaría de Gobierno del Estado de Chiapas, "Censo General" (1862), *BSMGE*, vol. 10; José Fernando Ramírez, "Noticias históricas y estadísticas de Durango (1849–1850)," *BSMGE*, 5.

46. *Memoria que presenta el gobernador de Guanajuato . . . desde el 10 de mayo de 1824 hasta el 31 de diciembre de 1825,* especially Annex No. 5.

47. In some highly urban districts, such as León, this may give distorted, exceedingly rural, results.

48. The only apparent exception was the Villa de San Felipe, but there there must have been a mistake, because it is unlikely that in a villa there were no jornaleros, so their number must have been omitted from the

table. In "Elementos para formar el Censo y Estadística del Estado Libre y Soberano de la Puebla de los Angeles," published in *El Caduceo* (Puebla), Oct. 26, 1824, pp. 114–15, the three following categories were separated: labradores propietarios; labradores colonos o arrendatarios; jornaleros. Though there are no definitions of the categories, the differentiation is clear; on the other hand, the category of fabricante does not appear, probably being subsumed under that of jornaleros.

49. Morfi, *Viaje de Indios*, p. 42.

50. See also Dionisio Vera Quintana, "Noticias estadísticas de Salvatierra."

51. Raso, "Notas estadísticas del Departamento de Querétaro," especially pp. 198–215.

52. Santiago Ramírez, *Noticia histórica de la riqueza minera de México*; Claudio Ochoa and Isidro Gondra, "Apuntes para formar la estadística minera de la República Mexicana," *BSMGE*, 2; Viagero, "Las minas de México," *Anales de la Minería Mexicana*, vol. 1; A Resident, *Observations on Foreign Mining*; Francisco Hermosa, *Manual de laboreo de minas y beneficio de metales*; George Rickard, *Practical Mining: Fully and Familiarly Described*, pp. 69–70; Robert West, *The Mining Community in New Spain: The Parral Mining District*; Walter Howe, *The Mining Guild of New Spain and its Tribunal General, 1770–1821*; David Brading and Harry E. Cross, "Colonial Silver Mining: Mexico and Peru," *Hispanic American Historical Review* 52, 4, (Nov. 1972); *Escritura de asociación de la Compañía de Minas Zacatecano-Mexicana* (1835); *Convenio celebrado entre don Mariano Medina y Madrid y don Martín Bengoa . . . para el establecimiento de una compañía* (1838); *Información, presupuesto, bases y condiciones de la compañía de minas restauradora de Temascaltepec* (1838).

53. Joel R. Poinsett, *Notes on Mexico*, pp. 162–63, reproduces the much reduced population figures shown by a census of 1822. The total, including the nearby mines, came to 35,733 (of which 15,379 where in the city limits proper), contrasting with Humboldt's data for 1802, which were 70,600 and 41,000, respectively. Poinsett also gives the distances of the mines from the town: about 1,000 yards for Valenciana, and 135 yards for Rayas (probably measured from the town gates). The farthest away were the refining haciendas of Burras (4,854 people at 12,692 yards), Santa Rosa (1,943 inhabitants at almost 16,000 yards), Cuevas (population of 2,404 at 17,000 yards), and Santa Ana (1,626 people at over 7,000 yards), and the locality of Marfil, where 2,351 people lived at 5,000 yards from Guanajuato. When British capital started pouring in, later in the 1820s, the population picked up again.

54. Archivo Histórico de Hacienda, *Colección de documentos publicados bajo la dirección de Jesús Silva Herzog*, vol. 3: *Relaciones estadísticas de Nueva España*, pp. 75–81.

55. *Memoria en que el Estado Libre de los Zacatecas da cuenta . . . al Congreso del mismo estado* (1833); Guillermo Prieto, "Recuerdos de un viaje a Zacatecas," El Museo Mexicano, vol. 3 (1844); "Zacatecas," El Museo Mexicano, vol. 4 (1844); "Vetagrande," *El Museo Mexicano,* vol. 4 (1844), p. 466.

56. *Informe que da la Junta Menor Permanente de la Compañía de Minas Zacatecano Mexicana del estado de la negociación del Fresnillo.* See the *informes* for *tercer trimestre* 1837, p. 49, and for *primer semestre* 1838, p. 34. Also the *Informe dado por la Junta Permanente de la Compañía Zacatecano Mexicana a la de Fomento y Administrativa de Minería, sobre la negociación de Fresnillo* (1845):12; Packenham to Palmerston, Mexico, November 19, 1835, in FO/50, vol. 93, ff. 163–65; "El mineral de Fresnillo," El Museo Mexicano, vol. 1 (1843):206–16; Manuel Payno and Antonio del Castillo, "El Fresnillo y sus minas," *El Museo Mexicano,* vol. 2 (1843):5–14.

57. Report of Henry Ward to George Canning, Oct. 21, 1826, in FO/50, vol. 24, ff. 43–167, see f. 147; José Burkart, "Descripción del distrito de minas de Tlalpujahua y su constitución geológica," BSMGE, 2ª Epoca, vol. 1, p. 82. The Tlalpujahua mines, which had been abandoned, were "denounced" by José Mariano Michelena, José Rodrigo Castelazo, and others, in 1824, so as to lease them out to a British company.

58. Archivo Histórico de Hacienda, *Colección,* vol. 3, pp. 76–81; Guadalupe Nava Oteo, "Jornales y jornaleros en la minería porfiriana," *Historia Mexicana* 12, 45 (July–Sept. 1962); *Informe que da la Junta Menor Permanente de la Compañía de Minas Zacatecano-Mexicana,* Primer semestre 1840, pp. 11–12, and segundo semestre 1840, p. 10. Thomas A. Rickard, *Journeys of Observation* (1907), gives data for a later period, with some historical information, mentioning that salaries were lower in Great Britain than in Mexico.

59. In a brochure announcing the proposed reactivation of some mines, *Empresa de avio para la mina de San Nicolás alias El Jacal, en el mineral de Pachuca* (1841), three old workers who had been connected with them were induced to report on the old prosperity, indirectly making references to their occupational shifts between the categories of peón, *barretero,* and *rescatador* (buyer of minerals), owning a small *sangarro* to melt ores bought from workers. See also Francisco Xavier de Gamboa, *Comentarios a las ordenanzas de minas* (1761), ch. 17; "Noticia que manifiesta las denuncias, registros y posesiones de minas que hubo en la Diputación de Minería de Guanajuato en el año de 1860," *Anales de la Minería Mexicana* vol. 1 (1861); J. Lloyd Mecham, "The Real de Minas as a political institution," *Hispanic American Historical Review* 7, 1 (Feb. 1927).

60. Zerecero, *Memorias,* p. 159. The repartimiento was Mexico's equivalent of the Peruvian *mita,* though in Peru it was applied more in-

tensely. See *Fuentes para la historia del trabajo en la Nueva España,* ed. Zavala and Castelo, especially vol. 7, document no. CXCII (for 1639), and vol. 8, "Introducción," pp. XLII–XLVII and also pp. XXIII–XXVII, for the famous conflict in the Pachuca and Real del Monte area in 1766, and doc. no. LI (for 1687).

Chapter 2

1. Timothy E. Anna, *The Mexican Empire of Iturbide.*
2. See Cardoso, ed., *Formación y desarrollo de la burguesía;* Barbara A. Tenenbaum, *México en la época de los agiotistas, 1821–1857; Walker, Kinship, Business and Politics.*
3. Andrés Henestrosa, *Carlos María de Bustamante;* Victoriano Salado Alvarez, *La vida azarosa y romántica de Carlos María de Bustamante.*
4. Vicente Rocafuerte, *Ensayo sobre tolerancia religiosa* (1831); Jaime E. Rodríguez O., *The Emergence of Spanish America: Vicente Rocafuerte and Spanish Americanism, 1808–1832;* Bustamante, *Continuación del Cuadro,* vol. 4, pp. 11–13, 17–18, who also accused Rocafuerte of shady dealings during his stay in London as Mexican representative in charge of negotiating the loans and of having too much of a personal interest in getting government support for his gaslight company, which illuminated a few blocks of the capital (pp. 29–30).
5. Bustamante, *Continuación del Cuadro* 4:20–21, 48, 61; Manuel Gómez Pedraza, *Manifiesto* (1831).
6. *Continuación del Cuadro,* 4:42, 49, 53, 70. Joseph Welsh's own correspondence confirms his early enthusiasm for Santa Anna's revolt, which caused him problems with the British minister in Mexico. See his reports to Packenham, from Veracruz, from Jan. 4 to Febr. 11, FO/50 vol. 77, ff. 18–20, 25–30, 49–51, 59–60.
7. *Continuación del Cuadro* 4:23.
8. David Brading, *Los orígenes del nacionalismo mexicano.*
9. In 1824 the clerical faction, led by José María de la Llave, which won the national congressional election, accused Juan Nepomuceno Troncoso, then curate of the Sagrario parish, of being a heretic. See *El Caduceo de Puebla,* October 4, 1824.
10. In a *Carta al Pensador Mexicano,* signed by J.N.T. (obviously Juan Nepomuceno Troncoso), the author assumes solidarity with an anonymous Puebla pamphleteer who had taken the pen name of El Liberal (probably himself) and criticized El Pensador for his adulation of Viceroy Apodaca, who had granted elections but surely did not believe in them. Troncoso admonished El Pensador to make use of reason in his writings. See F.M., *El Liberal a los bajos escritores.* Another Puebla-produced pam-

phlet, signed by M.M.V., *Otro liberal a los escritores bajos*, joins the previously mentioned F.M. in counseling the "bajos escritores," that is, the liberal demagogues, to control themselves and avoid "hecatombs." It is not easy to tell whether M.M.V. and F.M. were pseudonyms for the Troncosos, but even if they were different people, they reveal a sector of opinion calling itself "liberal" but dissociating itself from the more agitational and demagogic variety of that ideology. Juan Nepomuceno Troncoso had been attacked in 1820 by Juan Martín de Juanmartiñena, noted member of the church censorship office, for his pamphlet *Dar que van dando*. See *La Abeja Poblana*, Supplement to no. 6, Jan. 4, 1821.

11. *Discusión habida en el Congreso de la Puebla*, Feb. 26, 1829.

12. *Abeja Poblana*, Nov. 22, 1821; *Testamento de Iturbide, que otorgó antes de embarcarse* (1823).

13. Robertson, *Iturbide*, p. 57; Bustamante, *Diario* 1:254. A *Proclama del gato maromero a sus discípulos* (March 23, 1823), published during the last weeks of Iturbide's reign, accused "a certain cleric of Guadalajara [obviously the bishop] who has just preached that the republicans are heretics." Guadalajara became, after the downfall of the empire, a focus of Iturbidista resistance, expressed in popular and military movements. See José Ignacio Dávila Garibi, *Biografía de un gran prelado, el Excmo Sr. Dr. D. Juan Cruz Ruiz de Cabañas y Crespo*.

14. Q.d'O., vol. 1, "Deuxième partie du précis historique de l'Amérique Espagnole. Révolution du Mexique," ff. 200–34 ("Notices biographiques"), a report prepared by the consul in Corunna (Spain), B. Barrère, in Nov. 1822; Manuel de la Bárcena, *Manifiesto al mundo sobre la justicia y la necesidad de la independencia de la Nueva España* (1821); Bustamante, *Diario* 1:190.

15. Bustamante, *Diario* 1:252, and his *Conversaciones del Payo y del Sacristán*, 2d series, nos. 5, 9, and 10, January and February 1825.

16. Bustamante, *Diario* 1:255; *Familia Imperial* (1822); Fernández de Lizardi, *Satisfacción del Pensador Mexicano al Soberano Congreso* (1822); Woodrow Borah, *Justice by Insurance*, p. 222.

17. Robertson, *Iturbide*, p. 174; Bustamante, *Diario* 1:163, 195, 199; Fernández Lizardi, *Exposición . . . al Superior Congreso contra la censura fulminada por F.F. Alatorre* (1822).

18. Ernesto de la Torre Villar, *La constitución de Apatzingán y los creadores del Estado mexicano*, p. 74; see also a pamphlet headed *Señor* (Nov. 3, 1821). Bustamante, despite their political differences, appreciated his solid virtues and his sermons. *Voz de la Patria*, vol. 3, no. 18, Aug. 14, 1830.

19. Q.d'O., vol. 2, "Copie d'une note . . ." Lucas Alamán, in his *Historia de Méjico*, constantly refers to a manuscript memoir by his brother about current events.

20. Q.d'O., vol. 1, "Notices biographiques," ff. 200–234, where "Terán" is described as a millionaire and an intriguer. Bataller, when things headed clearly in the direction of independence, parted company with Monteagudo and went back to Spain.

21. José M. L. Mora, *Revista Política,* in *Obras Sueltas,* p. 29.

22. Bustamante, *Diario* 1:165, 176–79, 193.

23. *Testamento de Iturbide;* Bustamante, *Diario* 1:176–77.

24. *El Archivista General* of April 10, 1824; "List of the Mexican Noblesse," in FO/50, vol. 11, ff. 18–22, Feb. 10, 1825. See also Ricardo Ortega y Pérez Gallardo, *Historia genealógica de las familias más antiguas de México;* Doris Ladd, *The Mexican Nobility at Independence, 1780–1826;* Carlos Macías, "El retorno a Valenciana. Las familias Pérez Gálvez y Rul," *Historia Mexicana* 36, 144 (April–June 1987); Brading, *Haciendas and Ranchos,* p. 136;.

25. Zerecero, *Memorias,* pp. 188–89. For Perez Gálvez's association with Calleja, see Rafael Montejano y Aguiñaga, *El Valle del Maíz,* pp. 146–47, but this was considered to be an unfounded opinion by Alamán, *Historia de Méjico* 1:90.

26. *Escritura de contrata y asociación de los señores accionistas del mineral de Guadalupe con el propietario de las minas D. José Mariano Larreategui* (1850), where Francisca de Paula Pérez Gálvez undertakes to complete a contract initiated by her deceased brother; *Plan de reorganización de la compañía de minas denominada Restauradora del Mineral de Catorce* (1851), which describes their attempt at reinvigorating the decaying interests of the San Luis Potosí branch (of Ignacio Obregón lineage).

27. Enrique Lafuente Ferrari, *El Virrey Iturrigaray y los orígenes de la independencia de México;* Bustamante, *Diario* 1:267–68; Brading, *Miners and Merchants,* p. 301; "The Mexican noblesse," FO/50, vol. 11, f. 19v; Moisés González Navarro, *El pensamiento de Lucas Alamán.* Alamán descended from Francisco Matías de Busto, a criollo miner of the early eighteenth century, who became the first marqués de San Clemente, and whose interests were eventually acquired by the Valenciana family. Alamán's combination of ministerial positions with the directorship of a foreign company, though a common practice at the time, was considered by his political opponents and some foreign observers as creating an incompatibility. See *El Atleta,* Jan. 9, 1830, and R. W. H. Hardy, *Travels in the Interior of Mexico,* p. 10.

28. The Quai d'Orsay had reports in 1824 about Arechederreta as a very respected monarchist, who met Alamán every day. See "Copie d'une note remise par M. le Cnel Schmaltz a M. Samonel, Lieutenant de Vaisseau en mission au Mexique," New Orleans, May 5, 1824, in Q.d'O., vol. 2, ff. 245–47, which gives a general account of influential people at the time.

29. Manuel Romero de Terreros, *El Conde de Regla, Creso de Nueva España*, and by the same author, *La Corte de Agustín I, Emperador de México*; Francisco Canterla y Martín de Tovar, *Vida y obra del primer Conde de Regla*; José Burkart [wrongly printed Juan], "Memoria sobre la explotación de minas en los distritos de Pachuca y Real del Monte," *Anales de la Minería Mexicana*, vol. 1; by the same author, "Resumen de los resultados obtenidos en la explotación de minas de Pachuca y Real del Monte durante los años de 1859, 1860 y 1861," *BSMGE* 2ª Epoca, vol. 2; Pedro de Terreros, *Representación que el ciudadano gral Pedro de Terreros hace . . .* (1836). In 1850 in the state of Mexico, 8,870 "jornaleros" were working in the mines, mostly in the nucleus formed by Real del Monte, Pachuca, and near-by Atotonilco el Chico, but including the reales of Zimapán, El Oro, and a few smaller ones. See Ochoa and Gondra, "Apuntes para formar la estadística."

30. He was appointed "Caballerizo Mayor" by Iturbide. See "List of the Mexican Noblesse," FO/50, vol. 11, ff. 18–22; *Familia Imperial* (1822); *Orden Imperial de Guadalupe* (1822).

31. Ladd, *Mexican Nobility*, p. 80; Brading, *Miners and Merchants*, p. 170.

32. Iturribarría, "Memoria geográfica y estadística del Departamento de San Luis Potosí," *BSMGE* 7; *Testamento de Iturbide que otorgó antes de embarcarse* (1823) and *Testamento liberal de Judas* (1823); Bustamante, *Diario* 1:264; "List of Mexican Noblesse," FO/50 f. 19v; Doris Ladd, *Mexican Nobility*, p. 136. Before the Insurgencia Moncada had had connections with people plotting for independence, but the viceroy helped him make up his mind by forcing him to take a prominent role in repression. Zerecero, *Memorias*, pp. 39 and 95.

33. Zerecero, *Memorias*, pp. 188–89; Bustamante, *Campañas del Gral Don Félix María Calleja*.

34. See José Luis Becerra López, *La organización de los estudios en la Nueva España*; Dorothy Tank de Estrada, *La educación ilustrada, 1786–1836*. For the close connections between miners and merchants in New Spain, see Brading, *Miners and Merchants*.

35. *El Sol*, Dec. 22, 1821.

36. Naredo, *Estudio geográfico* 1:52–54; Eugene L. Wiemers, Jr., "Agriculture and Credit in Nineteenth Century Mexico: Orizaba and Córdoba, 1822–71," *Hispanic American Historical Review* 65, 3 (Aug. 1985). In a *Contrata de tabacos, celebrada entre los comisionados de la empresa y los representantes del común de cosecheros de los distritos de Orizava y Córdoba* (1839), José Julián appears as one of the representatives for Orizaba in a negotiation with a company organized by several agiotistas to finance the government, taking in exchange the arrendamiento of the Renta. For an early statement of José María's ideas regarding the need to concentrate the nation's economy in mining and in the kind of agriculture

270 · NOTES TO PAGES 61–64

that sent its products abroad (not the "miserly" type that sold in the internal market), see his participation in a lower house tariff debate, *El Sol,* March 9, 1827.

37. Manuel B. Trens, *Historia de Veracruz* 3:278–80, cited in Enrique Florescano, "Estudio preliminar," in Luis Chávez Orozco and Enrique Florescano, *Agricultura e industria textil de Veracruz: siglo XIX,* p. 65.

38. *Proyecto de ley sobre contribuciones,* by J. M. G. (1821). Later on, in June 1822, José María Gutiérrez de Rosas, a lawyer associated with the Mexican Audiencia and erstwhile member of the Ayuntamiento, published an *Ensayo sobre rentas públicas del Imperio Mexicano* (1822), dedicated to José Antonio Andrade, military commandant of the capital, with similar ideas to those of J.M.G., so perhaps the initials stand for his name, shorn of the maternal patronimic. In any case, both represented the progressive "economists," tinged with a strong case of Enlightenment liberalism in the case of Maldonado, who cooperated with Iturbide. Similar ideas about concentrating revenues on a *contribución directa* and a stiff 100 percent import tariff were put forth by another anonymous *Memoria presentada a S.A.S. la Regencia del Imperio Mexicano sobre Hacienda Pública* (1822).

39. The initials J.M.G. might stand for Jose María Gutiérrez de Rozas, shorn of his maternal name, since the contents of both works have important points in common. I doubt the initials could stand for Jose María Guillén, a popular pamphleteer who would not be familiar with the price and productivity calculations recorded in the brochure. Similar ideas were put forth by another anonymous *Memoria presentada a S.A.S. la Regencia del Imperio Mexicano sobre Hacienda Pública* (1822), stating that the ideal system would be a high tariff and a *contribución directa,* but acknowledging that for the moment it was difficult to introduce those innovations.

40. For a classification of liberal groups in Spain, according to criteria similar to those here adopted, see Raymond Carr, *Spain, 1808–1939,* pp. 130–31, 158–67, 178–79, 228–30; Artola, *La burguesía revolucionaria;* Concepción de Castro, *La revolución liberal y los municipios españoles.*

41. Odoardo returned to Spain soon after independence. In August 1822, as a member of the congressional committee that had to preside over the Pensador's excommunication, he argued that the Tribunal de Censura Eclesiástica had a right to sanction Lizardi (see *Satisfacción del Pensador Mexicano*). Yáñez was a close friend of Alamán and of his half-brother Arechederreta (Q.d'O., vol. 2, ff. 245–47), which placed him in the border between moderate liberalism and conservatism.

42. Bustamante, *Diario,* vol. 1, p. 215.

43. After the downfall of the empire in March 1823, a triumvirate was established while the constitution was being discussed. When this was finished, in late 1824, the former insurgent Guadalupe Victoria was elected

president by the Congress (as an exemption to the common procedure, which provided for the state legislatures voting, each one having two votes). He tried to bring factions together and make them share the ministries, which was not easy, due to the intense antagonism between Escoceses and Yorkinos, with the latter allied to most of the old Iturbidistas.

44. He was made caballero gran cruz of the Order of Guadalupe, dean of the Council of State, and teniente general of the army. See the brochure *Orden Imperial de Guadalupe* (1822).

45. Rodríguez, *The Emergence of Spanish America*; Bustamante, never mincing his words, said about Rocafuerte that he "was endowed with a great talent and a fertile imagination, most of the time delirious," *Continuación del Cuadro Histórico*, vol. 4, p. 17.

46. José Servando Teresa de Mier Noriega y Guerra, *Memorias*, his *Historia de la Revolución de Nueva España*, written under the pseudonym José Guerra, and his *Profecía política . . . con respecto a la Federación Mexicana* (1823); Nettie Lee Benson, "Servando Teresa de Mier, Federalist," *Hispanic American Historical Review* 28, 4 (Nov. 1948).

47. Juan López Cancelada, *Ruina de la Nueva España si se declara el comercio libre con los extranjeros*. A protectionist and industrialist position was also expressed very clearly by a Veracruz resident, Joaquín Pérez de Arceo, who warned the authorities against the undue introduction of British merchandise. He was conscious, though, that his ideas would not be very popular in Veracruz, at any rate among the merchant community. See Guadalupe Nava Oteo, *Cabildos y ayuntamientos en la Nueva España en 1808*, pp. 158–66.

48. Alejandro Villaseñor y Villaseñor, *Los condes de Santiago*; Paul Ganster, "La familia Gómez de Cervantes: Linaje y sociedad en el México colonial," *Historia Mexicana* 31, 122 (Oct.–Dec. 1981); Bernardo García Martínez, *El marquesado del Valle*.

49. During his second presidency, in August 1838, by invoking a decree of Santa Anna of 1833, he had the mortal remains of Iturbide brought to the capital and received amid great pomp and, of course, a great mass of léperos, according to Bustamante, *El gabinete mexicano* 1:87–89.

50. See "Sumaria información sobre averiguar los autores y cómplices de una conspiración proyectada para trastornar el gobierno establecido y substituirlo por uno republicano," in Apéndice of *Documentos para la historia de la guerra de independencia*.

51. See *Diario* 1:183.

52. Q.d'O., vol. 2, ff. 245–47.

53. Alfonso Noriega, *Francisco Severo Maldonado, el Precursor*; Paulino Machorro Narváez, *D. Francisco Severo Maldonado*; Juan B. Iguíniz, "Apuntes biográficos del Dr. D. Francisco Severo Maldonado," *Anales del Museo Nacional de Arqueología, Historia y Etnografía* (Mexico City) vol. 3, 17 (1911); Francisco Severo Maldonado, *El Pacto Social*,

propuesto a España, and his *Contrato de Asociación para la República de los Estados Unidos del Anáhuac* (1823). He also edited *El Fanal del Imperio o Miscelánea Política* during 1822 and 1823, and published in Guadalajara in 1832, *El triunfo de la especie humana,* which apparently has been lost.

54. *Diario* 1:235.

55. On Prissette see the initial prospect of a paper he later edited, *El Archivista General,* 1824. For the evolution of *El Aguila* see Costeloe, *La Primera República,* p. 61 n. 54.

Chapter 3

1. For a recent review of several works on this subject, see Eric Van Young, "To see someone not seeing: Historical studies of peasants and politics in Mexico," *Mexican Studies/Estudios Mexicanos* 6, 1 (Winter 1990).

2. See Gino Germani, *Authoritarianism, Fascism, and National Populism* for the concept of social mobilization.

3. The integrative or "social-control" effects of rural life, even on large properties, are well known and have been commented on by Van Young, in his *Hacienda and Market,* pp. 264–69.

4. *Memoria de hacienda del Ayto de Mexico,* 1830.

5. Bustamante, *Diario* 1:183, says Iturbide showed himself there, during the last months of the empire, in his attempt to elicit popular support for his cause.

6. Jelinger C. Syms, *Arts and Artisans at Home and Abroad,* pp. 116–17.

7. Guillermo Prieto, *Memorias de mis tiempos* 1:46–47; Tank de Estrada, *La educación ilustrada; Sentencia pronunciada contra el regidor Ignacio Paz, con inserción de la declaración del capitán Vargas* (1827); José Ignacio Paz, *Contestación documentada que da José Ignacio Paz . . .* (1827); José Ignacio Paz, *El estupendo grito de la acordada* (1829).

8. See José Joaquín Fernández de Lizardi, *Obras* 1:7–75; Fernández de Lizardi, *El Pensador Mexicano,* with Estudio Preliminar by Agustín Yáñez; Luis González Obregón, *Novelistas mexicanos: José Joaquín Fernández de Lizardi (El Pensador Mexicano);* Jefferson R. Spell, *The Life and Works of José Joaquín Fernández de Lizardi;* Margarita Palacios Sierra, *Estudio preliminar e índices del periodismo de José Joaquín Fernández de Lizardi;* Paul Radin, ed., *An Annotated Bibliography of the Poems and Pamphlets of José Joaquín Fernández de Lizardi;* Paul Radin, ed., *The Opponents and Friends of Lizardi.* A collection of eight bound volumes of tracts by El Pensador, in the British Museum, cataloged 1570/1874, has been used as source material for many of his works here quoted.

9. See "Estudio Preliminar" by Agustín Yáñez, in *Fernández de Lizardi, El Pensador Mexicano*, esp. pp. 96–101 and 139–43; and Fernández de Lizardi's *La muralla de México en la protección de María Santísima* (1811) and *El aviso patriótico a los insurgentes a la sordina* (1811).

10. Fernández de Lizardi, *Proclama del Pensador a los habitantes de México* . . . (1813). It was widely believed at the time that Calleja (especially before assuming the viceroyalty) had some sympathies toward a "moderate" form of independence, with him at its head, of course.

11. Mexico, 1820. Fernández de Lizardi was at that time commended as an example of moderation by other writers, such as José M. de Estrada, who in his *Justa defensa contra una acusación inicua* (1820) was taking issue with a more radical antagonist of the government, who under the pseudonym Observador wrote an attack, *La libertad de imprenta prohibida*, against the local commandant, José de la Cruz.

12. Yermo had in his haciendas some six hundred blacks, to whom he had given freedom without losing a single one of them, as reports went, since they remained very loyal to him. During the wars of independence, they persistently sided with the Spaniards, mobilized by their erstwhile owner and patrón.

13. Fernández de Lizardi, *Conversaciones Familiares del Payo y del Sacristán*, 2d series, nos. 16–21 and 24, May to July 1825.

14. *Chamorro y Dominiquín: Diálogo joco-serio sobre la independencia de la América* (March 1, 1821); the series continued with a few more issues and was restarted after independence, with just one number, after Iturbide's coup, favoring his coronation.

15. El Irónico, *La chanfaína sequita: Carta al Pensador Mexicano*, nos. 1 and 2 (1820), authored by Azcárate, according to Steele and Costeloe; and Raz y Guzmán, *Sal y pimienta a la chanfaína* (1820), signed by N., and attributed to Raz y Guzmán in a manuscript marginal note in the British Museum copy.

16. *Al que le caiga el saco: carta al Pensador Mexicano* (1821). In a later pamphlet Lizardi himself referred to Gregorio Torres Palacios as author of "la del saco."

17. *Carta de . . . Iturbide al Pensador Mexicano* (1821) and *Contestación del Pensador a la carta que se dice dirigida a él por el Coronel Iturbide* (1821). On June 4, 1821, just before the official suppression of freedom of the press, a pamphlet signed by J. A. M. (probably Fernández de Lizardi; see end of this note), *Proclama de un americano amante de su patria* (1821), denounced the imprisonment of Fernández de Lizardi, José Ballarta, Rafael Dávila, Luis Antepara, and others, which put an end to the idyl between the viceroy and the supposedly "loyal" opposition. On October 5, with the capital already liberated, J. A. M. published a *Segunda proclama* (Oct. 5, 1821), stating that he had escaped to Iturbide's camp

when the authorities had tried to imprison him (which is what happened to Fernández de Lizardi).

18. "Diálogo fingido de ciertas cosas, entre una muchacha y Tata Pablo," *El Pensador Mexicano* vol. 2, no. 13, Jan. 1, 1813.

19. El Casillero, *Pan libre y cuartazo al panadero* (1820), who referred to an article in *El Noticioso* of June 28, proposing the elimination of the casillas. He thanked not only El Pensador but also some members of the previous Ayuntamiento for their support, admonishing the new constitutional one not to be misled by petitions from interested parties. See also *Legislación del trabajo,* ed. Genaro Vásquez, Reglamento del gremio de panaderos (1770), which is very different from that of the other guilds, as here the panaderos are merchants rather than artisans, though they do make bread. Little is said about maestros or apprentices, the positions can be sold, and it is said that "from now on" the trade should be converted into a real gremio, with diputados in charge of controlling quality and the entry of new people into the strictly controlled business.

20. J. V. G., *Pregunta al Pensador Mexicano sobre pensiones de casas y coches* (1820); *Clamores de los vendedores de la Plaza del Mercado* (1821); see also M.N.C., *Ilustre Sr; Sabio Consistorio: Beneméritos Padres de la Patria: a V.S.S. se dirije pues mi torpe pluma* (1820).

21. J. M. A. B., *Motivos para que mueran los pasaportes y licencias de caballos* (1820); Fernández de Lizardi, *Plática de los perros en defensa de los vinateros, feteros y fonderos* (1820). See also, in connection with the problems faced by the Indians, his *Carta de los indios de Tontonapeque al Pensador Mexicano* (1820), and *Hasta los mudos se quejan al piadoso emperador* (1822). During the constitutional period inaugurated in 1820, a number of other pamphleteers wrote in favor of a reconsideration of the dignity of the Indians, notably the anonymous *Consuelos a los indios, y aliento a los ciudadanos* (1820); *De la naturaleza del indio* (1820); *De la liberalidad del indio* (1820); *Al Indio Constitucional, un ciudadano español íntimo amigo suyo* (1820).

22. Fernández de Lizardi, *Conversaciones familiares del Payo y del Sacristán,* vol. 2, no. 3 (Jan. 22, 1825), set as answers to queries from his friend the Payo del Rosario; Fernández de Lizardi, *Consejo de Guerra a los ingleses, por el Pensador Mexicano* and *Sentencia del Consejo de Guerra sobre los ingleses* (1825). The title was a bit sensationalist, as it banked on the confusion created in the hearer's mind by the words "Consejo de guerra." These were the days when the British mining interests were being installed in Mexico, and public opinion was very much divided as to the convenience of letting them in and allowing them to own lands in the country.

23. Gabriel Guarda, *La implantación del monacato en Hispanoamérica: Siglos XV–XIX*; José García Oro, *La reforma del clero español en tiempo*

de los Reyes Católicos; Lino Gómez Canedo, *La provincia franciscana de Santa Cruz de Caracas*; Pedro Nolasco Pérez, *Religiosos de la Merced que pasaron a la América Española (1514–1777)*; Michael Thomas Destefano, *Miracles and Monasteries in Mid-Colonial Puebla, 1600–1750*.

24. Alipio Ruiz Zavala, *Historia de la Provincia Agustiniana del Santísimo Nombre de Jesús de México* 1:165, 180.

25. Pedro Nolasco Pérez, *Historia de las misiones mercedarias en América*, pp. 473–78.

26. Palafox y Mendoza, *Alegaciones en favor del clero . . .* (1650). The scheming friars, according to Palafox, had tried to get support from the viceroy conde de Salvatierra, their object being to gain access to the income-producing curatos and to get rid of conventual discipline.

27. Elsa Malvido, "Los novicios de San Francisco en la ciudad de México: La edad de hierro (1649–1749)," *Historia Mexicana* 36, 144 (April–June 1987), gives the social origins of entrants as mostly middle class, including artisans, with a few of rural origin; Francisco Morales, *Ethnic and Social Background of the Franciscan Friars in Seventeenth Century Mexico*, chapters 4, 7, describes a broad range of social origins, but with few members of the nobility and a large percentage of artisans. In general it would seem that mestizos were underrepresented, making the regular orders a place for "poor white" predominance, the status of the members suffering a secular decline.

28. See for example the *Regla de N.S.P.S. Francisco . . .* (1837); Joseph de Castro, *Directorio para informaciones de los pretendientes de el santo habito de N.S.P.S. Francisco* (1737); *Constituciones de la Provincia de San Diego de México . . .* (1698).

29. Luis Morote, *Los frailes en España*; Juan Sáenz Marín, *Datos sobre la Iglesia española contemporánea, 1768–1868*; Rafael Gómez Hoyos, *La Iglesia de América en las leyes de Indias*; Luis Barbastro Gil, *El clero valenciano en el Trienio Liberal, 1820–1833*.

30. For a very interesting case of a conflict based on the visit to a Caracas convent by a representative from the provincial superiors, see Lucas Castillo Lara, *Los mercedarios y la vida política y social de Caracas en los siglos XVII y XVIII* 2:77–229. See also *Memorial ajustado . . . del pleito que siguió el Ilmo. Sr. Don Benito Crespo . . .* (1738).

31. Jacques Le Goff, "Ordres mendiants et urbanisation dans la France médiévale," *Annales: Economies, Sociétés, Civilisations* 25, 4 (July–Aug. 1970); John B. Freed, *The Friars and German Society in the Thirteenth Century*; Joseph H. Lynch, *Simoniacal Entry into Religious Life from 1000 to 1260*; Daniel R. Lesnick, *Preaching in Medieval Florence*; Jeremy Cohen, *The Friars and the Jews*; *La povertá del secolo XII e Francesco d'Assisi*, Atti del II Convegno Internazionale, Assisi, 17–18 October 1974.

32. Some impressive data about the low ages at death of friars in a

Lima convent can be found in *Libro de incorporaciones del Colegio de Propaganda Fide de Ocopa (1752–1907)*.

33. Miguel Artola, *La burguesía revolucionaria (1809–1869)*, pp. 63 and 142; Alejandra Moreno Toscano, "México," in Richard M. Morse, ed., *Las ciudades latinoamericanas* 2:174, quoted in Ciro Cardoso, ed., *México en el siglo XIX (1821–1910)*, p. 54.

34. For some statistical data bearing on the statement that about half the population was adult (eighteen years old or more), see Raso, *Estadística del Departamento de Querétaro*, where out of a total male population of 95,331 there were 45,790 over eighteen years old; and Alejandro Villaseñor y Villaseñor, *Memoria política*, Doc. no. 1, where out of a total of 113,841 inhabitants, 41,175 are between the ages of eighteen and fifty; Secretaría de Gobierno del Estado de Chiapas, "Censo General" (October 21, 1862), *BSMGE* 10, p. 69, where "muchachos, chicos y solteros" add up to 58 percent of the total.

35. The 1849 census of the city of Mexico analyzed by Shaw in *Poverty and Politics*, gives 1 percent as the proportion of clerics in the male occupied population. Shaw believes the real figure might have been somewhat higher, closer to 5 percent, as many clerics tried to avoid identification. If the proportion of middle classes, as reported by Shaw in that study, is taken to be 20 percent, then supposing that the adult males are all employed, the 5 percent of the total corresponds to 25 percent of the middle class. This figure is somewhat high, but it may be corrected by considering the middle class closer to 30 percent (see chapter 1), in which case the clerics would make up 15 percent of the middle class in the city of Mexico, a more realistic figure, especially taking into account that by that time many friars had been defrocked. However, these data from the city of Mexico, based on an impressionistic assumption to correct what might have been an undercount, must await further evidence for its confirmation.

36. Ann Miriam Gallagher, *The Family Background of the Nuns of Two Monasteries in Colonial Mexico*.

37. Dionisio Victoria Moreno, *Los Carmelitas Descalzos y la conquista espiritual de México, 1585–1612*, pp. xxxvi and 189–90; Alfonso Martínez Rosales, "La provincia de San Alberto de Indias de Carmelitas Descalzos," *Historia Mexicana* 31, 124 (April–June 1982), p. 513.

38. In Miguel Artola, *Los orígenes de la España contemporánea* 1:42.

39. Cirilo Alameda, *Representación que el general de N.S.P.S. Francisco ha hecho . . .* (Sept. 19, 1820); Cándido Alesua, *Cuatro cartas . . .* (1820); Alesua, *Piquete suavecito . . .* (Aug. 9, 1820).

40. *Aviso importante al pueblo católico* (1821); *Carta de un religioso liberal a un amigo suyo* (1821); Fernández de Lizardi, *Impugnación y defensa . . .* (1821); Manuel Gómez Marín, *Cumplimiento del desafío teológico* (January 9, 1821).

41. Melchor de Macanaz, *Testamento de España*. His arguments were answered in *Vindicación y defensa de las religiones* (1820) by J. V. M.; Juan Rosillo de Mier Quatemoczín, *Manifiesto* ... (Nov. 3, 1821), *Enseñar al que no sabe* (Puebla, Nov. 10, 1821), and *Lo dicho, dicho* (1822). In the latter work, Rosillo answered his respected teacher Hormedes (author of the tract he was answering), lamenting that the old man had been induced by his prejudiced entourage to write a defense of the hierarchical structure of the regular orders. In passing, he added a lot more about his own life and the events leading to the supposed suicide, but surely murder, of a friar in the convent near Mexico from which he had fled. He admitted that he had lived only for a short time in convents, but that was enough to know what life was like in them. His career had been spent mostly in missions or among the military as capellán.

42. Alamán, *Historia* 1:552; Bustamante, *Diario* 1:206; *Se acabaron los gendarmes porque marchan al presidio* (1826).

43. Fernández de Lizardi, *Defensa de los francmasones* (February 13, 1822); Jose M. L. Mora, *Disertación sobre la naturaleza y aplicación de las rentas y bienes eclesiásticos* (1833). The anonymous *Examen crítico de las causas de la persecución que han experimentado los francmasones* (1822) and *Ilustración sobre la sociedad de los francmasones* (January 22, 1822), were allegedly republished by their Mexican editors only for information, while a more defiantly entitled *Discurso masónico en que se da una idea del origen, progresos y estado actual de la masonería en Europa* (1822), the editor pretended that he was only giving those materials to the presses in order that they might be impugned.

44. Fernández de Lizardi, *Exposición al Superior Congreso [sobre la] censura fulminada por Félix F. Alatorre* (March 11, 1822), *Carta primera del Pensador al Papista* (1822), and *Tercer ocurso* (March 23, 1822).

45. El Papista, *Cascabeles al gato* (1822); Fernández de Lizardi, *Carta[s] del Pensador al Papista* (1822); El Papista, *Carta[s] segunda, tercera, cuarta del Papista* (1822). See Rafael Dávila, *Justo castigo y destierro del Pensador Mexicano* (August 19, 1822), for a description of the events associated with this dispute. Dávila said that he defended the right of the Pensador to publish, not his ideas; he added the news, possibly false, that Fernández de Lizardi was preparing to leave town and had asked for a "passport" in preparation for being banned.

46. Fernández de Lizardi, *Satisfacción del Pensador al Soberano Congreso* (August 19, 1822). Antonio Mier was a determined Iturbidista who had been responsible for hanging a portrait of the Liberator in the provisional junta's building and who maintained that he "had eaten Iturbide's bread," an expression that earned him the nickname of "zampatortas" (*Testamento de Iturbide*).

47. Hermenegildo Fernández, *La desgraciada muerte del Pensador Mexicano* (August 25, 1822); *Prisión y trabajos del pobrecillo Pensador* (1822), where he is attacked, together with his "escudero" the Payo del Rosario; *Defensa del Pensador por su aprendiz* (1822), where the supposed apprentice commented that he had been engaged in the "café de calle de Manito, barrio de San Pablo," obviously an ill-famed joint, judging by its location.

48. Fernández de Lizardi, *Delirio del San Pableño* (September 15, 1822); *El San Pableño, Un guapo desafía al guapo que le salió al Pensador* (1822); *Primer limonazo del sanpableño al guapo destapado en favor del Pensador Mexicano* (1822), a tract equivocally titled, as usual, because it should have had a comma after destapado to make sense; Fernández de Lizardi, *El Pensador llama a juicio a sus necios enemigos* (1822).

49. Fernández de Lizardi, *Segunda defensa de los francmasones* (October 29, 1822).

50. The sermon was delivered on Sunday, April 27, 1823.

51. Fernández de Lizardi, *Protestas del Pensador Mexicano ante el público y el Sr. Provisor* (July 19, 1825), *Observaciones que el Pensador Mexicano hace a las censuras* (October 5, 1825), and *Horrorosos atentados de una parte del clero de Guatemala contra la independencia general* (January 19, 1826).

52. Aza had written a republican pamphlet the very day of Iturbide's coronation, during which a lépero hit him on the head for not taking off his hat. Though Aza had very serious differences with the Pensador, apparently he respected him and was one of the few to mourn him at the moment of his death, together with the Payo, Zerecero, and José María Guillén.

53. José María Aza, *Enójanse los compadres y se sacan las verdades*, 11 parts (1825–26); its first number must have appeared at the end of November and the last one on February 1, 1826.

54. Aza, *Cayó el pobre Pensador del partido liberal*, no. 4 of *Enójanse los compadres*.

55. Fernández de Lizardi, *Respuesta del Pensador al defensor del Payo del Rosario, ciudadano José María Aza* (December 1, 1825), *Cuartazo de don Joaquín a un grosero gachupín* (December 6, 1825), *Lavativa a un gachupín y a Cabrera su arlequín* (December 10, 1825), *Se le quedó al gachupín la lavativa en el cuerpo* (December 24, 1825), *Cedió el Pensador al fin, la victoria al gachupín* (January 5, 1826), an equivocally titled tract where, however, Lizardi admitted having had intolerant attitudes in the past, due to his education, but that he had overcome them.

56. See Aza's *Muerte del escudero Aza intentada por el Pensador Mexicano en la imprenta de Cabrera*, no. 11 of *Enójanse los compadres*.

57. Fernández de Lizardi, *Hagan bien tilín tilín por la alma del gachupín* (February 4, 1826); José María Aza, *Carrera militar y literaria del Pensador*

Mexicano (March 1, 1826).

58. Fernández de Lizardi, *Defensa del Payo del Rosario por el Pensador Mexicano* (May 22, 1826) and *Verdadera defensa de los francmasones* (May 20, 1826).

59. For the application of the rules to the first Mexican election under the new constitutional period in 1820, see *Instrucciones que para facilitar las elecciones parroquiales y de partido* (1820); for Puebla, the process is also specified in great detail in *La Abeja Poblana* of Nov. 30, 1820.

60. Antonio Annino, "Pratiche creole e liberalismo nella crisi dello spazio urbano coloniale: Il 29 novembre 1812 a Cittá del Messico," and Mario Bellingieri, "Dal voto alle baionette: Esperienze elletorali nello Yucatán costituzionale ed independente," both in Annino and Romanelli, *Notabili, elettori, elezioni* , pp. 727–63 and 765–85; Nettie Lee Benson, "The Contested Mexican Elections of 1812," *Hispanic American Historical Review* 26, 3 (August 1946). For a reaction to the annulment of the elections and comments on their resumption in April 1813, see also the anonymous *Alcance a los documentos para la historia* (1820).

61. Fernández de Lizardi, *Reflexión patriótica sobre la próxima elección* (Dec. 4, 1813).

62. "Derecho de reunión," a series of articles purportedly extracted by an anonymous T. T. T. from a rare book and published in the weekly *El Poblano* from March 25 to May 20, 1827.

63. José María Luis Mora, "Discurso sobre la necesidad de fijar el derecho de ciudadanía en la República, y hacerlo esencialmente afecto a la propiedad," in *Obras Sueltas,* pp. 630–39.

64. *Abusos de las elecciones populares* (1820); *Victoria de los serviles, y honrosa retirada del partido liberal* (1820); *Análisis del papel titulado 'Aviso a los sres electores de Mechoacán'* (1820); *Filónomo vindicado* (1820). For a later statement of the moderate liberals' diffidence toward political parties, though admitting their role in a consolidated free polity provided they were not "extreme," see *El Anteojo,* Sept. 9, 1835.

65. J. E. Fernández (D.J.E.F.), *Proyecto de nuevo reglamento para las elecciones de los representantes del pueblo en las primeras Cortes* (Oct 12, 1821).

66. Fernández de Lizardi, *Ideas políticas y liberales* (1821); *Cincuenta preguntas del Pensador Mexicano a quien las quiera responder* (Nov. 18, 1821).

67. J. E. Fernández, El Cohetero (D.J.E.F.), *Busca-pies al Pensador Mexicano, sobre sus Ideas políticas y liberales* (1821).

68. Fernández de Lizardi, *Primer bombazo por el Pensador al Dr. D.F.E. Fernández* (1821).

69. *Oyen y callan, pero a su tiempo hablan* (1821). The judges were also asking for an increase in their almost nonexistent salaries, or to be allowed to ply their trade as lawyers.

70. Agustín de Iturbide, *Pensamiento que en grande ha propuesto el que suscribe* (November 8, 1821).

71. *Semanario Político y Literario de México* 4, 3, Dec. 5, 1821; *La Diputación de Puebla dirige una representación al Soberano Congreso* (1823), where a previous request of November 16, 1821, is copied; *Crítica del Hombre Libre. Diálogo entre un religioso y su pilhuanejo* (1821). The latter brochure was published separately from the main body of the newspaper.

72. *La Regencia Gobernadora Interina del Imperio Mexicano a todos sus habitantes* (November 18, 1821); *Decreto de la Regencia sobre las elecciones* (November 18, 1821); Vicente Fuentes Díaz, *Origen y evolución del sistema electoral.*

Chapter 4

1. Manuel María Ramírez de Arellano, *Legal solicitud importantísima o salva triple de artillería imperial* (1821); *Contestación de un Americano al manifiesto del Sr. D. A. de Iturbide* (Oct. 11, 1821); *El derecho del pueblo mexicano para elegir Emperador* (1821); *Derechos convincentes para elegir emperador americano* (1821); *El importante voto de un ciudadano* (1821); *Realizado en Puebla el importante voto de un ciudadano* (1821); *El grande asunto de hoy* (1821).

2. *Yo no entiendo estas cosas* (1821); José Domínguez, *No paga Iturbide con condenarse* (Dec. 13, 1821); *En qué vendrán a parar Iturbide y Volívar?* (1822), a great eulogy of both liberators, accompanied by an imprecation against the Spanish Cortes, who were the "greatest thieves and murderers known in centuries," and who, like all Europeans, only respected money; *Tribuno de la Plebe, o Escritor de los Pelados.*

3. See "La voluntad general puede errar?" *La Abeja Poblana*, January 25, 1821. After Puebla was liberated by the Trigarante Army, the Troncoso brothers started another short-lived serial, *El Amigo del Pueblo*, subtitled "Segundo periódico que se publica en esta ciudad de Puebla en uso de los derechos gloriosamente reestablecidos" (September 1 to 22, 1821), supporting the idea of an empire.

4. *Rasgo de generosidad* (March 22, 1821); Gerónimo Torrescano, *Cuarto Alcance al Mosquito Tulancingueño no. 18* (October 12, 1821).

5. *El Primer Jefe del Ejército Imperial a la Guarnición de México* (Sept. 12, 1821), and *Advertencia* (April 6, 1822), the latter also addressed to the rebellious Spanish troops waiting for reembarkment to their home country, who had attempted "to seduce some negroes from the lowlands."

6. The other commandants were Manuel de la Sotarriva for Mexico (replaced, when he was designated minister of war, by Luis Quintanar and then by José Antonio Andrade); Pedro Negrete for Nueva Galicia;

Anastasio Bustamante for the Provincias Internas (based in San Luis); Domingo Luaces and, at his death, José Antonio Echávarri, for Oaxaca. Later on Melchor Alvarez was designated for Yucatán.

7. Fernández de Lizardi started publishing *Un puñado de verdades a nuestros enemigos* (Sept. 12, 1821), and then *El Pensador Mexicano al Excmo Sr. Gral del Ejército Imperial D. Agustín de Iturbide* (Sept. 29, 1821), where he proposed Iturbide's crowning only a few days after entering the capital; for the pamphlet literature of the times, see Lynda Carol Spielman, *Mexican Pamphleteering and the Rise of the Mexican Nation, 1808–1830.*

8. Pablo Villavicencio, *Lo que nos importa a todos, que lo remedie el gobierno* (1822).

9. Carlos María de Bustamante, *Continuación del Cuadro Histórico* 4:21.

10. See Pablo Villavicencio, *O se destruye el coyte o mata nuestras gallinas* (1824) and *El hijito del coyote que cuidaba a las gallinas* (1824). See also Harold Sims, *La expulsión de los españoles de México, Descolonización en México,* and *La reconquista de México.*

11. Iturbide, *Carrera militar y política de Don. A. de Iturbide, o sea Memorias que escribió en Liorna* (1827); Unos Liberales, *Defiende su libertad la patria contra Iturbide* (1827); Luis Espino (Spes in Livo), *Reclama viles injurias la patria por Iturbide* (1827).

12. Bustamante, *Conversaciones del Payo y del Sacristán,* 2d part, no. 1 (1825); *Diario,* p. 246.

13. Licenciado Andrés Quintana Roo (L. A. Q. R.), *Indicaciones sobre gobierno* (1822).

14. *Dictamen de las comisiones de hacienda . . .* (March 15, 1822). *El Sol,* in its issue of January 12, 1821, stated that the bases for the new polity ought to be the organization of citizens' militias and the reorganization of the public credit, condemning the recourse to forced loans, which impaired confidence; against this "Florete" tried to argue in a popular vein that forced loans were sometimes a necessity, invoking as an authority even the name of J.B. Say in, *Qué haremos con los préstamos forzosos* (1822).

15. Un Verdadero Americano, *Bosquejo ligerísimo de la revolución de Méjico desde el grito de Iguala hasta la proclamación imperial de Iturbide* (1822). See also *El Congreso Constituyente a la Nación Mexicana* (May 21, 1822), where the members of Congress who had accepted the imposition explained their action, arguing that once Spain had rejected the treaty of Córdoba, they were free to proclaim Iturbide emperor.

16. Vicente Gómez Farías was a medical doctor from Guadalajara but with important connections in Zacatecas and Aguas Calientes. It was in the latter city (at the time and until 1857 a part of Zacatecas, with a short period as a federal territory) that he started practicing his profession. He

owned the majority-share capital of a small mine in Nieves (which he tried to sell to the state in a time of distress, in 1835) and some land. His activities are profusely documented in his archive at the University of Texas, Austin (hereinafter VGF Archive). A catalog of the manuscripts has been published by Pablo Max Ynsfran, *Catálogo de los Manuscritos del Archivo de Don Valentín Gómez Farías obrantes en la Universidad de Texas, Colección Latinoamericana,* listing the documents in chronological order. References will be given using the Ynsfran number (preceded by a Y), followed by the folder and document numbers. See receipts of payments for share capital, VGF Archive, Y53-55, F44A 72–74, of 1832, and Manuel González Cosío (governor of the state) to Gómez Farías, from Zacatecas, March 11, 1835, saying the state did not have funds for the purchase, Y378, F45 342.

17. Espinosa de los Monteros contributed, a few months later (in August), to drafting the list of the deputies who were to be jailed. See Ezequiel A. Chávez, *Augustín de Iturbide,* p. 138. Quintana Roo, as undersecretary of relaciones, signed the orders of detention. The Quai d'Orsay classed him, in a report of 1828, as an erstwhile advisor of Iturbide, explaining in this way his lack of influence in the early states of the republic. Actually having been a strong Iturbidista did not detract from prominence in republican times, as evidenced by Gómez Pedraza. See Q.d'O., vol. 3, ff. 127–28.

18. Zerecero was imprisoned with the jailed deputies in August 1822, but some of the latter believed he had informed on them and was jailed to eliminate suspicions. See Miguel Santamaría, *Despedida del público mexicano* (1822), who says that "a certain Cerecero" accused him of being the inspirer of the supposed plot against Iturbide. The Pedrazista antiyorkino tract *Semblanzas de . . . la Cámara de Diputados . . . en el bienio de 1827 y 1828* (1828) repeated the accusation that Zerecero had denounced the republicans to Iturbide. As for Antonio Valdés, a Cuban federalist who supported Iturbide, a certain informer who was confronted by fray Servando (also jailed) said that the friar had been heard maintaining that Valdés was the only "servile" (that is, Iturbidista) who belonged to the Mountain, the "name by which the left side is known." Fray Servando, in order to gain time and add confusion, answered to the questioning that he could never have said such a thing, since the Mountain was the right side. See "Sumaria información" in *Documentos para la historia de la guerra de independencia.*

19. *El amigo de la paz y de la patria,* no. 1. The series only consisted of two numbers, both in 1822.

20. Fernández de Lizardi, *Ideas políticas y liberales por el Pensador Mexicano* (1821); Francisco Lagranda, *Consejo predente sobre una de las garantías* (1821); *Representación que los generales y jefes del Ejército . . .* (Dec. 1821).

21. Fernández de Lizardi (el Pensador Mexicano), *La nueva tonada del trágala-trágala* (1822).

22. Fernández de Lizardi, *El sueño del Pensador no vaya a salir verdad* (1822). As often happened with those by Lizardi, this pamphlet produced comments or reactions by other authors. He was supported by an anonymous *No son sueños del Pensador* (1822).

23. Fernández de Lizardi, *Segundo sueño del Pensador Mexicano* (1822). In it he maintained that "imperial dignity only means being bound with chains of gold."

24. Fernández de Lizardi, *Alerta mexicanos, no nos perdamos* (July 18, 1822) and *Defensa de los diputados presos* (Sept. 27, 1822). Many of Lizardi's (and other pamphleteers') titles were ambivalent or even contrary to their contents, as a means of stimulating potential readers' interest or luring additional buyers from a rival public. This was the case with the *Defensa*, which was not really a defense, except in the slightest meaning of the word.

25. See Villavicencio's ironically titled *El señor Generalísimo pensó acertarla y la erró* (1822); and *Zorzico a la tierna despedida del león hispano y el águila del imperio mexicano* (1822). In *Llegada del león al castillo de San Juan de Ulúa* (1822) the Payo versified about "a well-merited throne for the hero who saved it," and in *Desafío del Castillo de Ulúa y respuesta de la América Septentrional* (1822), he included a sonnet praising Augustín I and at the same time singing "eternal glory to the liberal heroes."

26. Villavicencio, *Teman unos, callen otros, que yo he de hablar la verdad aunque la vida me cueste* (1822) and *Versos contra quien quiere despotismo* (1822), which were not directed against Iturbide but against his clerical flatterers, and *Ya matan a testimonio a Santana y a Victoria* (1823), where he argued that things would have gone better if after the dissolution of Congress by Iturbide in October 1822 new elections had been held immediately.

27. In *Maromeros, voltereta, que el dado se va cambiando* (1822), the clerical author expressed his hopes that the emperor would defeat his enemies and made a list of the fence sitters, among them the "maldito Payo," who was made fun of as announcing a pamphlet entitled "Equilibrios."

28. See the Payo's reply in Villavicencio, *Cuántas vidas y coronas cuestan los malos ministros* (Feb. 26, 1823), where he treated Iturbide as a modern Trajan, led astray by his entourage.

29. *La escarlatina del Soberano Congreso* (Nov. 1822). The anonymous author was obviously clerical, as he accused congressmen of being silly followers of Rousseau, Montesquieu, Necker, Constant, and Bentham,

by comparison to whom Voltaire would have been a master of morality, when what was needed was a simple constitution and wise religious men. The brochure is bound with others in an eight-volume collection of pamphlets by the Pensador Mexicano in the British Museum, which includes some who are only attributed to him. Fernández de Lizardi, who as well as the Payo was accused by some of authoring the libel, denied it explicitly. See his *Sólo un ruin perro acomete a otro perro rendido* (1822). On March 1, 1823, during the last month of the empire, with confusion allowing more press freedom, an *Epitafio contra el Soberano Congreso glosado por un liberal* (March 1, 1823), was published by J. F. A., who attributed the original Escarlatina to the Payo del Rosario. The latter denied it in his already mentioned *Ya matan a testimonio a Santana y a Victoria*.

30. Iturbide, *Carrera militar y política*, pp. 25–26 and 47–48.

31. Dávila, *Sea el Iturbide al descubierto* (1823), in *The Early Pamphlets of Rafael Dávila*.

32. Bustamante, *Diario* 1:177. See Manuel Barrera *Exposición que acerca de la contrata de vestuario . . .* (1827) and *Bases de la contrata de limpia de calles y barrios . . .* (1844), the latter contract suscribed together with José María, a son of Manuel, and Luis Bracho, representing the deceased Mariano. Manuel Barrera also invested in shares of the Compañía Minera Zacatecana Mexicana, formed in 1835 with national capital, to work the Fresnillo veins, with support from the Santa Anna government. In 1825 José María was an alcalde auxiliar, and by 1835 he had branched out into contracting the lighting service for the capital, which was still in his hands by 1840. See *Representación de los alcaldes auxiliares al Excmo Ayuntamiento* (April 29, 1825); *Contrata de vestuarios y otras prendas para el ejército . . .* (Jan. 27, 1832); *Al Público . . .* (Nov. 10, 1835) BMMT 9770.aa.2; José M. Mejía, *Manifestación que hizo . . .* (1840). By 1841 José María was used by the tottering Bustamante administration to arouse the barrios in a last-moment attempt at saving his regime by declaring in favor of federalism. See *Diálogo, Un cívico y su compadre* (1841), where the Barrera family is said to have "dressed the army and undressed the public treasury."

33. *Testamento liberal de Judas*; José María Guillén, *Muerte y entierro de Agustín Primero*. The anonymous author of *Ya se va Agustín Primero, desterrado y sin corona* (1823) recalled that "only a faction of the dregs of the people" supported Iturbide and criticized him for his issues of paper bills and for the silver conducta appropriated from Spanish merchants. The *Ilustrador Extraordinario*, vol 1, no. 14, when one year had elapsed from the coup, recalled that in those days the people of Mexico received the law from the "turba descamisada" and from the "insolent *chusma* of an obscure barrio."

34. *Pasquín sedicioso* (1823) BMMT 9770k7(152).

35. Iturbide, *Orden Imperial del 3 de junio de 1822, Al Ejército y al pueblo* (1822); Jorge D. Frías, *Pío Marcha, el sargento que proclamó un imperio*, p. 28; Jorge Flores D., *Pío Marcha, parva figura de un gran retablo*.

36. *Consulta del gobierno al Soberano Congreso sobre que se establezca un tribunal especial . . . dedicado a juzgar exclusivamente las causas de sedición contra el Estado . . .* (1822); *Dictamen de las Comisiones Unidas . . .* (1822).

37. See "Sumaria información sobre averiguar los autores y cómplices de una conspiración proyectada para trastornar el gobierno establecido y subsituirle el republicano," in *Documentos para la historia de la guerra de independencia, 1810–1822*, Apéndice; *El oficio que la Comisión del Soberano Congreso presentó a Su Majestad y su contestación* (1822).

38. *Epitafio; Sólo un ruin perro . . .* His *Defensa de los francmasones*, of February 13, 1822, is one of the "intermediate writings" he once referred to as comprising his republican period between the early Iturbidismo and the later support for the coup d'état. He had always been quick at picking a fight with the clericals; a long series of pamphlets and counterpamphlets ensued, ending in excommunication, which was only lifted in October 1823, through intervention by the Supreme Court. Among those "intermediate writings" was one called *También en el Sol hay manchas* (of May 1822), in which he said that he had defended the freemasons (identified with *El Sol*) and had read their paper with pleasure, but now he could not approve of them when they said (in their issue of May 11, 1822) that monarchy was convenient, according to Montesquieu, in countries with a low degree of enlightenment. Fernández de Lizardi then restated his preference for a federal republic, but only a week afterward he would accept the fait accompli of the empire. For the full argument of *El Sol*, see its issues of April 27, May 11, and May 15, 1822.

39. Villavicencio, *Ya matan a testimonio a Santana y a Victoria; Prisión del ministro Herrera y del Intendente de San Luis* (1823).

40. *Lista de los Señores Diputados designados por S.M.I. para que compongan la Junta* (Nov. 1, 1822).

41. Bocanegra, *Memorias* 1:85–94; Zavala, *Ensayo Crítico*, p. 149.

42. Bustamante, *Diario* 1:240.

43. *Representación del ciudadano síndico lic. Ramón Gamboa . . . (1829)*; Robertson, *Iturbide*, p. 192; Guillermo Gallardo, *Joel Roberts Poinsett, agente norteamericano*.

44. Antonio Medina, minister of hacienda, "Extracto de valores de los Ramos de Hacienda Pública . . ." (October 28, 1822), and "Prospecto General del Estado de los Recursos de la Hacienda Nacional." Papers of Agustín de Iturbide, reel 9, ff. 274–79 and 280–95.

45. *Proyecto del Plan de Hacienda para el año de 1823* (December 6, 1822), which proposed for the poor a yearly capitación of 4 reales per adult person under sixty years of age, and for the "rich" (and middle classes) a contribución directa of 10 percent of their income, which was estimated as four times the amount paid in rent. It also proposed an increase in the alcabala, applying it also to the efectos del viento, and the issue of 4 million pesos in paper money, amortizable in one year by allowing payments to the state to be made one-third in paper. Zavala was one of the five signers of this Proyecto. See also the *Diario Redactor de México,* founded by the Iturbidista (of radical liberal persuasion) Antonio José Valdés in January 1823, which continued to support the emperor but argued that it would be impossible to pay the projected contributions (Jan. 13 and 31, 1823). The idea of issuing paper money had already been proposed in August 1822 by a well-known Iturbidista, Francisco de Paula Tamariz, who was in charge of provisioning the army. See his *Proyecto sobre un establecimiento de papel moneda* (August 29, 1822), signed F. de P. T.; Q.d'O., vol. 2, "Dechiffrement Mexique 1823," ff. 176–83; *Si sigue el papel moneda perecen pobres y ricos* (1823); Zavala, *Ensayo crítico,* pp. 150 and 154.

46. *Plan o indicaciones para reintegrar a la nación* (1823); Nettie Lee Benson, "The Plan of Casa Mata," *Hispanic American Historical Review* 25, 1 (Feb. 1945). In his first pronunciamiento of December 2, Santa Anna had declared for a republic, but in the jointly authored plan of Veracruz, that part was dropped and only a recall of Congress was demanded.

47. *Decreto de convocatoria para el Congreso General Constituyente del Imperio Mexicano* . . . (Jan. 20, 1823); Vicente Fuentes Díaz, *Origen y evolución del sistema electoral.*

48. The *Proyecto de Reglamento Político de Gobierno del Imperio Mejicano* . . . (1823) was prepared by a three-member group formed by the clerical conservative Toribio González from Guadalajara, the radical-liberal Cuban Antonio José Valdés, and the Iturbidista stalwart Ramón Esteban Martínez de los Ríos, an old lawyer from Querétaro associated through his legal profession with the república de indios of Querétaro, for which he had signed a declaration of loyalty to the crown in 1810. The reglamento gave the provincial deputations the responsibility for making plans for the division of fiscal and common lands (except the minimum necessary for ejidos) among Indians and other industrious persons (art. 90).

49. Antonio José Valdés, the Cuban radical liberal who continued to support Iturbide (he was considered by fray Servando to be the "only servile in the Mountain") accused Zavala of being inconsistent, with his previous acceptance of the establishment of the Junta Instituyente.

50. Austin's father had already been to Mexico to obtain concessions from the Spanish government, in early 1821. His son was finally able to get the ratification of the previous concession from Iturbide, who found time, eight days before his abdication, to sign the decree. See Robertson, *Iturbide*, pp. 149 and 219.

51. *El público de esta capital* . . . (January 28, 1823); Villavicencio, *Zurra al papel embustero de la muerte de Guerrero* (1823); *Verdadera noticia de la muerte de Guerrero* (1823).

52. See his *Viva el Gral Santana porque entregó Veracruz* (1822). The title of the pamphlet was ironic, accusing Santa Anna of conniving with the Spaniards to surrender Veracruz to them, but it also gave the newsboys the opportunity to go about screaming "Viva Santa Anna," causing confusion, irritating the authorities, and increasing sales.

53. *Manifestación que un amante de su patria hace* . . . *de los últimos acontecimientos* (Jan. 25, 1823).

54. Apart from his compadrazgo, Gómez Navarrete had maintained a long professional association with Iturbide, reflected in great detail in the latter's papers. Navarrete had been since 1810 apoderado of the two parcialidades of San Juan and Santiago in Mexico City. See the power of attorney given to him on January 22, 1810, and notarially attested again on January 16, 1819, by Manuel Santos Vargas Machuca, Francisco Antonio Galicia, Mateo de los Angeles Alvarado, and Marcos Mendoza, respectively governors and first alcaldes of the two parcialidades. This important job gave him precious contacts with the Indian leadership in the barrios, for whom, according to an undated letter "Relación de méritos," he conducted many lawsuits defending lands about whose possession there had been "tumults and casualties," thus helping to "maintain loyalty to the King among the Indians . . . despite the rebels' efforts to seduce them." Papers of Agustín de Iturbide, reel 11, ff. 26–47 and 65–68.

55. See *Sesión extraordinaria del Congreso* (March 15, 1823). The two most important military figures supporting Iturbide almost to the end were Anastasio Bustamante, captain general and jefe político of a broad zone stretching from San Luis Potosí, Zacatecas, and Guanajuato to the eastern and western provincias internas, practically a "viceroy" of the north, as his namesake Carlos María called him; and Luis Quintanar, captain general and jefe político in Mexico, replacing José Antonio Andrade. Negrete, captain general and jefe político of Nueva Galicia, defected earlier.

56. Quintana Roo, *Opinión del Ministerio de Estado sobre la convocatoria* (Feb. 23, 1823); *Dos palabras al Sr. Quintana Roo sobre su modo de caer parado* (1823), by J. M. R., most probably Juan Manuel Riesgo, a member of "Iturbide's abominable camarilla," according to

Bustamante (*Diario* 1:164); Manuel Crescencio Rejón, *El Yucateco a don Andrés Quintana* (1823).

57. Villavicencio, El Payo del Rosario, *Tres palabritas al Sr. Andrade y sus 17 firmones* (1823) and *Otras tres palabritas del Payo del Rosario* (1823). At the very end of the empire, the Payo left for San Agustín de las Cuevas, publishing an enthusiastic ode to the immortal Santa Anna, Victoria, Guerrero, Echávarri, and Morán. See his *Serviles, metan las manos, que se desploma el templo* (1823).

58. *La conspiración de ayer que se atribuyó a los barrios* (March 1, 1823), a flyer signed by J. M. S; *Carta del Capitán Pío Marcha a don Guadalupe Victoria* (1823); El Pensador, *Por la salud de la Patria se desprecia una corona* (March 7, 1823); Luis Espino (Spes in Livo), *Oiga el público verdades, que el autor no tiene miedo* (February 1823); Villavicencio, *Si no se rompe la unión se pierde la libertad* (1823), a pamphlet that must contain a typographical error (accidental or purposeful), because its contents are not congruent with the word *no*.

59. "Defensa del Coronel [Santiago] Menocal dirigida al Sr. Cnel Dn Francisco De Paula Alvarez, Secretario Particular de S.M.I. con el objeto de que imponga al Soberano de ella," Papers of Agustín de Iturbide, reel 9, ff. 82–92; and Bustamante, *Diario* 1:195–96.

60. Bustamante, *Diario* 1:177; see also two letters, both of January 29, 1823, by Luciano Castrejón (signed in a very unlettered hand), informing the emperor that he had the barrios ready for action and that he was preparing an answer to Guadalupe Victoria's desertion. Papers of Agustín de Iturbide, reel 8, ff. 349–52.

61. *Ya agoniza el despotismo y otorga su testamento* (March 8, 1823).

62. *El indulto de los Barreras* (1823); Bernardo González Angulo, *Satisfacción al público sobre la libertad de los Barreras* (April 11, 1823); *Ataque bien sostenido contra el libertador de tres tapados* (1823), by M. B. In the June 17, 1823, issue of *El Sol*, an announcement appeared, signed by José Mariano Barrera, offering his services (as he had been left without employment), asking interested persons to contact him at the *tocinería* of Manrique and Donceles streets; *El Sol* is such an unlikely place to put that type of ad that it may have been an ironic invention on the part of the editors.

63. See Bustamante, *Diario* 1:180.

64. *Ni se ha instalado el Congreso ni tenemos libertad* (1823).

65. Bustamante, *Diario* 1:185–86 and 193–94.

66. *Bando dado en Puebla el 15 de marzo de 1823* (1823).

67. *Levantamiento del Emperador en Tulancingo contra las tropas del Sr. Bravo* (1823) and El Sanpableño desengañato, *Proclama de un sanpableño*.

68. Bustamante, *Diario* 1:205–06; *Prisión de Pío Marcha en el barrio del Salto del Agua*, by F. D. (1823). Pío Marcha had run into trouble with

the emperor, who had him jailed between July and October of 1822; he was again arrested for a few days in the final phase of the imperial regime, for having raided an opposition printing press, but he soon was pardoned and given a pension by Iturbide. During Guerrero's government he obtained a promotion in rank, along with a higher retirement pay. Later on he rallied people to favor the Jalapa plan and was granted further promotions by Bustamante. During the final period of the Bustamante regime, in March 1832, the oppositionist *El Duende* said that Pío Marcha had been jailed, but that this was in order to get information from other political prisoners. He was well treated by Maximilian, but afterward was pardoned again by Juárez. When he died in 1878, *El Monitor Republicano* referred to him as a hero. See Jorge D. Frías, *Pío Marcha, el sargento que proclamó un imperio.*

Chapter 5

1. *Conducta del Sr. Iturbide* (1823); El liberal juicioso, *Respuesta al sangriento papel Conducta del Sr Iturbide* (1823); Fernández de Lizardi, *La nueva revolución que se espera de la nación* (1823); El Ciudadano Franco, *Reverente representación . . .* (May 16, 1823).

2. Already in April the regiment in Guadalajara had been accused of starting a commotion with vivas to Iturbide, which they denied. See José María López and others, *El coronel y oficiales del regimiento provincial . . .* (April 10, 1823); Bustamante, *Diario* 1:251–52; *Declaración del Estado libre de Jalisco* (June 16, 1823); Manuel María Giménez, *Representación al Congreso contra los diputados serviles* (April 15, 1823); "Introduction" to *The Political Pamphlets of Pablo de Villavicencio,* ed. James C. McKegney.

3. Fernández de Lizardi: *El Payaso de los Periódicos,* 1823, pp. 7–8; *Felicitaciones y reflexiones a los padres de la patria* (1823); *Conversaciones familiares del Payo y del Sacristán,* 2d series, nos. 16–24 (1825).

4. Colima became a territory in January 1824; in 1836 it joined Michoacán; and it reverted to territory status in 1846, though losing some of its districts; only in 1857 did it become an autonomous state. A *Representación del Congreso de Jalisco al Congreso Nacional* (March 9, 1824) urged changes in the triumvirate, concentrating its attacks on Michelena, who was said to lack any respect among his peers and on Negrete, who through his satellites, Colonels Brizuela and Correa, promoted the separation of Colima.

5. Bustamante, *Diario* 1:264; *El Avechucho, papel volante (1823).*

6. Antonio López de Santa Anna, *Plan de República Federada* (June 5, 1823) and *El Sol,* June 15, July 1, 2, 12, 13, 1823, for Santa Anna's plan and his unsuccessful confrontation with the local commandant, Gabriel Armijo.

7. See Querétaro's initial proposal to Guanajuato and Michoacán (*El Sol*, June 19, 1823) and the gathering of military commandants of these states (or their representatives, including one from Santa Anna and another from his opponent, Armijo), who met at Celaya, July 1, 1823, under the leadership of Miguel Barragán ("Acta de la Villa de Celaya," Doc. No. 9, in Bocanegra, *Memorias* 1:268–69; also *El Sol*, July 9, 11 and 12, 1823). Though the Acta de Celaya declared in favor of supporting the central government, it was through an organization of their own making and under a military commandant of their choice. Finally Santa Anna declared himself satisfied with the convocation of a new Congress, and lay down his arms.

8. *Que aguarde el nuevo Congreso la venida de Iturbide* (September 11, 1823), a tract with an ambiguous title that accused the Iturbidista plotters, including the Guadalajara authorities, who had recently "taken off their mask."

9. Robert A. Humphreys, *British Consular Reports on the Trade and Politics of Latin America, 1824–1826*.

10. *Guía de Hacienda de la República Mexicana (1826)*, which reproduces the estimates made in 1822. Of the total for the state of Mexico, I have allotted 10 percent to Querétaro (which was not separate at that time).

11. *Correo de la Federación*, January 23, 1829, statement by the Jalisco legislature; *El Sol*, June 19, 1823, declaration by the joint Diputación, Ayuntamiento, and military commandant of Querétaro, on June 11 and 12, inviting Guanajuato and Valladolid (Michoacán) to form a league, with a military force headed by Miguel Barragán and Luis Cortázar; Bustamante, *El gabinete mexicano* 2:58. See chapters 10 and 11 for other cases, and Bazant, *Cinco Haciendas*, p. 37, for the potential for San Luis Potosí to become a separatist region, banking on its access to the sea via Tampico.

12. *Lista fidedigna de individuos . . .* (1823).

13. "Acta de la conspiración para la restauración de la libertad," Mexico, Oct. 31 to Nov. 2, 1823, HyD 1806; instructions for the day of the coup, HyD 1810–17, 1826, 1913, 1915–23; draft of a proclama, Nov. 11, 1823, HyD 1822 and 1914; see also a series of reports between February and August of 1824 by Francisco Antonio de Narváez, signed Tinaono de Zaverna, from the Hacienda de la Compañía in Chalco (which had been leased by the government to Iturbide), HyD 1951–52, 1954, 1959, 1963, 1966, 1982, 1999, 2027–28, 2189, 2200–2201, 2212, 2218. Narváez was administrator of the Hacienda de la Compañía, having acted in that position since Iturbide's time. See an undated letter by him to the emperor, in a group of documents classified as coming from the administration of that hacienda, in The Papers of Agustín de Iturbide, reel 8, ff. 959–62.

14. Nov. 19, 1823, and Jan. 16, 1824, HyD 1845 and 1969. For a later analysis of the evolution of Iturbidismo toward a coalition with the federalists, and its tranformation "into a masonic rite," see *El Anteojo*, August 1, 12, and 23, 1835.

15. *El Sol*, Dec. 23, 1823, and Jan. 5–8, 1824.

16. José María Lobato, *Habitantes de México* (Jan. 24, 1824). Lobato had been active in the imperial army sent against Santa Anna and signed the proclamation *El Brigadier José María Lobato a su división* (December 6, 1822). He was a radical yorkino, appreciated by the most extreme members of that faction. When he died in 1829, impressive funeral rites were held, attended by personalities such as Guerrero and Alpuche, the latter singing the mass, though they were all freemasons, in Carlos María de Bustamante's opinion. See his *Voz de la Patria* 3, 20 (August 21, 1830). The Payo del Rosario (Villavicencio) wrote on that occasion an *Oración fúnebre encomiástica a la muerte del Gral D. J.M. Lobato* (March 15, 1829).

17. Reyes to Lobato, Texcoco Jan. 23, 1824,; his proclama in Chalco and Texcoco, Jan. 23; and Lobato to Reyes accepting his support. HyD 1978–79, 1984; Robertson, *Iturbide*, p. 276.

18. Vicente Guerrero, general commandant of the south, to Mariano Bello (probably a jefe político in Tixtla), Jan. 18, 1824, announcing from Cuernavaca the revolt by various personalities, including the Pensador, HyD 1973. The plan itself, of Jan. 16, proposing the Spaniards' elimination from public employment, declared against an empire and a one-man executive and in favor of federalism and the recognition of past services during the Insurgencia, HyD 1970.

19. Unsigned circular, surely from Reyes, to a group of sergeants in the capital, and a series of instructions for the organization of the Ejército Restaurador, March 19–21, 1824; letters from Narváez (Tinaono de Zaverna), March 8, 1824, and from Juan Francisco Zequeira, March 13, 1824. HyD 2104, 2112–15; 2028, 2094.

20. He was now publishing the *Archivista*, which despite its title was actively involved in politics. See *El Archivista General*, March 13 and April 12, 1824; Pablo de Villavicencio, *O se destierra el coyote . . .* (1824) and *El hijito del coyote que cuidaba a las gallinas* (March 24, 1824); José M. Guillén, *Fuga y alcance del Payo del Rosario* (April 2, 1824); Bustamante, *El Centzontli*, no. 156 (1824); Fernández de Lizardi, *Carta[s] del Pensador al Payo del Rosario . . .* (1824) and *Conversaciones familiares del Payo y del Sacristán* 2, 2 (Jan. 1825).

21. To discredit Iturbide, pamphlets were published accusing him, among other things, of being prepared to cede both Californias to the Russians in exchange for money and armaments, because he was unsuccessful in getting them from Great Britain. See *Planes del Sr. Iturbide para la nueva reconquista de América* (1824).

22. He had authored a *Pacto Federal del Anáhuac,* published in July 1823, proposing a federal republic.

23. *Manifiesto del Congreso Constituyente del Estado de Jalisco a sus habitantes* (April 30, 1824).

24. *Prisión del Sr. Iturbide en Londres* (1824), an ambiguously titled pamphlet to attract buyers, which really concerned itself with the Jalisco separatist attempt; Fernández de Lizardi, *Pronóstico político del Pensador Mexicano . . .* (May 12, 1824).

25. Villavicencio, *Cosas que jamás se han oído* (1825), written against Carlos María de Bustamante. The Executive Power had banned the Payo for eight months during 1824, as a reprisal for his incendiary pamphlets against the Spaniards, depicted as coyotes.

26. Q. d'O., vol 2, ff. 174–75; Ezequiel A. Chávez, *Agustín de Iturbide,* p. 205; Carlos María de Bustamante, *El Gral Don Felipe de la Garza . . .* (1826).

27. See Jaime Olveda, *El iturbidismo en Jalisco.* According to Carlos María de Bustamante, Eduardo García was a nephew of Iturbide; see his *El Gral Don Felipe de la Garza,* p. 47.

28. The Basilisio Valdés affair became famous and fed the presses because of its possibility of being exploited as "social realism." Apparently Valdés had robbed because of his poverty, and trying to escape punishment attempted to make his crime "political," hoping to get the usual amnesty. In the event the authorities took him seriously and shot him, on April 5, 1824. That date happended to coincide with Prissette's expulsion. See Bustamante, *El Gral Don Felipe de la Garza,* p. 34. Fernández de Lizardi could not pass up making out the "young patriot" Valdés to be an innocent victim of the power-hungry triumvirate centralists. See his *Conversaciones* 2, 2 (January 19, 1825). He also took up the case of Generals Anastasio Bustamante and Luis Quintanar, the leaders of the foiled Jalisco resistance, whose careers suffered a temporary setback because of their participation (*Conversaciones* 2, 3 (Jan. 22, 1825).

29. *Manifiesto que el Congreso Constitucional del Estado Libre de Jalisco dirige a sus habitantes* (July 7, 1824).

30. Carlos María de Bustamante, *El gabinete mexicano* 1:87–89, describes the reception of Iturbide's remains in Mexico City, in September 1838, with the usual accompaniment of "an immense *leperada* of idle people attracted by the gathering and novelty to see what they could fish . . . [and pickpocket]."

31. Garcia Yllueca was a lawyer associated with the military, with a long career as a moderately liberal bureaucrat in the service of the Spanish crown, to which he had been loyal until a very late period.

32. The above-named states, whose population was estimated in 1823 to be 2,399,663, that is, 39 percent of the national total, had obtained

only 49 deputies' seats in the previous Congress, or 30 percent of the total of 162.

33. Fernández de Lizardi, *Defensa del papel* . . . (1823), published in the Imprenta del Ciudadano Lizardi.

34. *Decreto del Soberano Congreso Mexicano sobre elecciones* (1823).

35. Bustamante, *Diario* 1:221; *El Mensajero Comercial de Méjico,* November 1, 1826, quoted Arrillaga as saying that the public debt was not excessively large by international standards.

36. *El Sol,* Nov. 17–18, 1823.

37. *El Archivista General,* April 8 and 22, 1824.

38. Fernández de Lizardi, *No hay porqué tener temor, siendo justo el Director* (1824). See also his previous *Aunque haya nuevo congreso, qué con eso?* (Nov 10, 1823), where he contributed to distrust of the legislative body.

39. José Servando Teresa de Mier Noriega y Guerra, "Voto particular del Dr. Mier" (1823) and his *Profecía política*; Nettie Lee Benson, "Servando Teresa de Mier, Federalist," *Hispanic American Historical Review* 28, 4 (Nov. 1948). In his proposal fray Servando would have the provincial elected diputaciones propose three names for the most important national posts in their areas, including the "prefects," the equivalent of governors. The prefects would have control of the local militia.

40. Robertson, *Iturbide,* p. 276; *El Archivista General,* April 8 and 22, 1824.

41. The central government also retained the 15 percent contribution foreign products paid on entering the country (apart from the 25 percent tariff), after which they were exempt from alcabala; the state of Yucatán kept the proceeds from taxing the exports of its own products. *El Archivista General,* April 14, 1828.

42. Roberto Crichton Wyllie, *México: Noticia sobre su Hacienda Pública.*

43. *El Sol* reported the event without much comment but continued to depict the Venezuelan Liberator in a favorable light (May 26, 1824).

44. "Extrait d'une lettre du Mexique," Q.d'O., vol. 2, ff. 299–301; and letter from M. Alex Martin, French representative in Mexico, to A. Ferronnays, French foreign minister, June 30, 1828, Q.d'O., vol. 3, ff. 202–05.

45. Fernández de Lizardi, *Disputa de los dos congresos* (October 26, 1824), and his *Conversaciones* 2, 2 (January 1825), where he condemns the state government's intention to expel the national authorities but expresses relief at the fact that they have finally tolerated their presence in the city.

46. *Representación del Excmo Ayuntamiento constitucional de la ciudad de México a la Cámara de Diputados de la Federación, sobre que no se derogue ni altere la ley que la ha declarado distrito federal de la nación* (January 25, 1825); and *El Ayuntamiento de la ciudad de México . . . hace presente a la Cámara de Diputados . . .* (October 31, 1825). When the federal district was established, it was not allowed either repre-

sentation in the senate or a vote in presidential elections; it was granted the power to elect representatives to the lower house, however.

47. José M. Bausa, "Bosquejo geográfico y estadístico del Partido de Papantla," *BSMGE, 5.*

48. Jan Bazant, *Historia de la deuda exterior de México, 1823–1946;* Jaime E. Rodríguez O., *The Emergence of Spanish America;* José Ignacio Esteva, *Crisol de la Memoria de Hacienda en el examen de los análisis de ella: año de 1825* (1825), p. 48.

49. Tomás Murphy, Mexican minister in Paris, to Vicente Rocafuerte, minister in London, September 8, 1825, and to Lucas Alamán, June 26, 1825. Embajada Mexicana, docs. no. 37 and 36.

50. "Extrait d'une lettre de M. Louis Sultzer, directeur de la Cie Rhénane au Mexique," Mexico, November 19, 1825; Q.d'O., vol. 2, ff. 327–28.

51. Already in 1824 French official observers thought that though in Cuba many people favored independence, all property holders were against it, because they felt that it "could not be established without bringing in licence and the loss of their properties." See "Copie d'un rapport fait au Gral. Duzelaz . . . ," Martinique, 1824, Q.d'O., vol. 2, ff. 268–74; "Reflexiones de un amante de la independencia de las Américas . . . ," Embajada Mexicana, doc. no. 158, annex to no. 157 of June 7, 1827; and Tomás Murphy to Vicente Rocafuerte, January 13, 1826, and to Villele, March 3, 1826, Embajada Mexicana, docs. no. 45 and 512.

52. The French minister in Mexico reported that "the country has made in the last three years incredible progress. Order has been established in the administration and the greatest peace reigns [in it]"; "Extrait d'une depeche de Mr Alex Martin a Mr l'Amiral Baron Duperre, Commandant la force navale du Roi aux Antilles," Mexico City, June 24, 1826. Q.d'O., vol. 2, f. 353.

Chapter 6

1. See the following tracts by Villavicencio: *De coyote a perro inglés voy al coyote 8 a 3* (Feb. 11, 1825); *El loco de las Tamaulipas o segunda parte del Coyote a perro inglés* (1825); *Si no se van los ingleses hemos de ser sus esclavos* (November 11, 1825); *Los coyotes de España vendrán,* 3 pts. (1826), of which the 2nd part is of August 26; *Plan de desgachupinar* (1826) and *Si vienen los godos nos cuelgan a todos* (1826). By Fernández de Lizardi, *Sentencia del consejo de guerra sobre los ingleses* (November 29, 1825), and *Un coyote convertido les predica a las gallinas* (August 18, 1826). For a speech by Senator Vargas, a political friend of Gómez Pedraza, accusing El Payo of being supported by the Spaniards, see *El Sol,* Feb. 18, 1826.

2. Francisco Molinos del Campo, *Informe del Gobernador del Distrito Federal* . . . (Jan. 2, 1826); Juan Zelaeta, *El Ayuntamiento no miente* (Jan. 14, 1826); Juan Zelaeta, *El ciudadano* . . . *o últimos hechos del Sr. Molinos* (April 10, 1826).

3. *La libertad en la ley, o ejecución de justicia* (March 5, 1826); *Los amigos de la igualdad ante la ley, Roben a los extranjeros y verán como hay garrote* (March 8, 1826).

4. *Memoria sobre el Estado de la Hacienda Pública* . . . (January 4, 1825). The calculated income from customs includes the tariffs plus an extra *derecho de internación* of 18.75 percent (15 percent incremented by one-fourth) in lieu of alcabala, which was collected by the federal government, in contrast to the alcabalas, which were granted to the states. Export duties were mostly levied on silver, but they were only 3 percent of value, thus yielding scarcely 300,000 pesos, given the current level of silver exports of 10 million pesos. The allowed ports of entry at the time, according to the Memoria, were Veracruz, Tampico, Alvarado, Soto la Marina, Refugio, and Campeche on the Atlantic; Acapulco, San Blas, Mazatlán, and Guaymas on the Pacific.

5. *Análisis de la Memoria presentada por el Sr. Secretario del Despacho de Hacienda* . . . (April 10, 1825).

6. *Análisis de la Memoria del Ministro de Hacienda* . . . (May 20, 1825). The members were the Escoceses José Agustín Paz and Manuel Heras Soto (both from the state of Mexico), the Iturbidista Bernardo González Angulo (from Puebla), Antonio Monjardín (also from Puebla), and José María Covarrubias (from Jalisco).

7. *Observaciones sobre la Memoria que el E. M. de Hacienda leyó* . . .(1825).

8. *Ocios de Españoles Emigrados* (London) 4, 18 (Sept. 1825), and 20 (Nov. 1825).

9. Esteva, *Crisol de la Memoria de Hacienda en el examen de los análisis de ella* (1825); *A los españoles ociosos en Londres un mexicano ocupado* (1825); *Carta sobre el Crisol de la Memoria de Hacienda* (1825), by M.P. (probably a pseudonym of Esteva himself), and *Carta de M.P. sobre el comunicado del Observador* . . . (1825); *Contestación que da la Comisión de la Cámara de Senadores al Impreso titulado Crisol* (August 26, 1825).

10. *Memoria del Ramo de Hacienda Federal de los EEUU Mexicanos* (1826); *Dictamen de la Comisión de Hacienda de la Cámara de Senadores* . . . (March 20, 1826); *Manifiesto de la administración* . . . (January 10, 1827); Esteva, *Apuntaciones* (1827); and the furious criticisms against his whole administration in *Observaciones sobre la Memoria de la Hacienda Mexicana para 1827* (March 1827).

11. Embajada de México, Docs. Nos. 812 and 823, of April 18 and May 10, 1826, reporting the positive reaction in business circles to the reform of the tariff, and the Bordeaux Chamber of Commerce petition in favor of normalizing relations with Mexico.

12. Fernández de Lizardi, *Se acercan las elecciones, cuidado con los borbones* (July 26, 1826); *El Iris,* May 13, 1826.

13. *El Iris,* April 8, July 5 and 8, 1826; Orazio de Attelis, baron of Santangelo, *Las cuatro primeras discusiones del Congreso de Panamá,* pp. 33, 68–69, 85, 146.

14. Santangelo, *Las cuatro primeras discusiones,* dedication; *El Iris,* June 10 to 28, 1826. At this point Heredia, the Cuban poet and coeditor with the Italians Linati and Galli, parted company with them and attacked Santangelo vehemently. See *Gaceta del Gobierno,* July 1, 1826, and Alpuche e Infante, *Grito contra la inhumanidad.* Later that year the Yorkino *El Correo* published a long series (from November 15 to December 5, 1826) of laudatory comments by Antonio Leocadio Guzmán on the "Bolivian" constitution, with occasional editorial support, though condemning its imposition through force or massive petition (as Bolívar's friends were trying to do at the time in Colombia). Both *El Sol* and the Pedrazista *El Aguila* usually expressed scorn for Bolívar's "ill-conceived" code. See for example *El Aguila,* December 15, 1826.

15. *Gaceta del Gobierno,* July 4, 1826, written by the Cuban José María Heredia, who had parted company with Linati and Galli, his erstwhile associates in the *Iris;* Fernández de Lizardi, *Si a Santangelo destierran ya no hay justicia en la tierra* (July 4, 1826); Alpuche e Infante, *Acusación del Sr Alpuche contra D. Sebastián Camacho . . .* (1826); *El Iris,* July 5, 1826; John Jordan, *Serious Actual Dangers of Foreigners and Foreign Commerce in the Mexican States; El Iris,* August 2, 1826.

16. Bustamante, *Diálogo entre un barbero y su marchante* (1826).

17. Fuentes Díaz, *Origen y evolución del Sistema electoral.*

18. *Manifiesto del Congreso Constituyente . . . de la Puebla.*

19. *Memoria presentada al Congreso Primero Constitucional de Puebla; A los habitantes del Estado de Puebla.*

20. Fernández de Lizardi, *Ya en Oaxaca y en Durango acabó la libertad* (1826), and *Entre bobos anda el juego: llevóselo todo el diablo* (Sept. 23, 1826); Villavicencio, *Ya tenemos en Oaxaca parte de la Santa Liga* (Sept. 1826), pp. 600, 601, 602, 605.

21. *Documentos importantes tomados del espediente* (1826), p. 42, for the religious-Zavalista outburst; Robertson, *Iturbide,* p. 53. Francisco Lombardo, the minister of relaciones under Gómez Farías, informed the Mexican representative in Paris, in early 1834, that in the south there had been a rebellion led by Piedra and Carlos Tepixcoco, aimed at "provoking a war among Mexicans of different colors," but that they had been defeated and were in hiding. Embajada Mexicana, Doc. No. 5879, Feb. 8, 1834. Many years later, in 1861, Piedra narrowly escaped being shot by General O'Horan of the invading armies. He died in 1873 after a long and agitated life.

22. Letter from Robert Auld to James Vetch (still the company's chief executive at the time, resident in Real del Monte), of November 3, 1826. FO/50 vol. 27, f. 266.

23. FO/50 vol. 27, ff. 266–266v.

24. FO/50 vol. 27, annexes in ff. 269–71v. These events were covered in the Mexican press. *El Mensajero Comercial de México* (of a moderate-liberal orientation) of January 1, 1827, commenting on the general evolution of the country in the year just finished, lamented that miners forgot that they owed their prosperity to foreigners and that they had come to the point of "forging conspiracies . . . and . . . arming themselves in public places under the view and the toleration of local authorities, who with their silence seemed to authorize [them]."

25. See Vicente Fuentes Díaz, *Origen y evolución del sistema electoral* and the *Instrucciones para elecciones parroquiales y de partido* (July 10, 1820).

26. FO/50 vol. 27, f. 267v. The complete letter with its annexes is found on ff. 265–71v.

27. Letter from the directors of the Anglo Mexican company in Guanajuato, J. W. Williamson, E. Jones, and J. Murphy to R. Packenham, received in Mexico on July 20, 1827. FO/50 vol. 34, ff. 271–74v.

28. Correspondence between Minister Juan de Dios Cañedo and Packenham, April 26 and 29, 1828, in FO/50 vol. 43, ff. 223–25v.

29. *Memoria presentada al Congreso de Puebla*. The newly appointed governor stated that the militias, established in order to consolidate the government's authority, would easily have turned against it, as had happened recently in Europe, where their "execrable" role had become apparent to all.

30. *Alerta contra serviles* (1820).

31. *Aguila*, December 17 and 18, 1826; Zerecero, *Memorias*, p. 189. *El Sol* said, just before the final election, that making "Colonel B." alcalde would be like "giving the church to Luther," because of his role as impresario at the theater, and contractor of military apparel (December 17, 1826).

32. Martin to Damas, November 30, 1827, Q.d'O. vol. 3, ff. 137–39.

33. See comments against Espinosa de los Monteros and Ramos Arizpe, *Correo*, Dec. 8 and 28, 1826.

34. Arenas, *Prisión violenta y satisfacción que da al público el R.P.F. Joaquín Arenas* (1820); Joaquín Arenas, *Fraile contra fraile a cara descubierta* (April 22, 1823); El visionario, *El jarave loco del padre Arenas* (May 23, 1827); Un tlapaneco, *La sombra del padre Arenas que Iturbide encontró en penas* (1827), signed Oc Felnara Milsono, an acrostic I have been unable to decipher; *Ejecución de justicia en el religioso dieguino Fr. Joaquín Arenas* (1827); the Porrúa dictionary adds that he was a money counterfeiter.

35. *Sentencia pronunciada contra el regidor Ignacio Paz* (1827); Paz, *Contestación documentada* (1827); *El Sol*, Febr. 18 and 20, 1827; Espino, *Plan legítimo del padre Arenas para revolucionar a favor de España* (May 1827), and *Debilidad del gobierno y embrollos del padre Arenas* (June 1827); Fernández de Lizardi, *Si muere el fraile traidor, que sea en la Plaza Mayor* (April 1, 1827).

36. *Rueguen a Dios por Arenas que ahora sí es cierta su muerte* (March 14, 1827); El visionario, *El jarave loco*; Un tlapaneco, *La sombra*.

37. Espino, *Complicidad de 5 senadores en el crimen de Negrete* (1827); Villavicencio, *Defensa del hijo de Iturbide ante el Congreso de Veracruz* (May 1827); Iturbide, *Carrera militar y política*; Villavicencio, *Manifiesto del Payo del Rosario a sus compatriotas* (1827), and *Tristes recuerdos del hombre de Iguala, por el Payo del Rosario* (September 16, 1827); Fernández de Lizardi, *Testamento y despedida del Pensador Mexicano*, 2 parts (1827), the first one dated April 27.

38. See Harold D. Sims, *La expulsión de los españoles de México*, and the related works by the same author, *Descolonización en México* and *La reconquista de México*. Also Romeo R. Flores Caballero, *La contrarrevolución en la independencia*.

39. Martin to Damas, May 15, 1827, Q.d'O. vol. 3, ff. 86–87.

40. Villavicencio, *No sea el bando del gobierno sacarnos del purgatorio y meternos al infierno* (May 1827); El Costeño de Acapulco, *La ejecución de justicia contra el coronel Mangoy* (1827); Un americano enemigo de la esclavitud, *Defensa de los gachupines por los editores del Sol* (May 1827); Espino, *Paño de lágrimas de los gachupines y cebollas a los mexicanos* (June 1827); El mismísimo que no puede ver el Sol ni pintado, *Parabién a la nación y pésame a los coyotes* (May 16, 1827).

41. This commonplace was often repeated by the French minister, for example in his report of January 28, when he reported that Veracruz was "the richest in the federation, and with its own resources it is master of those of the Supreme Government, because it controls the customs house." Martin to Damas, January 5, 1828, Q.d'O. vol. 3, ff. 155–56.

42. Poinsett published a *Defense* against such slander, on July 4; see *El Sol*, July 7, 1827.

43. *El Aguila,* June 12 and 23, 1827.

44. See *El Correo*, July 1, 1827, for Vicente Gómez Farías as a possible candidate, supported by the provincial federalists.

45. Martin to Damas, Nov. 30, 1827, Q.d'O. vol. 3, ff. 137–139.

46. *El Amigo del Pueblo* published five volumes, from Aug. 1, 1827, to Sept. 3, 1828. See issues of Aug. 22, 1827; Sept. 26, 1827 and Feb. 6, 1828; Aug. 15, 1827; Nov. 28, 1827; Aug. 8 and 15, 1827; Aug. 1, 1827, Feb. 27, 1828. For a very outspoken earlier defense of political parties, see also José María Tornel's article in *El Correo*, December 27, 1826.

47. Tornel later claimed to have suspended the publication in order not to stir the fire of factionalism, but he was writing a sort of *apologia pro vita sua.* See his *Manifestación del ciudadano Tornel* (May 10, 1833), p. 4.

48. Both Tornel and Bocanegra were ministers during most of the 1841–44 Santa Anna–dominated period; Tornel continued to support increasingly authoritarian measures under Paredes and the final Santa Anna regime of 1853–55; for the article justifying "armed petitions," see *El Amigo* of December 26, 1827.

49. *Correo,* October 20, 1827.

Chapter 7

1. Soon Rubio passed on the contract to the stronger financial house of Agüero González y Cía. See Embajada Mexicana, Document 3736, letter from José María de Bocanegra, Minister of Relaciones, to Máximo Garro, Minister in Paris, Mexico, December 31, 1843, informing him about the operation. To forestall criticisms from local cotton producers, Rubio took on the obligation of buying up the whole Veracruz crop, arguing that it was not sufficient to satisfy the needs of the textile industry. The government promised not to give other concessions for 1844 and 1845.

2. Rubio had leased the mines in 1835 and bought them in 1842 for over 300,000 pesos; he also wanted the monopoly for salt provisioning in the area, thus provoking the reaction of the other smaller miners, or "denunciadores." See *Comunicados y documentos . . . relativos al ruinoso contrato . . .sobre las salinas del Peñón Blanco.*

3. See Quintana, *Estevan de Antuñano,* who reproduces several of his pamphlets.

4. Bazant, *Antonio Haro y Tamariz.*

5. In Embajada Mexicana, Doc. No. 2606, "Apuntes sueltos," reference is made to Felipe Neri del Barrio's monarchist convictions by early 1829; Mora, *Revista política,* p. 172; Tomás López y Pimentel, *Cálculo de una fábrica de tabaco en Aguas Calientes* (Mexico City, 1837).

6. Randall, *Real del Monte,* pp. 210–12; Gustavo Baz and E. L. Gallo, *Historia del Ferrocarril Mexicano.*

7. Prieto, *Indicaciones sobre el origen* (1851), pp. 217–18; Manuel Payno, *Proyecto de arreglo de gastos de la Hacienda Pública y contribuciones para cubrirlos* (1848); Luis de la Rosa, *Observaciones sobre varios puntos concernientes a la Administracion Pública del Estado de Zacatecas* (1851); J. M. Carranza, *Proyecto de ley de clasificación de rentas de la República Mexicana* (1855).

8. *Lista de los señores vocales de la Sociedad Económica Mexicana de Amigos del País* (March 1822). Already from 1820 the Semanario Político y Literario de Mexico, supported by the Fagoagas, was proposing the formation of a Sociedad Económica de Amigos del País (September 13, 1820). The Iturbidista *La Sabatina Universal* reported on the formation of the society (July 6, 1822).

9. Ortiz, *México considerado como nación independiente y libre*; Embajada Mexicana, doc. nos. 1442, 3427, and 3918; Q.d'O., vol. 3 (1827–28), from A. Martin to Ferronnays, August 25, 1828, ff. 231–34; Ernesto de la Torre Villar, *La labor diplomática de Tadeo Ortiz*; Tarsicio García Díaz, *El pensamiento político, económico y social de Don Tadeo Ortiz de Ayala*; Wilbert H. Timmons, "Tadeo Ortiz, Mexican Emissary Extraordinary," *Hispanic American Historical Review* 51, 3 (Aug. 1971); "Noticias estadísticas del Istmo de Tehuantepec," and "Ventajas de una comunicación oceánica en el istmo americano y preferencia que merece para este objeto el territorio de Tehuantepec sobre los de Panamá y Nicaragua," *El Ateneo Mexicano* (1844).

10. Embajada Mexicana, doc. nos. 1747, 1749–51, 1755–56, 2081, 2093 about the joint declaration; and no. 1582 on the shipping line.

11. Fernández de Lizardi was arguing their case in *Conversaciones*, vol. 2, no. 2, Jan. 19, 1825, complaining that they were being furloughed due to their Iturbidismo (based mostly on their behavior at the helm of affairs in Jalisco, during its revolt from central control in 1823 and 1824).

12. Sims, *La expulsión de los españoles* and *La descolonización en México*; Michael Costeloe, *La Primera República*, p. 106; Martin to Damas, Nov. 30, 1827, Q.d'O., vol. 3, ff. 137–39.

13. In the commission the proposal was promoted by a combination of Yorkinos and former Iturbidistas: Juan José Romero, José Manuel Herrera, Casimiro Liceaga, José María Tornel, Andrés Quintana Roo, and Manuel Crescencio Rejón.

14. See Embajada Mexicana, doc. nos. 2582, 2599, and 2702, all from Murphy (Jan. 5 and April 10, 1828, and May 12, 1829); "Apuntes sueltos," doc. no. 2606, unsigned and undated, but surely by Murphy Jr. and probably from late 1828; doc. nos. 2603 and 2607, of July 6, 1828, and Feb. 19, 1829, from Murphy Jr. to the Mexican Secretary of Relations, and doc. no. 2605, of Feb. 21, 1829, from Murphy to Ouvrard; doc. 2583, from the Mexican Secretary of Relations to Murphy, of December 18, 1828.

15. Martin do Damas, April 10 and 25, 1828, Q.d'O., vol. 3, ff. 177–85; Villavicencio, *Testamento de don Nicolás Bravo* (1828), *El perdón de Bravo no es moco de pavo* (January 16, 1828), and *Concluye el testamento del Sr. Bravo* (January 25, 1828).

16. The legislatures voted for two men, without reference to president

or vice-president, and the one who had the most votes was the winner. The likely result was therefore that the vice-president would be the main rival of the president, not his running mate. This mechanism was based on a failure to recognize the system of political parties as intermediaries in running candidates and on the fiction that the "best" people would be considered for the top position. See reports of the election procedures in Martin to Ferronnays, June 30, 1828, Q.d'O., vol. 3, ff. 202–05; Packenham to Aberdeen, Sept. 26, 1828, FO/50, vol. 45, f. 134.

17. *El Correo de la Federación* published its version of the events in its issue of April 19, 1828. It had already given attention to the subject the year before.

18. Both the newspaper's version, favorable to Zavala, and those of his opponents, the subprefecto and the juez de letras of Tenancingo, coincide in describing the role of the militias. See *El Correo*, April 17, 18, and 19, 1828. The judge gave an ampler report of the events in *Documentos que manifiestan la conducta que observó el ciudadano lic. Miguel Macedo* (May 15, 1828).

19. Robert W. Randall, *Real del Monte: A British Mining Venture in Mexico*, ch. 7; Torcuato S. Di Tella, "Las huelgas en la minería mexicana, 1826–1828."

20. Letter from Tindal to Packenham, August 27, 1827, including a note by Vetch to the alcalde and the answer by the juez de letras. FO/50 vol. 35, ff. 282–86.

21. Letter from Packenham to the Foreign Office, July 24, 1827, in FO/50, vol. 34, ff. 318–22v.

22. The ayuntamientos of Jalapa and Orizaba were induced by Santa Anna to put pressure on the Veracruz state congress, which had an anti-Guerrero majority, to ask the national congress to invalidate the votes in favor of Gómez Pedraza (the president was elected by the state legislatures, each one having two votes). On September 12, 1828, Santa Anna openly declared himself against the government, and three days later he seized a silver conducta taking government funds to Jalapa.

23. Letter from Tindal to Packenham, August 26, 1828 (ff. 15–16), and September 19 (ff. 17–17v.), included in Packenham's report to the Foreign Office, FO/50, vol. 45, ff. 1–17v. From mid-September there were war actions against Santa Anna, which at first were successful and forced Santa Anna to abandon Veracruz and withdraw toward Oaxaca.

24. Randall, *Real del Monte*, pp. 142–43.

25. See Moisés González Navarro, *La anatomía del poder en México, 1848–1853*, pp. 197–205; Di Tella, "Las huelgas en la minería," pp. 605–08.

26. The British chargé in Mexico already knew the unofficial results of the legislatures' votes by mid-September and communicated them to London. FO/50, vol. 45, f. 134.

27. On April 19, 1828, *El Aguila* reported the Vetagrande events, quoting an unnamed member of the Zacatecas legislature, who said that "the loss is a *friolera*, but these situations make us lose our credit, and are due to the Englishmen's lack of knowledge, due to the fact that every month there are new directors. Each one wants to innovate according to his whim and [following] the advice of those who are seeking better jobs." On April 23 it referred again to the subject, copying an article from the *Correo de Zacatecas*, which predicted that "if the English do not soften up their rules, if they do not adapt to the country's customs, troubles will not cease."

28. Letter of April 11, 1828, from Kerrison to his superior in the company, Charles Tindal, then resident in Real del Monte, where he had been promoted from his earlier post in Zacatecas. FO/50, vol. 43, ff. 160–65.

29. FO/50, vol. 43, ff. 150–51.

30. *El Correo de la Federación* on April 20 rebuked the enemies of liberty, who exaggerated any event so as to show that the country was in anarchy; it explained that in Vetagrande "the workers . . . were forced to protest as a body the fraud committed against them" and that things took a turn for the worse "due to the Englishmen's indiscretion." *El Sol*, moderate liberal and generally favorable to foreign investors, also criticized in its April 27 edition the excessively rigid attitude adopted by some administrators of the company, taking them to be responsible for the turn of events.

31. *El Correo de la Federación*, April 27, 1828.

32. Alex Martin, reflecting in his dispatches the views usual among moderate circles in Mexico, had the worst impression of Espinosa, to whose bad advice he attributed Iturbide's downfall; he believed Cañedo to be an enlightened and moderate man, but apt to suffer excesses of instability; the displaced Ramos Arizpe was "a man of *esprit*, learning, intrigue, and experience," who had attracted the wrath of the Yorkinos due to his ability; as for Pedraza, Martin was disappointed by what he thought to be his betrayal of the moderate cause. In fact, though, Pedraza was starting a strategy of convergence with the moderates, weaning the more amenable types from among the Yorkinos and the federalists. Martin to Damas, March 25, 1828, Q.d'O., vol. 3, ff.170–73.

33. See José María Alpuche e Infante, *Manifestación . . . de su conducta pública en la cámara en la elección de presidente celebrada en favor de Don Vicente Guerrero* (Sept. 16, 1830). When news about Pedraza's victory were confirmed, Alpuche foresaw trouble due to the confrontation the new president would have with "the people and the army united" (p. 5).

34. A detailed report of these events is found in Bustamante, *Continuación del Cuadro Histórico*, vol. 3.

35. *El Aguila*, September 14, 1828; *El Correo*, Sept. 22, 1828; Bustamante, *Continuación del Cuadro Histórico*, vol. 3, p. 186. The terms

"democratic" and "popular" were used almost as synonyms by many observers in those days to refer to the radical party. Martin to Damas, January 25 and March 15, 1827, Q.d'O., vol. 3, ff. 17–18 and 32–33.

36. José María Tornel y Mendívil, *Manifestación*; *El Correo*, Jan. 14, 1829.

37. He had been made marqués de la Cadena by the emperor, but the title was revoked immediately after the overthrow of the monarchy. Before the end of the Acordada revolt, he changed his mind and gave himself up to the government. See Alamán, *Historia* de Méjico, vol. 5, p. 777, and José María Tornel y Mendívil, *Breve reseña histórica de los acontecimientos más notables de la Nación Mexicana*, pp. 383–84. A Luis Velázquez de la Cadena, born in 1796, probably related to José Manuel, was administrator of the comunidades de indios of Tlatelolco and Tenochtitlan from 1835 to 1849, which may give an idea of the family's sensitivity to opinion among the lower orders. See Lira, *Comunidades indígenas*, pp. 90–95; Guillermo Porras Muñoz, "La calle de la Cadena en México," in *Estudios de Historia Novohispana* 5:143–91.

38. Tornel, *Manifestación* (May 10, 1833), p. 13, and *Breve reseña histórica*, pp.382–95; Silvia M. Arrom, "Popular Politics in Mexico City: The Parián Riot, 1828." *Hispanic American Historical Review* 68, 2 (May 1988).

39. Martin to Ferronnays, June 30, 1828, Q.d'O, vol. 3, ff. 202–05. The French representative remarked on the number of enlightened and patriotic people who shared this attitude, which he thought was wrong.

40. José Ignacio Basadre, a prominent Yorkino from Veracruz, who had become Guerrero's secretary in the War ministry and remained as the dominant figure in that office, sent a letter to Filisola, prominently displayed in *El Correo* (January 6, 1829), in which he treated him in a very friendly way and tried to persuade him to join the lights of the century and accept the new authorities. To this Filisola first answered that he did not see any light in a general pillage nor in forcing constitutional proceedings, but later on acknowledged the inevitable, in order to avoid worse results. Meanwhile the rebellious Puebla cívicos had sacked a conducta that was about to leave for the coast (*El Correo*, Jan. 11, 1829). See also Bustamante, *Voz de la Patria* 3:13, and *Continuación del Cuadro Histórico* 3:217.

41. The editors of *El Correo* (Zavala and Gondra among them) were forgetting that Zavala had been a collaborator of the emperor for much longer. Involved in the same condemnation as turncoats from the ranks of progressive liberalism were José Ramón Pacheco Leal, Juan Tames, and Vicente Romero, who had been joined by the pamphleteer Rafael Dávila. See *El Correo*, Jan. 8 and 23, 1829.

42. *El Correo*, January 12, 1829.

43. On January 6, 1829, the Jalisco legislature, which was ending its term, issued a report explaining that it had sent an offer to the neighbor-

ing states to organize a defensive league under a single military command (*El Correo*, Jan. 23, 1829). In Zacatecas a similar attitude had been dominant, but in January the newly elected governor, Francisco García, acknowledged that the measures adopted were unjustified (*El Correo*, Jan. 11, 1829). San Luis had refused from the outset to take part in such a coalition (*El Correo*, Jan. 3, 1829). Later on in 1829, another league was attempted under the leadership of Jalisco, to prepare for defense against the Spanish invasion, but it also was short-lived.

44. Pedraza had proffered his resignation of the presidency in the knowledge that the Senate, where he had a majority, would not accept it. The lower house thus was led to ignore the resignation and pursue a legal strategy by stating that Pedraza was incapable of exercising the presidency and that it had been wrong for many legislatures to vote for him, flaunting national opinion.

45. Bustamante, *Continuación del Cuadro Histórico*, vol. 3, pp. 221–26, 229. According to Villavicencio, the author of the tract was Juan Bautista Escalante, attorney for various Indian comunidades in the capital. See his *Octava función de maroma en casa de Doña Prudencia de Mendiola* (1829), in *The Political Pamphlets*, vol. 3, pp. 993–1017, and Bustamante, *Voz de la Patria*, vol. 3, no. 16 (Aug. 4, 1830).

46. For some examples, see *El Correro*, Jan. 2, 4, and 31, 1829, where the displaced Cañedo was scorned as being the source of "disposiciones antinacionales," or the Veracruz government said to be in the hands of a "facción anti-nacional." The references to Iturbide were somewhat ambivalent, but usually highly respectful: "always memorable emperor and general" (Jan. 28), "the hero of Iguala" (Jan. 23), while condemning his hangers-on and sycophants, such as Antonio Terán and Carlos Montes de Oca. In a long series on public credit (probably by Zavala), a cryptic comment states (Jan. 6) that at the inception of independence, the country was in the very expert hands of two people, one in charge of politics and the other of its wealth, presumably Iturbide and Rafael Pérez Maldonado, an old "haciendista" from Jalisco, who had many years' experience in the viceregal administration and was minister of hacienda from independence until mid-1822. Concerning the latter, by contrast, Carlos María de Bustamante says that he was "*chocho*" and as such opposed the abdication of Iturbide until the very end (*Diario*, vol. 1, p. 195). For Zavala's attempt at removing himself from Guerrero, see his *Manifiesto*.

47. Tornel, in a later pamphlet explaining his participation in the events, said that with some foresight one might have predicted a bad end to the new government, given the very contradictory elements included, of whom he spoke well only of Bocanegra. Tornel, *Manifestación*, p. 27.

48. Bustamante, *Voz de la Patria*, vol. 3, no. 19 (Aug. 18, 1830); *El Correo*, Jan. 1, 5, and 28, 1829, and Villavicencio, *Décima función de*

maroma, in *The Political Pamphlets,* vol. 3, pp. 1039–56. Deputy José Domínguez is wrongly referred to in the index of Bustamante's *Continuación del Cuadro Histórico,* vol. 3, as José Miguel Domínguez (p. 469), the former Corregidor of Querétaro, who in fact was at the time a member of the Supreme Court and more usually known as Miguel Domínguez.

49. However, the Senate finally discharged him from any blame, as a result of the able defense by the Iturbidista lawyer (also judge and industrialist) José Manuel Zozaya Bermúdez. See Tornel, *Manifestación,* p. 11. The attitude of the Yorkinos toward Bustamante is reflected in several tracts by the Pensador and the Payo, who had words of praise for him, due to his association with Iturbide and his being an alternative military pole to the one formed by the Escoceses and their colaborators. See Villavicencio's *Testamento de la República Mexicana por la presidencia del Sr. Gómez Pedraza* (Aug. 16, 1828), where after condemning a long list of Escoceses and Pedrazistas, he urges Zavala, Bustamante, Quintanar, and Filisola to join Guerrero and his *pintos* and hang the *soleros.*

50. Guerrero, *Manifiesto del ciudadano Vicente Guerrero* (April 1, 1829).

51. Napoleon was during those days often invoked by the Payo. In addition to putting him in the same category as Washington, Bolívar, and Iturbide, he quoted his saying that "the interests of the State must sooner or later overcome petty passions," a jejune enough statement, which might have been put in anybody else's mouth. See his *Grandes bailes y maromas en casa de doña Prudencia de Mendiola: Diálogo 3° entre ésta y D. Antonio* (1829), in *The Political Pamphlets* 3:1163–75. Other words of wisdom were put in verse form: "Hay muchos que maldicen la opresión/ porque oprimir no pueden—Napoleón," in *Grandes bailes: Diálogo 1°,* pp. 1135–51, p. 1147.

52. Rafael Dávila, the noted anti-Iturbidista pamphleteer of Yorkino sympathies (until before the Acordada), who had now become an oppositionist, hinted later in the year, through one of his invented characters (a scarcely Spanish-speaking Indian) that if "Pretendiente" Guerrero were not careful, minister "Perrera" (Herrera) might occasion him some grief with "el Iturbidito" (Iturbide's son, whose return to the country had been solicited by the Payo since 1827 and had been again proposed unsuccessfully by Domínguez in early 1829). See Rafael Dávila, "Siguen las hijas del Cojo retozando en el Parián," published in September 1829 and reprinted as *Diálogo 3°* of *El Toro,* vol. 1 (1830).

53. Wyllie, *México: Noticia sobre su Hacienda Pública;* Murphy Jr. to De Launnay, July 21, 1830, Embajada Mexicana, doc. no. 3658, explaining later changes in the above legislation; "Analyse de la correspondance du Consul de France au Mexique 1826–29," Q.d'O., Fonds Divers, vol. 40, Amérique, Mémoires et Documents: Mexique 1826–29, ff. 4–23 (see esp. ff. 19–20); Bustamante, *Continuación del Cuadro Histórico* 3:293.

54. Costeloe, *Primera República,* p. 231, gives examples of rates as high as 200 or 500 percent or more per year. See Bazant, *Historia de la deuda exterior,* and Tenenbaum, *México en la época de los agiotistas.*

55. Bocanegra, *Memorias* 1:543–52. Zavala, however, proceeded soon afterwards, in conjunction with Antonio Mejía, to sell most of those lands to an American company, which was illegal and set him on the course that ended up in his participating in Texas's independence.

56. See *El Correo,* Jan. 11 and 28, 1828, the latter with an address by Lucas Balderas to his artilleros, to whom he promised that some would remain on duty, thus giving permanent employment to the more needy ones.

57. *American Annual Register for the Years 1829–1830,* p. 220.

58. Ramón Gamboa, *Representación . . . al Ayuntamiento* (August 3, 1829); Charles W. Macune, Jr., *El Estado de México y la Federación Mexicana,* pp. 166–67.

59. Tornel, *Manifestación* (May 10, 1833).

60. Bocanegra, *Memorias* 2:39; Bustamante, *Continuación* 3:291.

61. Bocanegra, *Memorias* 2:40–42; Bustamante, *Continuación* 3:293.

62. Bustamante, *Continuación* 3:324; Bocanegra, *Memorias* 2:120–31. During the attempted resistance, Severiano Quesada, one of the civic and popular leaders, was assasinated. Alamán argues that Esteva, despite his official position, was no longer trying to organize any resistance, but rather favored Quintanar's pronunciamiento by reducing his vigilance. Alamán does not really support this assertion with any evidence except his own statement that Esteva sent an aide reporting on the situation and urging him to act quickly. See his *Historia* 5:783, 976–81.

63. Packenham to Aberdeen, Nov. 2, 1828, FO/50, vol. 45, ff. 228–32.

Chapter 8

1. Costeloe, *Primera República,* pp. 251, 257–62, 265–69; Manuel Posadas, *Alegato de defensa . . . del Sr. diputado D. José María Alpuche e Infante* (1830).

2. In "Copie d'une note remise par M. le Cnel Schmaltz," New Orleans, May 5, 1824, in Q.d'O., vol. 2, ff. 245–47. Rafael Mangino was described as a pro-French and pro-Spanish monarchist.

3. Murphy Jr. to De Launnay, July 21, 1830, Embajada Mexicana, doc. no. 3658, informing him of the exceptions enacted in May 1830 to the prohibitive law of May 22, 1829.

4. Murphy Jr. to Secretary of Relations, August 11 and November 27, 1830, Embajada Mexicana, doc. nos. 2280 and 2304. Alamán himself, bowing to the spirit of the times, thought that the initial French liberal revolution was commendable and that it would be a pity if the new devel-

opments "discredited the wondrous July revolution and the principles it had imposed"; Alamán to Murphy Jr., April 6, 1831, doc. no. 4504.

5. Bustamante, *Voz de la Patria* 3, 20 (Aug. 21, 1830).

6. Alamán to Murphy Jr., October 6, 1831, Embajada Mexicana, doc. no. 4519.

7. See *Dictámenes de los ciudadanos síndicos* (1830), a report mainly written by the well-known jurist Manuel Gamboa, who concluded that nonnaturalized foreigners could only practice trade after ten years' residence (according to Spanish law).

8. Alamán to Murphy Jr., March 27, 1830, Embajada Mexicana, doc. no. 3575. In fact it took more than ten years for the subject to be reactivated, during the Santa Anna regime of 1841–44. See Alley de Cipreye to Guizot, April 23, 1843, and April 25, 1844, in Q.d'O., vol. 24, f. 15, and vol. 26, ff. 189–93; in the latter the French representative was prepared to use the prohibition of retail trade (if it had been enacted, which it was not) as an issue for armed intervention.

9. Bustamante, *Continuación del Cuadro Histórico* 4:11–17; Vicente Rocafuerte, "Ensayo sobre la tolerancia religiosa" (1831), in *Colección Rocafuerte*, vol. 7.

10. Bustamante, *Continuación del Cuadro Histórico* 4:24–27, 28–29. For Inclán's role as a moderate Yorkino trying to control excesses in the Acordada, see Tornel y Mendívil, *Breve reseña*, p. 385, and Bustamante, *Voz de la Patria* 3, 10; for his later "voltereta," supporting the revolt against the Bustamante regime that would bring back his old political friend Pedraza, see Bustamante, *Continuación del Cuadro Histórico* 4:66, and *O auxiliamos al gobierno o la patria se va al infierno, tercera parte* (October 30, 1832).

11. Vicente Rocafuerte, *Consideraciones generales sobre la bondad de un gobierno* (1831); Jaime Rodríguez O., *The Emergence of Spanish America*; Lucas Alamán, *Un regalo de año nuevo para el Sr. Rocafuerte* (1832).

12. Joseph Welsh, the British consul at Veracruz, was quite sympathetic to the rebel general's cause and was reprimanded by the British representative in Mexico. See his reports, from January 5 to February 25, 1832, in FO/50, vol. 77, ff. 15–69. He emphasized Santa Anna's popularity among the country people and his capacity to rely on the jarochos, or "cossacks" (ff. 19, 26, 49v, 51, 53v, 59–60, 66–67, 69).

13. According to General Mier y Terán, local merchants favored the uprising because it was an opportunity to pay off their arrears with the customs at a high discount. He thought the British were also part of this and had produced a newspaper, written in English and Spanish, *La Gazeta de Tampico*, especially to this effect. Writing to Estevan Moctezuma on March 21, 1832, he denounced the paper as a "hotbed of anarchy," and

the rebels' object the formation of a dictatorship under Santa Anna, with the argument that Mexico "could only be a Republic if first it is regenerated by an arbitrary power." See copy of his letter in a report by the English consul in Tampico, Joseph Crawford, FO/50, vol. 77, ff. 129–31, of April 16, 1832, and of the newspaper, in FO/50, vol. 77, ff. 121v–23.

14. Bustamante, *Continuación del Cuadro Histórico* 4:65–68.

15. Bustamante, *Continuación del Cuadro Histórico* 4:84. Cuesta was in fact arbitrating between the progressive liberal government of José Ignacio Cañedo y Arróniz (a relation of Juan de Dios Cañedo) and the populist opposition led by Juan José Tames. An anonymous letter of August 14, 1832, in the Gómez Farías archive, describes the disturbances accompanying the elections in Guadalajara in 1832 and reports that Tames held a position similar to that of Guerrero in 1828. See "A un amigo," VGF Archive, Y58, F44A 77.

16. Bustamante, *Voz de la Patria*, 3, 19 and 20 (Aug. 18 and 21, 1830), referring to Febr. 1829.

17. See letter from General Juan Morales (a friend and a reputed representative of Francisco García) to García, Mexico, August 11, 1832, in VGF Archive, Y57, F44A 76.

18. Bustamante, *Continuación del Cuadro Histórico* 4:86.

19. The uprising on the outskirts of the capital was led by one "General Alcachofa" and a certain Espinosa, as reported by Bustamante, *Continuación del Cuadro Histórico* 4:97–98. Bustamante usually refers to General Miguel Cervantes y Velasco, marqués de Salvatierra (also marqués de Salinas) as Miguel Salvatierra, probably reflecting a common usage.

20. *O auxiliamos al gobierno, o la patria va al infierno*, pp. 609–11, 618, 623, and 628–29. For the need to leave the regular troops free to face the enemy, relieving them from the maintenance of internal order, which should be entrusted to a hastily recruited militia led by the more solid sectors of the population, see pp. 630–32.

21. Carlos María de Bustamante, *El peligro ya se acerca, y nosotros lo llamamos* (1832), pp. 645–55; *Reflecsiones sobre el manifiesto de D. Anastasio Bustamante dado en 14 de agosto de 1832* (1832); also in *Catalogue of Mexican Pamphlets*.

22. See letters from Pedraza and from Ramos Arizpe to Gómez Farías, from Puebla, December 1832; VGF Archive, Y75–77, F44A 66, 85–86. For Parres, see Chávez, *Iturbide*, p. 130. In fact there were some tensions between García and Gómez Farías, the latter being the leader of the more "avanzado" party in the state, which tried to install him as governor, replacing García in 1832. García was able to thwart the maneuver, and he recounted it to his colleague José Urrea, of Durango. Urrea sent a copy of the correspondence to Gómez Farías, with less than saintly motiva-

tions. See Francisco García to José Urrea, Zacatecas, Dec. 1, 1832, and Urrea to Garcia, Durango, Dec. 7, 1832 (copies), in VGF Archive, Y71–72, F44A 10–11.

23. Tornel y Mendívil, *Manifestación*, p. 58; Ana María Huarte de Iturbide, *Representaciones . . . al Supremo Poder Legislativo de los Estados Unidos Mexicanos* (March 1, 1833). The previous year her attorney Gómez Navarrete had published an *Exposición promoviendo el cumplimiento del decreto de la Junta Soberana Gubernativa de 21 de febrero de 1822* (April 1832), detailing his demands for payment of the million pesos and the twenty leagues in Texas granted by the first Congress to the Liberator. The answer then had been that the million pesos were to be given in real estate from the Inquisition, but as this had already been sold, it was necessary to wait for better times for any payment to be made. Meanwhile they decided to increase the pension given to the widow. Now the latter recalled the whole story and more concretely demanded that her pension actually be paid. She also added that Iturbide's name was no longer divisive, and her sons had been educated "in democracy," so their exile should be terminated. Finally she was legally allowed to return to Mexico with her family, but she was asked by the envoy to the United States, Joaquín M. del Castillo y Lanzas, not to use that right. She answered that she needed to remain in the United States and would think of returning only if the government did not pay her pension, which was necessary for the education of her children. See Ana M. H. de Iturbide to Gómez Farías, Philadelphia, Feb. 24, 1834, in VGF Archive, Y281, F45, 251.

24. *La Verdad Desnuda*, Feb. 27 and March 6, 13, and 16, 1833.

25. *El Mono*, March 26, 1833. The editor also wondered whether the armed forces would tolerate being led by a provincial quack who would surely fly at the first confrontation, like his friend Bocanegra had done while provisional president at the end of the Guerrero regime.

26. Carlos García to Gómez Farías, Puebla, May 12, 1833, VGF Archive, Y113, F44A 44. In Spanish "hacer la cama," at least in present-day usage, means to prepare a snare for someone to fall into. The exact words were "prepararle una cama, a más de aquella en que pensamos." Admittedly other interpretations are also possible. For Carlos García's Iturbidista connections, see his letter of farewell to the exile, from Puebla, April 12, 1823, in HyD doc. no. 1647; the letters to him from Minister José Manuel Herrera, May 19 and 21, 1822, announcing the proclamation of the empire and urging him to prepare a celebration, in Archive of Carlos García, Genaro García Collection, University of Texas Library; and the letter from José Antonio Gutiérrez de Lara, Padilla, July 28, 1824, regretting the death of their "hero," in the same collection.

27. VGF Archive, Y226, F63 4720, diploma of Oct. 26, 1833.

28. *El Fénix,* August 27, 1833; it was answered by the *La Columna,* making a *racconto* of the early common struggles of both papers in the "causa nacional" and promising to ignore its rival in the future.

29. *La Columna,* Nov. 4, 1833.

30. See *Ocursos de los acreedores* (1835); *Documentos que demuestran la justicia de los ocursos hechos por los acreedores al Peaje de Veracruz* (1835). The loans had been contracted in 1807, and though the consulado had been extinguished, the mortgage was still valid, and the decision to award the contract without passing on the responsibility for repayment was deemed illegal. It was also argued that the contract with Garay had been arranged by Relaciones and not by Hacienda, as it should have been. The problem is recounted in *Exposición que la Junta de Peajes del Camino de Toluca a Veracruz hizo al Sr. Presidente de la República* (1852), in *Proposiciones para la derogación del decreto del 31 de Mayo de 1842* (1849), and in Empresa del Camino de Toluca a Morelia, *Informe que la Junta Directiva de esta empresa dió a la General de Accionistas* (1850–55).

31. The expulsion list included most Escocés notables, plus Anastasio Bustamante and some well-known Iturbidistas such as Juan Nepomuceno Gómez Navarrete, Carlos Beneski, and José Domínguez Manso.

32. Packenham to Palmerston, June 11, 1833, FO/50 vol. 79, ff. 241–46; see also Mora, *Revista Política,* pp. 48–49.

33. Costeloe, *Primera República,* p. 395. The pro–Santa Anna *La Lima de Vulcano* referred to this coalition, declaring it anticonstitutional, in its issue of May 24, 1834, soon after Santa Anna's takeover and ouster of Gómez Farías.

34. Costeloe, *Primera República,* pp. 359–60, 374, 380.

35. Costeloe, *Primera República,* p. 379.

36. *El Monitor del Pueblo,* July 10, 1833.

37. *El Fénix* strongly supported Bocanegra and Carlos García, both of whom apparently were reluctant to accompany Gómez Farías in his last effort at mobilizing all possible sources of support in a radical program of reform. See the issues between Dec. 15 and 31, 1833, on Bocanegra, and of Dec. 15 on Carlos García.

38. Juan José del Corral later published a series of articles on this subject in *La Lima de Vulcano,* a pro–Santa Anna conservative-liberal paper (Oct. 9 to Nov. 4, 1834). Garay maintained a long-standing relation with Gómez Farías, concerning money matters. Already in March 1833 he was advancing him some funds, which he later collected from the vice-president's salaries (VGF Archive, Y362, 349–50; F45 327, 313–14). He was instrumental in collecting friends' donations to help finance the exile's trip abroad in 1835 (Y383, F45 347) and had interviews with President Barragán to stop local authorities' harrassment of Gómez Farías (Y394–96, F45 357–59). During the latter's exile in New

Orleans, Garay sent funds, partly his and partly from a group of friends (Y449, 457, F45 401, 411, both of 1837). In 1840, after the failed revolt led by Gómez Farías in Mexico City, Garay again collected funds (Y700, 893, 896, 907, F47A 623, 747, 750, 760). He also took care of repairing and renting the vice-president's house in Mixcoac between 1840 and 1845 (Y911, 914, 923, 1240–42, 1253, 1257, F47B 764, 768, F65B 5227, F48 1066–67, 1073, 1079, 1086). No wonder Gómez Farías was very concerned about his benefactor's apparently serious illness in 1842 (Y1038, 47B 871). When Gómez Farías returned in triumph in 1846, he offered a position in the government to Garay, but the latter could not accept, because he had to face a meeting of creditors and could not set his mind to anything else (Y1784, F50 1724).

    39. *El Fénix,* Jan. 4, 1834.

    40. David W. Walker, *Kinship, Business, and Politics,* p. 219; *Eco de Yucatán en México* (July 17 to August 7, 1829).

    41. Carlos María de Bustamante did not like him and had been particularly incensed at his defense of a common thief who had stolen a sacred chalice from a church (*Continuación del Cuadro Histórico* 4:48), a subject he took up with Congress.

    42. Mora, *Revista Política,* p. 139.

    43. Santangelo was for a while lodged by Mejia, who also helped him install a new school. See a copy of Santangelo's letter to *El Fénix,* in *La Columna,* Oct. 9, 1833, and his rejection of the slander in *La Columna,* Nov. 30, 1833.

    44. See *La Lima de Vulcano,* August 12, 1834.

    45. See VGF Archive, Y271, F62 5034, anonymous letter to the vice-president, Febr. 5, 1834, from Puebla, denouncing the plot and signaling González Angulo, Gómez Pedraza, Bocanegra, Quintana Roo, Carlos García, General Herrera, and Tornel y Mendívil as taking part in it. A few weeks earlier an obscure resident of Huajuapan, self-defined as a ranchero and signing himself Carlos García (obviously not the minister of the same name), had warned Gómez Farías that the Bourbonists, centralists, "apostólicos," and Escoceses were preparing to assassinate both the president and the vice-president. See VGF Archive, Y 242, F63 4715, letter from a certain Carlos García to Gómez Farías, Dec. 18, 1833.

    46. See *Lista de los hombres de bien que tiene la República Mexicana* (1827), a Yorkino tract despite its title; and letter from Lombardo to Murphy Jr., Mexico, Feb. 8, 1834, Embajada Mexicana, doc. no. 5879.

    47. Zerecero, *Memorias,* p. 62.

    48. *La Lima de Vulcano,* August 10, 1834.

    49. Costeloe, *Primera República,* pp. 432–33. Francisco García, however, would soon turn against Santa Anna, when the centralist constitutional legislation known as the Siete Leyes began to be elaborated, militia

strength severely limited, and a military force sent to the provinces under the command of Santa Anna.

50. Miguel Barragán, a real nullity in politics and religion, according to the French legation, came from a very influential family in San Luis Potosí. See Montejano y Aguiñaga, *El Valle del Maíz*; Q.d'O., vol. 10, Baron Deffaudis to Achille Broglie, March 3, 1836, ff. 36–39.

51. Packenham to Wellington, Mexico, June 2, 1835, with extract of letter from Zacatecas to O'Gorman, FO/50, vol. 92, ff. 163–69; and June 25, ff. 201–02v, reporting the intensification of anti-British feelings. The British minister reported that now Santa Anna was ruling with the clear support of the "powerful party [of] the Clergy and wealthy classes of the community." May 1, 1835, FO/50, vol. 92, ff. 71–75. See also Josefina Z. Vázquez, "Iglesia, ejército y centralismo," *Historia Mexicana* 39, no. 153 (July–Sept. 1989), where the power and influence of the church in the formation of governments in Mexico during these years are said to be less than usually assumed.

52. Packenham to Wellington, Mexico, July 28, 1835, FO/50, vol. 92, ff. 268–70. The *Enciclopedia de los Sans Culottes,* which appeared between March and May 1835, defined a series of words with humor and implicit ideology. Thus Zacatecans were defined as devils, the south (from Tlalpan to Zacatula) as heretic, plebeyan as "an honorific title." When it reported news about the Zacatecan disaster, it appeared with a black margin, and under "necrology" announced the decease of two thousand honest citizens. After expressing its desire for vengeance and the horror inspired by the "holiest grandmother of Jesus" it ceased publication, claiming to be ready to face the dungeons, where its colleagues already lay.

53. Packenham to Palmerston, Mexico, November 19, 1835. FO/50, vol. 93, ff. 163–65.

54. Baron Deffaudis to Duc de Broglie, Mexico, January 2, 1836, Q.d'O., vol. 10, ff.4–7.

55. *El Momo,* a satirical Yorkino paper, defended itself from this accusation (August 4, 1838).

56. Beginning in 1837 some federalists had been trying to exploit tensions within the ruling majority, attempting to draw Bustamante into the federalist camp. It must be recalled that Bustamante, as an Iturbidista, had been an early member of the Yorkino lodges and retained friends and sympathies in them, despite his betrayals. See *Bustamante y Federación: Esto pide la Nación* (1837). As a result of these maneuvers, José María Bocanegra was brought into the cabinet between the end of October 1837 and February 1838, first in Relaciones and then in Hacienda. In the latter ministry, he was replaced by Manuel Gorostiza, a very adaptable federalist.

57. *El Cosmopolita,* Aug. 22, 1838.

58. *El Momo*, Aug. 25 and Sept. 1, 1838.

59. Juan Rodríguez Puebla, "Tres días de ministerio," in *El Cosmopolita*, Dec. 19, 1838. He was answered by an anonymous *Verdadera noticia de los tres días de ministerio* (1839). See also Bustamante, *El gabinete*, vol. 1, pp. 145–50; Juan Ortiz Escamilla, "El pronunciamiento federalista de Gordiano Guzmán, 1837–1842." *Historia Mexicana* 38, no. 150 (Oct.–Dec. 1988).

60. Bustamante, *El gabinete* 2:62–81.

61. Letter from "Juan" to Gómez Farías, Mexico, October 10, 1837, where he says he visited the president and tried to convince him that he was "seriously vulnerable unless he confronted or even led the forces that threatened our social mechanism." VGF Archive, Y 467, F45 419.

62. "Verdadero pronunciamiento del Gral Santa Anna," *El Vigía*, 2 (no date, late Sept. or early Oct. 1841, by context).

63. "Acta patriótica, adicional a la celebrada el día 30 de setiembre, para restablecer la Constitución Federal," *Boletín Oficial*, Oct. 2, 1841. There was also an untitled Acta, beginning "En la ciudad de México, a los treinta días del mes de setiembre de 1841, reunidos los ciudadanos que abajo firman, pidieron al Sr. Prefecto del Centro se sirviese oirles la franca manifestación de su fe política . . . ," signed by a large number of rather unknown people, some of them representing "veinte individuos que no saben firmar," or "los comerciantes del barrio de San Pablo," and including one Félix Marcha, probably a relative of the sergeant. José María Barrera acted as secretary of this meeting, the record of which was published as a separate leaflet. See also Bustamante, *El gabinete* 2:180–84, 206–15; Costeloe, "The Triangular Revolt in Mexico and the Fall of Anastasio Bustamante," *Journal of Latin American Studies* 20, 2 (1988); Frías, *Pío Marcha*.

64. *Boletín de la Ciudadela*, no. 15, Oct. 1, 1841; *Diálogo: Un cívico y su compadre* (early October 1841, by context).

65. For the Bases de Tacubaya, see *Boletín Oficial* (Sept. 29, 1841), and *El Observador Judicial y de Legislación* 1, 1 (Feb. 17, 1842).

66. Prieto, *Indicaciones*.

67. Alleye de Ciprey to Guizot, Mexico, June 21 and August 28, 1843, and January 27 and March 30, 1844, Q.d'O., vol. 24, ff. 146–52, 161–64, and 305–08; and vol. 26, ff. 38–43 and 166–67.

68. On March 18, 1844, Alleye de Ciprey reported to Guizot that "Mexico is in such a situation that it requires European intervention and makes it very likely to succeed . . . But things should not be done halfway, an army is necessary, and in it acclimatized Havana soldiers, if possible, should be included." In an attached "Mémoire sur la situation du Mexique, Mars 1844," he added that only an absolutist monarchy would be capable of overcoming the resistances that were widespread in the country. Q.d'O., vol. 26, ff. 166–87.

69. Gómez Farías to Rejón, New Orleans, Nov. 19, 1844, and Rejón to Farías, Havana, Sept. 7 and Nov. 13, 1845, VGF Archive, Y1204, 1385 and 1449, F47B 1027, F48 1225 and 1069. In his letters Rejón, exiled in Cuba together with Basadre and Santa Anna, claimed not to have been responsible for the last-minute closure of Congress and that he was accompanied in the ministry by three other trusted federalists (Basadre in War, Trigueros or Haro y Tamariz in Hacienda, and Baranda in Justicia). In fact, soon enough after the short interludes of the moderate Herrera and the conservative Paredes (a total of one year and a half), the Gómez Farías–Bocanegra–Rejón entente was reconstituted (by mid-1846), with the purpose of using (at the cost of being used by) Santa Anna.

70. Bustamante, *Apuntes para la historia del gobierno del general D. Antonio López de Santa Anna*, pp. 362-65.

71. Ibid., p. 365.

72. *Archivo del General Paredes*; see letters from Arista to Paredes, Monterrey, July 13 and 26 and August 26, 1845, pp. 547, 557-58, 585-86.

73. Teófilo Romero to Paredes, Guanajuato, July 7 and Sept. 29, 1845, *Archivo del General Paredes*, pp. 542-44, 615-16.

74. Agustín Suárez Peredo, Mexico, Oct. 1, 1845, Pánfilo Galindo, Guadalajara, Oct. 7, 1845, and Donato Manterola, Mexico, Oct. 8, 1845, all to Paredes; *Archivo del General Paredes*, pp. 617, 624-26, 628.

75. Fray Manuel de San Juan Crisóstomo to Paredes, Mexico, Oct. 7, 1845, in *Archivo del General Paredes*, pp. 626-27.

76. Farías to Paredes, Mexico, Oct. 4, 1845, asking him to reply to a fictitious name, *Archivo del General Paredes*, pp. 621-22. Apparently Paredes responded to these advances, or made others on his own initiative, but Gómez Farías did not set much store on this extremely contradictory alliance. In December he was telling Rejón that a revolution against the Herrera government was necessary, but he was referring to the one planned by Rejón with Basadre and Santa Anna from Cuba, which would break out the following year (and then against Paredes); he informed his friend that attempts were being made to involve him in "another revolution," but to no avail. Farías to Rejón, Mexico, Dec. 1845, VGF Archive, Y1471, F48 1352.

77. José María Tornel to Paredes, Mexico, Oct. 15, 1845, *Archivo del General Paredes*, pp. 634-35; anonymous letter to Paredes, Oct. 14, 1845. For the two types of militia formed during 1845, see Pedro Santoni, "A Fear of the People: The Civic Militia of Mexico in 1845," *Hispanic American Historic Review* 68, 2 (May 1988), especially pp. 282-87.

78. Bustamante, *El nuevo Bernal Díaz del Castillo* 1:21-25, describes one attempt at mobilizing the barrios and some cívicos by pro–Santa Anna and federalist agitators in June 1845, which almost succeeded in imprisoning President Herrera.

79. For some indications of Gómez Farías's and his friends' antagonism toward Pedraza and the "filósofos" (as his friends the moderado
intellectuals were called), see letters from Farías to José Arteaga, Mexico,
Oct. 10, 1846, and from Manuel Doblado to Farías, Guanajuato, Oct.
19, 1846; VGF Archive, Y1970 and 2003, F51 1940 and 1988.

80. Letters from Ignacio Basadre to Francisco Modesto Olaguíbel,
Havana, Nov. 9, 1845, VGF Archive Y1446, F48 1302; from Rejón to
Crescencio Boves, Havana, March 8 and 9, Y1487–488, F49 1381, 1384,
and to Gómez Farías, June 6, 1846, Y1509 F49 1414; from Santa Anna
to Gómez Farías, Havana, April 23 and May 9, 1846, Y1501 and 1503,
F49 1400 and 1406, and to Fermín, June 9, 1846, Y1510, F49 1417.

81. Bustamante, *El Nuevo Bernal Díaz,* pp. 75–76, 100–102, 118–29.
Guillermo Prieto and Manuel Payno were also impressed by the way things
had changed suddenly, from a protomonarchical order to one that witnessed such innovations as the "meetings" (spelled in all possible ways)
at the University, where any thought could be expressed. See "Revista
política," in *Revista Científica y Literaria de Méjico* 2 (1846):261–62
and 310.

82. Michael Costeloe, "Church-State Financial Negotiations in Mexico
During the American War, 1846–1847," *Revista de Historia de América,*
60 (July–Dec. 1965), and his "The Mexican Church and the Rebellion of
the Polkos," *Hispanic American Historical Review* 46, 2 (May 1966).

Bibliography

1. Archives and Their Catalogues

Archive of Carlos García, at the University of Texas, Austin. Genaro García Collection, Folder 35.

Archive of Valentín Gómez Farías, at the University of Texas, Austin. It has been cataloged in Pablo Max Ynsfran, *Catálogo de los Manuscritos del Archivo de Don Valentín Gómez Farías obrantes en la universidad de Texas, Colección Latinoamericana*. Mexico City: Jus, 1968, which gives a serial number to all documents. Referred to as VGF Archive, with Ynsfran's number (preceded by a Y); the original folder and document numbers are given as they appear in the archive.

Archives du Ministère des Affaires Etrangères, Paris: Mexique. It includes the political (or diplomatic) correspondence, referred to as Q.d'O., plus volume number and folii, and a separate series of Mémoires et Documents, separately titled.

Archivo Histórico de la Embajada de México, Paris. It has been cataloged in Luis Weckmann, *Las relaciones franco-mexicanas. Archivo Histórico Diplomático Mexicano: Guías para la historia diplomática de México*, 3 vols. Mexico City: Secretaría de Relaciones Exteriores, 1961, which gives a serial number to each document. Referred to as Embajada Mexicana, plus Weckmann's document number.

Documentos para la historia de la guerra de independencia, 1810–1822: Correspondencia privada de D. Agustín de Iturbide y otros documentos de la época. Vol. 23 of Publicaciones del Archivo General de la Nación. Mexico City: Talleres Gráficos de la Nación, 1933.

Fuentes para la historia del trabajo en la Nueva España, ed. Silvio Zavala and María Castelo. 8 vols. Mexico City: Fondo de Cultura Económica, 1939–45.

El General Paredes y Arrillaga: su gobierno en Jalisco, etc., según su propio archivo, and *Archivo del General Paredes: La situación política, militar y económica de la República Mexicana al iniciarse su guerra con los Estados Unidos*, in *Documentos inéditos o muy raros para la historia de México*, pub. Genaro García, 2d ed., vols. 51, 54–56, 58–60 of Biblioteca Porrúa; vol. 56, pp. 1–128, 521–639. Mexico City: Porrúa, 1974.

Hernández y Dávalos Manuscript Collection, at the University of Texas, Austin. It has been cataloged in Carlos E. Castañeda and Jack Audrey Dabbs, *Independent Mexico in Documents: Independence, Empire, and Republic. A Calendar of the Juan E. Hernández y Dávalos Manuscript Collection*, the University of Texas Library. Mexico City: Jus, 1954, which gives a serial number to all documents. Referred to as HyD Collection, with the Castañeda-Dabbs number.

The Papers of Agustín de Iturbide, Library of Congress, Washington D.C., Manuscript Division, Mss 15,338. The archive is uncataloged, but in the microfilmed copy, each document has a serial number beginning with zero for each one of the twelve reels, which is used as reference.

Public Record Office: Archives of the Foreign Office, Mexico. London. Referred to as FO/50, plus volume number and folii.

2. Reference Works

Bosch García, Carlos. *Material para la historia diplomática de México (México y los Estados Unidos, 1820–1848)*. Mexico City: Escuela Nacional de Ciencias Políticas y Sociales, 1957.

Bravo Ugarte. *Periodistas y periódicos mexicanos*. Mexico City: Jus, 1966.

Castañeda, Carlos Eduardo, and Jack Autrey Dabbs. *Guide to the Latin American Manuscripts in the University of Texas Library*. Cambridge, Mass.: Harvard University Press, 1939.

Catalogue of Mexican Pamphlets in the Sutro Collection, with Supplements, 1605–1887. California State Library, Sacramento, Sutro Branch, San Francisco, 1939–41. New York: Kraus Reprint Co., 1971. (Nonstandard pagination in three series: Catalog, pp. 1–963; Supplement, pp. 1–289; Author Index, pp. 1–65.)

Charno, Steven M. *Latin American Newspapers in United States Libraries: A Union List*. Austin: University of Texas Press, 1968.

Colección de documentos para la historia del comercio exterior de México. 1st series, 7 vols.; 2d series, 4 vols. Mexico City: Banco Nacional del Comercio Exterior, 1943–62, ed. Luis Chávez Orozcó.

Correspondencia Diplomática Franco-mexicana, 1808–1839. Selección de E. de la Torre Villar. 3 vols. Mexico City: Colegio de México, 1957.

Costeloe, Michael P. *Mexico State Papers, 1744–1843: A Descriptive Catalogue of the G. R. G. Conway Collection in the Institute of Historical Research, University of London*. London: Institute of Latin American Studies/Athlone Press, 1976.

Diccionario Universal de Historia y de Geografía. 10 vols. Ed. by Manuel Orozco y Berra. Mexico: Escalante y Cía, 1854.

Documentos para la historia de México. 1st series, 7 vols. Mexico City, 1853–54.

García y Cubas, Antonio. *Atlas geográfico, estadístico e histórico de la República Mexicana, formado por Antonio García y Cubas*. Mexico City, 1858.

Humphreys, Robin A, ed. *British Consular Reports on the Trade and Politics of Latin America*. London: Royal Historial Society, 1940.

Integración Territorial de los Estados Unidos Mexicanos. Mexico City: Dirección General de Estadística, 1952.

La legislación del trabajo en los siglos XVI, XVII y XVIII. Ed. Genaro Vásquez. Mexico City: DAPP, 1938.

Mateos, Juan Antonio. *Historia parlamentaria de los Congresos Mexicanos de 1821 a 1857*. 25 vols. Mexico City: V.S. Reyes, 1877–1912.

O'Gorman, Edmundo. *Breve historia de las divisiones territoriales: México y sus constituciones*. Mexico City: Porrúa, 1937.

———. *Guía bibliográfica de Carlos María de Bustamante*. Mexico City: Centro de Estudios de Historia de México, 1967.

Olea, Héctor R. *Panfletografía de El Payo del Rosario: Semblanza de Pablo Villavicencio*. Mexico City: Testimonios de Atlacomulco, 1969.

Ordenanzas de gremios de la Nueva España. Compendio de los tres tomos de la Compilación Nueva de ordenanzas de la Muy Noble y Muy Leal e Imperial Ciudad de México hecha por Francisco del Barrio Lorenzot. Ed. Genaro García. Mexico City: Secretaría de Gobernación, 1920.

Palacios Sierra, Margarita. *Estudio preliminar e índices del periodismo de José Joaquín Fernández de Lizardi*. Mexico City: Facultad de Filosofía y Letras, Universidad Nacional Autónoma de México, 1965.

Radin, Paul, ed. *An Annotated Bibliography of the Poems and Pamphlets of José Joaquín Fernández de Lizardi*. Occasional Papers, Mexican History Series, no. 2, part 1, 2 sections. San Francisco: California State Library, Sacramento, Sutro Branch, 1940.

———, ed. *The Opponents and Friends of Lizardi*. Occasional Papers, Mexican History Series, no. 2, part 2. San Francisco: California State Library, Sacramento, Sutro Branch, 1939.

———, ed. *Some Newly Discovered Poems and Pamphlets of José Joaquín Fernández de Lizardi, El Pensador Mexicano*. Occasional Papers, Mexican History Series, no. 1. San Francisco: California State Library, Sacramento, Sutro Branch, n.d.

Steele, Colin, and Michael Costeloe. *Independent Mexico: A Collection of Mexican Pamphlets in the Bodleian Library*. London: Mansell, 1973.

Torre Villar, Ernesto de la. *Correspondencia diplomática franco-mexicana, 1808–1839*. 3 vols. Mexico City: El Colegio de México, 1957.

Velasco, Alfonso Luis. *Geografía y estadística de la República Mexicana*. 20 vols. Mexico City, 1891.

3. Newspapers and Journals

(Single-authored serials are listed under their authors' names in section 4, Other Primary Sources and Contemporary Publications)

La Abeja Poblana. Puebla, 1820–21. Moderate-liberal Iturbidista, published by Juan Nepomuceno and José María Troncoso.

El Aguila Mejicana. Mexico City, 1823–28. Started by Juan Nepomuceno Gómez Navarrete, Juan Wenceslao Barquera, and Germán Prissette, as Iturbidista with federalist and radical-liberal elements. It later became more radical, under Lorenzo de Zavala and Antonio José Valdés, and then Pedrazista, until it disappeared during the Acordada revolt.

El Ambigú Municipal de la Nueva España. Mexico City, 1821. A series with information on the workings of the constitutional municipal system under Spanish law.

American Annual Register for the Years 1829–1830. 2d ed. Boston: Grey and G. W. Blunt, 1832.

El Amigo del Pueblo. Puebla, 1821. Short-lived continuation of *La Abeja Poblana.*

El Amigo del Pueblo. Periódico semanario literario, científico, de política y comercio. Mexico City, 1827–28. Published by José María Bocanegra and José María Tornel, together with some Iturbidistas. It followed a progressive-liberal line, favoring at first Gómez Pedraza and then Guerrero for the presidency.

Anales de la Minería Mexicana. Mexico City, 1861.

El Anteojo. Mexico City, 1835. Moderate-liberal, attacking both Escoceses and Yorkinos and excesses of party conflict. Opposed to Santa Anna and especially to Tornel and Blasco in his and Barragán's cabinets.

El Archivista General. Mexico City, 1824 (Feb.–April). Published by Germán Prissette, liberal Iturbidista.

El Ateneo Mexicano. Mexico City, 1844–45. Scientific and cultural journal, organ of the association of the same name, which had been started in 1840 through the initiative of Spanish Ambassador Calderón de la Barca. It avoided political subjects, though it celebrated the overthrow of Santa Anna in 1844. Among others, Manuel Carpio, José M. Lacunza, and José María Lafragua published in it.

El Atleta. Mexico City, 1829–30. Liberal-federalist, launched to support the final stage of the Guerrero presidency, was closed down by the Bustamante regime after a few months.

Boletín de la Ciudadela. Mexico City, 1841 (Sept.–Oct.). Published by the local garrison, under General Gabriel Valencia's command, in concert with Santa Anna, against the Bustamante administration.

Boletín de la Sociedad Mexicana de Geografía y Estadística. Mexico City, several epocas, from 1838 to the present. Published by the Sociedad (earlier Instituto) Mexicana de Geografía y Estadística.

Boletín Oficial. See *Gaceta.*

El Caduceo de Puebla. Puebla, 1824–26. Semiofficial organ of the government.

El Cardillo. Mexico City, 1828 (no month specified). It concentrated on personal attacks against the Spaniards and their friends and was accused by them of being "anarchist."

El Cardillo de las Mujeres. Mexico City, 1828 (no month specified). Like the preceding.

El Cardillo de los Agiotistas. Mexico City, 1837 (March–May). It concentrated on personal attacks and exposés of fraudulent and abusive practices by financiers.

La Columna de la Constitución Federal de la República Mexicana. Mexico City, 1832–33. Radical-liberal, anti-Santanista, edited by Crescencio Rejón, polemicized with the more moderate *Fénix*, headed at this time by Gómez Pedraza.

El Correo de la Federación Mexicana. Mexico City, 1826–30. Radical liberal organ, published by Lorenzo de Zavala and Isidro R. Gondra, supported Guerrero against Gómez Pedraza, was suppressed by Bustamante.

El Cosmopolita. Mexico City, 1837–43. Moderate-liberal, headed by Gómez Pedraza and his group of "philosophers."

Diario Redactor de México. Mexico City, 1823. Radical liberal, pro Iturbidista, founded by Antonio José Valdés.

Enciclopedia de los Sans Culottes. Mexico City, 1835. Radical- liberal anti–Santa Anna, using satire to attack the government.

El Federalista. Mexico City, 1823. Published by Francisco Ortega, very moderately federalist, against provincial separatist attempts by federalists and Iturbidistas.

El Fénix de la Libertad. Mexico City, 1831–34. Published by Vicente Rocafuerte, with Crescencio Rejón and Juan Rodríguez Puebla, progressive liberals, opposed to the Bustamante regime and then promoting liberal reforms, but shunning "excesses." In 1832 Rejón separated himself from *El Fénix* and started *La Columna*.

Gaceta del Gobierno Supremo de la Federación Mexicana (changes names throughout the period considered: *Boletín Oficial, Diario del Gobierno, Diario Redactor de México, Boletín Oficial, El Telégrafo*, etc.). Mexico City, 1821–49.

El Hombre Libre. Mexico City, 1822. Published by Juan B. Morales, progressive-liberal anti-Iturbidista, close to *El Sol* but favoring a republic.

El Indicador de la Federación Mexicana. Mexico City, 1833. Published by José M. L. Mora, anticlerical liberal favoring Gómez Farías's reforms.

El Iris: Periódico crítico y literario. Mexico City, 1826. Published by Italian artists Claudio Linati and Florencio Galli, with Cuban poet José María Heredia. With a radical-liberal orientation, during the Santangelo crisis they broke up, Heredia joining the government *Gaceta*, and his partners shortly afterwards being expelled from the country.

El Liceo Mexicano. Mexico City, 1844 (Jan.–June). Apparently headed by Manuel Díez de Bonilla, conservative Santanista. Dealt with cultural matters, very little politics.

La Lima de Vulcano. Mexico City, 1834–37. Edited by Luis Espino (Spes in Livo), a pamphleteer of radical anti-Spaniard and Iturbidista involvements, supported Santa Anna's coup but rejected the conservative and clerical orientation that followed it.

La Luz. Mexico City, 1835–36. Moderate liberal, federalist, anti–Santa Anna, practically a continuation of *El Anteojo*.

El Mensajero comercial de Méjico. Mexico City, 1827. Commercial paper headed by the Spanish liberal Mateo Llanos, who left the country due to popular pressures against his compatriots.

La Minerva. Puebla, 1828 (Nov.–Dec.). Purportedly antipartisan, opposed Santa Anna's pronunciamiento in favor of Guerrero. Stopped due to the popular uprising supporting the Acordada revolt in Mexico City.

La Minerva Mexicana. Mexico, 1822. Published by Andrés Quintana Roo, progressive-liberal supporting Iturbide.

Miscelánea militar mejicana. Mexico City, 1820. Published by the "ciudadanos militares" Joaquín and Bernardo Miramón, it followed a liberal-constitutionalist line, supporting the organization of militias.

El Momo. Mexico City, 1837–38. Satirical radical-federalist, opposed to the Bustamante regime and to the moderate liberals led by Gómez Pedraza. It scorned being called pro-French by the "oligarchs."

El Monitor del Pueblo. Mexico City, 1833 (June–August). Radical- liberal, supporting the "causa popular," favoring balanced government.

El Mono. Mexico City, 1833. Satirical, critical of the radical liberals and also of Santa Anna. Polemicizes with *El Fénix*.

El Mosaico Mexicano. Mexico City, 1836–37, 1840–42. Cultural publication, first edited by Isidro R. Gondra, radical liberal, and then, in 1837, by the editor Ignacio Cumplido and the "Academia de Letrán" group of Guillermo Prieto, Manuel Carpio, José Bernardo Couto, and José María Lacunza. In its second period, from 1840, Manuel Payno and others joined. In 1842 it ceased publication, one of the groups from the Academia de Letrán, led by Prieto and Payno, continuing with *El Museo*.

El Museo Mexicano o Miscelánea de amenidades curiosas. Mexico City, 1843–45. Published by Guillermo Prieto and Manuel Payno, with support from the editor Ignacio Cumplido. Moderate-liberal anti-Santanista position, though including other shades of opinion. In 1845 Prieto and Payno left, to start the *Revista Científica y Literaria de México*. Cumplido continued in association with José María Lacunza, a more moderate liberal who evolved in a conservative direction.

El Nacional. Mexico City, 1836. Strongly Santanista, promoting a dictatorship as a response to a crisis of the republic.

Noticioso Poblano. Puebla, Nov. 1821.

El Observador de la República Mexicana. Mexico City, 1827–28, 1830. Moderate-liberal doctrinaire journal, published by José M. L. Mora with other Escoceses, supported by J. M. Fagoaga.

El Observador Judicial y de Legislación. Mexico City, 1842–43. Good reporting of legislation during most of the two years of its publication.

Ocios de Españoles Emigrados. London, 1825. Published by moderate-liberal Spanish émigrés, including the well-known economist Canga Arguelles, and apparently financed by the Mexican envoy Vicente Rocafuerte, who opposed Esteva.

El Poblano. Puebla, 1827. Clerical-conservative, actively opposed to "clubs."

El Popular: Periódico Político Económico. Mexico City, 1833. Strongly opposed to radical liberals, favored Santa Anna's coup against Gómez Farías.

Propagador mercantil. Mexico City, 1833–34. Commercial information, favoring industry and the promotion of artisans, but without interference with international trade.

El Restaurador Mexicano. Mexico City, 1838–39. Radical-federalist, supported the federal revolt by José Urrea in Tampico, opposed the expulsion of French residents by Bustamante. Also opposed Santa Anna's provisional presidency in 1839.

Revista Científica y Literaria de Méjico, publicada por los antiguos redactores del Museo Mejicano. Mexico City, 1845–46. Moderate-liberal, anti-Santanista. Published by Guillermo Prieto and Manuel Payno, it continued their work, begun in *El Museo,* after the break with Cumplido and Lacunza.

La Sabatina Universal. Periódico político y literario. Mexico City, 1822. Published by Germán Prissette, probably with support from Quintana Roo or Zavala, supported Iturbide from a liberal position.

Semanario artístico para los artesanos de Mexico. Mexico City, 1844–46.

Semanario de Agricultura. Mexico City, 1840 (Feb.–June).

Semanario de la industria mejicana que se publica bajo la protección de la Junta de Industria de esta capital. Mexico City, 1841 (May–Nov.), represented textile industrialists' interests.

Semanario Político y Literario de México. Mexico City, 1820–21. Moderate-liberal, supported by the Fagoaga family.

El Sol. Mexico City, 1821–32. Moderate-liberal anti-Iturbidista, becoming increasingly conservative.

La Verdad Desnuda. Mexico City, 1833. Conservative-clerical, strongly against Yorkinos and those Escoceses who cooperated with them. It welcomed Santa Anna as a liberator, but disappeared before the latter's assumption of full powers.

El Vigía. Mexico City, n.d. (late Sept. or early Oct. 1841 by context). Short-lived attempt, sponsored by Bustamante's government, to promote a return to the federal constitution and thus recruit popular support for the tottering regime.

4. Other Primary Sources and Contemporary Publications

Abad y Queipo, Manuel. "Escritos del obispo electo de Michoacán." In José María Luis Mora, *Obras sueltas de José María Luis Mora, ciudadano mexicano,* pp. 175–271. 2d ed. Mexico City: Porrúa, 1963.

Abusos de las elecciones populares. Mexico City, 1820.

Acusación que hacen ante el Soberano Congreso muchos profesores de medicina, cirugía y farmacia, contra el Sr. Gobernador del Distrito J. Gómez de la Cortina. Mexico City, 1836.

Agrícola. *Plan provisional de arreglo de vinaterías y pulquerías de esta Corte.* Mexico City, 1823.

Alamán, Lucas. *Historia de Méjico.* 5 vols. Mexico City: Jus, 1942; first published 1849–52.

———. *Un regalo de año nuevo para el Sr. Rocafuerte, o consideraciones sobre sus consideraciones, por uno que lo conoce.* Mexico City, 1832.

Alamán, Lucas, et al. *Manifiesto de la conducta de los capitulares que formaron el Excmo Ayuntamiento de esta Capital desde el 22 de julio hasta el 3 de diciembre de este año.* Mexico City, 1849.

Alameda, Cirilo. *Representación que el general de N.S.P.S. Francisco ha hecho a las Cortes acerca del proyecto de ley sobre reforma de regulares, en la parte que comprende a la Orden Seráfica.* Madrid, 1820, reprinted Mexico City, 1821.

Alcance a los documentos para la Historia. Mexico City, 1820.

El Alcanzador. *Alcance a D. G. de Yermo en el Noticioso General no. 63.* Mexico City, 1821.

Alerta contra serviles. Puebla, 1820.

Alesua, Cándido. *Cuatro cartas que en desahogo de su amor a la Constitución y a los americanos, ofendidos en el cuaderno que a principios de este año de 820 publicó el M.R.P. Provincial fray Manuel Agustín Gutiérrez, escribió el Br. Cándido Alesua, ciudadano en Querétaro. Dalas a luz . . . D. Josef María Fernández de Herrera, Regidor Constitucional de Querétaro.* Mexico City, 1820.

———. *Piquete suavecito de Alesua al Americano vindicante del R.P. Gutiérrez.* Querétaro, 1820.

Al Indio Constitucional, un ciudadano español íntimo amigo suyo, by J. V. G. Mexico City, 1820.

A los españoles ociosos en Londres un mexicano ocupado, contestando al número 20 de su periódico. Mexico City, 1825.

A los habitantes del Estado de Puebla: Su Congreso Constituyente. Puebla, 1825.

Al Público. Impreso a costa de los Sres capitulares del Excmo Ayuntamiento de esta capital. Mexico City, 1835.

Alpuche e Infante, José María. *Acusación del Sr Alpuche contra D. Sebastián Camacho por la expulsión del Sr. Santangelo.* Mexico City, 1826.

———. *Grito contra la inhumanidad del gobierno.* Mexico City, 1826.

———. *Manifestación que el ciudadano José María Alpuche e Infante hace de su conducta pública en la cámara en la elección de presidente celebrada en favor de Don Vicente Guerrero.* New York, 1830.

———. *Manifiesto que el ciudadano José María Alpuche e Infante, cura propio de Cunduacán de Tabasco, hace a la nación mexicana, de su escandalosa prisión.* Mexico City, 1838.

Al que le caiga el saco. Carta al Pensador Mexicano. Mexico City, 1821.

Un Americano enemigo de la esclavitud. *Defensa de los gachupines por los editores del Sol.* Mexico City, 1827.

Los Amigos de la igualdad ante la ley. *Roben a los extranjeros y verán como hay garrote.* Mexico City, 1826.

Anales del Ministerio de Fomento. *Industria agrícola, fabril, manufacturera y estadística general de la República Mexicana.* Vol. 1. Mexico City, 1854.

Análisis de la Memoria del Ministro de Hacienda, formado por la Comisión nombrada al efecto por la Cámara de Diputados. Mexico City, 1825.

Análisis de la Memoria presentada por el Sr. Secretario del Despacho de Hacienda al Primer Congreso Constitucional de los EEUU Mexicanos, hecho por la Comisión de Hacienda de la Cámara de Senadores, de cuya orden se imprime. Mexico City, 1825.

Análisis del papel titulado "Aviso a los sres electores de Mechoacán." Mexico City, 1820.

Archivo Histórico de Hacienda: Colección de documentos publicados bajo la dirección de Jesús Silva Herzog. 3 vols. Mexico City: Secretaría de Hacienda y Crédito Público. Dirección de Estudios Financieros, 1943–44.

Arenas, Joaquín. *Fraile contra fraile a cara descubierta.* Mexico City, 1823.

———. *Prisión violenta y satisfacción que da al público el R.P.F. Joaquín Arenas, religioso de la más estricta observancia de N.P.S. Francisco, capellán real del hospital militar de la villa de Chihuahua.* Mexico City, 1820.

Ataque bien sostenido contra el libertador de tres tapados, by M. B. Mexico City, 1823.

Las autoridades duermen mientras la patria perece. Mexico City, 1823.

El Avechucho, papel volante: Los frailes convencidos de republicanismo, o diálogo entre un fraile y un secular republicano. Mexico City, 1823.

Aviso importante al pueblo católico, o sea Centinela alerta para defensa de la religión. Puebla, 1821.

El Ayuntamiento de la Ciudad de México. . . hace presente a la Cámara de Diputados. . . Mexico City, 1825. In BMMT 9770k8 (165).

El Ayuntamiento de México manifiesta al público los motivos que ha tenido para suspender el ejercicio de sus funciones económicas. Mexico City, 1840.

El Ayuntamiento de México publica la resolución superior en la queja que contra el Excmo Sr Gobernador interpuso en 13 de Mayo último. Mexico City, 1840.

Aza, José María. *Carrera militar y literaria del Pensador Mexicano.* Mexico City, 1826.

———. *Cayó el pobre Pensador del partido liberal.* No. 4 of *Enójanse los compadres.*

——— *(El amigo de los desgraciados). Defensa hecha al Payo del Rosario contra su compadrito el Pensador Mexicano.* No. 1 of *Enójanse los compadres.*

———. *Enójanse los compadres y se sacan las verdades.* 11 parts. Mexico City, 1825–26.

———. *Muerte del escudero Aza intentada por el Pensador Mexicano en la imprenta de Cabrera.* No. 11 of *Enójanse los compadres.*

Azcárate, Miguel María. *Memoria de los principales ramos de la policía urbana y de los fondos de la Ciudad de México, presentada a la Sere-*

nísima Regencia del Imperio . . . por el prefecto Municipal. Mexico City, 1864.

———. *Noticias estadísticas que sobre los efectos de consumo introducidos en esta capital en el quinquenio de 1834 a 1838 presenta el Comandante del Resguardo de Rentas Unidas de México, coronel retirado de ejército, Miguel María de Azcárate.* Mexico City, 1839.

Balbontín, Juan María. "Notas formadas para la geografía y estadística del Departamento de Querétaro." *BSMGE,* vol. 7 (1859):493–534.

Banda, Longinos. "Estadística de Jalisco." *BSMGE,* vol. 2 (1865):199–216, 245–80, 305–44, 589–629.

Bando dado en Puebla el 15 de marzo de 1823. Puebla, 1823.

Bárcena, Manuel de la. *Manifiesto al mundo sobre la justicia y la necesidad de la independencia de la Nueva España.* Puebla and Mexico City, 1821.

Barrera, Manuel. *Bases de la contrata de limpia de calles y barrios . . .* Mexico City, 1844.

———. *Exposición que acerca de la contrata de vestuario para los cuerpos del Ejército Trigarante hace el que sucribe.* Mexico City, 1827.

Bausa, José M. "Bosquejo geográfico y estadístico del partido de Papantla." *BSMGE,* vol. 5 (1857):374–426.

Beristáin y Souza, José Mariano. *Biblioteca Hispanoamericana Septentrional.* 3 vols. Mexico City, 1816–21.

Berlandier, Luis, and Chovel Rafael. *Diario de viaje de la Comisión de Límites que puso el gobierno de la República bajo la dirección del . . . General Manuel Mier y Terán.* Mexico City, 1850.

Bocanegra, José María. *Memorias para la historia de México independiente.* 2 vols. Facsimile. Mexico City: Instituto Cultural Helénico/ Instituto Nacional de Estudios de la Revolución Mexicana, 1986–87; first posthumous ed., 1892.

Borrones y verdades sobre las elecciones. Mexico City, 1828.

Bosquejo de los fraudes que las pasiones de los hombres han introducido en nuestra santa religión. Mexico City, 1822.

Bosquejo histórico de la revolución de tres días en la Capital de los Estados Unidos Mexicanos, o sea las acusaciones de la conducta del ministro de Guerra D. Manuel Gómez Pedraza. Mexico City, 1828.

Burkart, José. "Descripción del distrito de minas de Tlalpujahua y su constitución geológica." *BSMGE,* 2ª Epoca, vol. 1 (1869):82–111.

——— [wrongly printed Juan]. "Memoria sobre la explotación de minas en los distritos de Pachuca y Real del Monte." *Anales de la Minería Mexicana* vol. 1 (1861):5–25, 41–65, 81–113.

———. "Resumen de los resultados obtenidos en la explotación de minas de Pachuca y Real del Monte durante los años de 1859, 1860 y 1861." *BSMGE,* 2ª Época, vol. 2 (1870).

Bustamante, Carlos María de. *La Abispa de Chilpancingo.* Serial. Mexico City, 1821–22.

———. *Apuntes para la historia del gobierno del general D. Antonio López de Santa Anna, desde principios de octubre de 1841 hasta 6 de diciembre de 1844, en que fue depuesto del mando por uniforme voluntad de la nación.* Mexico City, 1845.

———. *Campañas del Gral Don Félix María Calleja, comandante en jefe del ejército real de operaciones llamado del centro.* Mexico City, 1828.

———. *El Centzontli.* Mexico City, 1824.

———. *Continuación del Cuadro Histórico de la revolución mexicana.* Vols. 1–3, Mexico City: Publicaciones de la Biblioteca Nacional, 1953–54; vol. 4, Instituto Nacional de Antropología e Historia, 1963.

———. *Conversaciones del payo y del sacristán.* 2 series. Mexico City, 1824–25.

———. *Diálogo entre un barbero y su marchante.* 2 parts. Mexico City, 1826.

———. *Diario Histórico de México, Diciembre 1822–Junio 1823.* Tomo 1, vol. 1. Reedited. Mexico City: SEP/INAH, 1980.

———. *El gabinete mexicano durante el segundo período de la administración del Excmo Sr. D. Anastasio Bustamante hasta la entrega del mando al Excmo Sr. Presidente interino D. Antonio López de Santa Anna, y continuación del cuadro histórico de la Revolución Mexicana.* 2 vols. Mexico City, 1842.

———. *El General Don Felipe de la Garza vindicado de las notas de traidor e ingrato con que se le ofende en el papel público intitulado Catástrofe de Don Agustín de Iturbide.* Mexico City, 1826.

——— *El nuevo Bernal Díaz del Castillo, o sea Historia de la invasión de los angloamericanos en México compuesta en 1847.* 2 vols. Mexico City, 1847.

———. *El peligro ya se acerca, y nosotros lo llamamos* (1832). In *Catalogue of Mexican Pamphlets in the Sutro Collection*, pp. 645–55. New York: Kraus Reprint Co, 1971.

———. *Voz de la Patria.* Serial, 1830–31.

Bustamante, José Francisco. "Apuntes estadísticos relativos al Departamento de Querétaro" (1854). *BSMGE*, vol. 7 (1859):535–40.

Bustamante y Federación: Esto pide la Nación. Mexico City, 1837.

Calderón de la Barca, Fanny. *Life in Mexico: The Letters of Fanny Calderón de la Barca.* Ed. Howard T. Fisher and Marion H. Fisher. Garden City, N.Y.: Doubleday, 1966.

Los canes de Zorita, no teniendo a quien morder, uno a otro se mordían. Mexico City, 1839.

Canga Arguelles, José. *Diccionario de hacienda.* 5 vols. London, 1826–27.

———. *Elementos de ciencia de hacienda.* London, 1825.

Capmany y de Montpalau, Antonio. *Memorias históricas sobre la marina, comercio y artes de la antigue ciudad de Barcelona.* 4 vols. Madrid, 1778–92.

Carranza, J. M. *Proyecto de ley de clasificación de rentas de la República Mexicana . . . conforme a los conceptos del Sr. Luis de la Rosa y los del actual Sr. Ministro de Hacienda D. Guillermo Prieto, fundado en la experiencia y práctica de sus resultados en el Estado de Zacatecas.* Zacatecas, 1855.

Carta de . . . Iturbide al Pensador Mexicano. Mexico City, 1821.

Carta de un religioso liberal a un amigo suyo que le pide su dictamen sobre el papel titulado Bosquejo de los fraudes, by F. O. S. Mexico City, 1821.

Carta sobre el Crisol de la Memoria de Hacienda en el examen de los análisis de ella, by M. P. Mexico City, 1825.

Casas, Carlos. "Raíz de Jalapa." *BSMGE,* 2ª Epoca, vol. 1 (1869):6–8.

El Casillero. *Pan libre y cuartazo al panadero.* Mexico City, 1820.

Castro, Joseph de. *Directorio para informaciones de los pretendientes de el santo habito de N.S.P.S. Francisco.* Mexico City, 1737.

Centinela contra serviles, by F. M. Puebla, 1820.

El Ciudadano Franco. *Reverente representación que en uso de su acción popular dirige al Soberano Congreso de la Nación el menor de sus ciudadanos.* Puebla, 1823.

Clamores de los vendedores de la Plaza del Mercado. Mexico City, 1821.

Colección de los decretos y órdenes del Primer Congreso Constitucional del Estado de Querétaro. Querétaro, 1827.

Compañía de Minas Zacatecana. *Proyecto para la formación de una compañía que reúna el capital necesario . . .* Zacatecas, 1830.

Comunicados y documentos a que se refieren, relativos al ruinoso contrato que la Administración provisoria del Gral Santa Anna celebró con D. Cayetano Rubio sobre las salinas del Peñón Blanco y demás limítrofes del departamento de San Luis Potosí. Zacatecas, 1845.

Conducta del Sr. Iturbide. Veracruz, 1823.

El Congreso Constituyente a la Nación Mexicana. Mexico City, 1822.

La conspiración de ayer que se atribuyó a los barrios, by J. M. S. Mexico City, 1823.

Constituciones de la Provincia de San Diego de México de los menores descalcos de las más estrecha observacia regular de N.S.P.S. Francisco en esta Nueva España. Mexico City, 1698.

Consuelos a los indios, y aliento a los ciudadanos. Mexico City, 1820.

Consulta del gobierno al Soberano Congreso sobre que se establezca un tribunal especial en esta Corte y demás capitales de Provincias, dedicado a juzgar exclusivamente las causas de sedición contra el Estado, y mandada imprimir en sesión de 7 de agosto de 1822. Mexico City, 1822.

Contestación de un Americano al manifiesto del Sr. D. A. de Iturbide, Generalísimo de mar y tierra de las armas americanas, by J.A.M. Mexico City, 1821.

Contestación que da el Ayuntamiento de esta Capital al cuaderno publicado por el Excmo Sr Goberandor del departamento, sobre el negocio relativo a la tapada de la toma del agua de la casa de Bella Vista. Mexico City, 1840.

Contestación que da la Comisión de la Cámara de Senadores al Impreso titulado Crisol. Mexico City, 1825.

Contestaciones dadas por algunas corporaciones y autoridades del Imperio . . . [a la] reposición de la Sagrada Compañía de Jesús. Puebla, 1822.

Contrata de tabacos, celebrada entre los comisionados de la empresa y los representantes del común de cosecheros de los distritos de Orizava y Córdoba. Orizaba, 1839.

Contrata de vestuarios y otras prendas para el ejército, celebrada por la junta de almonedas de esta capital, en 2 de enero de 1832, con órdenes y aprobación del superior gobierno. Mexico City, 1832.

Controversia que suscitó el comercio de la Nueva España con los países extranjeros, 1811–21. In *Colección de documentos para la historia del comercio exterior de México,* 1st series, vol. 2. Mexico City: Banco Nacional del Comercio Exterior, 1959.

Convenio celebrado entre don Mariano Medina y Madrid y don Martín Bengoa . . . para el establecimiento de una compañía. San Luis Potosí, 1838.

Corona fúnebre del Sr. Dr. Pedro Escobedo, o sea colección completa de todas las producciones literarias publicadas con motivo de su muerte. Mexico City, 1844.

El Costeño de Acapulco. *La ejecución de justicia contra el Coronel Mangoy, la causa son los coyotes porque intentó su expulsión.* Mexico City, 1827.

Crisol de la Memoria de Hacienda en el examen de los análisis de ella. Año de 1825. Mexico City, 1825.

Crítica del Hombre Libre. Diálogo entre un religioso y su pilhuanejo. Mexico City, 1821.

Cuevas, Luis Gonzaga. *Porvenir de México.* Mexico City: Jus, 1954; first published in 3 vols., 1851–57.

Dávila, Rafael. *The Early Pamphlets of Rafael Dávila, 1820–1822.* Occasional Papers, Reprint Series no. 17. San Francisco: California State Library, Sutro Branch, 1940.

———. *Justo castigo y destierro del Pensador Mexicano.* Mexico City, 1822.

———. *Taller de cohetería. Diálogos crítico-alegóricos entre un cohetero y un tamborillero.* 3 vols. Mexico City, 1827.

———. *El Toro: Diálogos joco-serios entre un cohetero y un tamborillero.* 3 vols. Mexico City, 1829–32.

Dávila Garibi, José Ignacio. *Biografía de un gran prelado, el Excmo Sr. Dr. D. Juan Cruz Ruiz de Cabañas y Crespo.* Mexico City, 1912.

Declaración del Estado libre de Jalisco. Guadalajara, 1823.

Decreto de convocatoria para el Congreso General Constituyente del Imperio Mexicano, que deberá reunirse el día 10 de Agosto, e instalarse el 28. Mexico City, 1823.

Decreto de la Regencia sobre las elecciones. Mexico City, 1821.

Decreto del Soberano Congreso Mexicano sobre elecciones. Mexico City, 1823.

Defensa del Pensador por su aprendis. Mexico City, 1822.

De la liberalidad del indio. Mexico City, 1820.

De la naturaleza del indio. Mexico City, 1820.

El derecho del pueblo mexicano para elegir Emperador. Mexico City, 1821.

Derechos convincentes para elegir emperador americano. Mexico City, 1821.

Diálogo. Un cívico y su compadre. Mexico City, 1841.

Dictamen de la Comisión de Hacienda de la Cámara de Senadores de los EEUU Mexicanos sobre la Memoria presentada por el Secretario de Hacienda . . . en el año corriente de 1826. Mexico City, 1826.

Dictamen de la Comisión de Hacienda del Excmo Ayuntamiento, que contiene un proyecto de contribuciones para formar el fondo con que debe atenderse a los objetos del servicio público. Mexico City, 1848.

Dictamen de la Comisión de Hacienda del Honorable Congreso del Estado de Querétaro sobre la Renta del Tabaco. Querétaro, 1825.

Dictamen de las Comisiones de hacienda y comercio reunidas, sobre préstamo forzoso y arbitrio para subrogarlo. Mexico City, 1822.

Dictamen de las Comisiones Unidas de Constitución y Legislación sobre el proyecto de ley consultado al gobierno por el Consejo de Estado y comunicado por aquél al Soberano Congreso. Mexico City, 1822.

Dictámenes de los ciudadanos síndicos del excmo Ayuntamiento acerca de si los extranjeros pueden tener carnicerías, panaderías y otros comercios de esta clase. Mexico, 1830.

La Diputación de Puebla dirige una representación al Soberano Congreso. Puebla, 1823.

Dirección General de Agricultura e Industria. *Memoria sobre el estado de la agricultura e industria de la República Mexicana en el año de 1844.* Mexico City, 1845.

Discurso masónico en que se da una idea del origen, progresos y estado actual de la masonería en Europa. Mexico City, 1822.

Discurso pronunciado por el Excmo Sr. Gobernador al cerrarse las sesiones del H. Congreso en 23 del corriente. Puebla, 1826.

Discusión habida en la Sala de sesiones del H. Congreso de la Puebla, sobre el proyecto del ciudadano J.M. Godoy y Cía, . . . (1829). In *Colección de documentos para la historia del comercio exterior de México* (2d series, 4 vols), vol. 1: *El comercio exterior y el artesano, 1825–1830,* ed. Luis Chávez Orozco. Mexico City: Banco Nacional de Comercio Exterior, 1965.

Documentos importantes tomados del espediente instruido a consecuencia de la representación que varios electores a la junta general del Estado hicieron a su congreso constituyente pidiendo se anulen las elecciones verificadas en Toluca. Se publican de orden del mismo congreso constituyente del Estado. Mexico City, 1826.

Documentos que demuestran la justicia de los ocursos hechos por los acreedores al Peaje de Veracruz. Mexico City, 1835.

Documentos que manifiestan la conducta que observó el ciudadano lic. Miguel Macedo, como juez comisionado por la Excma Audiencia del Estado de México para ejecutar la sentencia de restitución de tierras dada a favor de la hacienda de Atenco, contra los pueblos del partido de Tenango del Valle. Mexico City, 1828.

Documentos relativos a las contestaciones entre el Superior Gobierno y el Excmo Ayuntamiento sobre el ejercicio de las prerrogativas de este cuerpo y motivos por los que ha cesado en sus funciones. Mexico City, 1843.

Domínguez Manso, José. *Discurso que el ciudadano José Domínguez Manso, ministro de la Suprema Corte de Justicia* . . . Mexico City, 1832.

———. *No paga Iturbide con condenarse.* Mexico City, 1821.

Dos millones de moneda para el Estado de Puebla . . . *Proyecto que presentaron unos ciudadanos y que a moción del Sr. Diputado Pedro Herrera ha pasado para su examen* . . . *a la H. Legislatura.* Puebla, 1849.

Dos palabras al Sr. Quintana Roo sobre su modo de caer parado, by J. M. R. Mexico City, 1823.

Durán, Rafael. "Memoria sobre el Censo de la República Mexicana" (read in 1863). *BSMGE,* vol. 9 (1862).

Eco de Yucatán en México contra la conducta política y ministerial del secretario de Hacienda don Lorenzo de Zavala. 7 pts. Mexico City, 1829.

Ejecución de justicia del reo que asesinó al Sr. Navarro. Mexico City, 1826.

Ejecución de justicia en cuatro gendarmes asesinos. Mexico City, 1826.

Ejecución de justicia en el religioso dieguino Fr. Joaquín Arenas. Mexico City, 1827.

Ejecución de justicia. . . en uno de los asesinos del presbítero D. J. M. Marchena. Mexico City, 1826.

Empresa de avio para la mina de San Nicolás alias El Jacal, en el mineral de Pachuca. Mexico City, 1841.

Empresa del Camino de Toluca a Morelia. *Informe que la Junta Directiva de esta empresa dió a la General de Accionistas.* 5 pts. Mexico City, 1850–55.

En qué vendrán a parar Iturbide y Volívar? Mexico City, 1822.

"Ensayo estadístico sobre el territorio de Colima." *BSMGE,* vol. 1 (3d ed., 1861):302–35.

Epitafio contra el Soberano Congreso glosado por un liberal, by J. F. A. Mexico City, 1823.

La escarlatina del Soberano Congreso. Mexico City, 1822.

Escritura de asociación de la Compañía de Minas Zacatecano-Mexicana. Mexico City, 1835.

Escritura de contrata y asociación de los señores accionistas del mineral de Guadalupe (del Tajo) con el propietario de las minas . . . *D. José Mariano Larreategui.* Mexico City, 1850.

Escudero, José Agustín de. *Noticias estadísticas del Estado de Chihuahua.* Mexico City, 1834.

Esparza, Marcos. *Informe presentado al gobierno superior del Estado por el ciudadano* . . . , *a consecuencia de la visita que practicó en los partidos de Villanueva y Juchipila.* Zacatecas, 1830.

Espino, Luis [Spes in Livo]. *Complicidad de 5 senadores en el crimen de Negrete.* Mexico City, 1827.

———. *Debilidad del gobierno y embrollos del padre Arenas.* Mexico City, 1827.

————. *Oiga el público verdades, que el autor no tiene miedo.* Mexico City, 1823.

————. *Paño de lágrimas de los gachupines y cebollas a los mexicanos.* Mexico City, 1827.

————. *Plan legítimo del padre Arenas para revolucionar a favor de España.* Mexico City, 1827.

————. *Reclama viles injurias la patria por Iturbide.* Mexico City, 1827.

————. *Viaje estático al mundo político.* A prospect and 10 parts. Mexico City, 1822.

————. *Vos del pueblo mexicano a su augusto emperador.* Mexico City, 1822.

Espínola, Miguel M. *Apuntes sueltos para la historia de la renta del tabaco.* Mexico City, 1830.

Esposición que dirige al Excmo Sr. General de División . . . Antonio López de Santa Anna la Asamblea Departamental de México pidiéndole la derogación del supremo decreto de 27 de junio que mandó demoler el Parián. Mexico City, 1843.

Esposición que los individuos que compusieron el próximo pasado Ayuntamiento hacen al público, en respuesta al informe que a nombre y por acuerdo del actual ha publicado el Sr. Don Lucas Alamán, presidente hoy de la Corporación. Mexico City, 1849.

Esteva, José Ignacio. *Apuntaciones que el ciudadano José Ignacio Esteva al separarse del despacho del Ministerio de Hacienda entrega a su sucesor el Excmo Sr D. Tomás Salgado.* Mexico City, 1827.

————. *Crisol de la Memoria de Hacienda en el examen de los análisis de ella. Año de 1825.* Mexico City, 1825.

Estrada, José M. de. *Justa defensa contra una acusación inicua.* Guadalajara, 1820.

Examen crítico de las causas de la persecución que han experimentado los francmasones. Mexico City, 1822.

Exposición a la augusta Cámara de Diputados que da idea de los perjuicios causados por la demolición del Parián a los comerciantes locatarios de ese edificio . . . Mexico City, 1844.

Exposición de la Excma Junta Departamental de México sobre el dictamen del Consejo de Gobierno que consulta se suspenda la ordenanza municipal. Mexico City, 1841.

Exposición de las razones que tuvo el Excmo Ayuntamiento [de 1841] para contratar la nueva obra que se está haciendo de la plaza del Volador. Mexico City, June 1842

Exposición de las ventajas en que abunda la villa y puerto de Tuspan para ser uno de los abiertos al comercio de todas las naciones. Mexico City, 1836.

Exposición del Ayuntamiento Constitucional de Tampico de Tamaulipas al Congreso de la Unión sobre reforma del arancel de aduanas y de todas las leyes comerciales. Tampico, 1833.

Exposición que la Junta de Peajes del Camino de Toluca a Veracruz hizo al Sr. Presidente de las Repúblicas sobre el decreto que le quita la administración del ramo. Mexico City, 1852.

Fages, Eduardo. "Noticias estadísticas del departmento de Tuxpán." *BSMGE*, vol. 4 (1854):187–205.

Familia Imperial. Mexico City, 1822.

Fernández, Esmeregildo. BMMT 9770.K.7(54). Mexico City, 1822.

Fernández, Hermenegildo. *La desgraciada muerte del Pensador Mexicano.* Mexico City, 1822.

Fernández, J. E. (El Cohetero). *Busca-pies al Pensador Mexicano, sobre sus Ideas políticas y liberales.* 5 parts. Mexico City, 1821.

———. *Proyecto de nuevo reglamento para las elecciones de los representantes del pueblo en las primeras Cortes.* Mexico City, 1821.

Fernández de Lizardi, José Joaquín (El Pensador Mexicano). *Alerta mexicanos, no nos perdamos.* Mexico City, 1822.

———. *El amigo de la paz y de la patria.* 2 nos. Mexico City, 1822.

———. *Aunque haya nuevo congreso, qué con eso?.* Tenochtitlán, 1823.

———. *El aviso patriótico a los insurgentes a la sordina.* Mexico City, 1811.

———. *Carta de los indios de Tontonapeque al Pensador Mexicano.* Mexico City, 1820.

———. *Cartas del Pensador al Papista.* Mexico City, 1822.

———. *Carta[s] del Pensador al Payo del Rosario por el cuento del coyote y zurra al Sr. Bustamante, con un epitafio a su Cenzontli.* 2 parts. Mexico City, 1824.

———. *Cedió el Pensador al fin, la victoria al gachupín.* Mexico City, 1826.

———. *Chamorro y Dominiquín: Diálogo joco-serio sobre la independencia de la América.* Mexico City, 1821.

———. *Cincuenta preguntas del Pensador Mexicano a quien las quiera responder.* Mexico City, 1821.

———. *Consejo de Guerra a los ingleses, por el Pensador Mexicano.* Mexico City, 1825.

———. *Contestación del Pensador a la carta que se dice dirigida a él por el Coronel Iturbide.* Mexico City, 1821.

———. *Conversaciones familiares del Payo y del sacristán,* 2 series. Mexico City, 1824–25.

———. *Correo Semanario.* Serial. Mexico City, 1826.

———. *Un coyote convertido les predica a las gallinas.* Mexico City, 1826.

———. *Cuartazo de don Joaquín a un grosero gachupín.* Mexico City, 1825.

———. *Defensa de los diputados presos.* Mexico City, 1822.

———. *Defensa de los francmasones.* Mexico City, 1822.

———. *Defensa del papel titulado Si dura mas el Congreso nos quedamos sin camisa.* Mexico City, 1823.

———. *Defensa del Payo del Rosario por el Pensador Mexicano.* Mexico City, 1826.

———. *Defensa del Pensador por su aprendiz.* Mexico City, 1822.

———. *Delirio del San Pableño.* Mexico City, 1822.

———. *Diálogos de los muertos.* 2 parts. Mexico City, 1825.

———. *Disputa de los dos congresos.* Mexico City, 1824.

——. *Entre bobos anda el juego; llevóselo todo el diablo*. Mexico City, 1826.

——. *Exposición . . . al Superior Congreso contra la censura fulminada por F.F. Alatorre*. Mexico City, 1822.

——. *Felicitaciones y reflexiones a los padres de la patria*. Mexico City, 1823.

——. *Un frayle sale a bailar*. Mexico City, 1823.

—— (El San Pableño). *Un guapo desafía al guapo que le salió al Pensador*. Mexico City, 1822.

——. *Hagan bien tilín tilín por la alma del gachupín*. Mexico City, 1826.

——. *Hasta los mudos se quejan al piadoso emperador*. Mexico City, 1822.

——. *Horrorosos atentados de una parte del clero de Guatemala contra la independencia general, o sea El Genio de la Anarquía*. Mexico City, 1826.

——. *Ideas políticas y liberales por el Pensador Mexicano*. 2 parts. Mexico City, 1821.

——. *Impugnación y defensa del folleto titulado 'Un bosquejo de los fraudes que las pasiones de los hombres han introducido en nuestra santa religión.'* Mexico City, 1821.

——. *Lavativa a un gachupín y a Cabrera su arlequín*. Mexico City, 1825.

——. *La muralla de México en la protección de María Santísima*. Mexico City, 1811.

——. *La música no es mala*. Mexico City, 1823.

——. *El negro sensible*. Mexico City, 1825.

——. *No hay porqué tener temor, siendo justo el Director*. Mexico City, 1824.

——. *La nueva revolución que se espera de la nación*. Mexico City, 1823.

——. *La nueva tonada del trágala-trágala*. Mexico City, 1822.

——. *Obras*. 9 vols. Mexico City: Centro de Estudios Literarios, Universidad Nacional Autónoma de Mexico, 1963–82.

——. *Observaciones que el Pensador Mexicano hace a las censuras que los sres doctores don Ignacio María Lerdo y don Ignacio Grajeda hicieron de sus "Conversaciones"* . . . Mexico City, 1825.

——. *El Payaso de los Periódicos*. Mexico City, 1823.

——. *El Pensador llama a juicio a sus necios enemigos*. Mexico City, 1822.

——. *El Pensador Mexicano*. Mexico City: Universidad Nacional Autónoma de México, Biblioteca del Estudiante, 1940.

——. *El Pensador Mexicano al Excmo Sr. Gral del Ejército Imperial D. Agustín de Iturbide*. Mexico City, 1821.

——. *Pésame por la muerte de Iturbide a sus apasionados*. Mexico City, 1824.

——. *La plática de los perros en defensa de los vinateros, cafeteros y fonderos*. Mexico City, 1820.

——. *Por la salud de la patria se desprecia una corona*. Mexico City, 1823.

———. *Preguntas interesantes del Pensador a D. Rafael Dávila*. Mexico City, 1826.

———. *Primer bombazo por el Pensador al Dr. D.F.E. Fernández*. Mexico City, 1821.

———. *Proclama del Pensador a los habitantes de México, en obsequio del Excmo Sr. D. Félix María Calleja del Rey*. Mexico City, 1813.

———. *Pronóstico político del Pensador Mexicano y explicación de otro igual que escribió en 1814*. Mexico City, 1824.

———. *Protestas del Pensador Mexicano ante el público y el Sr. Provisor*. Mexico City, 1825.

———. *Un puñado de verdades a nuestros enemigos*. Mexico City, 1821.

———. *Reflexión patriótica sobre la próxima elección*. Mexico City, 1813.

———. *Respuesta del Pensador al defensor del Payo del Rosario, ciudadano José María Aza*. Mexico City, 1825.

———. *Satisfacción del Pensador Mexicano al Soberano Congreso*. Mexico City, 1822.

———. *Se acercan las elecciones, cuidado con los borbones*. Mexico City, 1826.

———. *Segunda defensa de los francmasones*. Mexico City, 1822.

———. *Segundo sueño del Pensador Mexicano*. 2 parts. Mexico City, 1822.

———. *Se le quedó al gachupín la lavativa en el cuerpo*. Mexico City, 1825.

———. *Sentencia del consejo de guerra sobre los ingleses*. Mexico City, 1825.

———. *Si a Santangelo destierran ya no hay justicia en la tierra*. Mexico City, 1826.

——— (Cogitator). *Si dura más el Congreso nos quedamos sin camisa*. Mexico City, 1823.

———. *Si muere el fraile traidor, que sea en la Plaza Mayor*. Mexico City, 1827.

———. *Sólo un ruin perro acomete a otro perro rendido*. Mexico City, 1822.

———. *El sueño del Pensador no vaya a salir verdad*. Mexico City, 1822.

———. *También en el sol hay manchas*. Mexico City, 1822.

———. *Tercer ocurso . . .* Mexico City, 1822.

———. *Testamento y despedida del Pensador Mexicano*. Mexico City, 1827.

———. *Unipersonal del arcabuceado*. Mexico City, 1822.

———. *Verdadera defensa de los francmasones*. Mexico City, 1826.

———. *Ya en Oaxaca y en Durango acabó la libertad*. Mexico City, 1826.

Filónomo vindicado. Mexico City, 1820.

Flores, Manuel, and Ramón Gamboa. *Voto particular sobre la destrucción del Parián, leído en el Excmo Ayuntamiento la mañana del 29 de Enero próximo pasado*. Mexico City, 1829.

Florete. *Qué haremos con los préstamos forzosos*. Mexico City, 1822.

Fonseca, Fabián, and Carlos de Urrutia. *Historia general de Real Haci-*

enda, escrita por . . . por orden del Virrey Conde de Revillagigedo, obra hasta ahora inédita. 6 vols. Mexico City, 1845–53.

Foronda, Valentín de. *Cartas sobre los Asuntos más exquisitos de la Economía Política y sobre las leyes criminales.* 2 vols. Madrid, 1789–94.

Gamboa, Francisco Xavier de. *Comentarios a las ordenanzas de minas.* Madrid, 1761.

Gamboa, Ramón. *Dictámenes de los ciudadanos síndicos del excmo Ayuntamiento acerca de si los extranjeros pueden tener carnicerías, panaderías y otros comercios de esta clase.* Mexico City, 1830.

———. *Representación del ciudadano síndico lic. Ramón Gamboa al Ayuntamiento de esta capital suplicándole pida al Gobierno Superior despida de la República a Mr. Joel Poinsett, enviado de los Estados Unidos del Norte.* Mexico City, 1829.

García, José M. "Breves noticias estadísticas de Guadalupe Hidalgo." *BSMGE,* vol. 7 (1859):277–79.

García Conde, Pedro. "Ensayo estadístico sobre el Estado de Chihuahua." *BSMGE,* vol. 5 (1857):166–324.

Giménez, Manuel María. *Representación al Congreso contra los diputados serviles.* Mexico City, 1823.

Gómez Marín, Manuel. *Cumplimiento del desafío teológico.* Mexico City, 1821.

Gómez Navarrete, Juan Nepomuceno. *Exposición promoviendo el cumplimiento del decreto de la Junta Soberana Gubernativa de 21 de febrero de 1822.* Mexico City, 1832.

———. *Exposición que dirige al Congreso General el ciudadano José Gómez Navarrete como albacea del Excmo Sr. D. Agustín de Iturbide, promoviendo el cumplimiento del decreto de la Junta Soberana Gubernativa de 21 de febrero de 1822.* Mexico City, 1832.

Gómez Pedraza, Manuel. *Contestación del Ministro de Guerra D. Manuel Gómez Pedraza a los cargos que le hacen cinco señores senadores en el periódico titulado Observador de la República Mexicana.* Mexico City, 1827.

———. *Manifiesto que . . . , ciudadano de la República de México, dedica a sus compatriotas, o sea una reseña de su vida política.* New Orleans, 1831.

González Angulo, Bernardo. *Satisfacción al público sobre la libertad de los Barreras.* Mexico City, 1823.

El grande asunto de hoy. Mexico City, 1821.

Guerrero, Vicente. *Manifiesto del ciudadano Vicente Guerrero, segundo presidente de los Estados Unidos Mexicanos.* Mexico City, 1829.

Guerrero, Vicente, and Nicolás Bravo. *Plan o indicaciones para reintegrar a la nación . . . Veracruz, el 6 de diciembre de 1822, por Antonio López de Santa Anna y Guadalupe Victoria; lo reimprimen y propalan Vicente Guerrero y Nicolás Bravo en Chilapa.* Mexico City, 1823.

Guía de Hacienda de la República Mexicana. Año 1826. Parte Legislativa. Tomo I. Mexico City, 1826.

Guillén, José María. *Fuga y alcance del Payo del Rosario.* Mexico City, 1824.

———(J. M. G.). *Muerte y entierro de Agustín Primero*. Mexico City, 1823.

Gutiérrez de Rosas, José María. *Ensayo sobre rentas públicas del Imperio Mexicano*. Mexico City, 1822.

Harcort, Eduardo. *Noticias geográficas políticas del territorio de Colima, escritas por el Cnel Ingeniero Eduardo Harcort en el año de 1834, y publicadas en 1842 por Ramón de la Vega*. Mexico City, 1842.

Hardy, R. W. H. *Travels in the Interior of Mexico in 1825, 26, 27 and 28*. London, 1829.

Haro y Tamariz, Antonio. *Estracto del espediente sobre la conversión de la deuda exterior*. Mexico City, 1846.

Hay [sic] *va ese hueso que roer, y que le metan el diente*. 13 parts. Mexico City, 1826–27.

Hermosa, Francisco. *Manual de laboreo de minas y beneficio de metales, dispuesto para uso de los mineros y azogueros de la República Mexicana*. Paris, 1857.

Hernández y Dávalos, Juan E. "Materiales para un diccionario estadístico, geográfico, histórico y biográfico del Estado de Jalisco." *BSMGE*, 2ª Epoca, vol. 2 (1870):453–64.

Huarte de Iturbide, Ana María. *Representaciones que la viuda del Excmo Sr Agustín de Iturbide ha dirigido al Supremo Poder Legislativo de los Estados Unidos Mexicanos*. Mexico City, 1833.

Ibar, Francisco. *Muerte política de la República Mexicana, o cuadro histórico de los sucesos políticos acaecidos en la República desde el 4 de diciembre de 1828 hasta el 23 de agosto de 1829*. Mexico City, 1829.

———. *Regeneración política de la República Mexicana, o cuadro histórico crítico de los sucesos políticos acaecidos en ella desde el 23 de diciembre de 1829 hasta el 19 de junio de 1830*. Mexico City, 1830.

Ilustración sobre la sociedad de los francmasones. Mexico City, 1822.

Ilustre Sr; Sabio Consistorio: Beneméritos Padres de la Patria: a V.S.S. se dirije pues mi torpe pluma, by M. N. C. Puebla, 1820.

Imperiosa voz de la necesidad en la actual crisis de la patria. Mexico City, 1821.

El importante voto de un ciudadano. Mexico City, 1821.

El indulto de los Barreras. Mexico City, 1823.

Información, presupuesto, bases y condiciones de la compañía de minas restauradora de Temascaltepec. Mexico City, 1838.

Informe dado por la Junta Permanente de la Compañía Zacatecano Mexicana a la de Fomento y Administrativa de Minería, sobre la negociación de Fresnillo. Mexico City, 1845.

Informe de la Junta departamental al Superior gobierno en la representación del Sr. Alcalde primero don J.M. Mejía en que solicita se reforme la ordenanza sobre contratas publicada en 12 de mayo del corriente año. Mexico City, 1840.

Informe del Gobernador del Distrito Federal dirigido a S.E. el Presidente de los Estados Unidos sobre las quejas del Ayuntamiento del año de 1825. Mexico City, 1826.

Informe documentado que el gobierno del Departamento de México da al Supremo de la Nación sobre la queja que ante la superioridad tiene elevada el E. Ayuntamiento de la capital. Mexico City, 1840.

Informe que da la Junta Menor Permanente de la Compañía de Minas Zacatecano Mexicana del estado de la negociación del Fresnillo. 12 pts. Mexico City, 1837–42.

Instrucciones para elecciones parroquiales y de partido. Mexico City, 1820.

Instrucciones que para facilitar las elecciones parroquiales y de partido, que han de celebrarse con el objeto de nombrar Diputados en Cortes, para las ordinarias de los años de 1820 y 1821, ha formado la Junta Preparatoria de Méjico y remite a los pueblos de su comprehensión. Mexico City, 1820.

El Irónico. *La chanfaína sequita: Carta al Pensador Mexicano.* 2 parts. Mexico City, 1820.

Iturbide, Agustín de. *Carrera militar y política de Don. A. de Iturbide, o sea Memorias que escribió en Liorna,* with an introduction by the Payo del Rosario. Mexico City, 1827.

———. *Advertencia.* Mexico City, 1822.

———. *El Emperador a los Mexicanos.* Mexico City, 1823.

———. *El Primer Jefe del Ejército Imperial a la Guarnición de México.* Mexico City, 1821.

———. *Orden Imperial del 3 de junio de 1822. Al Ejército y al pueblo.* Mexico City, 1822.

———. *Pensamiento que en grande ha propuesto el que suscribe, como un particular, para la pronta convocatoria de las próximas Cortes.* Mexico City, 1821.

Iturribarría, Ciríaco. "Memoria geográfica y estadística del Departamento de San Luis Potosí," in *BSMGE,* 7 (1859):288–321.

Jordan, John. *Serious Actual Dangers of Foreigners and Foreign Commerce in the Mexican States.* Philadelphia, 1826.

Junta General celebrada en Mexico el 9 de agosto de 1808, presidida por el E. Sr. Virrey D. José de Iturrigaray. Mexico City, 1808.

Lagranda, Francisco. *Consejo prudente sobre una de las garantías.* Mexico City, 1821.

La Legislatura constitucional del Estado de Querétaro . . . pasa a elevar una nota . . . de los ingresos y egresos . . . desde el 16 de octubre de 1824 hasta el 3 de diciembre de 1825. Querétaro, 1826.

Lerdo de Tejada, Miguel. *Comercio exterior de México desde la conquista hasta hoy.* Mexico City, 1853.

Levantamiento del Emperador en Tulancingo contra las tropas del Sr. Bravo. Mexico City, 1823.

El Liberal a los bajos escritores, by F. M. Puebla, 1820.

Unos Liberales. *Defiende su libertad la patria contra Iturbide.* Mexico City, 1827.

El Liberal juicioso. *Respuesta al sangriento papel Conducta del Sr Iturbide.* Mexico City, 1823.

La libertad en la ley, o ejecución de justicia. Mexico City, 1826.

Lista de los hombres de bien que tiene la República Mexicana. Mexico City, 1827.

Lista de los Señores Diputados designados por S.M.I. para que compongan la Junta que ha de substituir al extinguido Congreso Mexico City, 1822.

Lista de los señores vocales de la Sociedad Económico Mexicana de Amigos del País. Mexico City, 1822.

Lista fidedigna de individuos . . . comprendidos en la conspiración preparada para el día 2 del corriente octubre. Mexico City, 1823.

Lobato, José María. *El Brigadier José María Lobato a su división: Contra el visoño . . . Brigadier Santana y su plan. Que no, no, no haya república.* Córdoba, 1822.

———. *Habitantes de México.* Mexico City, 1824.

López, José María et al. *El coronel y oficiales del regimiento provincial de infantería de esta ciudad expresan que ven con escándalo papeles que los acusan de vivar "al héroe de Iguala con la denominación de absoluto."* Dirigido al Sr. Luis Quintanar, Capitán General y Jefe Político Superior. Guadalajara, 1823.

López Cancelada, Juan. *Ideas políticas económicas de gobierno: Memoria de instituto, formada por don Juan López Cancelada, secretario de la junta gubernativa, con cuya lectura han de abrirse sus sesiones en el año venidero de 1822.* Veracruz, 1821.

———. *Ruina de la Nueva España si se declara el comercio libre con los extranjeros. Exprésanse los motivos. Cuaderno segundo y primero en la materia por el lic . . . , redactor de la Gaceta de México.* Cádiz, 1811.

López y Pimentel, Francisco. *Memoria sobre las causas que han originado la situación actual de la raza indígena de México y medios de remediarla.* Mexico City, 1864.

López y Pimentel, Tomás. *Cálculo de una fábrica de tabaco en Aguas Calientes.* Mexico City, 1837.

Macanaz, Melchor de. *Testamento de España, por el Excmo Sr. D . . . Ministro que fue de Estado en la Corte de Madrid.* Mexico City, 1821.

Maldonado, Francisco Severo. *Contrato de Asociación para la República de los Estados Unidos del Anáhuac, por un ciudadano del Estado de Jalisco.* Mexico City, 1823.

———. *El Fanal del Imperio o Miscelánea Política.* Serial, Mexico City and Guadalajara, 1822–23.

———. *El Pacto Social, propuesto a España.* Mexico City, 1821.

Maniau, Joaquín. *Compendio de la historia de la Real Hacienda de Nueva España, escrito en el año de 1794 por J.M., oficial mayor en la contaduría general del tabaco . . . con notas y comentarios de Alberto Carreño.* Mexico City: Sociedad Mexicana de Geografía y Estadística, 1914.

Manifestación que un amante de su patria hace . . . de los últimos acontecimientos. Mexico City, 1823.

Manifiesto al público que hace el Ayuntamiento de 1840 acerca de la conducta que ha observado en los negocios municipales y del estado en que quedan los ramos de su cargo. Mexico City, 1840.

Manifiesto de la administración y progresos de los ramos de la hacienda federal mexicana desde agosto de 24 a Diciembre de 826. Mexico City, 1827.

Manifiesto del Ayuntamiento a los habitantes de la Capital, sobre las causas del mal estado que guardan los ramos puestos bajo cuidado de los capitulares. Mexico City, 1848.

Manifiesto del Congreso Constituyente del Estado de Jalisco a sus habitantes. Guadalajara, 1824.

Manifiesto del Congreso Constituyente del Estado Libre y Soberano de la Puebla de los Angeles a los habitantes de su distrito. Puebla, 1824.

Manifiesto que el Congreso Constitucional del Estado Libre de Jalisco dirige a sus habitantes. Guadalajara, 1824.

Marcha, Pío. *Carta del Capitán Pío Marcha a don Guadalupe Victoria.* Mexico City, 1823.

Maromeros, voltereta, que el dado se va cambiando. Mexico City, 1822, misprinted as 1821.

Martínez de Lejarza, Juan José. *Análisis estadístico de la provincia de Michoacán en 1822.* 2d ed. Morelia: Fimax Publicistas, 1974; first published Mexico City, 1824.

Mayer, Brantz. *México, lo que fue y lo que es.* Mexico City: Fondo de Cultura Económica, 1953; first published in English 1844.

McKegney, James C, ed. *The Political Pamphlets of Pablo de Villavicencio, "El Payo del Rosario."* 3 vols. Amsterdam: Rodopi N.V., 1975.

Mejía, José M. *El Alcalde primero del Excmo Ayuntamiento publica la manifestación que hizo ante el superior gobierno con motivo de las providencias superiores relativas a que los ramos municipales se administren por contratos.* Mexico City, 1840.

———. *Contestación del Alcalde primero José María Mejía al editorial del no. 1 del periódico intitulado El Mosquito publicado el día 3 del presente, relativo al estado de los fondos municipales.* Mexico City, Jan. 9, 1840.

Memoria de hacienda del Ayuntamiento de México. Mexico City, 1830.

Memoria de los ramos municipales formada por los capitulares que hasta el 31 de diciembre de 1846 pertenencieron al E. Ayuntamiento de la Capital de la República. Mexico City, 1847.

Memoria del Ramo de Hacienda Federal de los EEUU Mexicanos leída en la Cámara de Diputados el 13 de Enero y en la de Senadores el l6 del mismo mes por el ministro respectivo. Año de 1826. Mexico City, 1826.

Memoria económica de la Municipalidad de México, formada de orden del Excmo Ayuntamiento por una comisión de su seno en 1830. Mexico City, 1830.

Memoria en que el Estado Libre de los Zacatecas da cuenta . . . al Congreso del mismo estado. Zacatecas, 1833.

Memoria presentada al Congreso de Puebla de los Angeles por el Secretario del Despacho del Gobierno sobre el estado de la administración pública. Año de 1830. Puebla, 1830.

Memoria presentada al Congreso Primero Constitucional de Puebla de los Angeles por el Secretario del Despacho de Gobierno sobre el estado de la administración pública. Año de 1826. Mexico City, 1826.

Memoria presentada a S.A.S. la Regencia del Imperio Mexicano sobre. . . Hacienda Pública. Mexico City, 1822.

Memoria que el Gobierno del Estado de Guanajuato formó . . . respecto al año de 1826. Mexico City, 1827.

Memoria que presenta el gobernador de Guanajuato al Congreso Constituyente . . . desde el 10 de mayo de 1824 hasta el 31 de diciembre de 1825. Mexico City, 1826.

Memoria sobre el estado de la Hacienda Pública, leída en la Cámara de Diputados y en la de Senadores por el Ministro del Ramo. Mexico City, 1825.

Memoria sobre los yorkinos. Mexico City, 1828.

Memorial ajustado . . . del pleito que siguió el Ilmo. Sr. Don Benito Crespo, Obispo que fue de Durango, . . . con la religión de N.P.S. Francisco, de la Regular Observancia . . . sobre visitar y ejercer los actos de la jurisdicción diocesana en la Custodia del Nuevo México. Madrid, 1738.

Mier Noriega y Guerra, José Servando Teresa de [José Guerra]. *Historia de la Revolución de Nueva España.* 2 vols. Mexico City: Instituto de Cultura Helénica/Fondo de Cultura Económica, 1986 (first published London, 1813).

———. *Memorias.* 2 vols. Mexico City: Porrúa, 1946.

———. *Profecía política del sabio Dr. D . . . , diputado por Nueva León, con respecto a la Federación Mexicana.* Mexico City, 1849 (originally delivered 1823).

———. "Voto particular del Dr. Mier." In *Plan de Constitución Política de la República Mexicana.* Mexico City, 1823.

Miramón, Joaquín de. *Plan en general para la reforma y nuevo arreglo de la Milicia Nacional del Estado Libre de México, formada por el C. . . . Comandante de escuadrón de ejército, oficial mayor de la segunda secretaría del Supremo Tribunal de Guerra y Marina de la Federación, quien lo dedica al mismo Estado.* Toluca, 1830.

El mismísimo que no puede ver el sol ni pintado. Parabién a la nación y pésame a los coyotes. Mexico City, 1827.

Molinos del Campo, Francisco. *Informe del Gobernador del Distrito Federal dirigido a S.E. el presidente de los Estados Unidos sobre las quejas del Ayuntamiento del año de 1825.* Mexico City, 1826.

Mora, José María Luis. "Cuestión Importante para el Crédito Público: Ocupados por el gobierno los bienes del clero y de los regulares, serán ellos bastantes para cubrir los gastos del culto y pagar la deuda pública?" In *Obras sueltas*, pp. 385–420.

———. *Disertación sobre la naturaleza y aplicación de las rentas y bienes eclesiásticos y sobre la autoridad a que se hallan sujetos en cuanto a su erección, aumento, subsistencia o supresión.* Mexico City, 1833.

———. *México y sus revoluciones.* 3 vols. Mexico City: Porrúa, 1950; vol. 1, 3, and 4 only, first published Paris, 1836.

———. *Obras sueltas de José María Luis Mora, ciudadano mexicano.* 2d ed. Mexico City: Porrúa, 1963.

———. *Revista Política de las diversas administraciones que la República Mexicana ha tenido hasta 1837.* In *Obras Sueltas,* pp. 5–172. Mexico City: Porrúa, 1963.

Morales, Juan Bautista. *El Gallo Pitagórico.* Mexico City: Manuel Porrúa, 1975; first published 1845.

Morfi, Juan Agustín de. *Viaje de indios y diario del Nuevo México.* Manuscript, 1777–78, ed. by Manuel Orozco y Berra as a supplement of the *Diario Oficial,* 1856, forming vol. 1 of *Documentos para la Historia de México.* Mexico City: Imprenta de D. Alfredo del Bosque, 1935.

Motivos para que mueran los pasaportes y licencias de caballos, by J. M. A. B. Mexico City, 1820.

Murguía y Galardi, Jose Maria. "Estadística antigua y moderna de la provincia hoy Estado libre, soberano e independiente de Guajaca" (1826–27). *BSMGE,* vol. 7 (1859):161–275.

Navarrete, Francisco Antonio. *Relación peregrina de la agua corriente . . . de Santiago de Querétaro.* Mexico City, 1739.

Navarro y Noriega, Fernando. *Memoria sobre la población del Reino de Nueva España, por don Fernando Navarro y Noriega, contador general de los ramos de arbitrios de estos reinos.* Mexico City, 1820.

Ni se ha instalado el Congreso ni tenemos libertad. Mexico City, 1823.

No son sueños del Pensador. Mexico City, 1822.

"Noticias estadísticas del Departamento de Aguascalientes, correspondientes al año de 1837." *BSMGE,* vol. 1 (3d ed., 1861):253–69.

"Noticias estadísticas del Departamento de Jalisco" (1842). *BSMGE,* vol. 6 (1858):265–380.

Nuestros sacerdotes malos fraguaban nuestras cadenas. Mexico City, 1822.

O auxiliamos al gobierno, o la patria va al infierno, by J. M. B. 4 parts (Oct. 15, 23, and 30 and Nov. 11, 1832). In *Catalogue of Mexican Pamphlets in the Sutro Collection.*

Observaciones sobre la Memoria de la Hacienda Mexicana para 1827 publicadas en el periódico El Sol por sus editores y reimpresas con algunas notas. Mexico City, 1827.

Observaciones sobre la Memoria que el E.M. de Hacienda leyó. . . respecto a derechos de mineria, by J. M. Mexico City, 1825.

Ochoa, Claudio, and Isidro Gondra. "Apuntes para formar la estadística minera de la República Mexicana." *BSMGE,* vol. 2 (3d ed., 1864): 176–219.

Ocursos de los acreedores al ramo de peajes del Camino de Veracruz, dirigidos al Superior Gobierno y Suprema Corte de Justicia. Mexico City, 1835.

El oficio que la Comisión del Soberano Congreso presentó a Su Majestad y su contestación. Mexico City, 1822.

Orden Imperial de Guadalupe. Mexico City, 1822.

Ordenanzas Municipales acordadas por la Excma Junta Constitucional del Depto de Guanajuato y por el gobierno del mismo, en observancia de lo dispuesto en el párrafo séptimo del artículo 14 de la Sexta Ley Constitucional. Mexico City, 1839.

Origen y progreso de la revolución de Sierra Gorda, by O. L. A. San Luis Potosí, 1849.

Ortiz, Tadeo. *México considerado como nación independiente y libre, o sean algunas indicaciones sobre los deberes más esenciales de los mexicanos.* Bordeaux, 1832.

Otero, Mariano. *Ensayo sobre el verdadero estado de la cuestión social y política que se agita en la República Mexicana.* Mexico City: Instituto Nacional de la Juventud Mexicana, 1964; first published 1842.

Otro liberal a los escritores bajos, by M. M. V. Puebla, 1820.

Oyen y callan, pero a su tiempo hablan. Representación dirigida a la Soberana Junta . . . por los Jueces de Letras foráneos, sobre vicios de los Ayuntamientos y nulidad de sus elecciones. Mexico City, 1821.

Palafox y Mendoza, Juan de. *Alegaciones en favor del clero . . . de Puebla. . . por su Obispo Don Juan de Palafox y Mendoza, en el pleito contra los religiosos de Santo Domingo, San Francisco y San Agustín en 1640.* Puebla, 1650.

El Papista. *Carta[s] segunda, tercera, cuarta del Papista.* Mexico City, 1822.

———. *Cascabeles al gato.* Mexico City, 1822.

"Partido de Casamaloapan, Departamento de Veracruz." *BSMGE,* vol. 4 (1854):111–15.

Pasquín sedicioso . . . Mexico City, 1823. BMMT 9770k7(152).

Payno, Manuel. "Memoria sobre el maguey mexicano y sus diversos productos." *BSMGE,* vol. 10 (1863):383–451, 485–530.

———. *Proyecto de arreglo de gastos de la Hacienda Publica y contribuciones para cubrirlos, presentados al Congreso General por el ciudadano M.P.* Mexico City, 1848.

———. "Un viaje a Veracruz en el invierno de 1843." *Museo Mexicano o Miscelánea de amenidades curiosas,* vol. 3 (1844):56–562 (with interruptions).

El Payo del Rosario. See Villavicencio, Pablo de.

Paz, José Ignacio. *Contestación documentada que da José Ignacio Paz, al papel que salió titulado: Cosas que jamás se han oído por boca del señor Paz.* Mexico City, 1827.

———. *El estupendo grito de la acordada.* 4 parts. Mexico City, 1829.

———. *Gemidos de la educación pública, que D. José Ignacio Paz, Capitán retirado y Director de su Estudio Académico de primera educación, presentó al Soberano Congreso, y para su interesante emulación lo imprime un amante de la juventud.* Mexico City, 1822.

———. *Plan de estudios, constituciones y egercicios . . . en base a su experiencia de nueve años en Xalapa y dos años en Puebla.* Mexico City, 1819.

El Pensador Mexicano. See Fernández de Lizardi, José Joaquín.

Piquero, Ignacio. "Apuntes para la corografia y la estadistica del Estado de Michoacan" (1849). *BSMGE,* vol. 1, 3d ed. (1861):142–237.

Plan de reorganización de la compañía de minas denominada Restauradora del Mineral de Catorce. Mexico City, 1851.

Planes del Sr. Iturbide para la nueva reconquista de América. Mexico City, 1824.

Plan o indicación para reintegrar a la nación. Mexico City, 1823.

Poinsett, Joel R. *Discursos pronunciados en la Cámara de Representantes de los Estados Unidos de América por el Hon. Sr. don J.R. Poinsett, actual enviado extraordinario y Ministro plenipotenciario cerca de la República Mexicana.* Mexico City, 1829.

———. *Notes on Mexico.* New York: Praeger, 1969; first published 1825.

Posadas, Manuel, *Alegato de defensa que el Sr. Dr. D. Manuel Posadas, cura del Sagrario de la Catedral, defensor del Sr. Diputado D. José Manuel Alpuche e Infante, presentó en la causa que se le sigue en la Alta Corte de Justicia.* Mexico City, 1830.

Posteriores reflexiones sobre la abolición o conservación del estanco del tabaco. Mexico City, 1831.

Pregunta al Pensador Mexicano sobre pensiones de casas y coches, by J. V. G. Mexico City, 1820.

Prieto, Guillermo. *Indicaciones sobre el origen, vicisitudes y estado que guardan actualmente las rentas generales de la Federación Mexicana.* Mexico City, 1850.

———. *Indicación que deja . . . sobre los negocios pendientes en la secretaría que estuvo a su cargo a su sucesor . . . J.M. Urquidi.* Mexico City, 1853.

———. *Memorias de mis tiempos.* 5th ed. Mexico City: Porrúa, 1969.

———. *Viajes de orden suprema: Años de 1853, 54 y 55.* 3d ed. Mexico City: Porrúa, 1970.

Primer limonazo del sanpableño al guapo destapado[,] en favor del Pensador Mexicano. Mexico City, 1822.

Prisión del Sr. Iturbide en Londres. Mexico City, 1824.

Prisión de Pío Marcha en el barrio del Salto del Agua, by F. D. Mexico City, 1823.

Prisión y trabajos del pobrecillo Pensador, by Q. F. Mexico City, 1822.

Proclama del gato maromero a sus discípulos. San Agustín, Mexico, 1823.

Proclama de un americano amante de su patria, by J. A. M. [probably Fernández de Lizardi]. Mexico City, 1821. Followed by a *Segunda proclama,* by the same pen-name, Mexico City, 1821.

Proposiciones para la derogación del decreto del 31 de mayo de 1842, por los diputados Manuel Zárate, José Ramón Pacheco y Manuel Payno, e informes y documentos que presentaron relativos al camino de fierro de Veracruz a San Juan, mandada imprimir por acuerdo de la Cámara. Mexico City, 1849.

Proyecto de ley sobre contribuciones, by J. M. G. Guadalajara, 1821.

Proyecto de policía para la Ciudad de México que un Europeo Americano presentó a Su Alteza Serenísima la Regencia del Imperio Mexicano, by B. T. Mexico City, 1821.

Proyecto de Reglamento Político de Gobierno del Imperio Mejicano presentado a la Junta Nacional Instituyente y leído en la sesión ordinaria del 31 de diciembre de 1822. Mexico City, 1823.

Proyecto del Plan de Hacienda para el año de 1823, presentado por su comisión y leído en sesión extraordinaria del 6 del presente mes. Mexico City, 1822.

El público de esta capital supo con sorpresa la repentina desaparición del General D. V. Guerrero. Mexico City, 1823.

Que aguarde el nuevo Congreso la venida de Iturbide. Mexico City, 1823.

El Quebrantahuesos. 21 parts. Mexico City, 1826–27.

Qué va que nos lleva el diablo por los pícaros serviles. Mexico City, 1823.

Quintana Roo, Andrés (L.A.Q.R.). *Indicaciones sobre gobierno*. Mexico City, 1822.

———. *Opinión del Ministerio de Estado sobre la convocatoria*. Mexico City, 1823.

Quirós, José María. *Ideas políticas económicas de gobierno. Memoria de Instituto, formada por don José María Quirós secretario de la Junta Gubernativa, con cuya lectura han de abrirse sus sesiones en el año venidero de 1822*. Veracruz, 1821.

———. *Memoria de estatuto. Idea de la riqueza que daban a la masa circulante de Nueva España sus naturales producciones en los años de tranquilidad y su abatimiento en las presentes conmo–ciones, por José María Quirós secretario del Real Consulado de Veracruz y leída en la primera junta de gobierno celebrada en 24 de enero de 1817*. Veracruz, 1817.

Ramírez, José Fernando. *México durante su guerra con los Estados Unidos*. Mexico City: Librería de la Vda de C. Bouret, 1905.

Ramírez, Santiago. *Noticia histórica de la riqueza minera de México y de su actual estado de explotación*. Mexico City: Secretaría de Fomento, 1884.

Ramírez de Arellano, Manuel María. *Legal solicitud importantísima o salva triple de artillería imperial*. Mexico City, 1821.

———. "Noticias históricas y estadísticas de Durango (1849–1850)." *BSMGE*, vol. 5 (1857):6–115.

Ramos Arizpe, Miguel. *Discursos, memorias e informes*. Notas biográfica y bibliográfica y acotaciones de Vito Alessio Robles. Mexico City: Universidad Nacional Autónoma, 1942.

Rasgo de generosidad. Orden general comunicada al Ejército de las tres garantías. Cuaulotitlán, 1821.

Raso, José Antonio del. *Estadística del Departamento de Querétaro relativa a la población, presentada a la Excma Asamblea Departamental*. Querétaro, 1846.

———. "Notas estadísticas del Departamento de Querétaro, formadas por la Asamblea Constitucional del mismo" (1845). *BSMGE*, vol. 3 (1852):168–236.

Raz y Guzmán, Juan Bautista (N.). *Sal y pimienta a la chanfaína*. Mexico City, 1820.

Realizado en Puebla el importante voto de un ciudadano, by E.D.L. Mexico City, reprinted from Puebla, 1821 by context.

Reflecsiones sobre el manifiesto de D. Anastasio Bustamante dado en 14 de agosto de 1832. Veracruz and Mexico City, 1832.

La Regencia Gobernadora Interina del Imperio Mexicano a todos sus habitantes. Mexico City, 1821.

Regil, José M. "Estadística de Yucatán," rev. by Alonso Manuel Peón. *BSMGE*, vol. 3 (1852):237–340.

Regla de N.S.P.S. Francisco y breve explicación de sus preceptos según las declaraciones de los Sumos Pontífices. Mexico City, 1837.

Reglamento de Auxiliares para la seguridad de las personas y bienes de los vecinos de esta capital y observancia de las leyes de policía. Reprint. Mexico City, 1829.

Reglamento de policía. Mexico City, 1811.

Reglamento para la Compañía Queretana de Industria. Querétaro, 1831.

Rejón, Manuel Crescencio. *El Yucateco a don Andrés Quintana*. Mexico City, 1823.

Relación sobre la economía de Querétaro y de su Corregidor Don Miguel Domínguez, 1802–1811, ed. David Brading. *Boletín del Archivo General de la Nación* (Mexico City) 2ª serie, vol. 11, nos. 3–4 (1970): 275–318.

Relaciones del siglo XVIII relativas a Oaxaca. Manuscript collected and published by Francisco del Paso y Troncoso. Mexico City: Vargas Rea, 1950.

Representación al Soberano Congreso: Los dueños y encargados de panaderías, vecinos de la capital . . . Mexico City, 1836.

Representación de los alcaldes auxiliares al Excmo Ayuntamiento. Mexico City, 1825.

Representación del Ayuntamiento de esta Capital en defensa de la industria agrícola y fabril de la República. Mexico City, 1841.

Representación del Congreso de Jalisco al Congreso Nacional (Guadalajara, 1824).

Representación del Excelentísimo ayuntamiento Constitucional de la ciudad de México a la Cámara de Diputados de la Federación, sobre que no se derogue ni altere la ley que lo ha declarado distrito federal de la nación. Mexico City, 1825.

Representación dirigida al Excmo Sr. Presidente provisional, D. Antonio López de Santa Anna, por la empresa del Camino a Cuernavaca. Mexico City, 1841.

Representación que el Ayuntamiento de esta Capital dirigió al Congreso General en defensa de los fondos municipales de la misma. Mexico City, Nov. 30, 1849.

Representación que elevaron al Superior Gobierno algunos propietarios de fincas urbanas en esta capital sobre contribuciones. Mexico City, 1849.

Representación que hacen al Congreso del Estado de México los propietarios de haciendas de caña del mismo Estado, con motivo de las contribuciones que la Comisión de Hacienda propone se establezcan en su dictamen de 18 de marzo de 1828. Mexico City, 1828.

Representación que la Junta de Fomento Comercial y de Instrucción dirije al Soberano Congreso de la Unión, sobre la reforma del arancel vigente y alza de las prohibiciones. Veracruz, 1851.

Representación que las maestras, oficialas y demás empleadas de la fábrica de tabacos de esta ciudad dirigen al Supremo Gobierno, pidiendo no se adopte el proyecto de elaborar puros y cigarros por medio de una máquina. Mexico City, 1846.

Representación que los dueños de las Casas de Matanza hacen al Soberano Congreso pidiendo que se derogue la ley que previene se paguen los derechos de la Hacienda pública con dos terceras partes de plata y una de cobre. Mexico City, 1836.

Representación que los generales y jefes del Ejército . . . Mexico City, 1821. BMMT 9770k6(30bis).

Representación que los mineros y vecinos de Zacatecas dirigen a la A. Cámara de Senadores, en sostén del decreto que expidió la H. Legislatura del Estado reglamentando la libre explotación de sales. Mexico City, 1851.

A Resident, *Observations on Foreign Mining.* London, 1838.

Respetable público: El antiguo Ayuntamiento de esta capital . . . Mexico City, 1820.

Reyes Veramendi, Manuel. *Vindicación del ciudadano Manuel Reyes Veramendi.* Mexico City, 1838.

Rickard, George. *Practical Mining: Fully and Familiarly Described.* London: Effingham Wilson, 1869.

Rivera y Mendoza, A. "Informe sobre el cultivo del café en el distrito de Jalapa." *BSMGE,* 2ª epoca, vol. 2 (1870).

Rocafuerte, Vicente. *Colección Rocafuerte. Homenaje a Don Vicente Rocafuerte en el primer centenario de su muerte.* 16 vols. Quito: Edición del Gobierno del Ecuador, 1947.

———. *Consideraciones generales sobre la bondad de un gobierno, aplicadas a las actuales circunstancias de la República de México.* Guadalajara, 1831.

———. *Ensayo sobre tolerancia religiosa.* Mexico City, 1831.

Rodríguez de Campomanes, Pedro. *Discurso sobre el fomento de la industria popular.* Madrid, 1774.

———. *Discurso sobre la educación popular de los artesanos y su fomento.* Madrid, 1775.

Rodríguez Puebla, Juan. "Tres días de ministerio." *El Cosmopolita,* Dec. 19, 1838.

Romero de Terreros, Pedro. *Representación que el ciudadano gral. Pedro Romero de Terreros hace al Augusto Congreso para los fines que en ella se expresan.* Mexico City, 1836.

Rosa, Luis de la. *Observaciones sobre varios puntos concernientes a la Administracion Pública del Estado de Zacatecas.* Baltimore, 1851.

Rosillo de Mier Quatemoczín, Juan. *Enseñar al que no sabe. Ad calumnias tacendum non est . . .* Puebla, 1821.

348   BIBLIOGRAPHY

————. *Lo dicho, dicho. Comprobación al manifiesto sobre la inutilidad de los provinciales que ha motivado el papel titulado . . . Desengaño de Preocupados y Abatimiento de Engreídos.* Puebla, 1822.

————. *Manifiesto sobre la inutilidad de los provinciales de las religiones en esta América.* Puebla, 1821.

Rueguen a Dios por Arenas que ahora sí es cierta su muerte, by A. F. A. Mexico City, 1827.

Sánchez Garayo, A. *Manifestación que el apoderado de los acreedores del Fondo Dotal de Minería hace al público.* Mexico City, 1850.

El Sanpableño. *Un guapo desafía al guapo que le salió al Pensador.* Mexico City, 1822.

El Sanpableño desengañado. *Proclama de un sanpableño a los barrios de esta corte.* Mexico City, 1823.

Santa Anna, Antonio López de. *Mi historia militar y política, 1810–1874: Memorias inéditas*, in *Documentos inéditos o muy raros para la historia de México*, pub. by Genaro García, 2d ed., vol. 59 of Biblioteca Porrúa, pp. 5–118. Mexico City: Porrúa, 1974.

————. *Plan de República Federada.* San Luis Potosí, 1823.

Santamaría, Miguel. *Despedida del público mexicano.* Mexico City, 1822.

Santangelo, Orazio de Attelis, Baron of. *Las cuatro primeras discusiones del Congreso de Panamá, tales como deberían ser*, trans. Lorenzo de Zavala. Mexico City, 1826.

Sartorius, Carlos. "Memoria sobre el estado de la agricultura en el partido de Huatusco." *BSMGE*, 2ª epoca, vol. 2 (1870).

Satisfacción que da el Ayuntamiento Constitucional de México a las imposturas con que lo ha injuriado una memoria impresa por su regidor D. Vicente Valdés sobre la enajenación de los potreros nombrados El Ahuehuete y El Medio, en el siguiente informe a Su Majestad Imperial. Mexico City, 1822.

Se acabaron los gendarmes porque marchan al precidio. Mexico City, 1826.

Secretaría de Gobierno del Estado de Chiapas. "Censo General", signed by Juan María Ortiz, San Cristóbal de las Casas, Oct. 21, 1862. *BSMGE*, vol. 10 (1863): fronting p. 69.

Segura, Manuel de. "Apuntes estadísticos del distrito de Orizaba, formados por . . . prefecto del mismo distrito, en 1839." *BSMGE* vol. 4 (1854):3–71.

Semblanzas de los individuos de la Cámara de Diputados de los años de 1825 y 26. Mexico City, 1827.

Semblanzas de los miembros que han compuesto la Cámara de Diputados del Congreso de la Unión de la República Mexicana en el bienio de 1827 y 1828. New York, 1828.

Semblanzas de los representantes que compusieron el Congreso Constituyente de 1836. Mexico City, 1837.

Sentencia pronunciada contra el regidor Ignacio Paz, con inserción de la declaración del capitán Vargas. Mexico City, 1827.

Señor. Mexico City, 1821. BMMT 9770.bb.9(21).

Servo, Luis M. "Apuntes estadísticos de Mazatlán." *BSMGE*, vol. 7 (1859):323–37.

Sesión extraordinaria del Congreso. Mexico City, 1823. BMMT 9770. k.7(142).

Shiels, Arturo. "El Partido del Carmen: breve reseña histórica, geográfica y estadística." *BSMGE,* 2ª epoca, vol. 2 (1870):661–701.

Si sigue el papel moneda perecen pobres y ricos. Mexico City, 1823.

Sigüenza y Góngora, Carlos de. *Glorias de Querétaro* (1680), reescritas por José María Zelaa e Hidalgo. Mexico City, 1803.

Suárez y Navarro, Juan. *Historia de México y del General Antonio López de Santa Anna.* Facsime. Mexico City: Instituto Nacional de Estudios Históricos de la Revolución Mexicana, 1987; first published 1850.

Syms, Jelinger C. *Arts and Artisans at Home and Abroad, with Sketches of the Progress of Foreign Manufactures.* Edinburgh, 1839.

Tamariz, Francisco de Paula (F. de P. T.). *Proyecto sobre un establecimiento de papel moneda.* Mexico City, 1822.

Tayloe, Edward Thornton. *Mexico, 1825–1828: The Journal and Correspondence of Edward Thornton Tayloe.* Ed. C. Gardiner. Chapel Hill: University of North Carolina Press, 1959.

El Tejedor y su compadre. 7 pts. and 1 supplement. Puebla, 1820.

Tercera representación dirigida al E. Ayuntamiento pidiendo no se lleven a cabo ciertas medidas, que tienden a monopolizar el ramo de tocinería. Mexico City, 1849.

Terreros, Pedro de. *Representación que el ciudadano gral Pedro de Terreros hace al Augusto Congreso para los fines que en ella se expresan.* Mexico City, 1836.

Testamento de Iturbide que otorgó antes de embarcarse. 2 parts. Mexico City, 1823.

Testamento liberal de Judas. Mexico City, 1823.

Thiéry de Menonville, Nicolas Joseph. *Traité de la culture du Nopal, et de l'éducation de la cochenille . . . précédé d'un Voyage a Guaxaca.* 2 vols. Cap Français, Paris, Bordeaux, 1787.

Un tlapaneco. *La sombra del padre Arenas que Iturbide encontró en penas.* Tlalpam, 1827.

Tornel y Mendívil, José María. *Breve reseña histórica de los acontecimientos más notables de la Nación Mexicana.* Mexico City, 1852.

———. *Manifestación del ciudadano José María Tornel.* Mexico City, 1833.

———. *Manifiesto del origen, causas, progresos . . . de la revolución del Imperio Mexicano.* Puebla and Mexico City, 1821.

Torrescano, Gerónimo. *Cuarto Alcance al Mosquito Tulancingueño no. 18.* Mexico City, 1821.

El Tribuno de la Plebe, o Escritor de los Pelados. 2 parts. Mexico City, 1821.

El triunfo de los francmasones. Mexico City, 1822.

Troncoso, Juan Nepomuceno. *Carta al Pensador Mexicano.* Puebla, 1820.

———. *Carta al Sr. D. Francisco Manuel Sánchez de Tagle.* Puebla, 1821.

———. *Derechos y obligaciones del ciudadano: comprende ocho artículos.* Puebla, 1821.

Tronó en el Senado el Cohete y salió un Domingo Siete. Mexico City, 1826.
Unzueta, Juan Antonio de. *Manifiesto que da al público en vindicación de los cargos que se le hacen . . . el contador general de las rentas de tabaco y pólvora.* Mexico City, 1820.
———. *Memoria sobre la renta de tabaco presentada al Soberano Congreso Constituyente del Imperio Mexicano.* Mexico City, 1822.
Vaya un pliego de papel conque se obsequia a Tornel. Mexico City, 1839.
Valle, José Cecilio del. *Antología. Introducción, selección y notas de R. Oqueli.* Tegucigalpa: Editorial Universitaria, 1981.
Vera Quintana, R. "Noticias estadísticas de la ciudad de Salvatierra. Año de 1865." *BSMGE,* 2ª epoca, vol. 1 (1869):579–94.
Verdadera noticia de la muerte de Guerrero. Mexico City, 1823.
Verdadera noticia de los tres días de ministerio. Mexico City, 1839.
Un Verdadero Americano. *Bosquejo ligerísimo de la revolución de Mégico desde el grito de Iguala hasta la proclama imperial de Iturbide.* Philadelphia, 1822.
Viagero. "Las minas de México." *Anales de la Minería Mexicana o sea Revista de minería, metalúrgica, mecánica y de las ciencias de aplicación a la minería,* vol. 1 (1861).
Victoria de los serviles, y honrosa retirada del partido liberal. Puebla, 1820.
Villarroel, Hipólito. *México por dentro y fuera bajo el gobierno de los virreyes, o sea Enfermedades políticas que padece la capital de la Nueva España en casi todos los cuerpos de que se compone, y remedios que se deben aplicar para su curación.* Edited by Carlos María de Bustamante. Mexico City, 1831.
Villaseñor y Sánchez, Joseph Antonio de. *Theatro Americano.* 2 vols. Mexico City, 1746.
Villaseñor y Villaseñor, Alejandro. *Memoria política y estadística de la Prefectura de Cuernavaca.* Mexico City, 1850.
Villavicencio, Pablo de. *Concluye el testamento del Sr. Bravo.* Mexico City, 1828.
———. *Cosas que jamás se han oído, por el Payo del Rosario, o quien llama al toro, sufra la cornada.* Mexico City, 1825.
———. *Los coyotes de España vendrán pero los de casa nos la pagarán.* 3 parts. Mexico City, 1826.
———. *Cuántas vidas y coronas cuestan los malos ministros.* Mexico City, 1823.
———. *De coyote a perro inglés voy al coyote 8 a 3.* Mexico City, 1825.
———. *Defensa del hijo de Iturbide ante el Congreso de Veracruz.* Mexico City, 1827.
———. *Desafío del Castillo de Ulúa y respuesta de la América Septentrional.* Mexico City, 1822.
———. *En Mixcalco y en mi casa he de hablar del mismo modo.* Mexico City, 1825.
———. *Funcion[es 1ª to 12ª] de maroma en casa de Doña Prudencia de Mendiola: Diálogo[s 4° to 15°] entre ésta y Don Antonio* (1829). In McKegney, *Pamphlets,* vol. 3, pp. 865–1092.

———. *El gallo se halla durmiendo y los coyotes velando* (1825). In McKegney, *The Political Pamphlets* 1:422–32.

———. *Grandes bailes y maromas en casa de Doña Prudencia de Mendiola: Diálogo[s 1°, 2° 3°] entre ésta y D. Antonio* (1829). 3 parts. In *The Political Pamphlets* 3:1135–75.

———. *El hijito del coyote que cuidaba a las gallinas.* Mexico City, 1824.

———. *Llegada del león al castillo del San Juan de Ulúa o segunda parte del Aguila.* Mexico City, 1822.

———. *El loco de las Tamaulipas, o segunda parte del Coyote a perro inglés.* Mexico City, 1825.

———. *Manifiesto del Payo del Rosario a sus compatriotas, o sea Suplemento a la memoria del Sr.Iturbide.* Mexico City, 1827.

———. *No sea el bando del gobierno sacarnos del purgatorio y meternos al infierno.* Mexico City, 1827.

———. *O se destruye el coyote o mata nuestras gallinas.* Mexico City, 1824.

———. *Oración fúnebre encomiástica a la muerte del Gral D. J.M. Lobato, por su amigo el Payo del Rosario.* Mexico City, 1829.

———. *Otras tres palabritas del Payo del Rosario.* Mexico City, 1823.

———. *El perdón de Bravo no es moco de pavo.* Mexico City, 1828.

———. *Plan de desgachupinar.* 3d part of *Los coyotes de España vendrán.* Mexico City, 1826.

———. *The Political Pamphlets of Pablo de Villavicencio, "El Payo del Rosario."* Ed. James C. McKegney. 3 vols. Amsterdam: Rodopi N.V., 1975.

———. *Prisión del ministro Herrera y del Intendente de San Luis.* Mexico City, 1823.

———. *Lo que nos importa a todos, que lo remedie el gobierno.* Mexico City, 1822.

———. *Satisfacción del Payo del Rosario al señor Obispo Mier* (1826). In McKegney, *The Political Pamphlets* 2:623–27.

———. *Segunda conversación de Doña Prudencia de Mendiola con el jefe de los indios bárbaros: Diálogo 17° entre los concurrentes en casa de Doña Simplicia.* In McKegney, *The Political Pamphlets* 3:1112–13.

———. *El señor Generalísimo pensó acertarla y la erró.* Mexico City, 1822.

———. *Serviles, metan las manos, que se desploma el templo.* San Agustín de las Cuevas, 1823.

———. *Se va a descubrir la facción de gachupines que sedujo al Payo del Rosario para escribir contra los ingleses.* Mexico City, 1826.

———. *Si no se rompe la unión se pierde la libertad.* Mexico City, 1823.

———. *Si no se van los ingleses hemos de ser sus esclavos.* Mexico City, 1825.

———. *Si van tropas a la Habana nos hacen aquí la fiesta* (1825). In McKegney, *The Political Pamphlets* 1:433–40.

———. *Si vienen los godos nos cuelgan a todos.* Mexico City, 1826.

———. *Teman unos, callen otros, que yo he de hablar la verdad aunque la vida me cueste.* Mexico City, 1822.

————. *Testamento de Don Nicolás Bravo y herencia que deja a los esco-ceses y novenarios.* Mexico City, 1828.

————. *Testamento de la República Mexicana por la presidencia del Sr. Gómez Pedraza.* Tlalpan, 1828.

————. *Tres palabritas al Sr. Andrade y sus 17 firmones.* Mexico City, 1823.

————. *Tristes recuerdos del hombre de Iguala.* San Agustín de las Cuevas, 1827.

————. *Ultima [13ª] función de maroma y primera tertulia de unos indios bárbaros con Doña Prudencia de Mendiola: Diálogo 16° entre ésta y D. Antonio* (1829). In McKegney, *The Political Pamphlets* 3:1093–1112.

————. *Versos contra quien quiere despotismo.* Mexico City, 1822.

————. *Ya matan a testimonio a Santana y a Victoria.* Mexico City, 1823.

————. *Ya tenemos en Oaxaca parte de la Santa Liga* (1826). In McKeg-ney, *The Political Pamphlets* 2:598–607.

————. *Zorzico a la tierna despedida del león hispano y el águila del im-perio mexicano.* Mexico City, 1822.

————. *Zurra al papel embustero de la muerte de Guerrero.* Mexico City, 1823.

Vindicación y defensa de las religiones, en contraposición del papel titu-lado "Testamento de España," by J. V. M. Mexico City, 1821.

Vindicación y retractación del síndico. Verdad sabida, y buena fe guar-dada. Puebla, 1820.

El Visionario. El jarave loco del padre Arenas. Mexico City, 1827.

Viva el general Santana porque entregó Veracruz. Mexico City, 1822.

Voto de los barrios de la Capital. Mexico City, 1823.

Ward, Henry G. *Mexico in 1827.* 2 vols. London, 1828.

Wyllie, Robert. *México: Noticia sobre su Hacienda Pública bajo el gobi-erno español y después de la Independencia.* Mexico City, 1845.

Ya agoniza el despotismo y otorga su testamento. Mexico City, 1823.

Ya se va Agustín Primero, desterrado y sin corona. Mexico City, 1823.

Yo no entiendo estas cosas, by C.S.C.R. Mexico City, 1821.

Zavala, Lorenzo de. *Ensayo crítico de las revoluciones de México desde 1808 hasta 1830.* Reedited. Mexico City: Porrúa, 1969; originally published in 2 vols., Paris, 1831, and New York, 1832.

————. *Juicio imparcial sobre los acontecimientos de México en 1828 y 1829.* New York, 1830.

————. *Manifiesto del gobernador del Estado de México, ciudadano Lo-renzo de Zavala.* Tlalpam, 1829.

Zelaeta, Juan. *El Ayuntamiento no miente, o informe que ha estendido el síndico más antiguo . . . sobre los acontecimientos de la Inquisición.* Mexico City, 1826.

————. *El ciudadano . . . , al excmo Sr Victoria, o últimos hechos del Sr. Molinos.* Mexico City, 1826.

Zerecero, Anastasio. *Memorias para la historia de las revoluciones en México.* 2d ed. Mexico City: Universidad Nacional Autónoma de México, 1975.

5. Secondary Sources

Aguirre Beltrán, Gonzalo. *La población negra de México: Estudio etno-histórico.* Mexico City: Fondo de Cultura Económica, 1972.

Albi, Julio. *La defensa de las Indias, 1764–1799.* Madrid: Instituto de Cooperación Iberoamericana, 1987.

Altman, Ida. *Emigrants and Society: Extremadura and America in the Sixteenth Century.* Berkeley: University of California Press, 1989.

Anderson, Rodney D. *Guadalajara a la consumación de su independencia: estudio de su población según los padrones de 1821–1822.* Guadalajara: Gobierno de Jalisco, Secretaría General, 1983.

————. "Raza, clase y capitalismo durante los primeros años de la Independencia." In Carmen Castañeda, ed., *Elite, clases sociales y rebelión en Guadalajara y Jalisco, siglos XVIII y XIX*, pp. 59–72. Guadalajara: El Colegio de Jalisco, 1988.

————. "Raza, clase y ocupación: Guadalajara en 1821." In Carmen Castañeda, ed., *Elite, clases sociales y rebelión en Guadalajara y Jalisco, siglos XVIII y XIX*, pp. 73–96. Guadalajara: El Colegio de Jalisco, 1988.

Anna, Timothy. *The Fall of Royal Government in Mexico City.* Lincoln: Nebraska University Press, 1978.

————. *The Mexican Empire of Iturbide.* Lincoln: Nebraska University Press, 1990.

Annino, Antonio and Raffaelle Romanelli, eds. *Notabili, elettori e elezioni.* Quaderni Storici Nuova Serie 69, December 1988.

Archer, Christon. *The Army in Bourbon Mexico, 1760–1810.* Albuquerque: University of New Mexico Press, 1977.

Arrom, Silvia M. "Popular Politics in Mexico City: The Parián Riot, 1828." *Hispanic American Historical Review* 68, 2 (May 1988): 245–68.

————. *The Women of Mexico City, 1790–1857.* Stanford: Stanford University Press, 1985.

Artola, Miguel. *La burguesía revolucionaria (1809–1869).* Madrid: Alianza Universidad, 1973.

————. *Los orígenes de la España contemporánea.* 2 vols. Madrid: Instituto de Estudios Políticos, 1959.

Assadourian, Carlos Sempat. *El sistema de la economía colonial. El Mercado interior. Regiones y espacio económico.* Mexico City: Nueva Imagen, 1983.

Barbastro Gil, Luis. *El clero valenciano en el Trienio Liberal, 1820–1833: Esplendor y ocaso del estamento eclesiástico.* Alicante: Instituto de Estudios Juan Gil-Albert, Excma Diputación Provincial, 1985.

Baz, Gustavo, and E. L. Gallo. *Historia del Ferrocarril Mexicano.* Mexico City, 1874.

Bazant, Jan. *Alienation of Church Wealth in Mexico: Social and Economic Aspects of the Liberal Revolution.* Cambridge: Cambridge University Press, 1971.

———. *Antonio Haro y Tamariz y sus aventuras políticas, 1811–1869.* Mexico City: Fondo de Cultura Económica, 1968.

———. *Cinco haciendas mexicanas: Tres siglos de vida rural en San Luis Potosí (1600–1910).* Mexico City: El Colegio de México, 1975.

———. *Historia de la deuda exterior de México (1823–1946).* Mexico City: El Colegio de México, 1968.

———. "Peones, arrendatarios y aparceros en México, 1851–1853." *Historia Mexicana* 23, 90 (Oct.–Dec. 1973):330–57.

Becerra López, José Luis. *La organización de los estudios en la Nueva España.* Mexico City: Editorial Cultura, 1963.

Benson, Nettie Lee. "The Contested Mexican Elections of 1812." *Hispanic American Historical Review* 26, 3 (Aug. 1946):337–50.

———. *La diputación provincial y el federalismo mexicano.* Mexico City: El Colegio de México, 1955.

———, ed. *Mexico and the Spanish Cortes: 1810–1822.* Austin: University of Texas Press, 1966.

———. "The Plan of Casa Mata." *Hispanic American Historical Review* 25, 1 (Feb. 1945):45–56.

———. "Servando Teresa de Mier, Federalist." *Hispanic American Historical Review* 28, 4 (Nov. 1948):514–25.

Borah, Woodrow. *Justice by Insurance: The General Indian Court of Colonial Mexico and the Legal Aides of the Half-Real.* Berkeley: University of California Pres, 1983.

Bosch García, Carlos. *Historia de las relaciones entre México y los Estados Unidos, 1819–1848.* 2d ed. Mexico City: Secretaría de Relaciones Exteriores, 1974.

Bracamonte y Sosa, Pedro. "Haciendas y ganado en el Noroeste de Yucatán, 1800–1850." *Historia Mexicana* 37, no. 148 (April–June 1988): 613–39.

Brading, David. *The First America: The Spanish Monarchy, Creole Patriots, and the Liberal State, 1492–1866.* Cambridge: Cambridge University Press, 1992.

———. *Haciendas and Ranchos in the Mexican Bajío: León, 1700–1860.* Cambridge: Cambridge University Press, 1978.

———. *Miners and Merchants in Bourbon Mexico, 1780–1810.* Cambridge: Cambridge University Press, 1971.

———. *Los orígenes del nacionalismo mexicano.* Mexico City: Era, 1980.

———. "Relación sobre la economía de Querétaro y de su Corregidor Don Miguel Domínguez, 1802-1811." *Boletín del Archivo General de la Nación* (Mexico), 2ª serie, vol. 11, 3–4 (1970).

Brading, David, and Harry E. Cross. "Colonial Silver Mining: Mexico and Peru," *Hispanic American Historical Review* 52, 4 (Nov. 1972): 545–79.

Brand, Donald. *Quiroga, a Mexican Municipio.* Smithsonian Institution, Institute of Social Anthropology, Publication no. 11. Washington, D.C.: U.S. Government Printing Office, 1951.

Brister, Louis E. *In Mexican Prisons. The Journal of Edward Harcort.* College Station: Texas A and M University Press, 1986.

Bronner, Fred. "Urban Society in Colonial Spanish America: Research Trends." *Latin American Research Review* 31, 1 (1986):7–72.

Brungardt, Maurice, "The Civic Militia in Mexico, 1820–1835." Unpublished paper, University of Texas, Austin, n.d.

Bulnes, Francisco. *Las grandes mentiras de nuestra historia: la nación y el ejército en las guerras extranjeras.* Mexico City: Editora Nacional, 1951.

———. *Juárez y las revoluciones de Ayutla y de Reforma.* Mexico City: Editora Nacional, 1972.

Calderón, Francisco. "El pensamiento económico de Lucas Alamán." *Historia Mexicana* 34, 135 (Jan.–March 1985):435–59.

Canterla y Martín de Tovar, Francisco. *Vida y obra del primer Conde de Regla.* Sevilla: Escuela de Estudios Hispano-Americanos, 1975.

Carabarín Gracia, Alberto. *El trabajo y los trabajadores del obraje en la ciudad de Puebla, 1700–1710.* Cuadernos de la Casa Presno. Puebla: Centro de Investigaciones Históricas y Sociales, Universidad de Puebla, 1984.

Cardoso, Ciro Flamarión S., ed. *Formación y desarrollo de la burguesía en México, siglo XIX.* Mexico City: Siglo XXI, 1978.

———, ed. *México en el siglo XIX (1821–1910): Historia económica y de la estructura social.* Mexico City: Nueva Imagen, 1983.

Carr, Raymond. *Spain, 1808–1939.* Oxford: Clarendon Press, 1966.

Carrera Stampa, Manuel. *Los gremios mexicanos: La organización gremial en Nueva España, 1521–1861.* 4 vols. Mexico City: ediapsa, 1954.

Carrillo Azpeitía, Rafael. *Ensayo sobre la historia del movimiento obrero mexicano, 1823–1912.* 2 vols. Mexico City: Centro de Estudios de Historia Social del Movimiento Obrero, 1981.

Castillo Lara, Lucas. *Los mercedarios y la vida política y social de Caracas en los siglos XVII y XVIII.* 2 vols. Fuentes para la Historia Colonial de Venezuela. Caracas: Academia Nacional de la Historia, 1980.

Castro, Concepción de. *La revolución liberal y los municipios españoles.* Madrid: Alianza, 1979.

Chance, John K. *Race and Class in Colonial Oaxaca.* Stanford: Stanford University Press, 1978.

Chance, John K., and William B. Taylor. "Estate and Class in a Colonial City: Oaxaca." *Comparative Studies in Society and History* 19 (1977): 454–87.

Chávez, Ezequiel A. *Agustín de Iturbide, Libertador de México.* 2d ed. Mexico City: Jus, 1962.

Chávez Orozco, Luis. *Conflicto de trabajo con los mineros de Real del Monte, año de 1776.* Mexico City: Instituto Nacional de Estudios Históricos de la Revolución Mexicana, 1960.

———. *Historia de México (1808–1836).* Mexico City: Editorial Patria, 1947.

Chávez Orozco, Luis, and Enrique Florescano. *Agricultura e industria textil de Veracruz: siglo XIX.* Xalapa: Universidad Veracruzana, 1965.

Chevalier, Francois. *Land and Society in Colonial Mexico: The Great Hacienda.* Ed. L. B. Simpson. Berkeley: University of California Press, 1966.

Coatsworth, John. "Obstacles to Economic Growth in Nineteenth Century Mexico." *American Historical Review* 83, 1 (Feb. 1978):80–100.

———. "Railroads, Landholding and Agrarian Protest in the Early Porfiriato." *Hispanic American Historical Review* 54, 1 (Feb. 1974): 48–71.

Cohen, Jeremy. *The Friars and the Jews: The Evolution of Medieval Antijudaism.* Ithaca: Cornell University Press, 1982.

Contreras Cruz, Carlos, and Juan Carlos Grosso. "La estructura ocupacional y productiva de la ciudad de Puebla en la primera mitad del siglo XIX." In *Puebla en el Siglo XIX: contribución al estudio de su historia*, pp. 111–76. Puebla: Centro de Investigaciones Históricas y Sociales, Instituto de Ciencias, Universidad Autónoma de Puebla, 1983.

Cook, Sherburne F., and Woodrow Borah. *Essays in Population History: Mexico and the Caribbean.* 2 vols. Berkeley: University of California Press, 1971.

Costeloe, Michael P. *Church and State in Mexico: A Study of the Patronage Debate, 1821–1857.* London: Royal Historical Society, 1978.

———. "Church-State Financial Negotiations in Mexico During the American War, 1846–1847." *Revista de Historia de América* 60 (July–Dec. 1965).

———. *Church Wealth in Mexico: A Study of the "Juzgado de Capellanías" in the Archbishopric of Mexico, 1800–1856.* Cambridge: Cambridge University Press, 1967.

———. "Los generales Santa Anna y Paredes y Arrillaga en México, 1841–1843: Rivales por el poder o una copa más," *Historia Mexicana* 39, 154 (Oct.–Dec. 1989):417–40.

———. "The Mexican Church and the Rebellion of the Polkos." *Hispanic American Historical Review* 46, 2 (May 1966):170–78.

———. *La Primera República Federal de México.* Mexico City: Fondo de Cultura Económica, 1975.

———. "The Triangular Revolt in Mexico and the Fall of Anastasio Bustamante, August–October 1841." *Journal of Latin American Studies* 20, 2 (Nov. 1988):337–60.

Covarrubias, José. *La trascendencia política de la reforma agraria.* Mexico: Antigua Imprenta de Murguía, 1922.

Cuevas, Mariano. *Historia de la Iglesia en México.* 5th ed. 5 vols. Mexico City, 1947.

Deans-Smith, Susan. "Compromise and Conflict: The Tobacco Workers of Mexico City and the Colonial State, 1770–1810." Paper presented to a seminar on People, State and Nation in Mexico. Institute of Latin American Studies, University of Texas, Austin, April 1990.

Destefano, Michael Thomas. *Miracles and Monasteries in Mid-Colonial Puebla, 1600–1750: Charismatic Religion in a Conservative Society.* Ph.D. diss., University of Florida, 1977.

l

Díaz Díaz, Fernando. *Caudillos y caciques: Antonio López de Santa Anna y Juan Alvarez.* Mexico City: El Colegio de México, 1972.

Di Tella, Torcuato S. "The Dangerous Classes in Early Independent Mexico." *Journal of Latin American Studies* 5, 1 (1973):79–105.

———. "Las huelgas en la minería mexicana, 1826-1828." *Desarrollo Económico* 26, 104 (Jan.–March 1987):579–608.

———. *Latin American Politics: A Theoretical Framework.* Austin: University of Texas Press, 1990.

Domínguez, Jorge. *Insurrection or Loyalty: The Breakdown of the Spanish American Empire.* Cambridge, Mass.: Harvard University Press, 1980.

Dusenberry, William H. *The Mexican Mesta: The Administration of Ranching in Colonial Mexico.* Urbana: University of Illinois Press, 1963.

"El Ejército de Nueva España a fines del siglo XVIII." *Boletín del Archivo General de la Nación* 9, 2 (1938).

"El Ejército de Nueva España en 1780." *Boletín del Archivo General de la Nación* 8, 2 (1937).

Estep, Raymond. *Lorenzo de Zavala, profeta del liberalismo mexicano.* Mexico City: Librería de Porrúa, 1952.

Extremos de México: Homenaje a Don Daniel Cossío Villegas. Mexico City: Centro de Estudios Históricos, Colegio de México, 1971.

Farriss, Nancy M. *Crown and Clergy in Colonial Mexico, 1759–1821.* London: Athlone Press, 1968.

Fernández de Córdoba, Joaquín. *Pablo de Villavicencio, 'El Payo del Rosario,' escritor sinaloense precursor de la Reforma en México: Ensayo bio-bibliográfico.* Mexico City: El Libro Perfecto, 1949.

Fisher, Lillian Estelle. *The Intendant System in Spanish America.* Berkeley: University of California Press, 1929.

Flores Caballero, Romeo. "La consolidación de vales reales en la economía, la sociedad y la política novohispanas." *Historia Mexicana* 18, 71 (Jan.–March 1969):334–78.

———. *La contrarrevolución en la independencia: Los españoles en la vida política, social y económica de México, 1804–1838.* Mexico City: El Colegio de México, 1969.

Flores D., Jorge. *Pío Marcha, parva figura de un gran retablo.* Mexico City: Jus, 1980.

Florescano, Enrique, ed. *Haciendas, latifundios y plantaciones en América Latina.* Mexico City: Siglo XXI, 1975.

Florescano, Enrique. *Origen y desarrollo de los problemas agrarios de México, 1500–1821.* Mexico City: SEP/Era, 1986.

———. *Precios del maíz y crisis agrícolas en México, 1708–1810.* Mexico City: Colegio de México, 1969.

Florescano, Enrique, et al. *La clase obrera en la historia de México: De la colonia al imperio.* Mexico City: Siglo XXI, 1981.

Freed, John B. *The Friars and German Society in the Thirteenth Century.* Cambridge, Mass.: Medieval Academy of America, 1977.

Frías, Jorge D. *Pío Marcha, el sargento que proclamó un imperio.* Mexico City: Jus, 1980.

Fuentes Díaz, Vicente. *Gómez Farías, padre de la Reforma.* 2d ed. Mexico City: Comité de Actos Conmemorativos del Bicentenario del Natalicio del Dr. D. Vicente Gómez Farías, 1981.

———. *Origen y evolución del sistema electoral.* Mexico City: Imprenta Arana, 1967.

Gallagher, Ann Miriam. *The Family Background of the Nuns of Two Monasteries in Colonial Mexico: Santa Clara, Querétaro, and Corpus Christi, Mexico City, 1724–1822.* Ph.D. diss., Catholic University of America, 1972.

Gallardo, Guillermo. *Joel Roberts Poinsett, agente norteamericano.* Buenos Aires: Emecé, 1984.

Ganster, Paul. "La familia Gómez de Cervantes: Linaje y sociedad en el México colonial," *Historia Mexicana* 31, 122 (Oct.–Dec. 1981): 197–232.

García Bernal, Manuela Cristina. *La sociedad de Yucatán, 1700–1750.* Seville: Escuela de Estudios Hispanoamericanos, 1972.

García Díaz, Tarsicio. *El pensamiento político, económico y social de Don Tadeo Ortiz de Ayala.* Mexico City: Universidad Nacional Autónoma de México, 1962.

García Martínez, Bernardo. *El marquesado del Valle: Tres siglos de régimen señorial en Nueva España.* Mexico City: El Colegio de México, 1969.

García Martínez, Bernardo, et al. *Historia y Sociedad en el mundo de habla española. Homenaje a José Miranda.* Mexico City: Colegio de México, 1970.

García Oro, José. *La reforma del clero español en tiempo de los Reyes Católicos.* Madrid: Consejo Superior de Investigaciones Científicas, 1971.

Germani, Gino. *Authoritarianism, Fascism, and National Populism.* New Brunswick, N.J.: Transaction Books, 1978.

Gibson, Charles. *The Aztecs under Spanish Rule: A History of the Indians of the Valley of Mexico, 1521–1810.* Stanford: Stanford University Press, 1964.

Goldfrank, Walter L. "Theories of Revolution and Revolution without Theory: The Case of Mexico." *Theory and Society* 7, 1 and 2 (Jan.–March 1979):135–65.

Gómez Canedo, Lino. *La educación de los marginados durante la época colonial: Escuela y colegios para indios y mestizos en la Nueva España.* Mexico City: Porrúa, 1982.

———. *La provincia franciscana de Santa Cruz de Caracas: Cuerpo de documentos para su historia (1513–1837).* Fuentes para la Historia Colonial de Venezuela. Caracas: Academia Nacional de la Historia, 1974.

Gómez Ciriza, Roberto. *México ante la diplomacia vaticana: El período triangular, 1821–1836.* Mexico City: Fondo de Cultura Económica, 1977.

Gómez Hoyos, Rafael. *La Iglesia de América en las leyes de Indias.* Madrid: Instituto Fernández de Oviedo–Instituto de Cultura Hispánica de Bogotá, 1961.

Góngora, Mario. *Origen de los "inquilinos" de Chile central.* Santiago de Chile: Editorial Universitaria, 1960.

González, Luis. *Pueblo en vilo.* Mexico City: El Colegio de México, 1968.

———. "Tierra caliente." In *Extremos de México. Homenaje a Don Daniel Cossío Villegas,* pp. 115–49. Mexico City: Centro de Estudios Históricos, Colegio de México, 1971.

González Angulo, Jorge. "Los gremios de artesanos y la estructura urbana." In Alejandra Moreno Toscano, ed., *Ciudad de México: Ensayo de construcción de una historia,* pp. 25–36. Mexico City: SEP/INAH, 1978.

González de Cossío, Francisco. *Xalapa: breve reseña histórica.* Mexico City: Talleres Gráficos de la Nación, 1957.

González Navarro, Moisés. *La anatomía del poder en México, 1848–1853.* Mexico City: El Colegio de México, 1977.

———. *El pensamiento de Lucas Alamán.* Mexico City: Colegio de México, 1952.

———. *Raza y Tierra: La Guerra de Castas y el Henequén.* Mexico City: El Colegio de México, 1970.

González Obregón, Luis. *Novelistas mexicanos: José Joaquín Fernández de Lizardi (El Pensador Mexicano).* Mexico City: Editorial Botas, 1938; first published in 1888.

González Sánchez, Isabel. *Haciendas y ranchos de Tlaxcala en 1712.* Mexico City: Instituto Nacional de Antropología e Historia (Serie Historia, no. 21), 1969.

Green, Stanley C. *The Mexican Republic: The First Decade, 1823–1832.* Pittsburgh: University of Pittsburgh Press, 1987.

Guarda, Gabriel. *La implantación del monacato en Hispanoamérica: Siglos XV–XIX.* Anales de la Facultad de Teología, no. 24, Cuaderno 1. Santiago de Chile: Universidad Católica, 1973.

Guerra, Francois Xavier. *México: del Antiguo Régimen a la Revolución.* 2 vols. Mexico City: Fondo de Cultura Económica, 1988.

Gutiérrez Casillas, José. *Historia de la Iglesia en México.* Mexico City: Porrúa, 1984.

Hale, Charles. *Mexican Liberalism in the Age of Mora: 1821–1853.* New Haven: Yale University Press, 1968.

Halperín Donghi, Tulio. *De la revolución de independencia a la confederación rosista.* Buenos Aires: Paidós, 1972.

———. *El ocaso del orden colonial en Hispanoamérica.* Buenos Aires: Sudamericana, 1978.

———. *Reforma y disolución de los imperios ibéricos: 1750–1850.* Madrid: Alianza Editorial, 1985.

———. *Revolución y guerra: formación de una élite dirigente en la Argentina criolla.* Buenos Aires: Siglo XXI, 1972.

Hamill, Hugh M., Jr. *The Hidalgo Revolt: Prelude to Mexican Independence.* Gainesville: University of Florida Press, 1966.

Hamnett, Brian R. *Politics and Trade in Southern Mexico, 1750–1821.* Cambridge: Cambridge University Press, 1971.

———. *Revolución y contrarrevolución en México y el Perú: Liberalismo, realeza y separatismo, 1800–1824.* Mexico City: Fondo de Cultura Económica, 1978.

———. *Roots of Insurgency. Mexican Regions: 1750–1824.* Cambridge: Cambridge University Press, 1986.

Harris, Charles H. *A Mexican Family Empire: The Latifundio of the Sánchez Navarros.* Austin: University of Texas Press, 1975.

Henestrosa, Andrés. *Carlos María de Bustamante.* Mexico City: Senado de la República, 1986.

Herrera Canales, Inés. *El comercio exterior de México, 1821–1875.* Mexico City: Colegio de México, 1977.

Howe, Walter. *The Mining Guild of New Spain and its Tribunal General: 1770–1821.* Cambridge, Mass.: Harvard University Press, 1949.

Hutchinson, C. Alan. *Valentín Gómez Farías: La vida de un republicano.* Guadalajara: Gobierno de Jalisco, 1983.

Iguíniz, Juan B. "Apuntes biográficos del Dr. D. Francisco Severo Maldonado." *Anales del Museo Nacional de Arqueología, Historia y Etnografía* (Mexico City) 3, 17 (1911):131–54. Offprint.

Iturriaga, José. *La estructura social y cultural de México.* Mexico City: Secretaría de Educación Pública, 1987; 1st ed., Fondo de Cultura Económica, 1951.

Jiménez Codinach, Guadalupe. "Veracruz, almacén de plata en el Atlántico. La casa Gordon y Murphy: 1805–1824." *Historia Mexicana* 38, 150 (Oct.–Dec. 1988):325–53.

Junco, Alfonso. *Insurgentes y liberales ante Iturbide.* Mexico City: Jus, 1971.

Katz, Friedrich, ed. *Riot, Rebellion and Revolution: Rural Social Conflict in Mexico.* Princeton: Princeton University Press, 1988.

Katz, Michael. "Occupational Classifications in History." *Journal of Interdisciplinary History* 3, 1 (Summer 1972):63–88.

Keremitsis Dawn. *La industria textil mexicana en el siglo XIX.* Mexico City: SepSetentas, 1973.

Kicza, John E. *Colonial Entrepreneurs: Families and Business in Bourbon Mexico City.* Albuquerque: University of New Mexico Press, 1983.

Ladd, Doris. *The Making of a Strike: Mexican Silver Workers' Struggles in Real del Monte, 1776–1775.* Lincoln: University of Nebraska Press, 1988.

———. *The Mexican Nobility at Independence, 1780–1826.* Austin: Institute of Latin American Studies, University of Texas, 1976.

Lafuente Ferrari, Enrique. *El virrey Iturrigaray y los orígenes de la independencia de México.* Madrid: Consejo Superior de Investigaciones Científicas, 1941.

Landázuri Benítez, Gisela, and Verónica Vázquez Mantecón. *Azúcar y Estado, 1750–1880*. Mexico City: Fondo de Cultura Económica, 1988.

Lavrín, Asunción. "Execution of the Law of Consolidación in New Spain: Economic Aims and Results." *Hispanic American Historical Review* 53, 1 (Feb. 1973):27–49

Le Goff, Jacques. "Ordres mendiants et urbanisation dans la France médiévale." *Annales: Economies, Sociétés, Civilisations* 25, 4 (July–Aug. 1970):924–46.

Lesnick, Daniel R. *Preaching in Medieval Florence: The Social World of Franciscan and Dominican Spirituality*. Athens: University of Georgia Press, 1989.

Libro de incorporaciones del Colegio de Propaganda Fide de Ocopa (1752–1907). With Introduction and Notes by Julián Heras OFM Lima: Imprenta Editorial S. Antonio, 1970).

Lindley, Richard B. *Haciendas and Economic Development: Guadalajara, Mexico at Independence*. Austin: University of Texas Press, 1983.

Lira, Andrés. *Comunidades indígenas frente a la ciudad de México. Tenochtitlán y Tlatelolco, sus pueblos y barrios: 1812–1919*. Zamora, Michoacán: El Colegio de México/El Colegio de Michoacán, 1983.

López de Sarrelangue, Delfina E. *La nobleza indígena de Pátzcuaro en la época virreinal*. Mexico City: Universidad Nacional Autónoma de México, Instituto de Investigaciones Históricas, 1965.

———. *Una villa mexicana en el siglo XVIII*. Mexico City: Imprenta Universitaria, 1957.

Ludlow, Leonor, and Carlos Marichal, eds. *Banca y poder en México (1800–1925)*. Mexico City: Editorial Grijalbo, 1986.

Lynch, John. "British Policy in Latin America: 1783–1808." *Journal of Latin American Studies* 1, 1 (May 1969):1–30.

———. *Spanish Colonial Administration: 1782–1810*. London: University of London/Athlone Press, 1958.

Lynch, Joseph H. *Simoniacal Entry into Religious Life from 1000 to 1260: A Social, Economic and Legal Study*. Columbus: Ohio State University Press, 1976.

Machorro Narváez, Paulino. D. *Francisco Severo Maldonado: Un pensador jalisciense del primer tercio del siglo XIX*. Mexico City: Editorial Polis, 1938.

Macías, Carlos "El retorno a Valenciana: Las familias Pérez Gálvez y Rul." *Historia Mexicana* 36, 144 (April–June 1987):643–59.

Macune, Charles W., Jr. *El Estado de México y la Federación Mexicana*. Mexico City: Fondo de Cultura Económica, 1978.

Malvido, Elsa. "Los novicios de San Francisco en la ciudad de México: La edad de hierro (1649–1749)." *Historia Mexicana* 36, 144 (April–June 1987):699–738.

Martínez Rosales, Alfonso. "La provincia de San Alberto de Indias de Carmelitas Descalzos." *Historia Mexicana* 31, 124 (April–June 1982): 471–543.

Mateos, José María. *Historia de la Masonería en México.* Mexico City: La Tolerancia, 1884.

McAlister, Lyle N. *The 'Fuero Militar' in New Spain: 1764–1800.* Gainesville: University of Florida Press, 1957.

———. "Social Structure and Social Change in New Spain." *Hispanic American Historical Review* 43, 2 (May 1963):349–70.

Mecham, J. Lloyd. "The Real de Minas as a Political Institution." *Hispanic American Historical Review* 7, 1 (February 1927):45–83.

Meyer, Jean. *The Cristero Rebellion.* Cambridge: Cambridge University Press, 1976.

———. "Haciendas y ranchos, peones y campesinos en el Porfiriato: algunas falacias estadísticas." *Historia Mexicana* 35, 139 (Jan.–March 1986):477–509.

Mills, Elizabeth Hoel. *Don Valentín Gómez Farías y el desarrollo de sus ideas políticas.* Mexico City: Universidad Nacional Autónoma de México, 1957.

Miño Grijalva, Manuel. "El camino hacia la fábrica en Nueva España: El caso de la 'fábrica de indianillas' de Francisco de Iglesias, 1801–1810." *Historia Mexicana* 34, 133 (July–Sept. 1984):135–48.

Miranda, José. "La población indígena de México en el siglo XVII." *Historia Mexicana* 12, 46 (Oct.–Dec. 1962):182–89.

Montejano y Aguiñaga, Rafael. *El Valle del Maíz, S.L.P.* Ciudad del Maíz: Imprenta Evolución, 1967.

Morales, Francisco. *Ethnic and Social Background of the Franciscan Friars in Seventeenth Century Mexico.* Washington, D.C.: Academy of American Franciscan History, 1973.

Moreno Toscano, Alejandra, ed. *Ciudad de México: Ensayo de construcción de una historia.* Mexico: SEP/INAH, 1978.

Morin, Claude. *Michoacán en la Nueva España del siglo XVIII: Crecimiento y desigualdad en una economía colonial.* Mexico City: Fondo de Cultura Económica, 1979.

Mörner, Magnus. *La Corona española y los foráneos en los pueblos de indios de América.* Stockholm: Almqvist and Wiksell, 1970.

Morote, Luis. *Los frailes en España.* Madrid: Imprenta de Fortanet, 1904.

Morris, Richard, Josefina Zoraida Vázquez, and Elías Trabulse. *Las revoluciones de la independencia en México y en los Estados Unidos: Un ensayo comparativo.* 2 vols. Mexico City: Secretaría de Educación Pública, 1976.

Muro Arias, Luis F. "Herreros y cerrajeros en la Nueva España." *Historia Mexicana* 5, 3 (Jan.–March 1956):337–72.

Naredo, José M. *Estudio geográfico, histórico y estadístico del Cantón y de la ciudad de Orizaba.* 2 vols. Orizaba: Imprenta del Hospicio, 1898.

Nava Oteo, Guadalupe. *Cabildos y ayuntamientos en la Nueva España en 1808.* Mexico City: Secretaría de Educación Pública, 1973.

———. "Jornales y jornaleros en la minería porfiriana." *Historia Mexicana* 12, 45 (July–Sept. 1962):52–72.

———. *Religiosos de la Merced que pasaron a la América Española: 1514–1777. Con documentos del Archivo General de Indias.* Seville: Tipografia Zarzuela, 1924.

Noriega, Alfonso. *Francisco Severo Maldonado, el Precursor.* Mexico City: Universidad Nacional Autónoma de México, 1980.

———. *El pensamiento conservador y el conservadurismo mexicano.* Mexico City: Universidad Nacional Autónoma de México, Instituto de Investigaciones Jurídicas, 1972.

Olveda, Jaime. *Gordiano Guzmán, un cacique del siglo XIX.* Mexico City: SEP/INAH, 1980.

Olveda, Jaime. *El iturbidismo en Jalisco.* Mexico City: Dirección de Estudios Regionales, SEP/INAH, 1974.

Ortega y Pérez Gallardo, Ricardo. *Historia genealógica de las familias más antiguas de México.* 3 vols. Mexico City: A. Carranza y Cía, 1908.

Ortiz Escamilla, Juan. "El pronunciamiento federalista de Gordiano Guzmán, 1837–1842." *Historia Mexicana* 38, 150 (Oct.–Dec. 1988): 241–282.

Ortoll, Servando, ed. *Colima: Una historia compartida.* Mexico City: SEP/Instituto de Investigaciones Dr. José María Luis Mora, 1988.

Osborn, Wayne S. "Indian Land Retention in Colonial Metztitlán." *Hispanic American Historical Review* 53, 2 (May 1973):217–38.

Othón de Mendizábal, Miguel. *Ensayos sobre las clases sociales en México.* Mexico City: Editorial Nuestro Tiempo, 1968.

Ots Capdequí, José María. *El Estado español en las Indias.* 7th ed. Mexico City: Fondo de Cultura Económica, 1986.

Palomino y Cañedo, Jorge. *La casa y mayorazgo de Cañedo de Nueva Galicia.* 2 vols. Mexico City: Editorial Atenea, 1947.

Parcero, María de la Luz. *Lorenzo de Zavala, fuente y origen de la Reforma liberal en México.* Mexico City: Instituto Nacional de Antropología, 1969.

Pérez, Pedro Nolasco. *Historia de las misiones mercedarias en América.* Madrid: Revista Estudio, 1966.

Pérez Verdía, Luis. *Biografía del Excmo Sr. Don Prisciliano Sánchez, primer Gobernador Constitucional del Estado de Jalisco.* Guadalajara, Tipografía de Banda, 1881.

———. *Historia particular del Estado de Jalisco: Desde los primeros tiempos de que hay noticia hasta nuestros días.* Guadalajara: Escuela de Artes y Oficios, 1910.

Porras Muñoz, Guillermo. "La calle de la Cadena en México." *Estudios de Historia Novohispana* (Instituto de Investigaciones Históricas, UNAM) 5 (1974):143–91.

Potash, Robert. *Mexican Government and Industrial Development in the Early Republic: The Banco de Avio.* Amherst: University of Massachusets Press, 1983.

La Povertá del secolo XII e Francesco d'Assisi. Atti del II Convegno Internazionale, Assisi, 17–18 October 1974. Assisi: Societá Internazionale di Studi Francescani, 1975.

Quintana, Miguel. *Estevan de Antuñano, fundador de la industria textil en Puebla.* Mexico City: Talleres de Impresión de Estampillas y Valores, 1957.

——. "Papel histórico de Puebla en el progreso industrial de Nueva España." *BSMGE,* 5ª epoca, vol. 62, 2 (Sept.–Oct. 1946):347–76.

Rabasa, Emilio. *La evolución histórica de México.* 2d ed. Mexico City: Porrúa, 1956.

Ramírez Lavoignet, David. "Arroyo Hondo." *Historia Mexicana* 12, 47 (Jan.–March 1963):404–26.

Randall, Robert W. *Real del Monte: A British Mining Venture in Mexico.* Austin: University of Texas Press, 1972.

Real de Dios, José J., and Antonia Heredia Herrera. "El Virrey Don José de Iturrigaray." In J. A. Calderón Quijano, ed., *Los virreyes de Nueva España en el reinado de Carlos IV,* pp. 183–331. Seville: Escuela de Estudios Hispanoamericanos, Universidad de Sevilla, 1972.

Reed, Nelson. *The Caste War of Yucatán.* Stanford: Stanford University Press, 1964.

"El Regimiento de Dragones de la Reina y la provisión de caballos para el ejército." *Boletín del Archivo General de la Nación* 6, 6 (1935).

Reyes Heroles, Jesús. *El liberalismo mexicano.* 3 vols. Mexico City: Universidad Nacional Autónoma de México, 1958.

Rickard, Thomas A. *Journeys of Observation.* San Francisco: Dewey Publ. Co., 1907.

Rivera Cambas, Manuel. *Historia antigua y moderna de Jalapa y de las revoluciones del Estado de Veracruz.* Mexico City: Citlaltepetl, 1959.

Robertson, William S. *Iturbide of Mexico.* Durham, N.C.: Duke University Press, 1952.

Rodríguez García, Vicente. *El Fiscal de Real Hacienda en Nueva España: Don Ramón de Posada y Soto, 1781–1793.* Oviedo: Secretariado de Publicaciones de la Universidad de Oviedo, 1985.

Rodríguez O., Jaime E. *The Emergence of Spanish America: Vicente Rocafuerte and Spanish Americanism, 1808–1832.* Berkeley: University of California Press, 1975.

——, ed. *The Independence of Mexico and the Creation of the New Nation.* Los Angeles: University of California, Los Angeles, Latin American XCenter Publications, 1989.

Romero de Terreros, Manuel. *El Conde de Regla, Creso de Nueva España.* Mexico City: Ediciones Xochitl, 1943.

——. *La Corte de Agustín I, Emperador de México.* Mexico City: Imprenta del Museo Nacional de Arquitectura, Historia y Etnografía, 1922.

Ros, María Amparo. "La real fábrica de puros y cigarros: organización del trabajo y estructura urbana." In Alejandra Moreno Toscano, ed., *Ciudad de México: ensayo de construcción de una historia,* pp. 47–55. Mexico City: SEP/INAH, 1978.

Rosenwein, Barbara H., and Lester K. Little. "Social Meaning in the Monastic and Mendicant Spiritualities." *Past and Present* 63 (1974): 4–19.

Ruiz Zavala, Alipio. *Historia de la Provincia Agustiniana del Santísimo Nombre de Jesús de México.* Mexico City: Porrúa, 1984.

Sáenz Marín, Juan. *Datos sobre la Iglesia española contemporánea: 1768–1868.* Madrid: Editora Nacional, 1975.

Salado Alvarez, Victoriano. *La vida azarosa y romántica de Carlos María de Bustamante.* Mexico City: Jus, 1968.

Salvucci, Richard J. *Textiles and Capitalism in Mexico: An Economic History of the Obrajes, 1539–1840.* Princeton, N.J.: Princeton University Press, 1987.

Samayoa Guevara, Héctor Humberto. *Los gremios de artesanos en la ciudad de Guatemala: 1524–1821.* Guatemala City: Editorial Universitaria, 1962.

Santoni, Pedro. "A Fear of the People: The Civic Militia of Mexico in 1845." *Hispanic American Historic Review* 68, 2 (May 1988): 269–88.

Sarrelangue, Delfina E. López de. *La nobleza indígena de Pátzcuaro en la época virreinal.* Mexico: Universidad Nacional Autónoma de México, Instituto de Investigaciones Históricas, 1965.

———. "La población indígena de la Nueva España en el siglo XVIII." *Historia Mexicana* 12, 48 (April–June 1963):515–30.

Shaw, Frederick J. "The Artisan in Mexico City" In Elsa Cecilia Frost, Michael C. Meyer, and Josefina Zoraida Vázquez, eds., *El trabajo y los trabajadores en la historia de México,* pp. 399–418. Mexico City: El Colegio de México/University of Arizona Press, 1979.

———. "Poverty and Politics in Mexico City: 1824–54." Ph.D. diss., University of Florida, 1975.

Sierra, Catalina. *El nacimiento de México.* Mexico City: Universidad Nacional Autónoma de México, 1960.

Simpson, Leslie B. *The Repartimiento System of Native Labor in New Spain and Guatemala.* Colección Iberoamericana 13. Berkeley: University of California Press, 1938.

Sims, Harold D. *Descolonización en México: El conflicto entre mexicanos y españoles (1821–1831).* Mexico City: Fondo de Cultura Económica, 1982.

———. *La expulsión de los españoles de México: 1821–1828.* Mexico City: Fondo de Cultura Económica, 1974.

———. *La reconquista de México: La historia de los atentados españoles, 1821–1830.* Mexico City: Fondo de Cultura Económica, 1984.

Spell, Jefferson R. *The Life and Works of José Joaquín Fernández de Lizardi.* Philadelphia: University of Pennsylvania, 1931.

Spielman, Lynda Carol. *Mexican Pamphleteering and the Rise of the Mexican Nation, 1808–1830.* Ph.D. diss., Indiana University, 1975.

Staples, Anne. *La Iglesia en la Primera República federal mexicana, 1824–1835.* Mexico City: Sepsetentas, 1976.

Stevens, Donald F. *Origins of Instability in Early Republican Mexico.* Durham: Duke University Press, 1991.

Tank de Estrada, Dorothy. "La abolición de los gremios." In Elsa Cecilia Frost, Michael C. Meyer, and Josefina Zoraida Vázquez., eds., *El trabajo y los trabajadores en la historia de México*, pp. 311–31. Mexico City: El Colegio de México/University of Arizona Press, 1979.

———. *La educación ilustrada, 1786–1836: Educación primaria en la ciudad de México*. Mexico City: El Colegio de México, 1977.

Tannenbaum, Frank. *The Mexican Agrarian Revolution*. New York: Macmillan, 1929.

Taylor, James Williams. *Socioeconomic Instability and the Revolution for Mexican Independence in the Province of Guanajuato*. Ph.D. diss., University of New Mexico, 1976.

Taylor, Paul S. *A Spanish-Mexican Peasant Community: Arandas in Jalisco*. Berkeley: University of California Press, 1933.

Taylor, William B. *Drinking, Homicide and Rebellion in Colonial Mexican Villages*. Stanford: Stanford University Press, 1979.

———. *Landlord and Peasant in Colonial Oaxaca*. Stanford: Stanford University Press, 1972.

Tenenbaum, Barbara A. *México en la epoca de los agiotistas: 1821–1857*. Mexico City: Fondo de Cultura Económica, 1985.

Thomson, Guy P. C. *Puebla de los Angeles: Industry and Society in a Mexican City, 1700–1850*. Dellplain Latin American Studies no. 25. Boulder, Colo.: Westview Press, 1989.

Timmons, Wilbert H. "Tadeo Ortiz, Mexican Emissary Extraordinary." *Hispanic American Historical Review 51*, 3 (Aug. 1971):463–77.

Toro, Alfonso. *Dos Constituyentes del año de 1824: Biografías de Don Miguel Ramos Arizpe y Don Lorenzo de Zavala*. Mexico City: Museo Nacional de Arqueología, Historia y Etnografía, 1925.

———. *La Iglesia y el Estado en México (Estudio sobre los conflictos entre el clero católico y los gobiernos desde la Independencia hasta nuestros días)*. Mexico City: Talleres Gráficos de la Nación, 1927.

Torre Villar, Ernesto de la. *La constitución de Apatzingán y los creadores del Estado mexicano*. 2d ed. Mexico City: Universidad Nacional Autónoma de México, 1978.

———. *Los Guadalupes y la independencia*. Mexico City: Jus, 1966.

———. *La independencia mexicana*. 3 vols. Mexico City: SEP/80, 1982.

———. *La labor diplomática de Tadeo Ortiz*. Mexico City: Secretaría de Relaciones Exteriores, 1974.

———. *Lecturas históricas mexicanas*. 3 vols. Mexico City: Empresas Editoriales, 1966–67.

Tovar, Hermes. "Orígenes y características de los sistemas de terraje y arrendamiento en la sociedad colonial durante el siglo XVIII: El caso neogranadino." In Jan Bazant et al., *Peones, conciertos y arrendamientos en América Latina*, pp. 123–53. Bogotá: Centro Editorial, Universidad Nacional de Colombia, 1987.

Trabulse, Elías, ed. *Fluctuaciones económicas en Oaxaca durante el siglo XVIII*. Mexico City: El Colegio de México, 1972.

———. *Francisco Xavier Gamboa: Un político criollo en la Ilustración mexicana, 1717–1794.* Mexico City: Colegio de México, 1985.

Trens, Manuel B. *Historia de Veracruz.* 8 vols. Jalapa: Enríquez, 1947.

Tutino, John. *From Insurrection to Revolution in Mexico: Social Bases of Agrarian Violence, 1750–1940.* Princeton, N.J.: Princeton University Press, 1986.

Van Young, Eric. *Hacienda and Market in Eighteenth-Century Mexico: The Rural Economy of the Guadalajaraa Region, 1675–1820.* Berkeley, University of California Press, 1981.

———. "Islands in the Storm: Quiet Cities and Violent Countrysides in the Mexican Independence Era." *Past and Present* 118 (Feb. 1988): 130–55.

———. "To See Someone Not Seeing: Historical Studies of Peasants and Politics in Mexico." *Mexican Studies/Estudios Mexicanos* 6, 1 (Winter 1990):133–59.

Vázquez, Josefina Zoraida. "Iglesia, ejército y centralismo." *Historia Mexicana* 39, 153 (July–Sept. 1989):205–34.

———. *Mexicanos y norteamericanos ante la guerra del 47.* Mexico City: Ateneo, 1977.

Velázquez, María del Carmen. *El estado de guerra en Nueva España: 1760–1808.* Mexico City: El Colegio de México, 1950.

Victoria Moreno, Dionisio. *Los Carmelitas Descalzos y la conquista espiritual de México: 1585–1612.* 2d ed. Mexico City: Porrúa, 1983.

———. "La provincia de los carmelitas descalzos de México y la guerra de indepedencia (seis documentos para su historia)." *Historia Mexicana* 37, 148 (April–June 1988):657–67.

Villaseñor y Villaseñor, Alejandro. *Los condes de Santiago: Monografía histórica y genealógica.* Mexico City: Tipografía de El Tiempo, 1901.

Walker, David W. *Kinship, Business and Politics: The Martínez del Río Family in Mexico, 1823–1867.* Austin: University of Texas Press, 1986.

Wasserstrom, Robert. *Class and Society in Central Chiapas.* Berkeley: University of California Press, 1983.

West, Robert. *The Mining Community in North New Spain: The Parral Mining District.* Berkeley: University of California Press, 1949.

Whitecotton, Joseph W. "Estamento y clase en el valle de Oaxaca durante el período colonial." *América Indígena* 30, 2 (1970): 375–86.

Wiemers, Eugene L. Jr. "Agriculture and Credit in Nineteenth Century Mexico: Orizaba and Córdoba, 1822–71." *Hispanic American Historical Review* 65, 3 (Aug. 1985):519–46.

Zavala, Silvio. *La encomienda indiana.* Madrid: Imprenta Helénica, 1935.

Zavala, Silvio, and María Castelo. *De encomiendas y propiedad territorial en algunas regiones de la América Española.* Mexico City: J. Porrúa e Hijos, 1940.

Index

Abad y Queipo, Bishop, 6
Acordada rebellion (1828), 206–9; contrasted with Santa Anna-Bocanegra-Rejón episode, 243; federalism after, 139; Gómez Pedraza election and, 200; José Ignacio Paz in, 77; Lucas Balderas in, 76
Acta constitutiva de la federación, 141, 149
Agiotistas, 187–89, 192–93, 229; Antonio Garay, 231, 233; coalitions and, 211; Guerrero and, 212, 213; interest rates, 213; liberals and, 234; in mining, 238. *See also* Financiers
Agitational leaders, 94, 100
Agreda, conde de, 66
Aguayo, marqués de, 30, 57–58, 68, 191
Aguilar, 54; as demagogue, 117; Iturbidista agitation and, 87; mutiny by, 130
Aguirrevengoa, Ignacio, 69
Alamán, Lucas: in Bustamante cabinet, 221, 226; C.M. Bustamante and, 47; as *desarrollista,* 43, 219, 220; as Director of Industry, 243; as dominant figure in Poder Ejecutivo, 146; as entrepreneur, 189; factory in Orizaba, 17; half-brother, 52–53, 57; influence weakened, 150; links to mining, 68–69; on mechanization, 26–27; Monteleone estate, 233; provisional executive and, 216; Rayas and, 56–57; in Relaciones, 144; in Victoria cabinet, 152
Alameda, Cirilo, 85
Alas, Ignacio, 226
Alcalde, functions of, 172
Alliances, patterns of, viii, 247–48

Almanza, Mariano de, 69, 191
Alpuche e Infante, José María: Alamán and, 153; Arenas conspiracy, 178; elected president of congress, 220; elections of 1826, 165; exiled, 222; jailed, 220; as liberal, 220; opposes Iturbide, 113; returns from exile, 239
Alquilados, 33–34
Alvarez, Juan, 222
Anáhuac, Republic of, 45
Anaya, Juan Pablo, 107, 229
Anaya, Pedro María, 246
Andrade, José Antonio "Cartuchera," dismissed, 129; imprisoned, 140; Iturbidista plotting, 143; in Iturbidista Right, 125; Jaliscan separatism and, 137
Anglo Mexican Company, 174
Anti-foreign agitation, 223, 237–38, 241
Anti-Spanish agitation: after Arenas conspiracy, 178–79; by Yorkinos, 177, 195–96; Cuernavaca plot, 141; Escoceses and, 183; in Jalisco, 196; land seizures, 198–99; legislation, 180; Lobato and, 141, 208; loss of capital, 183; Mexico City militias, 126; nativism among merchants, 131; Payo del Rosario and, 115; popular petition and, 185; second Spanish expulsion bill, 215
Antireligious propaganda, 85–87. *See also* Church, Religion
Antuñano, Esteban de: as *desarrollista,* 220; as industrialist and pamphleteer, 188; as militia colonel, 175; owner of Constancia factory, 20
Aparceros, 32, 34

369

About the Book and the Author

If ever there was an ungovernable country, it was Mexico following independence in 1821. The chaos of political life, epitomized by several decades of coups and uprisings led by generals and congressmen, is imaginatively reinterpreted as a struggle between the elites and the masses to control the affairs of government.

Professor Di Tella's focus is the connection between the class structure and the political system. In broad terms, Di Tella argues that Mexican politics in the years between 1820 and 1850 witnessed a continuation of the civil war unleashed by the War of Independence. Under intense pressure from the violence-prone lower class and the downwardly mobile among the middle class, political elites sought to marshal support by coopting various groups in the popular sector. Intense and often violent competition occurred as a result of the crisscross of alliances between a popular-conservative coalition, a liberal-bourgeois one, and a radical-liberal or populist faction.

"Di Tella is the first author to provide an overall interpretive key for the first thirty-five years of independence. . . . An immense accomplishment."—Timothy E. Anna, author of *The Mexican Empire of Iturbide*

Torcuato S. Di Tella is Argentina's leading sociologist and the author of ten books. He teaches at the University of Buenos Aires and is past president of the Instituto de Desarrollo Económico y Social.